Critical Survey of Poetry
French Poets

Editor

Rosemary M. Canfield Reisman
Charleston Southern University

Salem Press
A Division of EBSCO Publishing, Ipswich, Massachusetts

Cover photo:
Victor Hugo (© The Print Collector/Corbis)

Copyright © 2012, by Salem Press, A Division of EBSCO Publishing, Inc.
All rights in this book are reserved. No part of this work may be used or reproduced in any manner whatsoever or transmitted in any form or by any means, electronic or mechanical, including photocopy, recording, or any information storage and retrieval system, without written permission from the copyright owner except in the case of brief quotations embodied in critical articles and reviews or in the copying of images deemed to be freely licensed or in the public domain. For information address the publisher, Salem Press, at csr@salempress.com.

ISBN: 978-1-42983-658-6

CONTENTS

Contributors iv

French Poetry to 1700 1
French Poetry Since 1700 32

Guillaume Apollinaire 47
Louis Aragon 58
Charles Baudelaire 69
André Breton 80
Paul Celan 88
Paul Éluard 97
Victor Hugo 104
Jean de La Fontaine 118
Jules Laforgue 129
Alphonse de Lamartine 140
Stéphane Mallarmé 149
Marie de France 158
Gérard de Nerval 170
Saint-John Perse 181
Jacques Prévert 189
Pierre Reverdy 197
Rainer Maria Rilke 207
Arthur Rimbaud 218
Tristan Tzara 230
Paul Verlaine 240
François Villon 250

Checklist for Explicating a Poem 260
Bibliography 263
Guide to Online Resources 266
Category Index 269
Subject Index 272

CONTRIBUTORS

Peter Baker
Southern Connecticut State University

Lowell A. Bangerter
University of Wyoming

James John Baran
Louisiana State University-Shreveport

Dorothy M. Betz
Georgetown University

Franz G. Blaha
University of Nebraska-Lincoln

Steven E. Colburn
Largo, Florida

J. Madison Davis
Pennsylvania State College-Behrend College

Lillian Doherty
University of Maryland

Desiree Dreeuws
Sunland, California

Rodney Farnsworth
Indiana University

David Harrison Horton
Patten College

Tracy Irons-Georges
Glendale, California

Maura Ives
Texas A&M University

Karen Jaehne
Washington, D.C.

Judith L. Johnston
Rider College

Irma M. Kashuba
Chestnut Hill College

Rebecca Kuzins
Pasadena, California

Norris J. Lacy
University of Kansas

Raymond LePage
George Mason University

Marie-Noëlle D. Little
Clinton, New York

John D. Lyons
University of Massachusetts, Dartmouth

Leslie B. Mittleman
California State University, Long Beach

Sylvie L. F. Richards
Northwest Missouri State University

Paul J. Schwartz
Grand Forks, North Dakota

FRENCH POETRY TO 1700

The history of French poetry in the early centuries is in fact the history of French literature as a whole. Prose was not cultivated as a literary medium until the thirteenth century, and for centuries after that the poetic genres continued to predominate. It thus seems appropriate to begin this essay with a brief survey of the history of the French language and of the forces involved in the creation of the nation-state of France.

Before France, there was Gaul. The French language developed out of the popular form of Latin spoken in Gaul under the Roman administration, which went back to Caesar's conquest of the region in the first century B.C.E. and endured until the fifth century C.E. By the time the Western Roman Empire had succumbed to waves of barbarian immigration, this language had already developed a character of its own and could be distinguished from the "purer" Latin of the cleric, scholar, and diplomat (which was to remain the language of learning and international intercourse for many centuries—although it, too, continued to evolve). The barbarian group that assumed political leadership of Gaul in the sixth century was the Franks, and while they gave their name to the territory and the language, they introduced few changes in the latter, which they learned from the Gallo-Roman population. "French" continued to evolve quite rapidly and was the first of the Romance languages to be recorded in writing.

The oldest document in the French language, preserved in a tenth century manuscript, goes back to C.E. 842 and consists of the oaths sworn in ratification of a treaty by Charles the Bald and Louis the German, two grandsons of Charlemagne. From the late ninth or early tenth century there survives a sequence, or liturgical poem, on the martyrdom of Saint Eulalia. It is important to realize that at that time, and for many centuries thereafter, French was not a single language but a group of related dialects, divided along regional lines. By the eleventh century, these dialects could be said to fall into two broad groups, called *langue d'oc* (language of *oc*) and *langue d'oïl*, after the word for "yes" in each. The *langue d'oc*, or Occitan, as it is known to modern linguists, was spoken in the south of France and included Provençal, the dialect of the troubadours. The *langue d'oïl* was a group of northern dialects, used by the authors of the chansons de geste. The Parisian dialect, which eventually came to dominate the others, grew in importance from the late twelfth century to the fifteenth, when it became the literary language of the country as a whole.

The first French literature of real importance appeared in the eleventh century. By that time, several institutions that were to play major roles in the development of France—and of French literature—had been established. The most important of these institutions, whose power was enhanced by their alliance, were the Roman Catholic Church and the monarchy. A brief survey of their early history seems in order here.

The Church had the deeper roots and was the stronger of the two for many centuries.

The Christianization of Roman Gaul had begun as early as the first century C.E., although the new faith encountered persecution there as it did in Rome. (Saint Denis, who gave his name to the basilica where French kings were buried for twelve centuries, was an early martyr, about C.E. 250.) By about the year 400, Christianity was well established, and it was adopted, along with the vernacular, by the Germanic immigrant-invaders of the fifth century. Church organization, modeled on the Roman imperial administration, survived this turbulent period intact and remained a source of stability throughout the Dark Ages that followed.

The baptism of the Frankish chieftain Clovis in 496 created the first link between the Church and what was to become the French monarchy, for Clovis was the founder of the Merovingian Dynasty, which continued to rule the Franks until the mid-eighth century, adding Burgundy and Provence to their realm. The Carolingian Dynasty, which followed, likewise obtained the sanction and support of the Church: Pepin I, its first representative to reign, was anointed at Saint-Denis by the Pope himself, and Charlemagne, Pepin's son, was crowned Holy Roman Emperor in Rome in the year 800. Charlemagne's empire, though short-lived (it fell apart almost immediately after his death), was responsible for a brief revival of classical learning. Indeed, the renewed interest in the classical form of the Latin language at this time helped to preserve Latin as the instrument of scholarship and diplomacy for the rest of the medieval period. Another enduring legacy of the Carolingian Empire was created by the sense of heroic possibility and divine sanction, which was embodied in the figure of Charlemagne himself, who quickly assumed legendary proportions.

The ninth century saw the division of the kingdoms that were to evolve into the states of France and Germany; it also saw violent inroads by the Vikings, Muslims, and Magyars (ancestors of the Hungarians) into Western Europe. During this period of unrest, political control was often reduced to its lowest terms, which meant smaller units of organization based on land tenure and on the capacity for self-defense. When Hugh Capet, founder of the Capetian Dynasty, was anointed by the Archbishop of Reims and succeeded the last Carolingian in 987, the territory under his control amounted to roughly one-fiftieth that of modern France. The centuries to come would see a continuing struggle between kings and nobles as the former sought to increase their lands and influence at the expense of the latter. The alliance between Church and monarchy, already a firmly established historical precedent, would prove a powerful fulcrum in this struggle. The monarchy would triumph, however, only with the help of a "third estate" still to emerge: the bourgeoisie.

THE ELEVENTH CENTURY

French literature, like the literature of ancient Greece, may seem to have sprung up full-blown, for the earliest surviving works—the eleventh century chansons de geste—are epics of great power and considerable sophistication. Like the Greek epics, however, they reflect both a period of poetic development (to which they owe their form) and a sense of history—specifically, the sense of looking back to a heroic past. The poetic development is very difficult to trace because of the dearth of evidence; it seems to owe much to the Latin verse forms used in the liturgy of the Church, and it may also reflect the memories of classical (especially Vergilian) epic preserved by the more educated of the clergy, who continued to produce Latin narrative verse throughout the medieval period. The impetus behind the flowering of the chanson de geste seems, however, to have been largely historical and to some extent religious: Its appearance coincides with the beginning of the Crusades and with the consolidation of the feudal system, both eleventh century developments. Heroic songs celebrating the exploits of Charlemagne and his vassals may well have existed in Carolingian times and in the intervening centuries, yet it was in the eleventh century that these songs came into their own, and the glimpses they give of social and political organization correspond to the conditions prevailing during that period.

The heroic songs do not have anything to say (except incidentally) about the life of the peasant class, nor indeed much about the life of women of the noble class. They reflect the point of view and interests of the feudal lords for whose entertainment and edification they were composed. They also reflect to some extent the interests and teachings of the Church, for some were written by clerics, or at least by men of some education—and at this period all education was under the aegis of the Church. As Sidney Painter has demonstrated in his 1940 book, *French Chivalry*, there were conflicts throughout the Middle Ages between the views of the clergy and those of the secular nobility concerning the duties and virtues of a "true knight." However, within certain bounds, clerical writers on chivalric conduct tended to accommodate Church teachings to the realities of feudal existence, which of necessity were dominated by the interests of the knightly class.

Feudal society

The feudal system was neither created nor destroyed at a single blow; it evolved out of the confusion of the ninth and tenth centuries, reached its high-water mark in the eleventh, and declined gradually in the face of royal and bourgeois inroads over the course of the next four centuries. Because of its intimate connection with the chanson de geste and with the slightly later developments of romance and troubadour poetry, it deserves detailed consideration here.

The feudal social and political structure was based on land tenure and military might. These two factors were interdependent because of the technology of warfare: The knight needed both means and leisure to equip and train himself for combat on horseback in heavy armor. Because the economy was almost exclusively agricultural (until the twelfth century saw the revival of town life), knights depended for their income on the surplus produced by the peasants, serf or free, who tilled their lands. These lands were held as fiefs granted by the king or by one of the greater nobles in return for the knight's service in battle. Many fiefs were also held by the Church, and in early days bishops and powerful prelates were often themselves knights; a prominent literary example is Archbishop Turpin, one of the heroes of the *Chanson de Roland* (twelfth century; *The Song of Roland*, 1880). The system proved well adapted to an age in which the absence of any strong central authority left the field open for brigandage and made communication and travel difficult. Under these conditions, such control as could be exercised was usually local and based on force or the threat of force. The knight was not seen as a parasite but as a professional soldier who performed the vital service of protecting those who lived on his lands—that is, those who fed and clothed him. The lack of central authority also made him a virtual sovereign, responsible for keeping the peace, enforcing the law, and judging those who broke it within his domain.

From the perspective of the chansons de geste, the most important aspect of the feudal system is the network of relationships it fostered among the knights themselves or between the knights and their overlords. The relationship of vassalage, whereby a man vowed his allegiance and loyal service to a more powerful lord in return for a fief, had both Roman and Germanic antecedents. On the fringes of the empire, men were often given land in return for (ongoing) service in the Roman army, and the German chieftains gathered about them groups of loyal retainers, each of whom could in turn call on the freemen under his authority for help at need. Under the decentralized conditions prevailing after the breakup of Charlemagne's empire, local ties grew stronger, while allegiance to a far-off king grew tenuous. The effective control of much of France reverted to those barons, or lesser nobles, who were themselves the best fighters and could command the most loyal troops.

It is easy to see how important the friendships and rivalries between individuals might become in such a situation. Like Homer's warriors, the knightly heroes of the chansons de geste are bound by ties of strong affection and divided by fierce hatreds; each insists on his own prerogatives and is mortally offended by slights to his honor. It is probably no coincidence that Homer's age was also one of decentralized power and of recovery following the collapse of a palace-centered economy. In medieval France as in prehistoric Greece, these conditions gave an unusually wide scope to the ambitions of individual nobles. At the same time, the awareness in each case that a previous age (the Mycenaean for Homer, the Carolingian for the eleventh century poet) had seen achievements on a grander scale focused interest on heroic stories of the past. The historic accuracy of these stories is often questionable and sometimes nonexistent; the historic interest they convey is genuine and significant.

THE SONG OF ROLAND

One of the three major cycles, or series of related chansons, deals with the court of Charlemagne and in particular with the prowess of his nephew Roland; the best known, and indeed the earliest, is the *Chanson de Roland* (twelfth century; *The Song of Roland*, 1880), which describes his last battle. As in the *Iliad* (c. 750 B.C.E.; English translation, 1611), the hero of the poem is not the commander in chief but one of his younger retainers, whose strength and daring make him more valuable in battle than men with more lands or larger contingents. The tragic plot of the poem is set in motion by the resentment and hatred of Roland's stepfather, Ganelon, whom Roland nominates for a dangerous embassy. (Roland has himself volunteered for the embassy, but Charlemagne has refused on the grounds that he is too valuable to risk.) Ganelon betrays Roland by urging the Saracens to ambush him in the Pyrenees as he commands the rear guard, covering Charlemagne's retreat from Spain. Overly confident of his own strength, Roland refuses to sound his horn (to summon help) until it is too late; at last, surrounded by dead and dying comrades, he sounds the horn, so that their deaths may be avenged, and dies extending his glove to God in an ultimate act of homage.

In a book-length study, *The Chanson de Roland* (1969), Pierre Le Gentil has shown how complex are the motives of both heroes and villains in the poem, and how subtle are the poet's means of characterization. Because of the directness of the narrative and the relative simplicity of the language, the modern reader may be tempted to dismiss it as "primitive"—from a twenty-first century perspective, the absolute antagonism of Christian and "infidel" and the notion of "holy war" do seem both primitive and alien. To appreciate the poem's complexity and coherence, one must try to approach it on its own terms, within its eleventh century feudal context.

An important element of this context which remains to be discussed is the relationship between Christianity and the code of knightly conduct. The Church consistently tried to curb the excesses to which knights were prone, condemning tournaments and private war between Christians as vainglorious and homicidal. However, war for profit (through plunder and ransom) remained a common occupation of the barons as long as the power of the king and his chief vassals was weak, while tournaments grew in popularity as the possibility of waging local wars waned. The Church did succeed in promulgating two more limited curbs on private warfare: The *Pax Dei*, or "peace of God" (late tenth century), laid a curse on those who plundered churches or the poor or harmed women or clergy, and the *Truga Dei*, or "truce of God" (eleventh century), forbade private war from Wednesday night to Monday morning and during the seasons of Christmas and Easter. Beginning in the twelfth century, ecclesiastical writers also urged the inclusion of a religious ceremony in the dubbing of new knights, to make them aware of belonging to a special "order" bound to uphold the faith (and, of course, the Church) as well as the behests of their secular lords.

The Church's greatest success, however, was in galvanizing the nobility of France for two great series of Crusades—in Spain and in Palestine—against the Islamic world. Although it is clear that the hope of profit was as important a motive in these wars as in local campaigns among rival barons, it would be as wrong to discount the religious motive as to give it sole consideration. Nor should the hope of secular glory—which plays such an important part in the chansons de geste—be ignored. The truth is that in this case, religious duty and individual ambition or hopes of profit could be made to coincide. Thus, Roland's love of battle and craving for glory are justifiable when used in the service of God, and spoils taken from Saracens are not considered ill-gotten gains but rewards for upholding a sacred cause. Painter quotes an especially apt passage from the troubadour Aimeric de Pégulhan: "Without renouncing our rich garments, or station in life, courtesy, and all that pleases and charms, we can obtain honor down here and joy in Paradise." Although considerable opportunism was involved, there is no reason to read such a passage as merely cynical. The chansons de geste, no less than the Crusades, undoubtedly reflect, among other motives, a genuinely religious impulse. Like their pagan ancestors, these knights had no trouble reconciling piety and prosperity—or, as in the case of Roland, piety and glory.

Evolution of the feudal regime

The Crusades were only one factor, although an important one, in the prospects of the feudal class as they evolved over the course of the following centuries. In addition to carving out a Latin Kingdom of Jerusalem (whose first king, or "advocate," Godfrey of Bouillon, became the hero of several late chansons de geste), French knights led or took part in a number of foreign campaigns in the second half of the eleventh century which resulted in the creation of new fiefs and kingdoms: William of Normandy's invasion of England in 1066, Norman conquests in Sicily and southern Italy, Burgundian and Champenois inroads in Spain and Portugal. The younger sons of nobles, who had the least to gain by remaining at home, were drawn to these adventures in especially large numbers, and some slackening of feudal warfare at home ensued. During the same period, improvements in agricultural technique and equipment permitted the cultivation and resettlement of great areas within France that had lain fallow since the ninth century. This simultaneous external and internal expansion greatly increased the prosperity of France as a whole, and at first the knightly class was in a position to profit most by it. Alfred de Jeanroy, in *La Poésie lyrique des troubadours* (1934), has suggested that the resulting wealth and leisure were largely responsible for the rapid development of poetry in this period.

A further development of the age, however—the growth of a money economy—was to prove a transitory blessing to the lesser nobility, for it led, in the course of the following centuries, to a centralization of power in the hands of the king and his chief vassals, such as the dukes of Normandy and Burgundy and the counts of Flanders and Champagne. The growth of towns and the proliferation of trade fairs at first provided nobles with sources of cash in the form of rents and market tolls, but their increasing dependence on such sources of income was eventually to make them vulnerable to royal devaluations of currency (in the fourteenth and fifteenth centuries) and inflation (in the sixteenth century). Meanwhile, the greatest gains were being made by the lords whose dependencies included the largest towns, and within the towns a class was rising that would seriously undermine the financial and even the political position of the nobility. Already by the end of the twelfth century, the king and dukes of France were using armies composed largely of poorer knights, who fought not in return for land tenure but for cash. At the same time, the great lords employed townsmen—bourgeois—as overseers of their estates, while the king, mistrustful of noble ambitions, began to rely increasingly on bourgeois civil servants. The lesser nobility had had a taste of prosperity, and some were not ready to relinquish it, even if it meant abandoning their status as seigneurs and attaching themselves to the army or court of a richer lord. Thus, as Painter puts it, "the nobles of France entered on their metamorphosis into courtiers."

Prevented from waging private war, they increasingly engaged in tournaments for glory and profit, while those who had the leisure and the inclination cultivated the arts of poetry, music, and dance. The chanson de geste was not yet past its prime, but it began to face competition. At the richer courts, noble women took a more prominent social role and began to exert a distinct influence on ideals of chivalric conduct. The more powerful of these women, including Eleanor of Aquitaine and her daughter, Countess Marie of Champagne, became patrons of poets working in new lyric and narrative genres that gave a more prominent place to profane love. Originating in the south of France with the troubadours, the new theme soon spread to their northern counterparts, the trouvères; meanwhile, the "matter of France" (the Carolingian cycle) was gradually supplanted by the "matter of Britain" (tales of Arthur and his knights) and the "matter of Rome" (tales from classical mythology) as sources of plots for narrative verse. Thus, the chanson de geste was finally eclipsed by the roman (romance).

The role of the Church

The twelfth and thirteenth centuries saw the high-water mark of the Church's independence and secular power, as well as of its hold on the intellectual life of France. Its independence was the result of a papal effort, begun in the eleventh century, to wrest control of clerical appointments from the nobility and kings of Europe, who had come to consider bishoprics and monastic offices as political plums—a means of rewarding and enriching their favorites. Using the powerful threat of excommunication, popes and their legates had insisted on the right of monks to elect their abbots and of canons (clergy attached to a cathedral) to elect their bishops. Most Church property was also freed from feudal dues and appropriation. The new abbots and bishops were often men of integrity and considerable learning. In the eleventh and early twelfth centuries, the monastic orders of Cluny and Cîteaux took a leading role in the reform, and their efforts were largely responsible for the surge of church building known today as Romanesque.

During the course of the twelfth century, as towns grew in size and importance, leadership passed to the canons and bishops, and the Gothic phase of church building was focused on the cathedral. Episcopal schools also eclipsed the monasteries as centers of learning and became the seedbeds of what has been called the "twelfth century renaissance." In Chartres and Paris especially, there was a revival of classical learning and a spurt of literary activity in Latin, which remained the language of the schools (as the name of Paris's Latin Quarter recalls). An especially important development was the renewed interest in logic and dialectic as keys to learning. Thanks to contacts with Byzantium and with the Arabs, ancient texts that had been lost to the West were rediscovered, and an interest in Aristotle, the great logician, was stimulated by the commentaries of Islamic scholars. Logic was applied even to the "mistress of the sciences," theology, by Pierre Abélard and his students. Despite the fierce reaction this generated (under the leadership of the stern but charismatic Bernard of Clairvaux), the new schools continued to grow and to attract students from all over Europe; by the thirteenth century, Paris had become the intellectual capital of the West. (The Sorbonne, the first college of the University of Paris to be endowed, was founded in 1257.)

The thirteenth century was also the century of Saint Thomas Aquinas, and it saw the triumph of Scholasticism, a system of philosophy and theology that forged a synthesis of ancient (Aristotelian) and Christian learning. It was chiefly through the cathedral schools and universities that the vernacular literature of France was enriched by contact with the classical legacy of dramatic, lyric, and epic poetry. The tradition of Latin didactic verse, which had been maintained throughout the Middle Ages by such clerics as had any learning, also flowed into the vernacular mainstream at this time, inspiring historical chronicles and other didactic works, at first in verse and then in prose.

Lyric poetry

The first real flowering of lyric—as opposed to narrative or liturgical—poetry in France took place early in the twelfth century, in the southern regions of Aquitaine and Provence. This poetry was written not in the *langue d'oïl*—the language of the chanson de geste and the parent stock of modern French—but in the *langue d'oc*, often referred to as Provençal (something of a misnomer, since Provençal was only one of four dialects involved). It deserves more than a passing mention in the history of French poetry, and indeed in that of European poetry as a whole, for its influence on later poets was profound. This is especially true of its major theme—courtly love—but the complexity of its form was also admired and emulated for centuries, especially in France.

The south was at this period the most cosmopolitan region of France, thanks to its coastal towns, which carried on a growing trade with Italy, Spain, and the Middle East. The debt of troubadour poetry to Arabic forms of lyric is still a matter of some debate. It seems clear that there was at least some influence, traceable to contacts between the Occitan (southern French) and Islamic cultures in the course of the Spanish Crusades. In particular, the form known as the *zadjal* may have suggested the intricacy of verse forms and the theme of refined love characteristic of the troubadour lyrics. The influence of contemporary Latin verse, especially hymns, has also been demonstrated. Whatever its sources, this sudden flowering owed much to the newfound wealth and leisure of the nobles of Aquitaine and Provence in the early twelfth century; the first known troubadour was in fact the powerful duke of Aquitaine, Guillaume IX (grandfather of Eleanor), and nearly all troubadours were of the noble class. Indeed, the decline of troubadour poetry—and of the *langue d'oc* as a literary language—may well be linked to the so-called Albigensian Crusade of the early thirteenth century, which in suppressing the Catharist or Albigensian heresy destroyed many of the noble families of southern France.

Troubadour poetry—all of which was written to be sung, either by the *trobador* (poet) himself or by a *jonglar* (French *jongleur*, professional singer)—comprises a number of distinct genres, each with its characteristic form, vocabulary, and themes. Thus, for example, the *planh* laments the death of a noble knight (usually the poet's lord); the *sirventes* explores a political or moral issue (such as prospects for war or peace, or the virtues and vices of different groups—young and old, Italian and German); the *tenson* takes the form of a debate in which opposing views are presented in alternating stanzas. By far the most popular forms, however, were those devoted to the theme of love, such as the *alba* (the lovers' parting at dawn) and the *canso d'amor* (love song). Indeed, even the *tenson* was often devoted to the fine points of courtship. Within an amazingly short time, a highly elaborate system of conventions evolved, and the elaboration was deliberate and self-conscious. It suited both the courtly milieu in which the troubadours moved and their necessarily indirect praise of a passion that was often adulterous.

A key metaphor in this system of conventions was feudal: The knight vowed homage and service to the lady of his heart, as to his liege lord, and (at least in the earlier poems) he often had some hope of recompense—if not in the form of sexual favors, then at least in the form of smiles, looks, kind words, or other "platonic" tokens of affection. A common complaint is that the lady is cruel or haughty and will not respond, although the lover's happiness—indeed, his very existence—depends on her. Sometimes it emerges that she is not unmoved but must feign indifference to protect her reputation or deflect her husband's jealousy, for the nature of this courtly or refined love (*fin' amor*) is such that it is rarely compatible with marriage—an institution more often used to further economic or political ends than to gratify the desires of individual men and women.

Women in particular were rarely consulted about their destined marriage partners, and it is easy to understand their craving, as increased prosperity gave them leisure to imagine such things, for the attentions of men who were attracted not to their houses and lands but to their persons and sensibilities. Although by far the greater number of troubadours were men (there were a few women), noble women seem to have played a considerable part in elaborating the ethic of courtly love; at the very least, they must have come to see themselves as worthy of gentle treatment and long courtship, withholding their favors from men who did not approach them with the proper deference.

As Frederick Goldin has indicated in his anthology *Lyrics of the Troubadours and Trouvères* (1973), adherence to the new ethic very soon became a condition of acceptance into the exclusive circles where it prevailed. The result was a new definition of the man of worth. In addition to noble birth and prowess in battle, he was to demonstrate the courtly qualities of fair speech, good manners, and a certain delicacy of feeling; above all, he was to find in love the source and focus of the knightly virtues. One of the fullest expositions of this new code is the *De amore* of André le Chapelain. A Latin prose treatise of the twelfth century, the *De amore* was translated into French in the thirteenth century and later into Italian and German; its author, a northerner (probably a protégé of Marie of Champagne), was one of the men responsible for the diffusion of courtly ideals among writers in the *langue d'oïl*. Needless to say, there were many discrepancies between the ideal and the reality, but the troubadours themselves were the first to acknowledge that, adopting an array of poetic voices—from the resigned "platonic" lover to the coarse womanizer—and playing them off against one another, sometimes within a single poem.

Efforts have sporadically been made to associate the troubadour ethic with the so-called Catharist heresy, the violent suppression of which in 1209 decimated the southern nobility and broke up the courts that had bred and sustained the troubadours. Among the attributes of the poetry that suggest such a connection are its hermetic style (*trobar clus*), which permitted the expression, in a kind of literary code, of ideas and feelings the "vulgar" were not to share, and the quasi-mystical attitude taken by some troubadours toward their ladies. (Women could attain to the highest positions within the Catharist sect and could be counted among "the Perfect," who were considered living saints.) It is difficult, however, to reconcile the often frankly erotic content of troubadour verse with the ascetic practices of the Cathars ("the pure").

The heresy was able to gain ground because, despite the twelfth century reforms, the Church was still a secular power, with all the abuses of its own doctrines that fact entailed. The Cathars, by contrast, preached a return to the austerity, simplicity, and charismatic fervor of early Christianity. The sect earned the respect of the peasants, but most of its adherents were of the noble and bourgeois classes. The Church could not ignore such a powerful challenge to its authority, and when attempts at conversion failed, Pope Innocent III ordered the Cistercians to preach a crusade against the sect. Most of the nobles of northern France took part, spurred by regional antagonisms and hopes of gain as well as by religious promptings. (Many southern nobles were in fact dispossessed of their lands.) The bloodshed was fearful, and the victims included many women and children. In addition, libraries were destroyed, a fact that may account for the dearth of surviving chansons de geste in the Occitan dialects.

The troubadour poems survived because they were esteemed and emulated (and thus recopied) in Italy and in the north of France. In this way, they became the antecedents of the *stil nuovo* or "new style" of Dante and his contemporaries, as well as of the lyrics of the French trouvères and the German *Minnesänger*. The trouvères in particular took over much of the original system of "courtly" images, themes, and forms, although they were less given to the Hermetic style. As Frederick Goldin has shown, they also abandoned the troubadour's lively attention to his courtly audience, concentrating instead on the inner experience of the lover and "the possibilities of figurative language"—extended metaphor and simile. Finally, they enriched the repertoire of lyric forms by borrowing from folk song such genres as the *chanson de toile* (sewing song) and by reviving the classical taste for bucolic poetry (thus, the genre called the *pastourelle* portrayed knights wooing shepherdesses).

THE ROMANCE

In the mid-twelfth century, a new genre of narrative verse appeared which absorbed the courtly love ethic and fused it with plot material unknown in the chanson de geste. This was the romance. The chansons de geste did not disappear but were forced instead to yield first place in popularity to the new genre, which seems to have been inspired by the rediscovery of Roman epic (Vergil, Statius) and Greek romance (in Latin retellings). Another prominent influence was that of Ovid, whose interest in love and in the psychological states of his characters struck a chord in the courtly circles where romance took root. As in the chansons de geste, historical accuracy is not a matter of much concern; thus, one of the most famous romances, the twelfth century *Roman d'Alixandre* (from which the twelve-syllable line, or Alexandrine, may take its name) portrays Alexander the Great as a typical twelfth century knight, who holds tournaments and adheres to the chivalric code. Despite such contemporary elements, the world of the romances is largely a never-never land, a fabulous past in which magical powers operate and the courtly ideal is incarnated in "perfect knights." This is true not only of the classically inspired romances but also of the Arthurian group, the plots of which, borrowed from Celtic legend, probably entered French literature by way of the Anglo-Norman court of the Plantagenets (where, it should not be forgotten, Eleanor of Aquitaine reigned as queen during the second half of the twelfth century).

In the greatest romances, the flight from reality characteristic of the genre is mitigated by an interest in psychology—especially that of love—and by an exploration of real contradictions within the chivalric ethic. The work of Chrétien de Troyes (1150-1190) is outstanding in these respects. His romance *Érec et Énide* (c. 1164; *Eric and Enid*, 1913) probes the conflict between the demands of prowess and courtly love: Erec is distracted from knightly pursuits by his love for his young wife, and he tries to right the balance by forcing her to follow him—without speaking—as he goes in search of adventure. *Cligès: Ou, La Fausse Morte* (c. 1164; *Cligès: A Romance*, 1912) examines the quandary of a woman who is betrothed to a man she does not love and who has vowed fidelity to another. (Although a magic potion helps her keep her vow and evade her husband, her dilemma—and her husband's fierce jealousy—are unmistakably real.)

Lancelot: Ou, Le Chevalier à la charrette (c. 1168; *Lancelot: Or, The Knight of the Cart*, 1990), Chrétien's treatment of the Lancelot story, offers the most extreme version of the knight's "love service" to his lady and the frankest endorsement of adultery. It is interesting that Chrétien takes pains in his prologue to explain that his patroness, Marie de Champagne, suggested the story and the theme: It was at her command he says, that he undertook the work.

Finally, Chrétien's last (and unfinished) romance, *Perceval: Ou, Le Conte du Graal* (c. 1180; *Perceval: Or, The Story of the Grail*, 1983), undertaken for a later patron, Philip of Flanders, describes the process by which an untutored boy becomes one of Arthur's greatest knights. Despite its fairy-tale quality, the story deals realistically with the pains and pleasures of growing up, as Perceval struggles to assimilate the courtly ethic and reconcile it with his duties as a Christian. (The legend of the Grail quest, which appears in *Perceval* and other early French romances, was reworked by Wolfram von Eschenbach, the German *Minnesänger*—who in turn inspired Richard Wagner's *Parsifal*, 1882—and by English writers in verse and prose, of whom the last and best known was Sir Thomas Malory.)

THE ROMANCE OF THE ROSE

The romance continued to enjoy unabated popularity for centuries, but as early as the thirteenth century it began to be recast in prose, which would thenceforth eclipse verse as a medium for narrative. One of the last great verse romances, *Le Roman de la rose* (*The Romance of the Rose*, partial translation c. 1370, complete translation 1900), was composed in two sections from 1230 to 1240 (by Guillaume de Lorris) and from 1275 to 1280 (by Jean de Meung). It has been called "the most popular single work of the thirteenth century and perhaps of the whole medieval period" by Geoffrey Brereton in *A Short History of French Literature* (1954). It was also destined to enjoy great influence with the French poets of the sixteenth century. Its popularity seems to have resulted from the success with which it combined the dominant themes and interests of its age: the courtly, the didactic, and the satiric. The first of its two authors was of noble birth, the second bourgeois, and their attitudes toward their subject—the allegorical struggle of a lover to obtain the Rose of his desire—are antipathetic in several ways, yet complementary. Guillaume de Lorris, the greater poet of the two, is a faithful spokesperson for the courtly tradition, which he sums up with exquisite grace and psychological subtlety. Jean de Meung, a product of the University of Paris and its Scholastic learning, is a rationalist who looks on love somewhat cynically and indeed seeks to undermine, through satire, the courtly conventions and the supremacy of the class that produced them.

COMIC AND SATIRIC POETRY

Virtually all the works discussed thus far, with the exception of the second part of *The Romance of the Rose*, were written by and for the members of the noble class; similarly, nearly all the characters portrayed in them are noble. The fabliaux, short narrative poems written in the meter proper to romance (octosyllabic rhyming couplets), offer a different view of thirteenth century society, one that includes bourgeoisie, peasants, and the lower clergy as well as knights and ladies. Some of the fabliaux are known to have been the work of nobles and wellborn clerics, and the genre undoubtedly had a place in courtly circles as a kind of comic foil to romance. However, it was also used by the *jongleurs* and by the *goliards* (poor students, usually clerics), who tended to live from hand to mouth and were seldom of noble birth.

As the bourgeois class grew and prospered, it, too, sought the entertainment these itinerant singers had to offer, and found it in the down-to-earth fabliaux. Although the genre encompasses a wide variety of subjects, fabliaux may be distinguished from other short narrative genres, such as the courtly *lai*, pious *miracle*, and polemical *dit*, by their comic tone and ordinary, everyday setting. Although a good number end with a moral, the real focus of interest is usually the tale itself. Sometimes the moral is frankly ironic. In *De Brunain et de Blérain* (thirteenth century), a peasant and his wife give their cow to the local priest, who has assured them that God returns twofold what is offered him; when the cow breaks free and returns home leading the priest's cow, with which it has been tethered, the peasant is overjoyed and believes God has kept his promise. The poet closes with the moral the priest had preached—"He is rich who gives to God, not he who hides and buries [his goods]"—but its religious meaning, discounted by the story, is replaced by a worldly one: Nothing ventured, nothing gained. Although a satiric vein is often visible in the fabliaux, as a group they neither spare nor single out any one class. Covetous priests, arrogant nobles, credulous peasants, and grasping bourgeoisie are all portrayed; the joke may be on any or all of them, depending, presumably, on the sympathies of the poet and of his audience.

ROMAN DE RENART

The thirteenth century likewise saw the creation of longer and more directly satiric poems inspired by the various serious genres and by indignation at specific social abuses. Thus, the *Bible Guyot* (1205-1218), written by a monk, details the abuses of the clergy, while the mock-epic *Audigier*, in rebuttal of the romances and *chansons de geste*, portrays the nobility as cowardly and coarse. The most successful of all of these attempts, however, was the *Roman de Renart* (c. 1175-1205; *The Most Delightful History of Reynard the Fox*, 1681; most commonly known as *Roman de Renart*), which grew from an initial long poem into a vast cycle—indeed, into a veritable genre. Its oldest "branches," as they are called, were probably inspired by medieval Latin versions of the beast fable, a genre ultimately traceable to Aesop's fables (sixth century B.C.E.) but, as the shadowy figure of Aesop himself should indicate, owing much to folktale and thus susceptible to additions and reshapings from popular as well as literary sources.

The various poems of the cycle have in common a wily and unscrupulous hero,

Renart the fox—usually known as Reynard in English—whose ability to outwit his "betters" (including not only Ysengrim the wolf and Brun the bear but also King Noble the lion) suggested very early, if not from the beginning, a social satire in which the lower orders manage to get the better of their oppressors among the nobility and clergy. It is worth noting that the genre enjoyed its greatest popularity in the northeastern regions of Picardy and Flanders, where the bourgeois class was particularly strong and conscious of its rising economic power. However, Renart is not a comfortable hero, and in one poem, *Le Couronnement Renart* (coronation of Renart), written about 1250, he actually obtains the crown—only to favor the rich while continuing to oppress the poor. In later branches, as in *The Romance of the Rose*, the stories are increasingly allegorical and didactic, becoming almost encyclopedic in scope; at the same time, political and social criticism is less veiled, and *Renart le Contrefait* (fourteenth century; the title suggests both "Renart the Misshapen" and "Renart the Dissembler") has been seen as a foreshadowing of the Jacquerie, a fourteenth century peasant uprising.

THE FOURTEENTH AND FIFTEENTH CENTURIES

By the early fourteenth century, a series of strong Capetian monarchs had succeeded in extending the royal domain—the portion of French territory not held as fiefs but administered directly by the king—until it included almost three-fourths of the entire realm. With the help of the Church, which upheld the monarchy's "divine right" to rule, of the legal profession, which consolidated their power on the basis of Roman legal precedent, and of the bourgeoisie, who manned their civil service and whose growing wealth filled their coffers with tax revenues, the Capetians made themselves the most powerful monarchs of Europe. The apex of their fortunes was reached under Philippe le Bel (Philip the Fair, thanks to his good looks), who dared to defy the Pope—and carried the day.

The struggle began in 1296, when Boniface VIII declared that Philip had no right to tax the clergy without papal consent, and ended in 1303, when the aging Pope died, reputedly of shock, after being held under arrest by Philip's agents on charges that included heresy. The king's diplomatic maneuvers next secured the appointment of a French pope, Clement V, who actually transferred the papal court to Avignon in Provence, from which his French successors continued to reign until 1377. A number of important institutions of government were also established or strengthened during this period. Philip was the first French king to convene a meeting of the Estates General, made up of representatives of the country's three "estates," or classes: clergy, nobility, and bourgeoisie (referred to as the "third estate"). The first meeting, in 1302, was designed to align the nation solidly behind Philip in his struggle with the pope. Later meetings were usually convened to raise general taxes, for which the king had to obtain the consent of feudal lords and independent towns; through its control of taxation, the Estates General wielded considerable power in the fourteenth century and during the Hundred

Years' War. Although it lost this power to the monarchy in the late fifteenth century, the precedent had been set for a governing body that was to include representatives of the nation as a whole. Finally, Philip IV enhanced the authority of the Parlement of Paris (a court of justice, not a parliament in the British sense), to the detriment of the nobility, who lost many of their judicial rights; by the fifteenth century, it had become independent even of the king, over whose legislation it held de facto power of judicial review.

At the accession in 1328 of Philip VI, the first king of the Valois line, the monarchy seemed stable and powerful; the kingdom was prosperous, and even the peasantry seem to have been feeling the good effects of two centuries of economic growth. In the course of the next two centuries, however, France was to be ravaged by the long, cruel conflict known as the Hundred Years' War. The steady concentration of power in the hands of the monarchy would be interrupted, to the temporary advantage of the feudal class. At the same time, the self-esteem of the French as a people would be shaken, a deep hatred of the English would be sown among them, and the costs of war, in lives and in resources, would prove staggering.

None of this was apparent until the war was well under way. The source of conflict was the issue of the French royal succession after the Capetian line ran out. After initially acknowledging Philip of Valois (a first cousin of the last Capetian king, Charles IV), Edward III of England decided to press his claim (through his mother, Isabel, Charles IV's sister) to the throne of France. As duke of Aquitaine and Guyenne—which Eleanor had brought as a dowry to Henry II—Edward Plantagenet was a vassal of the French crown; the encroachments of the French monarchy on feudal privileges made some sort of confrontation between the two kings inevitable. At this date, Anglo-Norman, a dialect of the *langue d'oïl*, was still spoken by the ruling class of England, who shared a common culture with the nobility of France. Edward thus had no trouble picturing himself as king of France; he had everything to gain and relatively little to lose by the attempt. In the event, his success surprised even him. Although France was the richer kingdom, its army—composed of heavily armored knights—proved inferior to the English, whose longbows were able to pierce armor while permitting greater mobility. The battles of Crécy and Poitiers, in 1346 and 1356 respectively, were not only military victories for the English but also severe blows to the prestige and chivalric ideology of the French nobility.

A more serious blow to the French cause was the capture of Philip IV's successor, King John, who had to be ransomed at incredible cost. A striking proof that the chivalric code still had substance at this period is the fact that when one of John's sons, who had been sent to England as hostage pending full payment of his father's ransom, broke his word and escaped, John himself returned voluntarily to London. The Treaty of Calais (1360) gave the French a breathing space, and John's canny successor, Charles V, who renewed the conflict, might have driven the English from France had he lived; he died however, at the age of forty-three, leaving a twelve-year-old son, Charles VI, who went mad in his early twenties and became a puppet of his unscrupulous and ambitious uncles. The latter took advantage of the king's weakness to extend their own power, and a feudal order reemerged in which chronic struggles among the French lords themselves further bled the country.

The vigorous Henry V of England, capitalizing on this state of affairs, allied himself with the dukes of Burgundy and made deep inroads into France between 1415 (the date of the Battle of Agincourt) and 1429, when the tide was finally turned by Joan of Arc, who believed she had been called by God to cast the English out of France. Although she was captured by the Burgundians in 1430 and burned by the English as a witch in 1431, her military victories, and chiefly the coronation of Charles VII, which she brought about, restored French morale. By 1436, Charles was able to reenter Paris, which the English and Burgundians had occupied since 1418. The country was so exhausted by the long struggle that it took until 1450 to expel the English from Normandy and until 1453 to take Guyenne, their last stronghold. (Only Calais, on the Channel opposite Dover, remained in English hands.)

Despite their ultimate victory, the French suffered far more in the war than did their enemies, many of whom were enriched by the spoils they took and whose prestige as a nation waxed as that of France waned. The war was fought almost exclusively on French soil, and the civilian population was subjected to plundering by French as well as English soldiers. The war likewise interfered with the cultivation of crops and the distribution of food, so that famine was widespread. Still more victims were claimed by the Black Death, or bubonic plague, which reached France in 1348 and 1349, recurring, less severely, in 1361. The disease is believed to have killed about a third of the population of Europe, including half the inhabitants of Paris (fifty thousand people) and thousands more throughout France. The death toll was undoubtedly increased by ignorance of the process of contagion; the same ignorance, in the face of such devastation, fostered the conviction that God had chosen this means to punish his people for their sins. Many believed the end of the world was near. That the plague was no respecter of persons and did not respond to collective acts of penitence struck terror in the believers; the varied responses included fanatical outbreaks of anti-Semitism, attempts to legislate morality, and discontent with the clergy, some of whom avoided ministering to the dying for fear of catching the disease. Although there were upsurges of piety, so that the Church was enriched by bequests, it was seen as having failed to mitigate or even to explain the suffering.

For other reasons as well, the moral authority of the Church declined steadily in the course of the fourteenth century. Corruption was perhaps the greatest single factor: The hierarchy resorted increasingly to simony (the sale of Church pardons, appointments, and dispensations) to satisfy its taste for luxury. At the papal court in Avignon—which Petrarch, writing in the 1340's, called "the Babylon of the West"—cardinals and prelates vied with one another in extravagance of dress; many had private palaces and mistresses. The Avignon "captivity" of the Papacy, which lasted until 1377, was immediately followed by the Great Schism (1378-1417), during which two and even three rival popes simultaneously laid claim to the office. Still, the hold of Catholicism was not easily shaken. It continued to provide the terms in which most men understood their existence and the rituals with which they faced life's crucial moments. Like the idea of chivalry and the prestige of the knightly class, the moral ascendancy of the Church and the prestige of the clergy were undermined by events of the fourteenth and fifteenth centuries, but they did not collapse. Indeed, as Johan Huizinga argued in his important book *The Waning of the Middle Ages* (1924), the pomp of Church and court and the elaborate distinctions of rank observed by both may well have been alternatives to, or forms of compensation for, the widespread pessimism of the age. It was not an age of reform, and in that respect it was, as Huizinga saw, a prolongation of the Middle Ages.

Evolution of literary forms

The art and poetry of the fourteenth and fifteenth centuries reflect a similar tendency to elaborate old forms and themes rather than to seek new ones. In architecture and sculpture, the "flamboyant" style (so named for the flame-like motif it favored) was an outgrowth of the Gothic. In literature, the romance and even the chanson de geste were still in vogue, while the heirs of the trouvères continued to celebrate courtly love in intricate lyric measures. However, new trends were visible as well. Poetry no longer held a monopoly of the literary genres; narratives, including romances and historical chronicles, began increasingly to be written in prose. At the same time, while many poets still wrote works intended to be sung, lyric poetry began to disengage itself from song, as narrative poetry had done at the appearance of the romance. Finally, lyric poetry made room for a certain realism, inspired by the harsh conditions of the age. The supreme poetic achievement of the age is that of François Villon, who combined his contemporaries' attention to form with his own uniquely realistic perspective on the ills—and the sins—of his generation.

In the fourteenth century, the repertoire of lyric forms inherited from the trouvères was enriched by the ballade (not to be confused with the English ballad), the rondeau, and other fixed forms that were to predominate for several centuries. In contrast to the sonnet, a highly versatile form developed in Italy at this period (but which would not enter French literature until the sixteenth century), these forms were both complex and rigid. To borrow a comparison from Geoffrey Brereton,

> the composer of the shortest *ballade* has to find fourteen similar rhymes of one sort, six of another, and five of another—besides working in an identical line four times. The sonneteer needs a maximum of only four rhymes of the same sort and he does not have to repeat any of his lines.

It was inevitable that such forms should suggest a certain artificiality, especially in the hands of their less skillful practitioners. However, some skill in poetry was evidently expected of the average "gentleman," as in Elizabethan England, and a collection of one hundred ballades by various hands (none of them professional) attests a fairly high standard of competence.

There were also more or less professional poets attached to the courts of princes; thus, Guillaume de Machault (c. 1300-1377) was chaplain, secretary, and court poet to John, king of Bohemia, while Eustache Deschamps (c. 1346-1406) served at the courts of Charles V and of his son Louis, duke of Orléans. Jean Froissart was a protégé of Philippa of Hainault, the queen of Edward III of England; he is best known for his prose *Chroniques* (late 1300's; *Chronicles*, 1523-1525) of contemporary history, but he wrote lyric poetry as well. One of the most popular poems of the age, *La Belle Dame sans merci* (1424), was the work of Alain Chartier, secretary to Charles VI and historiographer of Charles VII. Although none of these men was of noble birth, they fully espoused and promoted the chivalric ideology still prevailing in the noble circles in which they moved. The same is true of Christine de Pizan, one of the first professional women of letters, who sought the patronage of various nobles in order to support her three children (she was widowed as a young woman). It is interesting that while these writers made autobiographical allusions in their prose works, most of them clung to conventional courtly themes—the lovers' debate, the allegorical journey—and put relatively little of their personal experience into their poetry.

Charles d'Orléans

The same may be said of the most talented of them, who happened also to be the highest-born: Charles d'Orléans (1391-1465), a nephew of Charles VI and father of Louis XII. Taken prisoner at the Battle of Agincourt, he spent twenty-five years in England because his family could not afford the ransom demanded. Thanks to his rank, he was not harshly treated, and he took advantage of his enforced leisure to cultivate his talents as a poet. Although he used the same rigid forms as his contemporaries, his verse is distinguished by an impression of spontaneity—which is the result, however, of a thorough mastery of his medium. With Charles d'Orléans, the medieval taste for allegory finds a culminating expression (his earliest poem is a kind of *The Romance of the Rose* in miniature) and at the same time begins to shift toward true metaphor. It seems fitting that the last great representative of the courtly tradition should have been—like the first, Guillaume IX, the troubadour—a *grand seigneur*, a high-ranking member of the class that tradition had celebrated.

François Villon

François Villon (1431-1463?), the other great poet of the fifteenth century and one of the greatest of all time, offers a striking contrast in every respect to his noble contemporary, whose court at Blois he seems to have visited. A poor boy, son of an illiterate mother (for whom he wrote a moving prayer to the Virgin), Villon was educated at the University of Paris, thanks to a priest who became his benefactor. He might have made a career in the Church but instead was drawn to the headier, if more dangerous, life of the tavern and the street. He was tried for various crimes, ranging from murder to church robbery, and was certainly guilty of some of them. Banished from Paris in 1458, he wandered about the country and may have belonged—as did two of his friends—to a gang of thieves. Certainly, he saw the miseries of the age at first hand, and he describes them in vivid detail, from the point of view of the poorest classes. Although he used the poetic forms current in his day and made no technical innovations, his subject matter and tone are strikingly new. There were precedents for confessional poetry in the thirteenth century works of Ruteboeuf (a poor student and defrocked cleric), Jean Bodel, and Adam de la Halle; the latter two wrote *congés* (leave-takings) that seem to look ahead to Villon's *Le Grand Testament* (wr. 1461, pb. 1489; *The Great Testament*, 1878). Villon's entire oeuvre, however, is infused with the confessional impulse.

It is especially revealing to compare Villon's entry in a poetic contest sponsored by Charles d'Orléans with Charles's own entry. The theme assigned to all, "I die of thirst beside the fountain," suggested to Charles the unreliability of Fortune, who leads him in good times and in bad, yet the terms of his complaint are general and his tone even, although melancholy. The one specific reference, to "the fire of lovers," even makes it possible to read the poem as a conventional lover's complaint, although this theme is not developed and a broader interpretation seems preferable. To Villon, however, the paradox of want in the midst of plenty immediately suggests his own precarious existence; as his refrain stresses, he is "bien recuilly, debouté de chascun" ("welcomed and rebuffed by everyone"). It has been suggested that the envoi, or closing stanza, addressed by convention to an unspecified "prince," is in fact an oblique appeal to Charles for support. In any case, the urgency of Villon's tone is unmistakable; he brings a new subject matter to the courtly form, to powerful effect. Of all the poets considered thus far, Villon offers the most immediate and compelling look at his own world. His poems capture the brutality and pessimism of the age that produced the *danse macabre* (a common motif in the visual arts—a procession containing people of all classes, being led away by Death, a grinning skeleton). However, Villon also sees, and makes his readers see, the humor and the faith that made it possible to survive in that world.

THE SIXTEENTH CENTURY

The sixteenth century in France was dominated by two related movements best known to twentieth century readers as the Renaissance and the Reformation. Both were made up of smaller and disparate movements, yet while it is important to acknowledge the diversity this implies, the labels have stuck because they point to consistent trends amid the diversity. The century was characterized by a revival of interest in forms of art and learning stemming from classical models, and it saw the appearance of "reformed" Christian churches whose definitive rejection of Roman Catholicism led to long and bloody struggles. Both movements affected the whole of Europe, and neither began in France. It makes sense to speak of a French form of each, however—particularly since the sixteenth century saw the first appearance of strong national feeling among the French. Although this feeling would be seriously threatened by the religious wars of the second half of the century, it would reemerge upon the accession of Henry IV, the first of the line of Bourbon kings.

The Renaissance or "rebirth" of arts and letters had economic underpinnings: It was made possible by a gradual recovery (after the Hundred Years' War), followed by a boom in trade that favored French merchants and artisans because they were in a position to provide the finished goods Europe was seeking. Spain had silver and gold from her New World colonies but wanted cloth, leather, tools, and even food (Spanish agriculture as well lagged behind that of the French). All of these commodities the French had for sale. This was the era in which the modern form of capitalism can be said to have made its appearance, as the merchant class assumed the upper hand in the disposition of the country's wealth: The nobles spent money lavishly, but the bourgeoisie loaned and invested—and earned. Since the reign of Louis XI (1461-1483), who had picked up (or stolen or bought back) the pieces of his realm after the Hundred Years' War, the bourgeoisie had also provided the backbone of the royal administration. The noble class might live extravagantly—indeed, were expected to do so—and win glory in foreign campaigns, but they were chronically in debt and thus dependent on both the bourgeoisie (the moneylenders) and the king (the dispenser of offices and pensions). Meanwhile, a new order of nobility—the *noblesse de robe*, so called because they held judgeships—was being culled from the ranks of the bourgeoisie by kings anxious to reward their faithful officers and to win allies among this newly powerful class. Although social distinctions were carefully maintained between the *noblesse de robe* and *noblesse de sang* (the hereditary nobility), the former imitated the latter as much as they could, and often lived more sumptuously, as did many of the *grands bourgeois*.

Despite these far-reaching changes in economic and social organization, French kings continued to rule by "divine right" and to have the final word in most policy decisions, especially those regarding foreign policy. Indeed, thanks to increased control over the debt-ridden nobility and the rising bourgeoisie, the power of the monarchy was more far-reaching than ever before, to the point that the term "absolute" is often applied to the monarchy of this and the following two centuries. The concordat, or agreement with the pope, of 1516 increased royal power and finances further by making the king the de facto head of the Church in France, with authority to name successors to all major ecclesiastical posts. Because of the concordat, French kings were not tempted to use the stirrings of religious reform as an excuse to break with Rome, as did Henry VIII of England. The early years of the century were thus years of relative tolerance, in which religious questioning was but one symptom of the new approach to intellectual inquiry.

A combination of surplus wealth, absolute control of foreign policy, and old chivalric ideas permitted three French kings in succession to invade Italy in the late fifteenth and early sixteenth centuries. Although their territorial gains were short-lived and costly, they brought back with them to France a passion for the way of life they had tasted in Italy and a determination to transplant it to their native soil. They and their officers patronized artists such as Raphael, Michelangelo, and Leonardo da Vinci (the latter died at Francis I's château of Amboise); they built new, airy palaces and decorated them in a style inspired by that of Renaissance Italy, then in its culminating phase. Above all, they collected books and manuscripts and patronized scholars who had rediscovered the learning of the ancient world. Nor was it a simple matter of recovering lost texts and cultivating skills that had waned (such as the knowledge of classical Greek); the old texts were read in a new spirit.

In the first place, an avid intellectual curiosity was fed by new admiration for the powers of the human mind. The work of establishing accurate texts and translations called for critical acumen and self-confidence; instead of resorting to unquestioned authorities, scholars such as Guillaume Budé and Lefèvre d'Étaples produced their own commentaries. They also tended to focus their studies on humanity rather than on God—but this does not mean that they were irreligious. Although most of them criticized the temporal abuses of the Church, only a few took the further step of rejecting its authority in spiritual matters. While marveling at the purely human virtues they saw in the old pagan authors, they also re-edited the Bible and translated it into French; the study of Hebrew was revived along with that of Greek. Moreover, when the first printing presses appeared in France in the late fifteenth century, the majority of works published were not the classics but missals and other devotional books.

As Lucien Fèbvre emphasized in his influential essays on Renaissance France, printing was from the first a business, requiring considerable capital and hinging on possibilities of profit. The classics were printed later, and in smaller quantities, because they appealed to a smaller public, clustered in a few centers of learning: Paris, the Loire Valley (where the new royal châteaus were rising), Lyons (the great trading center of the age). It is important to realize, however, that the new learning was not confined to the upper classes; in fact, the chivalric ideal, which maintained its hold despite—and perhaps in compensation for—the dwindling power of the nobility, valued social graces and feats of arms above learning, and proportionally fewer nobles than one might expect became scholars.

The Reformation owed as much to the revival of classical learning as it did to the rise of the bourgeoisie. To approach sacred texts in a critical spirit is ultimately to assert the autonomy of the scholar, and of his conscience. John (Jean) Calvin, who became the leader of the reform movement in France, was a student of the Humanist scholar Guillaume Budé; at the Académie, Calvin's seminary in Geneva (established in 1559), his preachers received a thorough training in the classics as well as in theology. The same was true, however, of the preachers recruited by Saint Ignatius and his Society of Jesus, founded in 1534 to stem the tide of the Reformation; reformers and counter-reformers alike turned to the classics as models of clear exposition and—perhaps most important—of effective argument. The struggle between them was a fierce one, and it was not confined to the lecture hall and the pulpit; as nobles, *grands bourgeois*, and even cities took sides, it immediately became a political issue, with bloody consequences.

During the first third of the century, as the ideas of Martin Luther began to circulate in France, Francis I took a tolerant attitude while remaining orthodox himself. (His sister, Marguerite of Angoulême, was still more receptive to the new doctrines, and not only patronized but also protected many of the Huguenot—French Protestant—writers, including the poet Clément Marot.) Francis did not adopt a policy of repression until 1534, when the so-called "affair of the placards" made him fear for his own power. His son, Henry II, pursued this policy in a more fanatic spirit, and great numbers of Protestants were executed as heretics—although martyrdom had the effect of reinforcing Protestant convictions.

The event that led to civil war, however, was the death of Henry II in 1559. His three sons, who succeeded him one after the other, proved unable to control the state, and feudal ambitions, newly fused with religious animosities, erupted in a series of eight wars between 1562 and 1598. Both sides were guilty of fanaticism and atrocities; the most appalling single incident was the massacre of Protestants that began on the feast of Saint Bartholomew in 1572. The struggle was further complicated and intensified by the participation of foreign troops (Spanish and Italian Catholics, English and German Protestants), whose ostensible motive was to aid their coreligionists but who were often used to further the ambitions of foreign monarchs.

With the death of Henry III in 1589, the dynasty of the Valois came to an end and was succeeded by that of the Bourbons, whose first representative, Henry IV, had to renounce his Protestant faith to secure the allegiance of Paris. The bourgeois Parlement, as well as the Estates General (convened in 1592), clearly expressed public resentment of foreign intruders and weariness of religious strife. The Edict of Nantes, which Henry promulgated in 1598, granted freedom of worship to Protestants and Catholics alike, while a treaty with Spain in the same year marked the end of foreign intervention. Henry was not slow to gather the reins of absolute power into his hands, thereby setting the stage for the glories and abuses of the century of Louis XIV.

A CENTURY OF POETS

The sixteenth century saw a great efflorescence in French poetry. Although none of the individual poets had quite the stature of Villon, there were so many of them, and of such high quality, that the term "Renaissance" may be applied without hesitation. It is doubly appropriate because the new poetry was both a reflection of Italian influence at the height of that country's Renaissance and a genuinely French development, infused with confidence in the literary potential of the French language.

The century began with a school of poets known to critics as the Rhétoriqueurs because of their fondness for elaborate rhetorical figures. They represent both the end of a phase of development—the obsession with form that had marked the lyric poetry of the fourteenth and fifteenth centuries—and the beginning of the new Renaissance phase. Thus, despite their fondness for old forms, whose complexity they increased wherever possible, and for old themes (allegorical treatments of courtly love), they also took pride in their native language. One of the most talented of them, Jean Lemaire de Belges, even composed a treatise interspersed with poems, whose object was to demonstrate the equality of literary merit between French and Italian. Finally, two of the Rhétoriqueurs, Jean Marot and Octovien de Saint-Gelais, had sons who became better poets than their fathers—but who owed to those fathers their early formation as poets.

French Renaissance poetry, like that of the Rhétoriqueurs, was superior to all court poetry. Most of its practitioners were not themselves nobles but courtiers, attached to noble patrons who appreciated the arts. The most coveted places were at the royal court, where some of the century's best poets, including Clément Marot and Pierre de Ronsard, served in various capacities. (Poetic excellence was not sufficient, however, to ensure permanent favor: Marot fell from grace because of his Huguenot sympathies, and Ronsard because of the death of his royal patron, Charles IX.) However, there were other milieus in which poetry could flourish. The new passion for learning gave rise to circles or salons among the bourgeoisie, of which the most famous was that of Louise Labé, called "la Belle Cordiére" because both her father and her husband were prosperous ropemakers. She was herself a poet of considerable merit, and her circle, in Lyons, attracted other poets of both genders who drew inspiration from the style of Marot and the Italian Petrarch. The circle of seven poets known as the Pléiade (after the constellation of the Pleiades) took shape at a school in Paris and was made up of students of the Humanist scholar Jean Dorat. Earlier in the century, before the Catholic repression set in, there had been circles united by an interest in religious reform as well as in Humanist learning; the most brilliant of these was the court of Marguerite of Angoulême, sister of Francis I.

The two most striking characteristics of the new poetry fostered by these circles were its adaptation of Italian and classical forms and its steadily increasing sophistication of style and tone. From Petrarch, the fourteenth century Italian poet, it borrowed the sonnet sequence, and as Petrarch had celebrated the stages of his idealized love for "Laura," so Maurice Scève explored his for "Délie" (1544) and Joachim du Bellay his for "Olive" (1549). Ancient forms of lyric verse were borrowed—the ode, the epistle, the elegy— and attempts were even made to revive the epic in its classical, Vergilian form. (Classical tragedy was also revived at this period, with considerable success.) A school of so-called neo-Latin verse flourished in Humanist circles, and many of the poets best known for their French verse also composed in Latin.

There was an ongoing debate concerning the relative merits of Latin and French, which prompted the members of the Pléiade to issue a kind of manifesto (composed by du Bellay) called *La Défense et illustration de la langue française* (1549; *The Defence and Illustration of the French Language*, 1939). In addition to defending the merits of French as a medium for great poetry, du Bellay recommended that it be further "ennobled" or "elevated" through emulation of the classical genres and by borrowings from Latin vocabulary and syntax. Because of differences in the structures of French and Latin, and notably because Latin (like Greek) is an inflected language, some of these borrowings proved too artificial and were not naturalized into the poetic repertoire of French. In general, however, the emulation of ancient models brought a new sophistication to French lyric, which is perhaps best appreciated by comparing the poetry of the earlier generations of Renaissance poets with that of the Pléiade. This is scarcely to denigrate Marot and his contemporaries, whose style some will prefer because it is less polished or more "Gallic" (Marot was, after all, the contemporary of François Rabelais). It is merely to acknowledge a prominent trend, which produced some outstanding results and set the tone for half a century of French verse.

It remains to acknowledge the striking range of theme and mood visible in French Renaissance poetry—a range corresponding to the variety of genres it rediscovered and adapted, but corresponding as well to the range of emotions generated by the events of the century. Thus, side by side with the graceful and often passionate love poetry inspired by Petrarch, one finds the melancholy but stately sonnets of du Bellay's *Les Regrets* (1558; *The Regrets*, 1984), inspired by classical elegy, and the unfinished epics attempted by Ronsard and Guillaume du Bartas; one also finds Ronsard's eloquent defense of his Catholicism in the *Discours des misères de ce temps*, 1562; discourse on the miseries of these times) and Agrippa d'Aubigné's fierce blend of satire and indignation (in the Protestant cause this time) in his *Les Tragiques* (1616). Not infrequently, a considerable range is to be found in the work of a single poet. Marot, for example, though best known for his badinage (or light, playful wit), was equally capable of fervent lyricism (as in his translation of the biblical Psalms) and of vehement satire in the vein of d'Aubigné ("L'Enfer," or "Inferno," was inspired by his imprisonment for his Protestant beliefs). For sheer versatility, Ronsard was unequaled; he tried his hand at dozens of genres, and even his failures—such as an attempt to emulate the Pindaric odes—are the result of lapses of taste rather than any lack of poetic vigor. The rediscovery of Greece and Rome had enriched the repertoire of poetic forms and themes, but the passion conveyed was the poets' own—the faith and the anguish, the loves and the ambitions of a turbulent century.

The seventeenth century

In the seventeenth century, the French monarchy, the ancien régime, reached its apogee and began its decline. In an important sense, Louis XIV can be held responsible for both of these developments, although it is arguable that he did more to hasten the decline than to gain the summit, which had been the long-sought objective of Cardinal Richelieu and Cardinal Mazarin before him (not to mention Henry IV and Francis I). It was Louis XIV, the Sun King, who sought to formalize and demonstrate his power in the visible symbol of Versailles—a court whose every grace and virtue (and extravagance and whim) was ultimately an expression of his own will. Clearly, this was in many ways a fiction, and a pernicious one insofar as it blinded Louis himself to important social and economic developments in his realm. It was, however, a fiction of great power, which many seventeenth and eighteenth century rulers tried to emulate and which left its mark on French culture well beyond the Revolution.

Like their predecessors since Philip IV, both Louis XIII and Louis XIV—whose reigns together spanned nearly the entire century—based their power on the employment of bourgeois ministers while reducing the nobility to the status of dependents of the crown. Because both acceded to the throne in childhood, two of their ministers, the cardinals Richelieu and Mazarin, were virtual rulers of France for long periods. Richelieu was responsible for rebuilding the French military, crushing noble intrigues against Louis XIII, and humbling the Habsburg dynasty in the Thirty Years' War, thereby securing the borders of France. Mazarin pursued Richelieu's policies after the latter's death, and, despite the four-year setback of the Fronde (1648-1652), managed to complete the submission of the nobility and the containment of Habsburg Spain.

The Fronde was in fact the last real attempt of the French nobility to recoup the power they had been steadily losing to the monarchy since the thirteenth century. By allying themselves with the bourgeois Parlement and the Parisian masses, incensed by Mazarin's attempts to tax them, a coalition of princes managed for a time to expel "the Italian," whose foreign birth inspired suspicion and hatred. A quarrel between the rebellious factions, however, which coincided with Louis XIV's coming of age, spelled the end of the uprising. Moreover, the fear and humiliation which the young Louis experienced during the Fronde made him determined never to share his power with the nobility—nor, indeed, with the higher clergy. After Mazarin's death, he served as his own first minister and chose his other ministers from among the lower classes. He refused to convene the Estates General, suppressed what political initiative the Parlement had acquired, and brought even provincial administration under his direct control by the use of agents known as *intendants*.

Considering himself the spiritual as well as the temporal head of the French Church, he took the disastrous step of revoking the Edict of Nantes. This had the practical effect of driving numbers of Huguenots into exile, to the great detriment of French industry. The worst abuse of Louis's reign, however, was his utter disregard of fiscal realities. In planning Versailles and in waging continual war for what he considered the greater glory of France, he stubbornly refused to count costs. When combined with a bureaucratic control of industry and a cruelly unfair system of taxation (which exempted the rich while crushing the peasantry), Louis's prodigality paved the way that was to lead, in another century, to revolution. (A number of tax revolts among the peasants marked the decade of the 1670's.)

Despite its claims to absolutism, the monarchy was not the only institution in seventeenth century France, nor did Louis have a monopoly on the ideas of the age. It was an age in which religion still held great power, not only over the minds of individuals but also over institutions (such as the Sorbonne) and intellectual life—though its premium on philosophical truth would be challenged in the course of the century. If the French Church was largely subordinate to the king in temporal matters, it retained much authority in spiritual matters and could use this authority to political as well as spiritual effect. Thus, the international order of the Jesuits played a role in both the Thirty Years' War and the revocation of the Edict of Nantes.

Louis XIV's confessor was a Jesuit, and the king seems to have been following his advice in suppressing the ideas of Cornelius Jensenius and his French followers. The Jansenists, though Catholics, had ideas on predestination that resembled those of John Calvin. Their adherents included brilliant men of letters such as Jean Racine and Blaise Pascal, whose *Lettres provinciales* (1656-1657; *The Provincial Letters*, 1657) were at once a defense of Jansenist teachings and an attack on the moral "casuistry" of the Jesuits. The Jesuits, and the pope, focused their attacks on the Jansenists' notion of grace, but there can be little doubt that the moral austerity and integrity of the latter also made them a source of embarrassment to a corrupt Church and a corrupt court. Among the orthodox, too, there were initiatives toward reform, such as the creation of new religious orders and of a secret society, the Compagnie du Saint-Sacrement, whose efforts ranged from charitable works to persecution of Protestants, Jansenists, and freethinkers—Jean-Baptiste Molière criticized its excesses in his verse play *Tartuffe: Ou, L'Imposteur* (pr. 1664; *Tartuffe*, 1732).

Religious questions were rendered still more pressing by the growth of skepticism or "libertinism." Pascal's *Pensées* (1670; *Monsieur Pascal's Thoughts, Meditations, and Prayers*, 1688; best known as *Pensées*) consists of notes for an ambitious project he never completed: a "Defense of the Christian Religion," addressed to the *mondain*, or "man of the world," who in Pascal's day would have been increasingly likely to doubt or neglect religious teachings. Both the hypocrisy of the clergy and the luxurious life of the court were factors in this skepticism, but a new factor was philosophical doubt, sown by the growing split between religious and scientific truth. The Copernican theory of the solar system, developed in the sixteenth century, had been reaffirmed by Galileo in 1632. Although the Inquisition forced Galileo to recant, this proved to be a rearguard action, and by 1687, Sir Isaac Newton had laid the foundations for a wholly new science of physics. Pascal himself was a great mathematician as well as religious thinker, contributing to the creation of calculus and probability theory. Pascal's own faith, and the sense of mission that drove him to undertake a defense of Christianity, took on urgency precisely because he glimpsed the vast, indifferent universe science was to reveal and could no longer accept the rationalistic proofs of God's existence offered by the Scholastics. The most influential thinker of the age in France was René Descartes, who was not a solitary genius but the most successful of his contemporaries in formulating the new philosophical problems. His work proved seminal because it provided not a system but a method of research, inspired by mathematics and rejecting the testimony of tradition—including religious tradition. Although Descartes himself was a religious man and made room in his theories for a Creator, others went further and denied the existence of God. Those who rejected tradition as the basis of their beliefs were commonly referred to as *libertins* (an epithet that originally meant simply "freethinkers"). An important group of *libertins* gathered about the philosopher Pierre Gassendi, who also espoused the Copernican theory but borrowed his ideas on physics from the ancient "atomists," Democritus and Epicurus. In addition to elaborating new theories, many of these seventeenth century scientists also conducted experiments and shared their results with one another through the creation of *académies*, or scientific societies. *Académies* flourished in Dijon, Rouen, and other provincial cities, as well as in the capital.

Thus, behind the facade of Louis XIV's absolutism, a variety of social, spiritual, and intellectual movements were struggling to define and maintain themselves. In this respect, the history of the eighteenth century was essentially a working out of trends already perceptible in the seventeenth.

An eclipse of lyric poetry

Great French poetry was written in the seventeenth century, but almost all of it was dramatic poetry—the tragedies of Jean Racine and of Pierre Corneille, the comedies of Molière. Even the fables of Jean de La Fontaine are narrative and satiric, rather than lyric, poetry. Granted that great lyric genius is rare and owes much to inborn gifts, there is still call to ask why this century should have failed to foster such talents as there were. (The sixteenth and nineteenth centuries offer especially striking contrasts in this regard.) At least a part of the answer lies in the milieus where poetry was produced.

From the beginning, French lyric poetry had flourished chiefly in aristocratic circles, whether the poets were themselves noble or not. This did not change in the seventeenth century; the new element was the overwhelming force of centralization drawing all such circles into the orbit of the king. Hippolyte Taine argued in his history of the ancien régime that the creation of a single court as the source of all royal patronage (and the simultaneous reduction of all aristocrats to dependency on the king) had a great effect on both language and thought, which extended throughout the eighteenth as well as the seventeenth century. Because the court was "worldly" but not learned, the more erudite

Renaissance borrowings from the ancient world were rejected as pedantic or eccentric; the sophistication that continued to be sought was of a social and not an intellectual order. The exploration of individual emotion, an essential element in most lyricism, was likewise discouraged, as art became preeminently public. Thus, while a certain elaboration of form and refinement of expression might be approved as proper to the exclusivity of court circles, ideas, themes, and syntax were to be clear, logical, and accessible.

This ideal of clarity was expressed both at the beginning and near the end of the century by two influential critics, François Malherbe and Nicolas Boileau-Despréaux. Both were poets, but they are best known as the theoreticians of French "classicism," which they did not invent but did much to propagate. Malherbe laid down a set of rules for the composition of verse that forbade hiatus (the juxtaposition of two vowels) and enjambment, while prescribing that rhymes and metrical breaks (caesuras and line ends) should coincide with syntactic breaks. Boileau wrote a treatise on the art of poetry that owed much to Aristotle and Horace, the ancient theoreticians of style, but his work is clearly a product of its own time in its emphasis on reason, which it exalts above the other faculties involved in the creation of poetry.

Although Boileau also upheld the ideal of sublimity and looked to the ancients, as well as to the Bible, for models, his emphasis on logic and his tendency to equate reason with common sense actually had a leveling effect. In Taine's assessment, Boileau and his contemporaries could insist on the transparency of "truth" and "nature" because they shared a language and a perspective shaped by the court, where intense social pressure eliminated both individual and regional ("provincial") idiosyncrasies. It is worth noting that the seventeenth century also saw the creation (by Cardinal Richelieu) of the French Academy, an officially sanctioned group of writers charged with maintaining the "purity" of the French language.

This is not to say that a dull uniformity of style prevailed in seventeenth century poetry. There were in fact a variety of different trends, yet each reflected to some degree the effects of court pressure. The trend sometimes identified as Baroque because of its affinity with that style in the plastic arts is chiefly concerned with appearances and their instability. Jean Rousset's *Anthologie de la poésie baroque française* (1968; anthology of French Baroque poetry), which offers a selection of this poetry, arranged by theme, includes sections on metamorphosis, disguise, bubbles, clouds, and water, both as a reflecting or shimmering surface and as a flowing—hence inconstant—element. The influence of Italian poetry, and in particular of Giambattista Marino (who lived in Paris from 1615 to 1622), is visible in these works, but the attention to surfaces is also a characteristic of court life. A curious feature of seventeenth century religious art, which Rousset associates with the Baroque tendency, is a fascination with death and physical decay. This feature is obviously related to the spiritual struggles of the age, but it, too, reveals an obsession with appearances, for the living—including the beautiful and the powerful—may be transformed at any time into corpses. Thus, the spiritual anguish of the age was perhaps increased by the contrast, inherent in court life, between apparent beauty, favor, or power, and its instability.

Some critics, however, deny the existence of a true Baroque style in France and speak instead of *préciosité* and burlesque. These related trends share an exaggerated concern for form, but whereas *préciosité* takes form seriously and makes its observance almost a point of honor, burlesque reveals its ridiculous side. The précieux poets flourished in the salons, which emerged as miniature courts in the orbit of the royal court. The most famous and influential of these was that of the marquise de Rambouillet, whose poor health often prevented her from going out and who, in compensation, assembled about her a circle of literary and social luminaries. During the years of its existence (1620-1665), her salon welcomed Richelieu, Malherbe, Marino, Corneille, and Madame de Sévigné, among others, as well as many of the higher aristocracy.

Though serious works were read and discussed, the salon was primarily a social gathering, where time might be spent in parlor games and above all in polite conversation. Other salons were formed in emulation of the Hôtel de Rambouillet; the most prominent was the bourgeois salon of Madeleine de Scudéry, author of multivolume novels in true précieux style. Though chosen for its original meaning, "of great price or value," the term précieux came to mean a style of writing or behavior that sought consciously to elevate its practitioners. Exotic or abstract words might be substituted for ordinary ones; farfetched or hyperbolic comparisons were sought; medieval poetic forms such as the ballade and rondeau were revived for the sake of their complexity. Insofar as most salons were organized by women and devoted considerable attention to the refined expression of love, they bear comparison with the courts where troubadour lyrics evolved. However, the fact that many courtly themes had become clichés forced poets to seek ever more exaggerated treatments of them, while the dependent, courtier status of the people involved offered an implicit contrast to the virtues convention ascribed to them.

The situation invited parody, and indeed some précieux poetry verges on self-parody. Writers in the burlesque vein took advantage of this situation, pushing précieux tendencies to ridiculous extremes or deflating them with doses of realism. It is interesting to note that the burlesque poets—Paul Scarron, Saint-Amant, Cyrano de Bergerac—tended to occupy more ambiguous or marginal positions in society, while virtually all were *libertins*. Although some of these men frequented the salons, they also gathered in the cabarets and cafés of Paris, where there were no refined standards of etiquette to repress their flights of satiric and obscene humor.

Jean de La Fontaine

Granted that the centralized court life of the age did not foster lyric poetry, it nevertheless had a positive effect on some other forms of literature, for it encouraged the close study of human character under what might almost be called laboratory conditions.

Thus, the genius of La Fontaine, the greatest nondramatic poet of the age, found ample matter in the observation of his fellow courtiers. Like Villon, La Fontaine is remarkable for the range of tone he achieved in a poetic idiom that imposed great formal restrictions. In contrast to Villon, however, La Fontaine is himself absent from his poetry, except as a sharp and sometimes pitiless observer of human foibles. His *Contes et nouvelles en vers* (1665; *Tales and Short Stories in Verse*, 1735) and *Fables choises, mises en vers* (1668-1694; *Fables Written in Verse*, 1735) have been compared to the great dramatic poetry of his age, which sought to portray universals of human behavior yet in so doing inevitably revealed much about its own time and place.

Thus, La Fontaine's fables manage to give vivid glimpses of contemporary life in the guise of the beast fable. La Fontaine has even been accused (by Jean-Jacques Rousseau, among others) of teaching his readers how to rise in the world by dissembling and well-placed flattery, yet it can more plausibly be argued that his fables unmask the baser motives of courtiers, by attributing these motives to animals and by identifying them in plain words. In fact, the most striking feature of the fables, given La Fontaine's proximity to the court of Louis XIV, is their directness; nor does it come as a surprise to learn that the king was cool toward the poet. It should be noted as well that La Fontaine—who was himself a bourgeois from the provinces—did not limit his purview to the court but peopled his menagerie from all the ranks of seventeenth century society. Although his models were classical, he thus rejoined the French medieval tradition of the fabliaux and the *Roman de Renart*, offering a pungent antidote to the artificiality of much court poetry.

Bibliography

Banks, Kathryn. *Cosmos and Image in the Renaissance: French Love Lyric and Natural-Philosophical Poetry*. London: Legenda, 2008. Explores the relationship between Renaissance imagery and poetic language and the ways that poetic language, in turn, influenced Renaissance thought. Bibliography and index. Bilingual edition.

Gaunt, Simon, and Sarah Kay, eds. *The Cambridge Companion to Medieval French Literature*. New York: Cambridge University Press, 2008. A guide to French literature from the ninth century to the Renaissance. Detailed analyses of major poetic works, from lyrics to romances. Chronology and suggestions for further reading.

Hollier, Denis, with R. Howard Bloch et al. *A New History of French Literature*. Cambridge, Mass.: Harvard University Press, 1994. A translation of *De la literature française*. A unique work, consisting of 164 succinct essays on a wide range of subjects, all written by scholars who are known for their extensive knowledge in a particular area. Bibliographical references and index.

Kay, Sarah, Terence Cave, and Malcolm Bowie. *A Short History of French Literature*. New York: Oxford University Press, 2003. A reliable but accessible overview of French literature, told as a series of stories that describe major writers and place them within the context of their times. Ideal for general readers as well as for more advanced students of French.

Kelly, Douglas. *The Art of Medieval French Romance*. Madison: University of Wisconsin Press, 1992. Uses statements made by the authors of medieval romances to answer questions about the genre that are raised by modern readers.

Kenny, Neil. *An Introduction to Sixteenth-Century French Literature and Thought: Other Times, Other Places*. London: Duckworth, 2008. This thoughtful study attempts to account for the fact that in the French Renaissance the writers whose primary concern was the improvement of their society so often wrote about other times and distant places. Illustrated. Bibliographical references and index.

Moss, Ann. *Poetry and Fable: Studies in Mythological Narrative in Sixteenth-Century France*. New York: Cambridge University Press, 2009. Through studying changes in the treatment of mythological subjects, the writer shows how both aesthetic theories and the attitudes of readers were changing during the period.

Shapiro, Norman R., ed. and trans. *French Women Poets of Nine Centuries: The Distaff and the Pen*. Baltimore: Johns Hopkins University Press, 2008. Introductions by Roberta L. Krueger, Catherine Lafarge, and Catherine Perry; foreword by Rosanne Warren. Contains more than six hundred poems by fifty-six different writers, with originals and translations on facing pages. A monumental volume.

Shaw, Mary Lewis. *The Cambridge Introduction to French Poetry*. New York: Cambridge University Press, 2003. An exhaustive survey of French poetry, with topics ranging from verse forms and genres to the relationship between poetry and politics. Glossary of poetic terms, bibliography, and indexes.

Stephens, Sonya, ed. *A History of Women's Writing in France*. New York: Cambridge University Press, 2000. A collection of essays, each focusing on a different period. Includes bibliography and a guide to more than 150 writers and their works.

Willett, Laura, trans. *Poetry and Language in Sixteenth-Century France: Du Bellay, Ronsard, Sébillet*. Toronto: Centre for Reformation and Renaissance Studies, Victoria University, 2004. Contains key texts in development of poetic theory. Introduction and notes by Willett. Bibliography.

Lillian Doherty

FRENCH POETRY SINCE 1700

It has often been said that the most poetic works of eighteenth century France were written in prose—works such as François de Salignac de la Mothe-Fénelon's *Télémaque* (1699; *The Adventures of Telemachus*, 1720), Jean-Jacques Rousseau's *La Nouvelle Héloïse* (1761; *Eloisa: Or, A Series of Original Letters*, 1761), and especially *Les R{ecirc}veries d'un promeneur solitaire* (1782; *The Reveries of a Solitary Walker*, 1783), Bernardin de Saint-Pierre's *Paul et Virginie* (1787; *Paul and Mary*, 1789), and Constanin Volney's *Les Ruines* (1791; the ruins). Here, true poetic feeling and sentiment, as those terms were defined by the Romantics, are indisputably present. However, the eighteenth century, turned toward reason and progress, was not without poetry of a different sort, and critics who view the period as a mere lacuna in poetry between classicism and Romanticism have not studied the major authors or their influence on the following centuries. There was indeed a great output of poetry, although in many cases quantity substituted for quality.

The eighteenth century was one of the most vibrant periods of French history, yet it has two faces: the face of the salon, the court, the ball, and the masque, preserving the past, and the forward-looking face of the philosophes. In the eighteenth century, France was the idol of culture; European monarchs spoke French and built imitations of Versailles. At the court of Louis XV, although luxury and frivolity flourished, so did such cultural accomplishments as the architecture of Jacques Gabriel, the paintings of François Boucher, Jean-Honoré Fragonard, and Antoine Watteau, and the exquisite cabinets and commodes of Georges Jacob and Jean-Henri Riesener. In Paris, men and women of society gathered in the salons of the Duchesse de Maine, the Marquise de Lambert, Madame de Tencin, and Madame de Geoffrin. It was here that much poetry of the period gained its inspiration; it was inferior to the great seventeenth century masterpieces and somehow displayed in its shallow forms the end of an era.

The more vibrant aspect of the *siècle des lumières*, the Age of Enlightenment, was the activity of the philosophes, the great thinkers and writers who ultimately affected the destiny of France and the modern world with their emphasis on reason and their belief in human progress. At first relatively restrained and committed to popularizing scientific discoveries, as in the works of Pierre Bayle (1647-1706) and Bernard le Bovier de Fontenelle (1657-1757), they began to address more delicate issues. Charles-Louis de Secondat, known by his title of Montesquieu (1689-1755), wrote an anonymous satire of religious and political institutions in his *Les Lettres persanes* (1721; *Persian Letters*, 1722) and produced a scholarly study on law in *De l'esprit des lois* (1748; *The Spirit of Laws*, 1750). The great Voltaire, who so dominated every aspect of the eighteenth century that it is known as the Age of Voltaire, used his clever and ironic pen to satirize virtually everything and everyone, particularly religious intolerance and superstition.

Denis Diderot (1713-1784), known especially as the editor of the great résumé of eighteenth century knowledge, *L'Encyclopédie* (1751-1780), was himself a writer of sensibility, already foreshadowing Romanticism, and a man of cold reason bordering on atheism. Finally, Rousseau (1712-1778) argued for a return to the simple life, to a new morality and religion based on the heart, and a new type of government under which equality would reign.

Although the philosophes used prose as their principal means of expression, they all began a literary apprenticeship with poetry, and Voltaire expressed many of his important ideas, and all of his tragedies, in verse. Poets touched philosophical ideas, often tangentially, especially in science, nature, and morals, and Voltaire judged each of them by their conformity to his ideas. Poetry, on the whole, kept to classical models, faithful to the precepts of Nicolas Boileau-Despréaux (1636-1711). The great genres—ode, elegy, eclogue, and satire—were the most practiced. Rhythm and rhyme were decorously employed, and allusions to antiquity proliferated. At the beginning of the century, subjects were rarely personal, but after 1750, sentiment and nature themes began to appear. Poems of circumstance were frivolous, sensual, and pagan in inspiration, illustrating the degradation of morals, yet there was a surprising quantity of religious poetry in this age of anticlericalism, Deism, and even outspoken atheism. The century ended with a more lyric poet, André-Marie Chénier, a victim of the very Revolution that he had supported in verse and in action.

Didactic and religious poetry

In the camp opposed to Voltaire and the philosophes were several didactic and religious poets. Among the best of the religious authors were Jean-Jacques Lefranc, marquis de Pompignan (1709-1784), and Louis Racine (1692-1763), son of the great Jean Racine, author of seventeenth century classical tragedies. Pompignan is known for his "Ode sur la mort de Jean-Baptiste Rousseau" (ode on the death of Jean-Baptiste Rousseau), but his best works are his *Poésies sacrées* (1734, 1751, 1763; sacred poems), paraphrases of biblical texts, many of which have real literary value. Their lyric accents and ease of versification anticipate the achievements of Alphonse de Lamartine.

Island-born French poets

Romantic exoticism characterized the works of three poets born in French semitropical islands: Nicolas-Germain Léonard (1744-1793), born in Guadeloupe, and Antoine Bertin (1752-1790) and Évariste-Désiré de Forges de Parny (1753-1814), both born on the Île Bourbon, now the Île de la Réunion. The *Idylles* (1766) of Léonard are dreamy and delicate, recalling James Thomson (1700-1748) and Oliver Goldsmith in inspiration, though not without a classical influence. Léonard's more descriptive passages anticipate Alfred de Musset and especially Lamartine, who knew and read his works. Bertin, a friend of Parny, is best known for his *Les Amours* (1780), written in the manner of the sixteenth century poet Pierre de Ronsard. They are erotic, lighthearted, and sensual, with overtones of melancholy such as one finds in Watteau's painting F{ecirc}tes galantes.

The best poet of the three was Parny. He was much appreciated by Voltaire, who—alluding to the Roman elegist Tibullus—called him "mon cher Tibulle"; to posterity, Parny was known by the less flattering diminutive, Tibullinus. A poet of love and sensuality, Parny took as his Elvire a woman named Eléonore, whom he was not permitted to marry. His best love poetry is found in *Poésies érotiques* (1778; erotic poems). He addressed patriotic themes in his "Épître aux insurgents de Boston" (1777). His most original works, however, are his *Chansons madécasses traduites en françois* (1787), which are really poems in prose, although the distinction of inventing the genre usually goes to Aloysius Bertrand. Sensual and even licentious in the manner of the eighteenth century, Parny's poetry is not without the melancholy that was to inspire nineteenth century Romantics.

Pre-Romanticism

As the nineteenth century dawned, minor poets already were writing in Romantic accents, yet Romantic poetry did not come into prominence until 1820. A transitional writer, Charles-Hubert Millevoye (1782-1816), began with classical epistles, translations of Vergil, and biblical and historical poems. Millevoye's "Chute des feuilles" (falling leaves), "La Demeure abandonnée" (the abandoned dwelling), "Le Poète mourant" (the dying poet), and "Priez pour moi" (pray for me) are true Romantic poems, distinguished by their melancholy, appreciation of nature, and meditations on death and by their early expression of the cult of the individual.

André-Marie Chénier

The eighteenth century, so little known for true poetic inspiration, ended with the voice of a real poet, André-Marie Chénier (1762-1794), whose brother Marie-Joseph Chénier (1764-1811) at first eclipsed him in fame. Born in Constantinople of a mother who falsely claimed Greek ancestry, Chénier was to be haunted throughout his life by the Greek concept of beauty. His early poetry, mostly elegiac, was written in the style of the eighteenth century, yet he gradually attained a masterful simplicity, especially in *Les Bucoliques* (wr. 1785-1787, pb. 1819). Aiming, like Voltaire, to write an epic, he began two, *Hermès* and *L'Amérique*, neither of which was ever completed, although *L'Amérique* shows his gift for cosmic vision. In 1794, Chénier wrote *Iambes*, attacking the Jacobine tyranny that would send him to the guillotine the same year.

Chénier was not a Romantic: There is in his verse no cult of the individual, no restless melancholy or evocation of nature and death. If anything, he was a classical poet: His own line, "Sur les pensers nouveaux, faisons des vers antiques" ("On new thoughts, let us make ancient verses"), sums up his aesthetic. Some of his finest poems, such as

"L'Aveugle" (the blind man), the story of a meeting of three shepherds with Homer, anticipate the work of Victor Hugo. "La Jeune Tatentine" (the young Tatentine), a classical story of a young woman drowned at sea, is told in sober and clear lines. "La Jeune Captive" (the young captive), inspired by Chénier's meeting with the young Aimée de Coigny in prison, expresses their desire to cling to the young and vibrant life that the revolution was about to snatch from them. Chénier was at least able to attain immortality through his work, for although Romantic poetry was not to follow his style, it did continue his genuine lyrical inspiration. More directly, the Parnassians emulated his sculptural beauty and his love of ancient Greece.

Romanticism

The nineteenth century in France, as in England, Germany, Poland, and Russia, opened under the sign of Romanticism. While this was the Romantic period par excellence, Romantic themes in literature and ideas ebb and flow in alternation with the serenity of classicism. It is the opposition of a Greek temple to a Gothic cathedral, one representing a single, perfect idea repeated endlessly; the other, freedom in original creativity. Authors such as Madame de Staël have romanticized Romanticism, seeing in it the Christian expression of melancholy, the incompleteness of existence, and the somber gray of foggy northern climates. Finally, Romanticism expresses the turbulence of the human spirit as it strives for independence and emancipation from the rules and restraints of classical order and reason.

In France, the Romantic period spanned a century, from the late eighteenth century to the late nineteenth, achieving its fullest expression during the first third of the nineteenth century. Romanticism first appeared in France during the years between 1760 and 1775, largely in prose rather than poetry. It was from England and Germany, however, rather than from Rousseau and Diderot, that the French Romantic movement, especially in poetry, was to take its primary inspiration.

Madamede Staël's *De l'Allemagne* (1810; *Germany*, 1813) places the roots of Romanticism in Germany, and in the years that followed, French Romantics such as Victor Cousin, Jules Michelet, Charles-Augustin Sainte-Beuve, Hugo, Lamartine, Musset, and others would visit Germany as a hallowed shrine. In France, the most influential German Romantics were Johann Wolfgang von Goethe (1749-1832), whose Werther was the ancestor of René and Adolphe; Friedrich Schiller (1759-1805); and especially the teller of fantastic tales, E. T. A. Hoffmann (1776-1822), whose influence is directly evident in the works of Charles Nodier, Gérard de Nerval, and Théophile Gautier.

For the French Romantics, English inspiration meant William Shakespeare, whom many authors, such as Stendhal in *Racine et Shakspeare* (1823, 1825; *Racine and Shakespeare*, 1962), were to exalt in place of the French classicists. Voltaire, in the eighteenth century, had already proclaimed Shakespeare's superiority; both poets and dramatists were to discover him in the nineteenth. The sentimental novelists of eighteenth century England, such as Samuel Richardson (1689-1761), not only influenced French Romanticism, but inspired changes in the literature of far-off Russia as well. The two greatest contemporary influences from England were Sir Walter Scott (1771-1832), whose novels of medieval chivalry inspired Vigny, Alexandre Dumas, père, Honoré de Balzac, Hugo, Prosper Mérimée, and Gautier as well as writers in Italy, Germany, and Russia, and Lord Byron (1788-1824). The Byronic hero became the model for Romantics throughout Europe.

Although literary historians usually date the flowering of French Romanticism from François-René de Chateaubriand's novels *Atala* (1801; English translation, 1802) and *René* (1802; English translation, 1813) and his treatise *Le Génie du christianisme* (1802; *The Genius of Christianity*, 1802), there was actually a prolonged silence in literary production from the beginning of the French Revolution in 1789 to the exile of Napoleon Bonaparte in 1815. With the exception of Chénier, there was practically nothing of great value in poetry during this period—in fact, not until Lamartine's *Poetical Meditations* in 1820. The intensity of the revolution was no doubt responsible for the early years of this lacuna, although poetry did not have a remarkable history in the eighteenth century. The role of Napoleon (1769-1821) in the history of Romanticism is more problematic. A classicist in taste and philosophy, he launched the most severe and correct of all styles, the Empire style, and he took the ancient Roman Empire as the model of his conquests. No one, however, understood better than he the message of the Revolution: liberty, equality, fraternity, the need for newness, mobility of class structure, patriotism. Although he dreamed of French supremacy in Europe, his "liberation" of Germany and Italy taught the inhabitants of these countries to seek their own roots, and thus he sowed the seeds of nationalism throughout Europe.

French Romanticism, not unlike the Romantic movements in England, Germany, Poland, and Russia, stressed freedom from classical restraints. Since the classical tradition was strongest in France, where the distinction between comedy and tragedy was adhered to with Aristotelian exactness, the call to freedom did not immediately abolish classical forms. Lamartine still wrote in Alexandrines and evoked pagan deities and classical heroes. It was through the emancipation of the theater that poetry was to find new forms of expression, although Hugo's early verse is marked by formal experimentation. Where classicism insists on universal themes, Romanticism stresses the individual: Racine's *Phèdre* (1677; *Phedra*, 1776) dramatizes every woman's jealousy; "The Lake" is Lamartine's personal lament at the loss of love. Classicism made reason the primary law—in the words of Boileau, "aimez donc la raison." Romanticism, echoing Pascal's "raisons du coeur," the reasons of the heart, insisted that emotion had a more powerful role to play.

French Romantic poetry also exalted nature. As Rousseau discovered the mountains of Switzerland, so Lamartine heard the echoes of the Lac du Bourget in the surrounding hills of Burgundy, and Vigny evoked the purple and gold of Mount Nebo in exotic grandeur. However, for the Romantics, nature is more than a setting or, as in the eighteenth century, an object of study. Rather, it reflects the moods of the poet: Chateaubriand's melancholy, for example, becomes the autumn leaves that he hopes will carry him off to the land of happiness and oblivion. Death, too, is a Romantic theme, perhaps best illustrated by Chateaubriand's cult of the tomb. The Romantics, for the most part, share a spiritual orientation, though most of them reject traditional religious forms. Like Rousseau's Savoyard Vicar, they call on the God of the heart, whom they find in nature as well. Hence, they believe in immortality and resurrection, with the possible exception of the stoic Vigny, who stresses the silence of God in response to man's sufferings.

The revolt against classicism further implied a rejection of antiquity and a preference for the Middle Ages. As writers examined their individual memories in meditative introspection, so nations sought their origins in what, until then, had been despised medieval institutions, and buildings. Gothic architecture was again respected. Eugène-Emmanuel Viollet-le-Duc (1814-1879) restored cathedrals and chateaus; medieval manuscripts were collected and studied. Folktales about Renard and *chansons de geste* about Roland were evoked more than Ulysses and Aeneas. Along with medieval themes, exoticism was cultivated. Chateaubriand idealized the New World, the domain of the noble savage; Lamartine and Vigny were inspired by the Holy Land; Eugène Delacroix's somber paintings took on the sunny skies of Algeria after his visit there.

Romanticism, as Madame de Staël observed, is profoundly bathed in melancholy. The French spoke of a pervasive mal du siècle, suggesting a mood of restlessness and ennui, a distaste for one's society, a superabundance of life. This state of mind anticipates the dilemma of modern humanity, overwhelmed by too many options and rejecting traditional and stable values: Romantic melancholy deepens and sours under Charles Baudelaire, and eventually becomes the Absurd of Albert Camus.

Although Chateaubriand was the most profoundly Romantic of all French writers, his works are in prose, albeit with a poetic rhythm and orientation. The great French Romantic poets are Lamartine (1790-1869), Vigny (1797-1863), Musset (1810-1857), and Hugo (1802-1885). Since Romanticism implies freedom, each one was very different, yet they, like all French writers, gravitated to a salon—in the early 1820's, to Charles Nodier's salon at the Arsenal, and after 1827, to Hugo's Cénacle, rue Notre-Dame-des-Champs. Their greatest period of literary productivity was between 1820 and 1850, although Hugo's major poetic works, *Les Châtiments* (1853) and *Les Contemplations* (1856) appeared later. This was a period of relative conservatism in France: The Restoration of the Bourbons had already taken place in 1815. The Revolution of 1830, however, which brought Louis-Philippe to power, inspired a wave of lyric poetry.

Parnassian poets

Romanticism was perhaps the last great literary movement. Others, such as Symbolism and Surrealism, have since appeared, but they have lacked the unity of doctrine and the sweeping appeal of Romanticism. Nevertheless, they have left a profound mark on modern society, itself fragmented and confused.

By 1850, Romantic themes had begun to lose favor. In the novel, realism had already made its appearance: Balzac, in his *La Comédie humaine* (1842-1848; *The Human Comedy*, 1896), showed men as pawns of social forces and victims of their own monomaniacal passions. Romantic emotion was still present, yet it was not the introspective *mal du siècle* of Chateaubriand's *René*. The cult of the individual broadened to a concern for society, particularly in Hugo's poems and novels, where the downtrodden and the unfortunate became heroes rather than the noble savage or the disillusioned noble. In *Le Rouge et le noir* (1830; *The Red and the Black*, 1898), Stendhal, too, had chosen for his protagonist a provincial young man who is a far cry from the Byronic heroes of Romantic fiction.

Although the novel was to turn to the middle class for its inspiration, a number of poets turned away from the changing society of the mid-nineteenth century to take refuge in a detached ethereal atmosphere. These Parnassian poets, as they were known, who never constituted a full-fledged literary school with a unified doctrine, edited a journal called *Le Parnasse contemporain* (contemporary Parnassus), named for the home of the Muses. Its first issue, in 1866, contained poems by Gautier, Théodore de Banville, Charles-Marie Leconte de Lisle, Baudelaire, José-Maria de Heredia, François-Édouard Coppée, Sully Prudhomme, Verlaine, and Mallarmé, several of whom were to gain fame as Symbolists or as talented independent writers. The Parnassians' second volume appeared in 1871; the third volume, issued in 1876, is little more than an anthology, with no unifying theme.

The single doctrine that loosely linked the Parnassian poets was their commitment to art for art's sake. Reacting against Hugo's metrical freedoms and Romantic introspection, the Parnassians proclaimed the necessity of perfection in form. They wished to remain objective, not revealing their personal emotions or opinions. They sought serenity, equilibrium, and purity in their work, striving for sculptural perfection and a close affiliation with the plastic arts in general. Often finding inspiration in classical sources, they did not abandon the Romantic cult of the Middle Ages or love of the exotic. Although the main representatives of Parnasse are Leconte de Lisle (1818-1894), Banville (1823-1891), Heredia (1842-1905), and Prudhomme (1839-1907), these poets acknowledged the inspiration of Gautier (1811-1872) and Nerval (1808-1855), whose individualistic voice was claimed by many poetic schools, ranging from the Symbolists to the Surrealists. The Parnassians also greatly admired André Chénier.

Prose poems

Romanticism, with its call for new forms and experimentation, coupled with Parnassian emphasis on style, provoked a new type of poetry in the mid-nineteenth century. Generally called the *poème en prose*, or prose poem, its origination is credited to

Aloysius Bertrand (1807-1841), although Parny, in his *Chansons madécasses traduites en françois* in 1787, had anticipated it by almost a century. Bertrand's *Gaspard de la nuit* was published in 1842, a year after his death. Delicate and exact like a sculpture or a miniature, his work inspired a flurry of interest in the prose poem. Two prose poems, *La Bacchante* and *Le Centaure*, by Maurice de Guérin (1810-1839), were published posthumously in 1840, and many critics regard Lamennais's *Paroles d'un croyant* (1834; words of a believer) as a prose poem. This work of mystical socialism expresses religious and political beliefs in vibrant and inspiring terms. It was, however, with Baudelaire, Lautréamont, and Arthur Rimbaud that the prose poem was to become an important literary form. Lautréamont (1846-1870), whose real name was Isidore-Lucien Ducasse, anticipated the Surrealist revolution in his *Chants de Maldoror*, a prose poem published in 1869.

Symbolism

Symbolism is more difficult to define than Romanticism or Parnassianism, although it shares elements with both. From the Romantics, the Symbolists inherited an emphasis on subjectivity and the image of the poet as seer, an isolated figure rejected by society. From the Parnassians, the Symbolists took the notions of perfection in art and the importance of language for its own sake. Symbolism is oriented toward the ideal, the vague, the world of dreams and unreality. Closely associated with Impressionism, Symbolism reflects the impression of a moment that changes; it poses the question of the relation of the individual to time. Subtlety, fluidity, harmony—all are Symbolist virtues. To name an object, says Mallarmé, is to deprive it of much of its interest. Opposed to the world of materialism and bourgeois society, the Symbolists sought the Platonic and Hegelian universe of the ideal. Mystical without religious aspirations, the Symbolists nevertheless recognized a world of the spirit. They were also closely allied with music: Verlaine proclaimed, "De la musique avant toute chose" (music before everything else), and his works inspired many composers. Mallarmé's *L'Après-midi d'un faune* (1876; *Afternoon of a Faun*, 1956) is perhaps better known to foreign readers through Claude Debussy's tone poem of the same name.

Unlike Romanticism, which came to France primarily by way of England and Germany, Symbolism was born on French soil. The critic Robert Sabatier (*La Poésie du XIXeme siècle*, 2 volumes, 1977) calls the Symbolist movement a "calm revolution." It accompanied the more violent battles of the Franco-Prussian War of 1870, followed by the bloody Commune of 1871. This struggle, shorter but more intense than the Revolution of 1789, eventually subsided into the tumultuous Third Republic. Social agitation was great; workers demanded their rights, protesting against low wages, child labor, and other evils. At first, it seems a contradiction to place Verlaine's "pure poetry" in *Romances sans paroles* (1874; *Romances Without Words*, 1921) into such an atmosphere; Symbolism, however, was predicated on a rejection of reality and a quest for perfection.

Decadent poets

Ironically, Baudelaire, Rimbaud, Verlaine, and Mallarmé, who represent the best of Symbolism, did not refer to themselves as Symbolists; the term was applied to them retrospectively. Around 1885, a group of less-skilled poets influenced by these masters grouped together to form what they called the Symbolist school. Today, they are known to the world of letters by such various names as Decadents and vers-librists. They wrote in ephemeral journals such as *L'Hydropathe*, *Tout-Paris*, *La Nouvelle Rive Gauche*, and *Lutèce*. They wrote manifestos, such as Jean Moréas's *Manifeste du symbolisme*, published in *Le Figaro* in 1886, and René Ghil's *Traité du verbe*. They produced poems of mixed quality but always inferior to the works of the great masters who preceded them.

Among those who were labeled Decadents, the most noteworthy are Charles Cros (1842-1888), a scientist, inventor, and poet, and Corbière (1845-1875), whose *Les Amours jaunes* (yellow loves) was published in 1873. Laforgue (1860-1887), despite the brevity of his life, was perhaps the best known of the group. His principal collections, *Les Complaintes* (1885; complaints) and *L'Imitation de Notre-Dame la lune* (1886; imitation of Our Lady of the Moon), are marked by poetic fantasy and deep sincerity. His later poems are written in free verse, with trivial familiarity, revealing at the same time a preoccupation with death and with the problem of evil. Tormented by the image of Hamlet, Laforgue sought unity through the double. Like Baudelaire, Laforgue observed the monotonous and sad existence of the city; T. S. Eliot acknowledged a considerable debt to Laforgue.

Early twentieth century poets

The period between 1905 and 1914 was a brilliant one for Paris. The city became, as in the seventeenth and eighteenth centuries, the center of European culture. Impressionists such as Claude Monet and Pierre-Auguste Renoir continued to paint; Paul Cézanne and Henri Matisse had already launched new artistic forms; Pablo Picasso had come to Paris from Spain. Maurice Ravel and Debussy wrote their music for orchestra and ballet; the dance was revolutionized by the appearance of the director Sergey Diaghilev and the Ballets Russes in 1909, with the impetuous and genial dancer Vaslav Nijinsky, and the collaboration of the great Russian composer Igor Stravinsky in *The Fire-Bird* (1910), *Petrouchka* (1911), and *The Rite of Spring* (1913). The theater resumed life again in André-Léonard Antoine's *Théâtre Libre* and Jacques Copeau's *Vieux Colombier* in 1913.

However, this high degree of culture, calling forth poets and artists from Europe and America, had its dark side. The year 1905 was a year of wars and strikes throughout Europe, especially in Russia, where the shadow of the Revolution was already threatening. European alliances were fragile, and Germany, a victor over France in 1870, was once again a menace. In 1914, World War I broke out. For France, it was a moment of patriotism. The war, however, was long and difficult; soldiers spent months and years in the trenches, and the final victory was marred by great losses, both human and financial. The years immediately following, the 1920's, were years of exuberance and exaltation, of joie de vivre and new beginnings. The 1930's, in contrast, were dismal, with the Depression, unemployment, and yet another threat of German rearmament.

It was only natural that poetry should respond in various ways to such circumstances. The great cultural renaissance of the prewar years kept alive the Symbolist quest for beauty in Valéry, Claudel, and Gide, and Proust's autobiographical novel in poetic prose, *À la recherche du temps perdu* (1913-1927; *Remembrance of Things Past*, 1922-1931, 1981). The *renouveau catholique* (Catholic renewal), which had already attracted Jammes, Ernest Psichari, Jacques Maritain, and others, drew Claudel and Charles-Pierre Péguy, for it promised stable values in a changing world. At the same time, the unprecedented carnage of the war led to a cult of destruction of all traditional values. Freudian discoveries provoked exploration of dreams, and here the Surrealists found inspiration for their poetry, following the leadership of Guillaume Apollinaire and his nineteenth century predecessors, Lautréamont and Rimbaud. Surrealism touched almost every major French poet during and after the 1920's, and it exercised a considerable international influence as well; no other school of comparable influence is identifiable in twentieth century French poetry.

SURREALISM

Only a few years before poets and antipoets came to explore these kingdoms, Apollinaire had subtitled his play *Les Mamelles de Tirésias* (pr. 1917; *The Breasts of Tiresias*, 1961) a *drame surréaliste*. The Surrealist movement, touching art, poetry, and music, traced its roots to Apollinaire, and even further back to Lautréamont and his *Chants de Maldoror*. Like Romanticism, Surrealism was an international movement, exerting a powerful influence on the development of modern poetry in Greece, Latin America, and other nations and regions with widely diverse poetic traditions.

In part, Surrealism was a reaction to World War I, reflecting a loss of faith in traditional values. At the same time, there was also a feeling of euphoria at the end of the war, a sense of limitless possibilities. There were discoveries to be made in other worlds, especially the world of dreams, opened by the work of Sigmund Freud.

Early Surrealism found a kindred spirit in the Romanian Tzara (Sami Roesenstock; 1896-1963), who, in 1916, in Zurich, launched a movement called Dada, which was aimed against all logic, reason, and social organization. In 1918, the Dadaists published a manifesto that expressed their gospel of destruction and celebrated the "fertile wheel of a universal circus in the real powers and fantasy of each individual."

The founding Surrealist group included Soupault (1897-1990), René Crevel (1900-1935), Robert Desnos (1900-1945), Paul Éluard (1895-1952), Louis Aragon (1897-1982), Benjamin Péret (1899-1959), and Francis Picabia (1879-1953), all of whom acknowledged Breton (1896-1966) as their master. In their manifesto of 1924, they defined Surrealism as "psychic automation . . . in the absence of any control exercised by reason, and outside of any aesthetic or moral preoccupation." Thus, one of their most important techniques was "automatic writing," in which one wrote whatever occurred to him, without any reflection or concern for sense, grammar, or punctuation. They also practiced a faithful transcription of dreams, the "other life" so exalted by Nerval.

Many artists became members or associates of the Surrealist group, including the Spaniard Salvador Dalí (1904-1989), who was also a poet and an essayist, and who baptized his method "paranoic-critic"; Marcel Duchamp (1887-1968), who brought Surrealist art to the United States; the German Max Ernst (1891-1976), who used collages, among other media of expression, and was interested in depth psychology; and the Belgian René Magritte (1898-1967), whose works evince a metaphysical and disconcerting character. The cinema was also an important vehicle of expression for Surrealism, especially the films of the Spanish director Luis Buñuel, such as *Le Chien andalou* (1928) and *L'Age d'Or* (1930). The Surrealists also produced periodicals, such as *La Révolution surréaliste*. In 1930, the name of this journal was changed to *Le Surréalisme au service de la Révolution*, marking an internal rupture in the Surrealist movement between those who wished to maintain an apolitical stance and those who had embraced communism.

The most faithful Surrealists were Breton, Péret, Soupault, and, erratically, Desnos. With the exception of Breton, the poets who remained within the Surrealist camp achieved only limited success. It is rather those who received their first inspiration and liberation through Surrealism, and who then followed their own creative instincts, who are among the most representative of modern poetry. Indeed, as noted above, there is hardly a modern French poet who was not touched in some way by Surrealism.

Modern poetry

All modern poetry goes back to Baudelaire, Mallarmé, and Rimbaud. Symbolists, Surrealists, and religious writers alike took their inspiration from a vague doctrine that none of these poets explicitly enunciated. The critic Wallace Fowlie, writing in the 1950's, defined the legacy of Symbolism as a quest for "purity" in poetic expression; in his view, the progressive "spiritualization" of modern art in all of its forms is the principal characteristic of modern-day poetry. Here, "spiritualization" is not meant in a religious sense; rather, it suggests the emancipation of poetry from a mission, from the necessity to signify, to point to a meaning, to deal with personal or social issues. Thus, the modern poet becomes not a prophet—the role played by Hugo and his contemporaries—but rather a magician or a visionary, in the tradition of Rimbaud, an explorer of hidden realms and of the interior kingdom of the subconscious. The modern poet is also in search of the lost paradise of childhood, in the tradition of Baudelaire.

The Surrealists, under the sign of Melusine, defined the poetic vocation as that of the seer and the magician. Poets are not to change society; they are, rather, to illuminate it, to show it visions of another life. The Surrealists insisted on the primacy of language, its independence and its importance in its own right—hence the *jeux de mots*, the startling juxtapositions, the fragmentation of sentences, the popularity of the prose poem, and the abolition of genre distinctions in the practice of what is called simply *écriture*, writing.

Robert Greene, writing at the end of the 1970's, saw a further distinction in contemporary French poetry. He divided contemporary poets into two groups, one associated with the journal *Tel Quel* (the title of which comes from Valéry's essays), increasingly Marxist in its orientation, and the journal *L'Éphémère* (1967-1972), with its successor *L'Argile*, founded in 1973. The *telquelistes* are Hermetic writers with links to the analytical and neoclassical tradition of Valéry; they regard the poem as a reflection on itself, with no structure or meaning other than that given it by the reader. Writers who share this orientation also consider themselves as successors to Lautréamont. They ignore all genre distinctions and view all types of writing simply as *écriture*. To this group, Greene assigns Francis Ponge and Marcelin Pleynet, both of whom are regular contributors to *Tel Quel*.

The second group in Greene's schema trace their descent from Rimbaud and Apollinaire. They are Orphic poets who seek adventure: For them, poetry exists to take humanity beyond the everyday to a realm of deeper knowledge. These poets continue the quest of the Surrealists for a reality beyond reality. Like Apollinaire and the Surrealists, they maintain close ties with the world of the plastic arts (Greene feels that the cover of *L'Éphémère*, with an emaciated nude by Alberto Giacometti, is especially significant). Greene sees Reverdy as a predecessor of this second group, which includes Yves Bonnefoy, René Char, Jacques Dupin, and André du Bouchet.

All modern French writers, whose principal works appeared after 1940 and Germany's occupation of France, are marked by the existentialism articulated by Camus and Sartre. Victims of a senseless war, profoundly humiliated by the Occupation, and psychologically and spiritually shaken by the apparent loss of values, they look for meaning in the fundamental solitude of existence. The fragmentation of society is visible in their fragmented lives; the poetry of such authors as Henri Michaux verges on the absurd, and the linguistic experimentation of Raymond Queneau (1903-1976), whose work knows no genre, expresses a revolution in language and has had a strong influence on modern writing. Other writers, such as Pierre-Jean Jouve (1887-1976), who really belongs to the preceding generation, Patrice de la Tour du Pin (1911-1975), and Pierre Emmanuel (1916-1984) are among the most important representatives of poetry with a religious orientation.

Beyond France

Female voices also emerged in Canadian literature in , where Anne Hébert (1916-2000), after having summed up her work with *Œuvre poétique, 1950-1990* (1992; poetic work, 1950-1990) continued with *Poèmes pour la main gauche* (1997; poems for the left hand). Nicole Brossard (born 1943) published *Vertige de l'avant-scène* (1997; dizziness from center stage). These represent only a sample of the poetry being written by women in Canada.

Meanwhile, the canon of French literature, so long focused on the writers of the mother country, has expanded to include works from a variety of former colonies. Following the immense attention to the poetry of Léopold Senghor (1906-2001), who, as president of Senegal, enjoyed a unique ability to be heard on the international level, Aimé Césaire of Martinique (1913-2008) found a wide audience for a poetic work ranging from his early *Les Armes miraculeuses* (1946; *Miraculous Weapons*, 1983) to *La poésie* (1994).

In some ways the twentieth century resembled the eighteenth in that other literary forms threatened to upstage poetry. The modern novel, with its many forms ranging from popular romance and adventure to more serious intellectual and psychological works, has proliferated. At the same time, new technology has brought films and other electronic forms of publication to be considered on a par with literature. Amid this diversity of forms, however, poetry continues both to be widely written and to cultivate new voices. For the first time since the Renaissance, a significant number of these voices are female. Global communication has brought poets from Canada, Africa, and the Caribbean into the cultural sphere of France. As these many voices are raised, readers will be able to choose from a rich variety of texts for the twenty-first century.

BIBLIOGRAPHY

Blackmore, A. M., and E. H. Blackmore, eds. *Six French Poets of the Nineteenth Century: Lamartine, Hugo, Baudelaire, Verlaine, Rimbaud, Mallarmé*. New York: Oxford University Press, 2000. Includes generous selections from the six nineteenth century French poets most often read in the English-speaking world today. Modern translations are printed opposite the original French verse, and the edition contains more than a thousand lines of poetry never previously translated into English.

Breunig, L. C., ed. *The Cubist Poets in Paris: An Anthology*. Lincoln: University of Nebraska Press, 1995. This compilation, a synthesis of the collaboration between cubist art and literature, draws mainly on the works of fifteen Parisian cubist poets of the first two decades of the twentieth century, including Guillaume Apollinaire, Max Jacob, and André Salmon, who, with Pablo Picasso, formed the nucleus of the French cubist movement.

Caws, Mary Ann, ed. *Surrealist Painters and Poets: An Anthology*. Cambridge, Mass.: MIT Press, 2001. Contains materials produced by self-defined surrealists, including memoirs, dreams, journal entries, poetry, and art. Lavishly illustrated. Bibliographical materials and index.

_____. *The Yale Anthology of Twentieth-Century French Poetry*. New Haven,

Conn.: Yale University Press, 2004. This excellent collection includes poets representing Symbolism, post-symbolism, cubism, simultanism, Dada, and L'Éphémère, and ends with the new generations writing from 1967 to 2002. Bilingual. Bibliography and indices.

Flores, Angel, ed. *The Anchor Anthology of French Poetry: From Nerval to Valéry in English Translation*. Rev. ed. New York: Doubleday, 2000. First published in 1958, this collection introduced an indispensable corpus of Western poetry to countless Americans. The poetic and cultural tradition forged by the Symbolist poets—Baudelaire, Rimbaud, Verlaine, Apollinaire, and others—reverberated throughout the avant-garde and countercultures of the twentieth century, including modernism, Surrealism, abstract impressionism, and the Beat movement, an influence examined in a new introduction by poet-singer Patti Smith.

Kay, Sarah, Terence Cave, and Malcolm Bowie. *A Short History of French Literature*. New York: Oxford University Press, 2003. A highly readable volume, presenting an overview of French literature in narrative form. Describes major writers, pointing out their relationship to the times in which they lived. An ideal starting point for students of the subject or for general readers.

Kelly, Michael G. *Strands of Utopia: Spaces of Poetic Work in Twentieth-Century France*. London: Legenda, 2008. An unusual study, drawing attention to the links between utopian themes and poetic practice, especially as seen in the works of Victor Segalen, René Daumal, and Yves Bonnefoy.

Metzidakis, Stamos, ed. *Understanding French Poetry: Essays for a New Millennium*. New York: Garland, 1994. Focusing on the ebbing influence of poetry, this volume provides the theoretical grounding for understanding how and why French verse has become overshadowed by critical and artistic prose. The essays included are mostly original contributions by some of the foremost scholars of French poetry currently writing in the English-speaking world.

Prendergrast, Christopher. *Nineteenth Century French Poetry: Introductions to Close Readings*. New York: Cambridge University Press, 1990. Essays on eleven different poets from Lamartine to Mallarmé and Laforgue, by eminent scholars representing a wide range of critical and theoretical viewpoints. Each of these essays focuses on the detailed organization of a single poem and opens pathways for further study and discussion.

Shapiro, Norman R., ed. and trans. *French Women Poets of Nine Centuries: The Distaff and the Pen*. Baltimore: Johns Hopkins University Press, 2008. Introductions by Roberta L. Krueger, Catherine Lafarge, and Catherine Perry; foreword by Rosanne Warren. Contains more than six hundred poems by fifty-six different writers, with originals and translations on facing pages. A monumental volume.

Shaw, Mary Lewis. *The Cambridge Introduction to French Poetry*. New York: Cambridge University Press, 2003. An exhaustive survey of French poetry, with topics ranging from verse forms and genres to the relationship between poetry and politics. Glossary of poetic terms, bibliography, and indices.

Sorrell, Martin, ed. and trans. *Elles: A Bilingual Anthology of Modern French Poetry by Women*. Afterword by Jaqueline Chénieux-Gendron. Exeter, Devonshire, England: University of Exeter Press, 1995. Introduces English-speaking readers to some of the best French poetry published by women during the last three decades of the twentieth century. Each poet introduces herself with an essay on her conception of poetry and her own position as writer.

Stephens, Sonya, ed. *A History of Women's Writing in* France. New York: Cambridge University Press, 2000. A collection of essays, including general essays on women writers of various periods and one specifically on twentieth century women poets. Includes bibliography and a guide to more than 150 writers and their works.

Thomas, Jean-Jacques, and Steven Winspur. *Poeticized Language: The Foundations of Contemporary French Poetry*. University Park: Pennsylvania State University Press, 1999. Explores the way in which contemporary French poetry places great emphasis on language itself and analyzes the innovations crafted by more than fifty writers. With its eleven chapters and extensive bibliography, this is one of the most comprehensive English-language introductions to French poetry.

Irma M. Kashuba
Updated by Dorothy M. Betz

GUILLAUME APOLLINAIRE

Born: Rome, Italy; August 26, 1880
Died: Paris, France; November 9, 1918
Also known as: Wilhelm Apollinaris; Guillelmus Apollinaris de Kostrowitzki

PRINCIPAL POETRY
Le Bestiaire, 1911 (*Bestiary*, 1978)
Alcools: Poèmes, 1898-1913, 1913 (*Alcools: Poems, 1898-1913*, 1964)
Calligrammes, 1918 (English translation, 1980)
Il y a, 1925
Le Guetteur mélancolique, 1952
Tendre comme le souvenir, 1952
Poèmes à Lou, 1955
Œuvres poétiques, 1956

OTHER LITERARY FORMS

Besides poetry, Guillaume Apollinaire (ah-pawl-ee-NEHR) wrote a number of prose works. Among the most significant of his short stories and novellas are *L'Enchanteur pourrissant* (1909; "the putrescent enchanter"), published by Henry Kahnweiler and illustrated with woodcuts by André Derain; *L'Hérésiarque et Cie.* (1910; *The Heresiarch and Co.*, 1965), a contender for the Prix Goncourt; and *Le Poète assassiné* (1916; *The Poet Assassinated*, 1923). They are contained in the Pléiade edition, *Œuvres en prose* (1977), edited by Michel Décaudin.

Apollinaire collaborated on numerous plays and cinema scripts. His best-known individual works in these genres are two proto-Surrealist plays in verse: *Les Mamelles de Tirésias* (pr. 1917; *The Breasts of Tiresias*, 1961), first published in the magazine *SIC* in 1918, and *Couleur du temps* (the color of time; pr. 1918), which first appeared in the *Nouvelle Revue française* in 1920. They are available in the Pléiade edition of *Œuvres poétiques*. Apollinaire also published a great deal of art criticism and literary criticism in journals, newspapers, and other periodicals. In 1913, the articles published before that year were collected in *Peintres cubistes: Méditations esthétiques* (*The Cubist Painters: Aesthetic Meditations*, 1944). In 1918, *Mercure de France* published his famous manifesto "L'Esprit nouveau et les poètes" ("The New Spirit and the Poets"), which later appeared, along with many other articles, in *Chroniques d'art, 1902-1918* (1960), edited by L. C. Breunig. This collection has been translated into English as *Apollinaire on Art: Essays and Reviews, 1902-1918* (1972).

ACHIEVEMENTS

After Guillaume Apollinaire, French poetry was never the same again. Writing at the end of the long Symbolist tradition, a tradition very apparent in his early works, Apollinaire moved into a new perception of the world and of poetry. In the world of his mature verse, spatial and temporal relations are radically altered. Apollinaire's was one of the first voices in French poetry to attempt to articulate the profound discontinuity and disorientation in modern society. At the same time, however, his works reflect hope, frequently ecstatic, in the promise of the future.

Apollinaire's sense of radical discontinuity was reflected in his formal innovations, analyzed in considerable depth by Jean-Claude Chevalier in *Alcools d'Apollinaire* (1970). Immediately before the publication of *Alcools*, Apollinaire went through the volume and removed all punctuation, a device that he continued to use in most of his later works. His most notable poems, such as "Zone," "Liens" ("Chains"), and "Les Fenêtres" ("Windows"), use free verse with irregular rhyme and rhythm; his most startling works are the picture poems of *Calligrammes*, a form that he falsely claimed to have invented. They consist of verses arranged to give both a visual and an auditory effect in an effort to create simultaneity.

Like the cubists and other modern painters who sought to go beyond the traditional boundaries of space and time, Apollinaire desired to create the effect of simultaneity. This ambition is evident in "Zone," with its biographical, geographical, and historical discontinuity. In this single poem, the poet leaps from his pious childhood at the Collège Saint-Charles in Monaco to the wonders of modern aviation and back to the "herds" of buses "mooing" on the streets of Paris. Perhaps his most obvious achievement in simultaneity, though less profound, is in "Lundi rue Christine" ("Monday in Christine Street"), which records overheard bits of conversation in a "sinistre brasserie," a low-class café-restaurant that Apollinaire had frequented as early as 1903.

The friend and collaborator of many important painters during the exciting years in Paris just before World War I, Apollinaire began associating with artists when he met Pablo Picasso in 1904, after which he frequented the famous Bateau-Lavoir on the rue Ravignan with Max Jacob, André Derain, Maurice Vlaminck, Georges Braque, and others. After 1912, he moved into the world of art criticism, not always appreciated by the artists themselves, as critic Francis Steegmuller has noted. Not unrelated to this interest was Apollinaire's tumultuous liaison with Marie Laurencin from 1907 to 1912. He frequently inspired works and portraits by artists, including Laurencin, Henri Rousseau, and Picasso. Apollinaire's own works further testify to his links with painters: *Bestiary* was illustrated by Raoul Dufy, and "Windows" was the introductory poem to the catalog of the Robert Delaunay exhibit in 1912. His poems often parallel the work of the painters in their spirit of simultaneity; in their subjects, such as the *saltimbanques* of Picasso; and in their moods, such as those of Marc Chagall's dreamworld and inverted figures.

After 1916, Apollinaire became the *chef d'école*, the leader of a new generation of poets and painters. Among them were Pierre Reverdy, Philippe Soupault, Jean Cocteau, André Breton, and Tristan Tzara. His own works appeared in the most avant-garde journals: Reverdy's *Nord-Sud*, Picabia's *391*, and Albert Birot's *SIC*. His lecture "The New Spirit and the Poets" called poets to a new prophetic vision, imploring them to create prodigies with their imagination like modern Merlins. Like Paul Claudel, Apollinaire regarded the poet as a creator. The modern poet, he believed, must use everything for his (or her) creation: new discoveries in science, in the subconscious and the dreamworld, and in the cinema and visual arts.

The Surrealists, in their desire to revolutionize art and literature, saw in Apollinaire their precursor. It was he who coined the word *surréaliste*, in the preface to his drama in verse *The Breasts of Tiresias*. In it, he explains that an equivalent is not always an imitation, even as the wheel, though intended to facilitate transportation, is not a reproduction of the leg. Apollinaire conveys his message with a lighthearted tone, employing incongruous rhythms, parody, and sexual imagery. This is essentially the technique he employs in his most avant-garde poetry, and *The Breasts of Tiresias* echoes poems from "Ondes" ("Waves," the first part of *Calligrammes*) such as "Zone," "Le Brasier" ("The Brazier"), "Les Fiançailles" ("The Betrothal"), and "Le Larron" ("The Thief"). Thus, Apollinaire indicated the path to follow in revolutionizing poetry, although much of his work was in some respects traditional. Like Victor Hugo, he served subsequent poets chiefly as a guide rather than as a model, but it was his "esprit nouveau" that gave considerable impetus to a new form of modern poetry.

Biography

Born in Rome on August 26, 1880, Guillaume Albert Wladimir Alexandre Apollinaire de Kostrowitzky was an illegitimate child; in "The Thief," he says that his "father was a sphinx and his mother a night." In reality, his mother was a Polish adventurer of noble ancestry, Angelique Kostrowicka, known in Paris mostly as "Olga." His father's identity has never been definitively ascertained. The most plausible supposition points to Francesco Flugi d'Aspermont, who was from a noble Italian family that included many prelates. This theory is based on the careful investigation of biographer Marcel Adéma. Apollinaire's mysterious and involved parentage haunted the poet throughout his life, leaving unmistakable marks on his character and works.

Apollinaire received his only formal education at the Collège of Saint-Charles in Monaco and the Collège Stanislas at Cannes, from 1890 to 1897, where he acquired a solid grounding in religious and secular knowledge. Although his Catholic training was to remain firmly implanted in his memory and is evident in his poetry, he moved away from any outward adherence to religious beliefs after 1897. In 1899, he arrived in Paris, his home for most of the next nineteen years of his life and the center and inspiration of his literary activity. First, however, he made a significant trip to Germany's Rhineland in 1901, as tutor to Gabrielle, the daughter of the viscountess of Milhau. There, he met and fell in love with Annie Playden, Gabrielle's English governess. This ill-fated romance and the beauty of the Rhineland inspired many of Apollinaire's early poems, which were later published in *Alcools*.

Apollinaire's return to Paris coincided with the beginning of friendships with artists and writers such as André Salmon, Alfred Jarry, Max Jacob, and especially Picasso. In 1903, he began his collaboration on many periodicals, which he continued throughout his lifetime. Most of his prose and poetry was first published in such journals, many of which—such as *Le Festin d'Esope* and *La Revue immoraliste*—were of very short duration. His works appeared under several pseudonyms, of which "Apollinaire" was the most significant. Others included "Louise Lalame," "Lul," "Montade," and "Tyl." In 1907, he met Marie Laurencin, an artist, whose talent Apollinaire tended to exaggerate. Their liaison continued until 1912 and was an inspiration and a torment to both of them. During this period, Apollinaire was deeply marked by the false accusation that he was responsible for the theft of the *Mona Lisa* from the Louvre. A series of six poems in *Alcools*, "À la Santé" ("At the Santé") describes his brief stay in the prison of La Santé in Verlainian imagery.

The year 1912 marked Apollinaire's break with Laurencin and his definite espousal of modern art, of which he became a staunch proponent. During the two years preceding World War I, he gave lectures and wrote articles on modern art and prepared *Alcools* for publication. The beginning of the war, in 1914, was to Apollinaire a call to a mission. Although not a French citizen until the year 1916, he embraced with great enthusiasm his *métier de soldat* as an artilleryman and then as an infantryman, according an almost mystical dimension to his military service. His poetry of these first two years reveals the exaltation of war and the idealization of two women, "Lou" (Louise de Coligny-Châtillon) and Madeleine Pagès, to whom he was briefly engaged.

Wounded in the head in 1916, Apollinaire required surgery and was then discharged from the service. He returned to the world of literature and art with numerous articles, lectures, two plays, and a volume of poetry, *Calligrammes*. In May of 1918, he married Jacqueline Kolb ("Ruby"), the "jolie rousse" ("pretty redhead") of the last poem in *Calligrammes*. The marriage was of short duration, however, as Apollinaire died of Spanish influenza on November 9 of the same year.

Analysis

In his poetic style, Guillaume Apollinaire might be characterized as the last of the Symbolists and the first of the moderns. He is considered a revolutionary and a destroyer, yet the bulk of his work shows a deep influence of traditional symbolism, especially biblical, legendary, and mythical. Very knowledgeable in Roman Catholic doctrine from his years with the Marianists at Monaco and Cannes, he uses extensive biblical imagery: Christ, the Virgin Mary, and the Holy Spirit in the form of a dove.

Robert Couffignal has analyzed Apollinaire's religious imagery in detail and considers his comprehension of the Bible to be "a cascade of superficial weavings." Scott Bates sees the Last Judgment, with its apocalyptic implications, as central to Apollinaire's works. The concept of messianism and the advent of a new millennium is evident in both the early works and the war poems, which predict a new universe. In the Symbolist tradition, the poet is the seer of the new kingdom.

Many of Apollinaire's symbols are from the realm of legend and myth. Rosemonde, the idealized woman of the Middle Ages, is present in several poems, though she appears also as a prostitute. In "Merlin et la vielle femme" ("Merlin and the Old Woman"), the medieval seer foreshadows Apollinaire's vision of the future. Ancient mythology is the source for Orpheus, under whose sign *Bestiary* is written. Orpheus is also the symbol of Christ and the poet, as is Hermès Trismègiste. Ancient Egypt appears in frequent references to the Nile, the Israelites in bondage, and Pharaoh, the image of the poet himself. The fantastic abounds in Apollinaire's works: ghosts, diabolic characters, and phantoms, as found, for example, in "La Maison des Morts" ("The House of the Dead") and especially in the short stories.

Much of Apollinaire's early symbolism is directed toward the quest for self-knowledge; his choice of the name Apollinaire is a clue to his search. Though it was the name of his maternal grandfather and one of the names given to him at baptism, he seems to have chosen it for its reference to Apollo, the god of the sun. Indeed, solar imagery is central to his poetry, and the introductory poem of *Alcools*, "Zone," ends with the words "Soleil cou coupé" ("Sun cut throat"). Bates argues that the violent love-death relationship between the sun and night, with its corresponding symbolism, is as crucial to the interpretation of Apollinaire as it is to a reading of Gérard de Nerval or Stéphane Mallarmé. Along with love and death is death and resurrection. Apollinaire chooses the phoenix as a sign of rebirth and describes his own psychological and poetic resurrection in "The Brazier" and "The Betrothal," poems that he regarded as among his best. Fire seems to be his basic image, with its multiple meanings of passion, destruction, and purification.

Passion as a flame dominated Apollinaire's life and poetry. Of the many women whom he loved, five in particular incarnated his violent passion and appear in his work: Playden and Laurencin in *Alcools*; Lou, Madeleine, and Jacqueline in *Calligrammes* and in several series of poems published after his death. Apollinaire is capable of expressing tender, idealistic love, as in the "Aubade chantée à Lætare un an passé" ("Aubade Sung to Lætare a Year Ago") section of the "La Chanson du mal-aimé" ("The Song of the Poorly Loved") and in "La Jolie Rousse" ("The Pretty Redhead"), which closes *Calligrammes*. In most cases, Apollinaire is the *mal-aimé*, and as he himself says, he is much less the poorly beloved than the one who loves poorly. His first three loves ended violently; his last was concluded by his death. Thus, the death of love is as important as its first manifestation, which for him resembles the shells bursting in the war.

Autumn is the season of the death of love, wistfully expressed in such nostalgic works as "L'Adieu" ("The Farewell") and "Automne" ("Autumn"). Because the end of love usually involved deep suffering for him, the image of mutilation is not uncommon. The beloved in "The Song of the Poorly Loved" has a scar on her neck, and the mannequins in "L'Émigrant de Landor Road" ("The Emigrant from Landor Road") are decapitated, much like the sun in "Zone." Apollinaire perceives love in its erotic sense, and in many cases he resorts to arcane symbolism, as in the seven swords in "The Song of the Poorly Loved." "Lul de Faltenin" ("Lul of Faltenin") is also typical, with its subtle erotic allusions. Such themes are more overt in Apollinaire's prose; indeed, Bates has compiled a glossary of erotic symbolism in the works of Apollinaire.

Apollinaire was both a lyric poet and a storyteller. In the lyric tradition, he writes of his emotions in images drawn from nature. His work is particularly rich in flora and fauna. *Bestiary* shows his familiarity with and affection for animals and his ability, like the fabulists, to see them as caricatures of people. *Alcools*, as the title indicates, often evokes grapes and wine; it also speaks of fir trees (in "Les Sapins") and falling leaves. "Zone" contains a catalog of birds, real and legendary. The Seine comes alive in Apollinaire's ever-popular "Le Pont Mirabeau" ("Mirabeau Bridge"). In *Calligrammes*, the poet often compares the explosion of shells to bursting buds.

Apollinaire was the author of many short stories, and he maintains a narrative flavor in his poetry. "The House of the Dead" was originally a short story, "L'Obituaire," and it reads like one. Many of the picture poems in *Calligrammes* tell a story; "Paysage" ("Landscape"), for example, portrays by means of typography a house, a tree, and two lovers, one of whom smokes a cigar that the reader can almost smell. Apollinaire's technique often involves improvisation, as in "Le Musicien de Saint-Merry" ("The Musician of Saint-Merry"). Although he claims almost total spontaneity, there are revised versions of many of his poems, and he frequently borrowed from himself, rearranging both lines and poems. In particular, Apollinaire tells stories of the modern city, imitating its new structures as Arthur Rimbaud did in his innovative patterns, and like Charles Baudelaire, Apollinaire peoples his verse with the forgotten and the poor, the prostitutes and the clowns.

Apollinaire had a remarkable sense of humor, displayed in frequent word-plays, burlesques, and parodies. The briefest example of his use of puns is the one-line poem "Chantre" ("Singer"): "Et l'unique cordeau des trompettes marines" ("and the single string of marine trumpets"). *Cordeau*, when read aloud, might be *cor d'eau*, or "horn of water," another version of a marine trumpet, as well as *corps d'eau* ("body of water") or even *cœur d'eau* ("heart of water"). The burlesque found in his short stories appears in poetry as dissonance, erotic puns, and irreverent parodies, such as in "Les Sept Epées" ("The Seven Swords") as well as in "The Thief," a poem that Bates interprets as parodying Christ. Apollinaire's lighthearted rhythm and obscure symbolism tend to prevent his verse from becoming offensive and convey a sense of freedom, discovery, and surprise.

BESTIARY

Bestiary is one of the most charming and accessible of Apollinaire's works. The idea for the poem probably came from Picasso in 1906, who was then doing woodcuts of animals. In 1908, Apollinaire published in a journal eighteen poems under the title "La Marchande des quatre saisons ou le bestiaire moderne" (the costermonger or the modern bestiary). When he prepared the final edition in 1911, with woodcuts by Raoul Dufy, he added twelve poems and replaced the merchant with Orpheus. According to mythology, Orpheus attracted wild beasts by playing on the lyre he had received from Mercury. He is the symbol of Gnosis and Neoplatonic Humanism and is also identified with Christ and poetry, in a mixture of mystical and sensual imagery.

Apollinaire himself wrote the notes to the volume and uses as its sign a δ (the Greek letter delta) pierced by a unicorn. He interprets it to mean the delta of the Nile and all the legendary and biblical symbols of ancient Egypt, also suggesting a *D* for Deplanche, the publisher, in addition to the obvious sexual symbolism. He added the motto "J'émerveille" ("I marvel"), thus giving a fantastic aura to the work. Roger Little sees in the volume a "delicious and malicious" wit, with metamorphoses, syncretism, pride in poetry, carnal love, and mysticism. Like all Apollinaire's early works, it is full of self-analysis. In "La Souris" ("The Mouse"), the poet speaks of his twenty-eight years as "mal-vécus" ("poorly spent").

The animals represent human foibles; the peacock, for example, displays both his best and, unbeknownst to him, his worst. They also speak of love: the serpent, the Sirens, the dove, and Orpheus himself. They point to God and things divine: the dove, the bull, or, again, Orpheus. They speak of poetry: the horse, the tortoise, the elephant, and the caterpillar. For Apollinaire, poetry is a divine gift. He concludes his notes by observing that poets seek nothing but perfection, which is God himself. Poets, he says, have the right to expect after death the full knowledge of God, which is sublime beauty.

ALCOOLS

The most analyzed and the best known of Apollinaire's works is *Alcools*, a slender volume published in 1913 with the subtitle *Poèmes, 1898-1913*. A portrait of Apollinaire, an etching by Picasso, serves as the frontispiece. Apollinaire chose fifty-five of the many poems he had written from his eighteenth to his thirty-third year and assembled them in an order that has continued to fascinate and baffle critics. Michel Décaudin says that the order in *Alcools* is based entirely on the aesthetic and sentimental affinities felt by the author, or their discrete dissonances. Very few poems have dates, other than "Rhénanes" (September, 1901, to May, 1902) and "At the Santé" (September, 1911); nevertheless, critics have succeeded in dating many, though not all, of the poems.

The poems have several centers, though not all of those from one group appear together. More than twenty were inspired by Apollinaire's trip to the Rhineland in 1901, including the nine in the cycle "Rhénanes." Several of these poems and some others, such as "The Song of the Poorly Loved," "Annie," and "The Emigrant from Landor Road," refer to his unhappy love affair with Playden. These poems and an interview with her as Mrs. Postings in 1951 by Robert Goffin and LeRoy Breunig are the only sources of information about this significant period in Apollinaire's life. Three poems, "Mirabeau Bridge," "Marie," and "Cors de chasse" ("Hunting Horns"), scattered throughout the volume, refer to Laurencin.

The poems exhibit great variety in form, tone, and subject matter. They range from the one-line "Chantre" to the seven-part "The Song of the Poorly Loved," the longest in the collection. Most of them have regular rhyme and rhythm, but "Zone" and "Vendémiaire," the first and the last, give evidence of technical experimentation. The poems range from witty ("The Synagogue") to nostalgic ("Autumn," "Hunting Horns") and from enigmatic ("The Brazier") to irreverent ("The Thief"). Critics have arranged them in various ways. Bates, for example, sees the volume as a "Dionysian-Apollonian dance of life in three major symbols: fire, shadow, alcools."

Apollinaire chose the beginning and concluding poems of the collection, "Zone" and "Vendémiaire," with great care. "Zone" is overtly autobiographical in a Romantic-Symbolist ambience, yet its instant leaps in space and time make it very modern. Also modern is the image of the city, where Apollinaire can see beauty in a poster, a traffic jam, and a group of frightened Jewish immigrants. The city is also the central focus in the concluding poem, "Vendémiaire" (the name given the month of vintage, September 22-October 21, in the revolutionary calendar), a hymn to the glory of Paris. The poet exuberantly proclaims his immortality and omnipresence: "I am drunk from having swallowed all the universe." Bates sees the end of the poem as a hymn to joy reminiscent of Walt Whitman and Friedrich Nietzsche.

The bizarre juxtapositions, the inner borrowings of lines from one poem to the next, and the absence of punctuation provoked various responses from critics. Cubists hailed Apollinaire as a great poet. Georges Duhamel, writing in the June 15, 1913, issue of *Mercure de France*, called the volume a junk shop. Critics such as Adéma, Décaudin, and Marie-Jeanne Durry analyze *Alcools* with depth and scholarship. They discover many platitudes and much mediocrity but find it redeemed by what Steegmuller identifies as a spirit of freedom.

CALLIGRAMMES

Intended as a sequel to *Alcools*, *Calligrammes* is much more unified than *Alcools*, yet its importance was seen only much later. It consists of six parts. The first part, "Waves," is the most innovative and was written before World War I in the frenzied stimulation of artistic activity in Paris. The other five contain poems inspired by the war and by the poet's love for Lou, Madeleine, and—in the final poem—his future wife, Jacqueline.

Philippe Renaud sees the difference between *Alcools* and "Waves" as one of nature rather than degree. Even the most enigmatic poems of *Alcools* follow a familiar plan, he maintains, whereas in "Waves" the reader is in unfamiliar territory, disoriented in space and time. In "Waves" one feels both the insecurity and the indefiniteness that can only be called modern art. The introductory poem, "Chains," uses the elements recommended by Apollinaire in "The New Spirit and the Poets" yet remains anchored in the past. It leaps from the Tower of Babel to telegraph wires in disconcerting juxtapositions, speaking of humankind's eternal, frustrating quest for unity. In "The Windows," the window opens like an orange on Paris or in the tropics and flies on a rainbow across space and time.

Beginning with "Waves" and throughout *Calligrammes*, Apollinaire uses what he calls ideograms, or picture poems. They are the most attractive pieces in the book, though not necessarily the most original. They became excellent vehicles for the war poems, where brevity and wit are essential. The theme of war dominates the majority of poems in *Calligrammes*. The war excited Apollinaire, promising a new universe. He experienced exhilaration as he saw shells exploding, comparing them in the poem "Merveilles de la guerre" ("Wonders of War") to constellations, women's hair, dancers, and women in childbirth. He saw himself as the poet-hero, the omnipresent seer, the animator of the universe. In "La Tête étoilée" ("The Starry Head"), his wound was a crown of stars on his head.

Apollinaire was as dependent on love as he was on air, and he suffered greatly in the solitary trenches of France. His brief romance with Lou was intense and violent, as his pun on her name in "C'est Lou qu'on la nommait" ("They Called Her Lou") indicates; instead of "Lou," the word *loup* (which sounds the same in French but means "wolf") is used throughout the poem. In his poems to Madeleine, he devours images like a starving man. The anthology ends serenely as he addresses Jacqueline, "la jolie rousse," the woman destined to be his wife, as poetry was destined to be his life. This final poem is also his poetic testament, in which he bequeaths "vast and unknown kingdoms, new fires and the mystery of flowers to anyone willing to pick them."

OTHER MAJOR WORKS

LONG FICTION: *L'Enchanteur pourrissant*, 1909; *Le Poète assassiné*, 1916 (*The Poet Assassinated*, 1923).

SHORT FICTION: *L'Hérésiarque et Cie.*, 1910 (*The Heresiarch and Co.*, 1965).

PLAYS: *Les Mamelles de Tirésias*, pr. 1917 (*The Breasts of Tiresias*, 1961); *Couleur du temps*, pr. 1918; *Casanova*, pb. 1952.

NONFICTION: *Peintres cubistes: Méditations esthétiques*, 1913 (*The Cubist Painters: Aesthetic Meditations*, 1944); *Chroniques d'art, 1902-1918*, 1960 (*Apollinaire on Art: Essays and Reviews, 1902-1918*, 1972).

MISCELLANEOUS: *Œuvres complètes*, 1966 (8 volumes); *Œuvres en prose*, 1977 (Michel Décaudin, editor).

BIBLIOGRAPHY

Adéma, Marcel. *Apollinaire*. Translated by Denise Folliot. New York: Grove Press, 1955. This is the prime source of biographical material, the bible of scholars researching the poet and his epoch.

Bates, Scott. *Guillaume Apollinaire*. Rev. ed. Boston: Twayne, 1989. This book offers detailed erudite analyses of Apollinaire's major works and informed judgments on his place in French literature and in the development of art criticism. It emphasizes the importance to the entire world of Apollinaire's vision of a cultural millennium propelled by science and democracy and implemented by poetry. Included are a chronology, a twenty-six-page glossary of references, notes, and selected bibliographies of both primary and secondary sources.

Bohn, Willard. *The Aesthetics of Visual Poetry: 1914-1928*. New York: Cambridge University Press, 1986. Chapter 3, "Apollinaire's Plastic Imagination," reveals the lyric innovations that Apollinaire brought to visual poetry with *Calligrammes*: new forms, new content, multiple figures in a unified composition, a dual sign system used to express a simultaneity, and a difficulty of reading that mirrors the act of creation. Chapter 4, "Toward a Calligrammar," offers a sophisticated structural and statistical analysis of the calligrammes to demonstrate metonymy as the principal force binding the visual tropes, whereas metaphor and metonymy occur evenly in the verbal arena.

_____. *Apollinaire and the Faceless Man: The Creation and Evolution of a Modern Motif*. Rutherford, N.J.: Fairleigh Dickinson University Press, 1991. Traces the history of Apollinaire's faceless man motif as a symbol of the human condition, from its roots in the poem "Le Musicien de Saint-Mercy" to its dissemination to the arts community through the unproduced pantomime "A quelle heure un train partira-t-il pour Paris?"

_____. *Apollinaire and the International Avant-Garde*. Albany: State University of New York Press, 1997. Chronicles the early artistic and critical reception of Apollinaire in Europe, North America, and Latin America. Especially interesting is the discussion of Argentina, exported through the Ultraism of Jorge Luis Borges, and Apollinaire's place in the revolutionary circles of Mexico.

Cornelius, Nathalie Goodisman. *A Semiotic Analysis of Guillaume Apollinaire's Mythology in "Alcools."* New York: Peter Lang, 1995. Examines Apollinaire's use of linguistic and mythological fragmentation and reordering to mold his material into an entirely new system of signs that both encompasses and surpasses the old. Chapters give close semiotic readings of four poems: "Claire de lune," "Le Brasier," "Nuit rhëane," and "Vendémaine."

Couffignal, Robert. *Apollinaire*. Translated by Eda Mezer Levitine. Tuscaloosa: University of Alabama Press, 1975. This is a searching analysis of some of Apollinaire's best-known works, including "Zone," strictly from the Roman Catholic point of view. It traces his attitude toward religion from his childhood to his death. The book contains a chronology; translations of ten texts, both poems and prose, with the author's comments; a bibliographical note; and an index.

Matthews, Timothy. *Reading Apollinaire: Theories of Poetic Language.* New York: Manchester University Press, 1987. Uses a variety of historical, biographical, and stylistic approaches to offer an accessible point of entry into often difficult texts. Matthews's detailed discussion of *Alcools* focuses heavily on "L'Adieu" and "Automne malade," which allows for a reading that may be transferred to the rest of the book. His chapter "Poetry, Painting, and Theory" offers a solid historical background that leads directly into his examination of *Calligrammes*.

Shattuck, Roger. *The Banquet Years.* Rev. ed. New York: Vintage Books, 1968. In the two long chapters devoted to Apollinaire, "The Impresario of the Avant-garde" and "Painter-Poet," the author gives a year-by-year and at times even a month-by-month account of his life, loves, friends, employment, writings, and speeches. The tone is judicial, the critical judgments fair and balanced. Includes a bibliography and an index.

Steegmuller, Francis. *Apollinaire: Poet Among the Painters.* New York: Farrar, Straus, 1963. This is an exhaustive, extremely well-documented, unbiased, and highly readable biography. Contains a preface, translations, numerous photographs and illustrations, two appendixes, notes, and an index.

Irma M. Kashuba
Updated by David Harrison Horton

LOUIS ARAGON

Born: Paris, France; October 3, 1897
Died: Paris, France; December 24, 1982

PRINCIPAL POETRY
Feu de joie, 1920
Le Mouvement perpétuel, 1925
La Grande Gaîté, 1929
Persécuté persécuteur, 1931
Hourra l'Oural, 1934
Le Crève-coeur, 1941
Brocéliande, 1942
Les Yeux d'Elsa, 1942
En Français dans le texte, 1943
Le Musée grévin, 1943
La Diane française, 1945
Le Nouveau Crève-coeur, 1948
Les Yeux et la mémoire, 1954
Le Roman inachevé, 1956
Elsa, 1959
Les Poètes, 1960
Le Fou d'Elsa, 1963
Les Chambres, 1969
Aux abords de Rome, 1981
Les Adieux, et autres poèmes, 1982

OTHER LITERARY FORMS

Louis Aragon (ah-rah-GAWN) was one of the most prolific French authors of the twentieth century, and although lyric poetry was his first medium, to which he always returned as to a first love, he also produced many novels and volumes of essays. As a young man, he participated in the Surrealist movement, and his works of this period defy classification. In addition to the exercises known as automatic writing, which had a considerable impact on his mature style in both prose and poetry, he wrote a number of Surrealist narratives combining elements of the novel (such as description and dialogue) and the essay. The most important of these, *Le Paysan de Paris* (1926; *Nightwalker*, 1970), is a long meditation on the author's ramblings in his native city and on the "modern sense of the mythic" inspired by its streets, shops, and parks.

In the 1930's, after his espousal of the Communist cause, Aragon began a series of

Louis Aragon
(Library of Congress)

novels under the general title of *Le Monde réel* (1934-1944), which follow the tenets of Socialist Realism. These are historical novels dealing with the corruption of bourgeois society and the rise of Communism. His later novels, however, beginning with *La Semaine sainte* (1958; *Holy Week*, 1961), show greater freedom of form and lack the explicit "message" characteristic of Socialist Realism; these later works incorporate an ongoing meditation on the novel as a literary form and on its relation to history and biography.

An important characteristic of Aragon's style that cuts across all his works of fiction and poetry is the use of spoken language as a model: His sentences reproduce the rhythms of speech, full of parentheses, syntactic breaks, and interjections, and his diction, especially in prose, is heavily interlarded with slang. This trait is true to some extent even of his essays, although the latter tend to be more formal to both diction and rhetorical strategy. His nonfiction works are voluminous, for he was an active journalist for much of his life, producing reviews and essays on politics, literature, and the visual arts for a variety of Surrealist and then Communist publications.

Achievements

Like most writers who have taken strong political stands, Louis Aragon was, during the course of his lifetime, the object of much praise and blame that had little to do with the literary value of his work. This was especially true of his series of novels, *Le Monde réel*, which was hailed by his fellow Communists as a masterpiece and criticized by most non-Communist reviewers as contrived and doctrinaire. He was, with André Breton, one of the leaders of the Surrealist movement; his poetry after the mid-1940's combined elements of Romanticism and modernism, but his style evolved in a direction of its own and cannot be identified with that of any one school.

After his Surrealist period, during which he wrote for an intellectual elite, Aragon sought to make his work accessible to a wider public and often succeeded. The height of his popularity was achieved in the 1940's, when his poems played an important role in the French Resistance: written in traditional meters and using rhyme, so that they might more easily be sung, they became rallying cries for French patriots abroad and in occupied France. (Many of Aragon's poems have, in fact, been set to music by writers of popular songs, including Léo Ferré and George Brassens.) Beginning in the late 1950's, Aragon's work became much less overtly political, which contributed to its acceptance by non-Communist critics. At the time of his death in 1982, Aragon was considered even by his political opponents as a leading man of letters. Writers of lesser stature have been elected to the French Academy, but Aragon never applied for membership, and it is hard to imagine such an ardent advocate of commoners, who used slang liberally in his own work, sitting in judgment on the purity of the French language.

For Aragon, who wrote his first "novel" at age six (and dictated a play to his aunt before he could write), writing was like breathing, a vital activity coextensive with living. He was a novelist whose eye (and ear) for telling detail never dulled, a poet whose lyric gifts did not diminish with age.

Biography

Until late in life, Louis Aragon was reticent about his childhood, and many biographical notices describe it as idyllic; in fact, his family (which consisted of his grandmother, mother, and two aunts) was obsessed with a concern for appearances that caused the boy considerable pain. The illegitimate son of a prominent political figure, Louis Andrieux, who chose the name Aragon for his son and acted as his legal guardian, Aragon was reared as his mother's younger brother, and although as a boy he guessed much of the truth, it was not until his twentieth year that he heard it from his mother (at the insistence of his father, who had previously insisted on her silence). Since his maternal grandfather had also deserted the family, his mother, Marguérite Toucas-Masillon, supported them all as best she could by painting china and running a boardinghouse. According to his biographer, Pierre Daix, the circumstances of Aragon's childhood left him with an instinctive sympathy for outsiders, especially women, and a great longing to be accepted as a full member of a group. This longing was first satisfied by his friendship with André Breton and later by Aragon's adherence to the Communist Party. (Indeed, his deep need to "belong" may help to account for his unswerving loyalty to the party throughout the Stalinist era.)

Breton, whom he met in 1917, introduced Aragon to the circle of poets and artists that was to form the nucleus of the Dadaist and Surrealist movements. Horrified by the carnage of World War I (which Aragon had observed firsthand as a medic), these young people at first embraced the negative impulse of Dada, an absurdist movement founded in Zurich by Tristan Tzara. Their aim was to unmask the moral bankruptcy of the society that had tolerated such a war. Realizing that a philosophy of simple negation was ultimately sterile, Breton and Aragon broke away from the Dadaists and began to pursue the interest in the subconscious, which led them to Surrealism. Through the technique of automatic writing, they tried to suppress the rational faculty, or "censor," which inhibited free expression of subconscious impulses.

Politically, the Surrealists were anarchists, but as they became increasingly convinced that profound social changes were necessary to free the imagination, a number of them, including Aragon, joined the French Communist Party. At about the same time (1928), Aragon met the Russian poet Vladimir Mayakovsky and his sister-in-law, the novelist Elsa Triolet, at the Coupole, a Paris café. As Aragon put it, describing his meeting with Elsa many years later, "We have been together ever since" (literally, "We have not left each other's side"). In Elsa, Aragon found the "woman of the future," who could be her husband's intellectual and social equal while sharing with him a love in which all the couple's aspirations were anchored. Aragon celebrated this love in countless poems spanning forty years; some of the most ecstatic were written when the two were in their sixties. Elsa introduced Aragon to Soviet Russia, which they visited together in the early 1930's; she also took part with him in the French Resistance during World War II, publishing clandestine newspapers and maintaining a network of antifascist intellectuals. Although he followed the "party line" and tried to rationalize the Soviet pact with the Nazis, Aragon was an ardent French patriot; he was decorated for bravery in both world wars and wrote hymns of praise to the French "man (and woman) in the street," who became the heroes of the Resistance.

After the war, Aragon redoubled his activities on behalf of the Communist Party, serving as editor of the Communist newspaper *Ce Soir* and completing his six-volume novel *Les Communistes* (1949-1951). In 1954, he became a permanent member of the Central Committee of the French Communist Party, and in 1957, the Soviet Union awarded him its highest decoration, the Lenin Peace Prize. He was vilified by many of his fellow intellectuals in France for failing to criticize Stalin; not until 1966, during the much-publicized trial of two Soviet writers, Andrei Sinyavsky and Yuli Daniel, did he venture to speak out against the notion that there could be a "criminality of opinion." In 1968, he joined with the French Communist Party as a whole in condemning the Russian invasion of Czechoslovakia. Throughout his life, Aragon continued to produce a steady stream of poetry, fiction, and essays. His wife's death in 1970 was a terrible blow, but he survived it and went on to write several more books in the twelve years that were left to him.

ANALYSIS

Despite the length of Louis Aragon's poetic career and the perceptible evolution of his style in the course of six decades, there is a remarkable unity in the corpus of his poetry. This unity results from stylistic as well as thematic continuities, for even when he turned from free verse to more traditional metric forms, he managed to preserve the fluency of spoken language. In fact, his most highly structured verse has some of the qualities of stream-of-consciousness narrative. There are a variety of reasons for this. Aragon began to write as a very young boy and continued writing, steadily and copiously, throughout his life. As critic Hubert Juin has observed, Aragon never needed to keep a journal or diary because "his work itself was his journal," into which he poured his eager questions and reflections on what most closely concerned him.

This confessional impulse was reinforced and given direction in Aragon's Surrealist period by experiments with automatic writing, a technique adapted for literary use primarily by Breton and Philippe Soupault. By writing quickly without revising and by resisting the impulse to edit or censor the flow of words, the Surrealistis hoped to tap their subconscious minds and so to "save literature from rhetoric" (as Juin puts it). Literature was not all they hoped to save, moreover, for "rhetoric" had poisoned the social and political spheres as well; in liberating the subconscious, Aragon and his friends sought to break old and unjust patterns of thought and life. They also expected this powerful and hitherto untapped source to fuel the human imagination for the work of social renewal. Although Aragon repudiated the Surrealist attitude (which was basically anarchistic) when he embraced Communism as the pattern of the future, he never lost the stylistic freedom that automatic writing had fostered, nor did he become complacent about the "solution" he had found. Like his relationship with his wife, in which his hopes for the future were anchored, Aragon's Communism was a source of pain as well as of fulfillment: the deeper his love and commitment, the greater his vulnerability. Thus, poetry remained for him, as it had been in his youth, a form of questioning in which he explored the world and his relation to it.

There were, nevertheless, perceptible changes in Aragon's style during the course of his career. After the Dadaist and Surrealist periods, when he wrote mainly free verse (although there are metrically regular poems even in his early collections), Aragon turned to more traditional prosody—including rhyme—in the desire to make his verses singable. At the same time, he sought to renew and broaden the range of available rhymes by adopting new definitions of masculine and feminine rhyme based on pronunciation rather than on spelling. He also applied the notion of enjambment to rhyme, allowing not only the last syllable of a line but also the first letter or letters of the following line to count as constituent elements of a rhyme. Partly as a result of the conditions under which they were composed, Aragon's Resistance poems are for the most part short and self-contained, although *Le Musée grévin* (the wax museum) is a single long poem, and the pieces in *Brocéliande* are linked by allusions to the knights of the Arthurian cycle, whom Aragon saw as the symbolic counterparts of the Resistance fighters.

Aragon's postwar collections are more unified, and beginning with *Les Yeux et la mémoire* (eyes and memory), they might almost be described as book-length poems broken into short "chapters" of varying meters. Many of these "chapters," however, can stand alone as finished pieces; good examples are the love lyrics in *Le Fou d'Elsa* (Elsa's madman), some of which have been set to music, like the war poems, and the vignette from *Le Roman inachevé* (the unfinished romance) beginning "Marguerite, Madeleine, et Marie," which describes Aragon's mother and aunts—whom he thought of as his sisters—dressing for a dance. Within his longer sequences, Aragon skillfully uses shifts of meter to signal changes of mood and does not hesitate to lapse into prose when occasion warrants—for example, when, in *Le Roman inachevé*, he is suddenly overwhelmed by the weariness and pain of old age: "The verse breaks in my hands, my old hands, swollen and knotted with veins." Such disclaimers to the contrary, Aragon was never in greater control of his medium than in these poems of his old age, culminating in *Elsa, Le Fou d'Elsa,* and *Les Chambres* (the rooms). *Le Fou d'Elsa* is perhaps his greatest tour de force, a kind of epic (depicting the end of Muslim rule in Spain, with the fall of Granada in 1492) made up of hundreds of lyric pieces, along with some dialogue and prose commentary. As Juin has remarked, Aragon tends to alternate between two tones, the epic and the elegiac, and *Le Fou d'Elsa* is a perfect vehicle for both. The grand scale of the book gives full sweep to Aragon's epic vision of past and future regimes, while the inserted lyrics preserve the reduced scale proper to elegy.

To appreciate the texture of Aragon's poetry—his characteristic interweaving of image and theme, diction and syntax—it is necessary to examine a few of his poems in detail. Choosing one poem from each of the three distinct phases of his career (the Surrealist, Resistance, and postwar periods), all dealing with his central theme, the love of a woman, makes it possible to demonstrate both the continuities and the changes in his poetry during the greater part of his career. All three poems are in his elegiac vein, the mode easiest to examine at close range and the most fertile for Aragon. The occasional false notes in his verse tend to be struck when he assumes the triumphalist pose of the committed Marxist. When he speaks of his wife, his very excesses suggest a shattering sincerity, especially when the subject is separation, age, or death.

"Poem to Shout in the Ruins"

"Poème à crier dans les ruines" ("Poem to Shout in the Ruins"), although addressed to a woman, is not addressed to Elsa, whom Aragon had yet to meet when it was written. The poem records the bitterness of an affair that has recently ended and from which the poet seems to have expected more than his lover did. Like most of Aragon's work, the poem is heavily autobiographical; the woman involved was American heir Nancy Cunard, with whom Aragon had lived for about a year, and the allusions to travel throughout the poem recall trips the couple had taken together. Although the poem opens with a passage that might be described as expository, and although it moves from particular details to a general observation and closes with a sort of reprise, it strikes the reader as more loosely organized than it actually is. This impression results from its rhythm being that of association—the train of thought created when a person dwells on a single topic for a sustained period of time. Because the topic is unhappy love and the bitterness of rejection, the process of association takes on an obsessive quality, and although the resulting monologue is ostensibly addressed to the lover, the title suggests that neither she nor anyone else is expected to respond. The overall effect, then, is that of an interior monologue, and its power stems not from any cogency of argument (the "rhetoric" rejected by the Surrealists) but from the cumulative effects of obsessive repetition. Thus, the speaker's memories are evoked in a kind of litany ("I remember your shoulder/ I remember your elbow/ I remember your linen."); later, struck by the realization that memory implies the past tense, he piles up verbs in the *passé simple* (as in "Loved Was Came Caressed"), the tense used for completed action.

The lack of a rhetorical framework in the poem is paralleled by the absence of any central image or images. Although many arresting images appear, they are not linked in any design but remain isolated, reinforcing the sense of meaninglessness that has overwhelmed the speaker. The "little rented cars" and mirrors left unclaimed in a baggage room evoke the traveling the couple did together, which the speaker now sees as aimless. Some of the details given remain opaque because they have a private meaning that is not revealed ("Certain names are charged with a distant thunder"); others seem to be literary allusions, such as Mazeppa's ride (described in a poem by George Gordon, Lord Byron) and the bleeding trees, which to a reader who knows the works of Dante suggest that poet's "wood of the suicides." (Not until many years later did Aragon reveal that he had attempted suicide after the breakup with Cunard.)

The use of such arcane personal and literary allusions was a legacy of the Symbolist movement; as a young man, Aragon admired both Arthur Rimbaud and Stéphane Mallarmé, two of the most gifted Symbolists. The Surrealist approach to imagery evolved directly out of Symbolism in its more extreme forms, such as "Le Bateau ivre" ("The Drunken Boat") of Rimbaud and the *Chants de Maldoror* (1869) of Comte de Lautréamont. Despite its hopelessness, "Poem to Shout in the Ruins" conveys the almost hallucinatory power the Surrealists saw in imagery: its ability to charge ordinary things with mystery by appealing to the buried layers of the subconscious. "Familiar objects one by one were taking on . . . the ghostly look of escaped prisoners. . . ." The poem also suggests, however, that Aragon is not content merely to explore his subconscious; he hungers for a real connection to a real woman. In his desperate desire to prolong the liaison, he tries fitfully to make a "waltz" of the poem and asks the woman to join him, "since *something* must still connect us," in spitting on "what we have loved together." Despite its prevailing tone of negation and despair, the poem anticipates two central themes of Aragon's mature works: the belief that love between man and woman should be infinitely more than a source of casual gratification and the awareness of mortality (which the finality of parting suggests). This awareness is not morbid but tragic—the painful apprehension of death in a man whose loves and hopes were lavished on mortal existence.

"Elsa's Eyes"

"Les Yeux d'Elsa" ("Elsa's Eyes"), the opening poem in the collection of that name, is a good example of the metrically regular pieces Aragon produced in the 1940's (and continued to produce, together with free verse, until the end of his life). It is particularly characteristic in that, while each stanza has internal unity, the stanzas do not follow one another in a strictly necessary order; like those of a folk song or lyrical ballad, they offer a series of related insights or observations without logical or narrative progression. Many of Aragon's mature poems *do* exhibit such a progression (notably "Toi qui es la rose"—"You Who Are the Rose"), but in most cases it is subordinated to the kind of associative rhythm observed in "Poem to Shout in the Ruins."

The imagery of "Elsa's Eyes" is more unified than that of the earlier poem. Taking his wife's eyes as the point of departure, the poet offers a whole array of metaphors for their blueness (sky, ocean, wildflowers), brilliance (lightning, shooting stars), and depth (a well, far countries, and constellations). The last four stanzas are more closely linked than the preceding ones and culminate in an apocalyptic vision of Elsa's eyes surviving the end of the world. The poem as a whole, however, cannot be said to build to this climax; its power stems from the accumulation of images rather than from their arrangement. It should be noted that Aragon's Surrealist formation is still very much in evidence here, not only in the hallucinatory quality of his images but also in their obvious connection with subconscious desires and fears. The occasional obscurities are no longer the result of a deliberate use of private or literary allusions; Aragon was already writing with a wider public in mind. Nevertheless, he continued to evoke his own deepest desires and fears in language whose occasional ambiguity reflects the ambiguity of subconscious impulses.

A relatively new departure for Aragon in this period, the serious use of religious imagery, is reflected in the references to the Three Kings and the Mother of the Seven Sorrows in "Elsa's Eyes." Although reared a Catholic, Aragon became an atheist in his early youth and never professed any religious faith thereafter. During World War II, however, he was impressed by the courage of Christian resisters and acquired a certain respect for the faith that sustained them in the struggle against fascism. For his own part, Aragon began to use the vocabulary of traditional religion to extol his wife. Thus, for example, in "Elsa's Eyes," Elsa is described as the Mother of the Seven Sorrows, an epithet of the Virgin Mary; at the same time, Elsa is assimilated by natural forces and survives the cataclysm of the last stanza like a mysterious deity. This is partly attributable to Aragon's rediscovery, at about this time, of the courtly love tradition in French poetry, in which the lady becomes the immediate object of the knight's worship, whether as a mediatrix (who shows the way to God) or as a substitute for God himself. Repeatedly in Aragon's postwar poetry, Elsa is endowed with godlike qualities, until, in *Le Fou d'Elsa*, a virtual apotheosis takes place: The "holy fool" for whom the book is named (a Muslim, not a Christian) is convicted of heresy for worshiping a woman—Elsa—who will not be born for four centuries.

Whenever he was questioned on the subject, Aragon insisted that his aim was not a deification of Elsa but the replacement of the transcendent God of traditional religions with a "real" object, a woman of flesh and blood who could serve as his partner in building the future. Thus, Elsa's madman tells his judge, "I can say of her what I cannot say of God: She exists, because she *will be*." At the same time, the imagery of "Elsa's Eyes" clearly indicates that on some level there is an impulse of genuine worship, compounded of love, fear, and awe, in the poet's relation to his wife; he turned to the courtly tradition because it struck a deep chord in him. From the very first stanza, Elsa is identified with forces of nature, not all of which are benevolent: "Your eyes are so deep that in stooping to drink/ I saw all suns reflected there/ All desperate men throw themselves there to die." In most of the early stanzas, emphasis is laid on her grief (presumably over the effects of war), which only enhances her beauty, but the insistence on her eyes also suggests that, like God, she is all-seeing. Aragon himself often referred to his wife as his conscience, and Bernard Lecherbonnier has suggested in *Le Cycle d'Elsa* (1974) that the circumstances of Aragon's upbringing created in him, first in regard to his mother and later in regard to his wife, "an obsession with self-justification that permitted the myth of god-as-love to crystallize around the person, and in particular the eyes, of Elsa." Such an attitude is especially suggested by the final images of the poem, that of "Paradise regained and relost a hundred times" and that of Elsa's eyes shining over the sea after the final "shipwreck" of the universe.

"You Who Are the Rose"

An attitude of worship can also be seen in "You Who Are the Rose," from the collection *Elsa*, but it is tempered considerably by the vulnerability of the rose, the central image around which the poem is built. Its tight construction makes this a somewhat uncharacteristic poem for Aragon, yet his technique is still that of association and accumulation rather than logical or rhetorical development. As in "Poem to Shout in the Ruins," short syntactic units give the impression of spoken (indeed, in this poem, almost breathless) language. With an obsessiveness reminiscent of the earlier poem, the speaker worries over the flowering of the rose, which he fears will not bloom "this year" because of frost, drought, or "some subterranean sickness." The poem has a clear dramatic structure: The tension of waiting builds steadily, with periodic breaks or breathing spaces marked by the one-line refrain "*(de) la rose*," until the miraculous flowering takes place and is welcomed with a sort of prayer. The images that accumulate along the way, evoked by the poet in a kind of incantation designed to call forth the rose, are all subordinated to this central image of flowering, yet by their startling juxtaposition and suggestiveness, they clearly reflect Aragon's Surrealist background. Thus, the dormant plant is compared to "a cross contradicting the tomb," while two lines later its roots are "like an insinuating hand beneath the sheets caressing the sleeping thighs of winter." The use of alliteration is excessive—as when six words beginning with *gr-* appear in the space of three lines—and although this serves to emphasize the incantatory quality of the verse, to hostile critics it may look like simple bad taste. Hubert Juin, a friendly critic, freely acknowledges that a certain kind of bad taste is evident in Aragon; he ascribes it to the poet's "epic" orientation, his desire to include as much of the world as possible in his design, which precludes attention to every detail. It seems more to the point to recall that for the Surrealists, editing was a kind of dishonesty; by writing rapidly and not revising, they sought to lay bare what was most deeply buried in their psyches. What often saves Aragon from *préciosité*, or literary affectation, is the realism of this stream-of-consciousness technique. Caught up in the speaker's own anxiety or fantasy, the reader does not stop to criticize the occasional banalities and lapses of taste; he follows in the poet's wake, eager to see where the train of thought will lead.

The poignancy of "You Who Are the Rose," as of so many of Aragon's late poems, stems from the contrast between his exaggerated hopes—still virtually those of a young man—and the fact of old age, which threatens to deprive him of his wife and of his poetic voice. There is also, in some of his later work, a hint of sadness (although never of disillusionment) at the failure of Communism to fulfill its promise within his own lifetime. It is worth noting that in France the rose has long been associated with Socialist ideals; the poet's fear for his wife in "You Who Are the Rose" may be doubled by a tacit fear that the promise of Marxism will not be fulfilled. The two fears are related, moreover, because Aragon saw the harmony between husband and wife as the hope of the future, the cornerstone of a just and happy (Communist) society. His anguish is that of the idealist who rejects the possibility of transcendence: His "divinity" is mortal, like him. This helps to account for the fact that he continued to write with undiminished passion until the very end of his life, for poetry held out the only prospect of immortality in which he believed. The rose is mortal, but she has a name, and the poet can conjure with it (as his conclusion emphasizes: "O rose who are your being and your name"). What is more, Elsa Triolet was herself a writer, and in the preface to an edition combining her own and her husband's fiction, she described their mutually inspired work as the best possible memorial to their love. Aragon will probably be remembered primarily as the poet of Elsa—"Elsa's Madman," perhaps, in his anguished self-disclosure—but above all as Elsa's troubadour, an ecstatic love poet who insists on the possibility of earthly happiness because he has tasted it himself.

OTHER MAJOR WORKS

LONG FICTION: *Anicet: Ou, le panorama*, 1921; *Les Aventures de Télémaque*, 1922 (*The Adventures of Telemachus*, 1988); *Le Paysan de Paris*, 1926 (*Nightwalker*, 1970); *Les Cloches de Bâle*, 1934 (*The Bells of Basel*, 1936); *Le Monde réel*, 1934-1944 (includes *Les Cloches de Bâle*, 1934; *Les Beaux Quartiers*, 1936; *Les Voyageurs de l'impériale*, 1942; and *Aurélien*, 1944); *Les Beaux Quartiers*, 1936 (*Residential Quarter*, 1938); *Les Voyageurs de l'impériale*, 1942 (*The Century Was Young*, 1941); *Aurélien*, 1944 (English translation, 1947); *Les Communistes*, 1949-1951; *La Semaine sainte*, 1958 (*Holy Week*, 1961); *La Mise à mort*, 1965; *Blanche: Ou, L'oubli*, 1967; *Théâtre/roman*, 1974.

SHORT FICTION: *Servitude et grandeur de français*, 1945; *Le Mentir-vrai*, 1981.

NONFICTION: *Le Traité du style*, 1928; *Pour une réalisme socialiste*, 1935; *L'Homme communiste*, 1946, 1953; *Introduction aux littératures soviétiques*, 1956; *J'abats mon jeu*, 1959; *Les Deux Géants: Histoire parallèle des États-Unis et de l'U.R.S.S.*, 1962 (with André Maurois; 5 volumes; partial translation *A History of the U.S.S.R. from Lenin to Khrushchev*, 1964); *Entretiens avec Francis Crémieux*, 1964; *Écrits sur l'art moderne*, 1982.

BIBLIOGRAPHY

Adereth, M. *Aragon: The Resistance Poems*. London: Grant & Cutler, 1985. A brief critical guide to Aragon's poetry.

_____. *Elsa Triolet and Louis Aragon: An Introduction to Their Interwoven Lives and Works*. Lewiston, N.Y.: Edwin Mellen Press, 1994. An introductory biography of Triolet and Aragon and their lives together including critical analysis of their work and a bibliography.

Becker, Lucille Frackman. *Louis Aragon*. New York: Twayne, 1971. An introductory biography of Aragon and critical analysis of selected works. Includes bibliographic references.

Benfey, Christopher, and Karen Remmler, eds. *Artists, Intellectuals, and World War II: The Pontigny Encounters at Mount Holyoke College, 1942-1944*. Amherst: University of Massachusetts Press, 2006. Contains a chapter on Aragon, Gustave Cohen, and the poetry of the Resistance. Provides a general perspective on World War II literature.

Josephson, Hannah, and Malcolm Cowley, eds. *Aragon, Poet of the French Resistance*. New York: Duell, Sloan and Pearce, 1945. A study of Aragon's poetic works produced between 1939 and 1945.

Lillian Doherty

CHARLES BAUDELAIRE

Born: Paris, France; April 9, 1821
Died: Paris, France; August 31, 1867

PRINCIPAL POETRY

Les Fleurs du mal, 1857, 1861, 1868 (*Flowers of Evil*, 1931)
Les Épaves, 1866
Petits Poèmes en prose, 1869 (also known as *Le Spleen de Paris*; *Poems in Prose*, 1905, also known as *Paris Spleen, 1869*, 1947)
Complete Poems, 2002

OTHER LITERARY FORMS

Collections of essays by Charles Baudelaire (bohd-uh-LEHR) on literature, art, aesthetics, and drugs appeared under the titles *Les Paradis artificiels* (1860; *Artificial Paradises*, 1996), *Curiosités esthétiques* (1868), and *L'Art romantique* (1868). Baudelaire also published translations of several volumes of the prose works of Edgar Allan Poe. The most convenient edition of most of his works is the Pléiade edition, *Œuvres complètes* (1868-1870, 1961), edited by Yves Le Dantec and Claude Pichois.

ACHIEVEMENTS

Although Charles Baudelaire is sometimes grouped with the Symbolists, a movement that constituted itself more than a decade after his death, he himself neither belonged to nor founded a school. It is probably fair, however, to designate him as one of the earliest exponents of modernism. He constantly sought, in both literature and painting, works that expressed a beauty specific to the reality of the moment, even if that reality was unpleasant or bizarre. His corrosive irony, his suggestive understatement of the metaphoric sense of his images, and his aggressive use of material drawn from the prosaic side of life have had a lasting success and influence. Movements as diverse as Symbolism, Dadaism, and the Italian neorealist cinema have claimed descent from his work.

BIOGRAPHY

Charles Pierre Baudelaire was born in Paris on April 9, 1821. His father, Joseph-François Baudelaire, was of modest origin but well educated, for he attended seminary and became a priest before the Revolution. Well connected, he became preceptor to the children of the duke of Choiseul-Praslin and, as a painter, was personally acquainted with Enlightenment figures such as Condorcet and Cabanis. After the Revolution, having left the priesthood, he worked on the administrative staff of the French senate. Caroline Archenbaut-Defayis, Baudelaire's mother, was thirty-four years younger than his

Charles Baudelaire
(Library of Congress)

father. Widowed, she remarried when her son was six years old. Baudelaire's stepfather, Jacques Aupick, was a career military officer who had Baudelaire placed in a series of boarding schools, first in Lyons, when the child was nine, and then in Paris, at the age of fifteen. The choice of schools permitted Baudelaire to be near his mother as the Aupick household moved in response to the officer's promotions.

As an adolescent, Baudelaire was friendly, religious, and studious. He won prizes in Latin verse composition (one of the poems in *Flowers of Evil* is in Latin). He seems to have had few serious disputes with his stepfather until after obtaining the *baccalauréat* in 1839. After that, however, the now successful general became progressively the object of Baudelaire's dislike and even hatred. Disapproving of the young man's friends and conduct, the general sent him on a long boat trip toward India, but Baudelaire, once embarked, refused to go farther than Mauritius. When Baudelaire reached legal majority in 1842, he broke with the Aupicks and lived prodigally on the money he inherited from his father. The life of ease of the young literary dandy lasted only two years, however, for the Aupicks had Baudelaire placed under conservatorship in 1844 on the grounds that he was incapable of managing his money. This deprivation of his full personal freedom had a devastating effect on Baudelaire, who attempted suicide the following year. Upon his recovery, he apparently resolved to write copiously and seriously, contributing to various reviews, especially *L'Artiste* and *Le Corsaire-Satan*.

Baudelaire was widely acquainted with important Romantic authors, including Charles Sainte-Beuve, Théophile Gautier, Victor Hugo, Gérard de Nerval, Théodore de Banville, Petrus Borel (the Wolf-man), and Champfleury. He was also close to the active painters of his day and spent much of his time in their studios. His essays on expositions and on individual artists, especially Eugène Delacroix and Constantin Guys, actually occupy twice as many pages in the complete works as his literary criticism. More intermittently, Baudelaire was involved in the political life of his day, staffing the barricades in the 1848 Revolution and distributing political tracts. His love of order, or rather his aspiration to order and hatred of disorder, kept him from fitting into the revolutionary cause, and his hatred of the bourgeoisie prevented him from siding with the conservatives.

By 1845, Baudelaire was already announcing a forthcoming volume of poetry, under the title "Les Lesbiennes." In 1848, he claimed to be working on a volume called "Les Limbes." Finally, in 1855, he settled on the title *Flowers of Evil*. When it appeared in 1857, the collection provoked a scandal that led to the prosecution of the poet and the publisher. Six of the poems were suppressed, and the poet was fined.

The death of General Aupick a few months before the appearance of *Flowers of Evil* led Baudelaire to a reconciliation with his mother. Although he never succeeded in putting his life in what he called order, living within his means and avoiding debts, his attempt to heal his rift with his respectable middle-class origins may explain the increasingly Christian and even Catholic orientation of his ideas in the last decade of his life. In 1866, while visiting Brussels, Baudelaire was stricken with partial paralysis and became aphasic. He died in Paris after more than a year of suffering.

Analysis

Although Charles Baudelaire was close to the major Romantic artists and poets, his work announced something new and difficult to describe. Baudelaire did not introduce a fundamentally new aesthetic principle but made important changes in the proportions of idealism and realism, formal beauty and attention to ideas, social commitment and alienation from society—all categories through which the Romantic poets had expressed their conception of literary art. More than most Romantics, he wrote poetry based on the ugliness of urban life and drew an intense beauty from the prosaic and the unspeakable. Although major Romantics, including Hugo, had broken down many restrictions on subjects that could be treated in poetry, Baudelaire went further, choosing such topics as crime, disease, and prostitution as his points of departure. Although many Romantics suggest a transcendent redemptive quality in art, a spiritual enlightenment that gives readers a kind of religious or social pathway to liberation, Baudelaire tantalizes the reader with religious hope but then pulls it away, suggesting that all hope is in the moment of artistic insight and not in the real future.

The image of the poet as prophet or spiritually superior dreamer, typical of Hugo or Alfred de Vigny, flickers occasionally through Baudelaire's work, but it generally yields to an image of the poet as a sensitive and marginal individual whose only superiority to his contemporaries is his consciousness of his corruption and decadence, something Baudelaire expressed as "conscience [or consciousness] in the midst of evil." Baudelaire thus prepared the way for the Decadent poets, and for those poets of the twentieth century who conceived of their work as primarily individual and not social. In this regard, it is significant that Baudelaire introduced Edgar Allan Poe to the French. Poe subsequently came to be a major influence on Stéphane Mallarmé and Paul Valéry and even played a role in contemporary French psychoanalysis.

In terms of poetic form, Baudelaire's major innovation was undoubtedly in the prose poem, which existed before him but achieved status as a major form principally through *Paris Spleen, 1869*. In his verse, Baudelaire often used the highly restrictive "fixed forms" with their set repetition of certain verses, such as the *pantoum*, in which the second and fourth verses of one stanza become the first and third of the following four-verse unit. Such forms were common among the Romantics, but Baudelaire's combination of this formal perfection with surprising and even shocking subjects produces a dissonant and unforgettable music. Baudelaire thus avoids the pitfalls of the school of art for art's sake, which he denounced for its exclusive attachment to surface beauty.

FLOWERS OF EVIL

Baudelaire insisted that *Flowers of Evil* should be read as a structured whole and not as a random collection of verse. Whatever one may think about the authority of such claims, the six major divisions of the book, beginning with the longest section, eighty-five poems, titled "Spleen et idéal" ("Spleen and Ideal"), and ending with the six poems of "La Mort" ("Death"), seem to outline a thematic and perhaps even chronological passage from aspirations toward a transcendence of pain, suffering, and evil (in the earliest section) through the exploration of various kinds of intoxication or escape—glimpsed in the sections "Le Vin" ("Wine"), "Flowers of Evil," and "Révolte" ("Rebellion")—only to end in death, seen itself as a form of escape from the disappointments or boredom of this world.

"TO THE READER"

Throughout *Flowers of Evil*, a major theme is the uncovering of humanity's own contradictions, hypocrisies, desires, and crimes: all the aspects of life and fantasy that the respectable middle class hides. In the very first poem of the book, "Au lecteur" ("To the Reader"), Baudelaire establishes an unusual relationship with his public. The poem begins with a list of vices—stupidity, error, sin, and stinginess—but instead of reproaching humanity and urging the reader to reform, the poet finishes the sentence with an independent clause containing a remarkable simile: "We feed our nice remorse,/ As beggars nourish their lice." Over this humanity presides the Devil, described two stanzas later as the magician, not Hermes but Satan Trismegistus (three-times great), who turns the rich metal of the will into vapor like an alchemist working backward. Building toward what will apparently be a crescendo of vice, Baudelaire, in stanza 7, lists sins that humanity would commit if people had the courage (such as rape, poisoning, stabbing, and arson) and then points to a still greater vice, which he names only three stanzas later in the conclusion: boredom (*ennui*). In the poem's striking concluding lines, Baudelaire claims that the reader knows this "delicate monster," and then calls the reader "Hypocritical reader, my likeness, my brother!"

This strange poem, borrowing so much of its vocabulary and rhetoric from the tradition of religious exhortation, does not choose between good and evil. Instead, it promotes a third term into what is usually a simple dilemma: Boredom, as the greatest of vices, is an aesthetic concept that replaces traditional moral concepts of evil as that which must be avoided at all costs, a vice that "could swallow the world in a yawn." In religious verse, the address to the reader as a brother is part of a call, first to recognize a common weakness and, second, to repent. Baudelaire does make an avowal of similarity but calls for an aesthetic rather than an ethical response.

"BEACONS"

The largest part of *Flowers of Evil* evokes a struggle against boredom through the artistic use of the ugliness of everyday life and ordinary, even abject, passions. The poem "Les Phares" ("Beacons") is an enumeration of eight great painters, including Peter Paul Rubens, Rembrandt, and Michelangelo, not as a celebration of human greatness but as a testimony to human sentiment and sensation, predominantly in the negative. Rubens is described, for example, as a "Pillow of fresh flesh where one cannot love" and Rembrandt as a "sad hospital full of murmuring." The last three stanzas seem at first to point to a religious purpose in this art that depicts a swarming, nightmare-ridden humanity, for Baudelaire uses terms from religion: malediction, blasphemy, *Te Deum*. Humankind's art is called a "divine opium," but this drug is not offered upward as incense to the Deity. It is, rather, an opium for human hearts. The purpose of art is ambiguous in this conclusion, for it is the best testimony to human dignity but is destined to die at the edge of God's eternity. In the historical context of French Romanticism, this vision of art serves at least to set Baudelaire apart from the partisans of art for art's sake, a movement that Baudelaire himself called the plastic school. Clearly, the visual beauty of the paintings alluded to is not their primary characteristic in "Beacons." These works of art are great because of their representative quality and for the tension between their beauty and the suffering on which they are based.

"A CARCASS"

The paradoxical search for an art that draws its beauty from ugliness and suffering appears in a spectacular way in another of the early poems of *Flowers of Evil*, titled "Une

Charogne" ("A Carcass"). Baudelaire's particular delight in the shocking combination of refined form with a crude and repugnant subject is noticeable in the very organization of the stanzas. There are twelve units of four lines each: The first and third lines of each stanza are rhyming Alexandrines (twelve-syllable lines), while the second and fourth lines are rhyming octosyllables. This division imposes a rhythm that heightens the contrast between refined gentleness and sickening sensations. As a whole, the poem is a monologue addressed to a person or character whom the speaker calls "my soul." Although there is a certain ambiguity about the significance of the term (it could represent a division of the self into two parts, a common Baudelairean theme), the poet's "soul" assumes the role of a woman to whom he speaks in words of endearment. He also recalls, however, the discovery, one summer morning, of a carcass lying near a pathway.

The poem's opening stanza illustrates the way in which a tension is created between contrasting tones. The first two lines are addressed to the soul in terms that allow one to expect some pretty image, something that would fit the context of a beautiful, mild summer morning. The end of the second Alexandrine, however, names the object: a "foul carcass." The discovery occurs as the speaker and his soul are coming around a bend in the path (*détour*), which parallels the transition from the first half of the stanza to the somewhat startling second half. The next eight stanzas continue to tell about the discovery of this cadaver in a tone that alternates, sometimes within stanzas and sometimes from one stanza to the next, between a distant aesthetic contemplation and a crude and immediate repulsion. The fourth stanza starts with a presentation of the point of view of the sky witnessing the "blossoming" of the carcass as if it were a flower, while the next two lines ("The stench was so strong that you thought you would faint on the grass") take a distinctly human point of view, even rather sadistically delighting in the soul's weakness. The speaker's reaction is represented as quite different, much closer to that attributed to the sky. In stanza 7, he compares the sounds coming from the carcass, eaten by organisms of decomposition, to flowing water and wind and to the sound of grain being winnowed. Not only does this comparison permit the poet to find beauty in ugliness, but it also permits him to pay homage to the bucolic poetry of the Renaissance (exemplified in such poems as Joachim du Bellay's "D'un vanneur de blé aux vents" ("From a Winnower to the Winds"), showing that classical themes can be presented in a thoroughly modern way.

In the following stanza, the speaker's drift continues from a purely aesthetic contemplation of the object to a comparison of the carcass to an artist's preliminary sketch in the artist's memory. This reverie is broken off in the ninth stanza by the return to the supposed summer morning scene and the recollection that a dog was waiting for the couple to leave so that he could get the "meat."

The last three stanzas are quite different, for they depart from the scene, which is in the past, and look forward to the future of the speaker's beloved "soul," foreseeing the time when she will be like that carcass. However, even in this section (a form of *envoi*, a traditional closing message to the addressee of a poem), the alteration of tone continues. In the tenth stanza, where the speaker declares "You will be like this filth," he still continues to refer to her as "my angel and my passion." This contrast leads toward the final stanza in which Baudelaire, again recalling the poetry of the French Renaissance, proclaims the immortality of his poetry ("I have kept the form and divine essence/ Of my decomposed loves") in contrast to the fleshly mortality of his "soul," his beloved.

It is impossible to assert that this conclusion is a straightforward poetic doctrine. Perhaps the poet, after having cast the "soul" in the paradoxical role of decomposition, is exercising a final irony toward his own poetry. In any case, it is clear that "A Carcass" represents Baudelaire's reworking of traditional texts from classical and Renaissance tradition. His way of using the tradition sets him apart from those Romantics he called the pagan school, who preferred to assume the posture of outright return to pre-Christian belief by denying historical evolution. One reason Baudelaire objected to this position was that he himself possessed a deeply tormented Christian character, described by some as Jansenist (that is, as belonging to the most severe, pessimistic, and ascetic form of seventeenth and eighteenth century French Catholicism), penetrated by the sense of sin and guilt. He could not imagine a simple return to classical "innocence." Baudelaire also had an acute sense of the passage of time and of historical change. In calling the work of the neopagans "a disgusting and useless pastiche," he was implicitly drawing attention to his own use of antiquity in a resolutely modernist manner, one that did not copy the ancients but assimilated their ideas into a representation of the reality of modern life.

"The Swan"

The poignancy that Baudelaire achieves with such an approach can be seen in his "Le Cygne" ("The Swan"), dedicated, like two other poems in the section "Tableaux parisiens" ("Parisian Pictures"), to Hugo, a deep believer in the historical movement of poetry. "The Swan" is divided into two numbered parts, one of seven and the other of six stanzas. In the first section, the speaker begins by addressing the legendary figure Andromache, the Trojan Hector's widow, captive in the city of Epirus. The Parisian speaker's memory, he says, has been made pregnant by the thought of the "lying Simoïs swelled by your tears." This allusion to the legends of Troy is the key to understanding the rest of the first part of the poem, most of which seems merely to tell of an event in the speaker's own life, an event without apparent connection with Andromache. He was walking across the new Carrousel Square when he recalled a menagerie that once stood on that spot. A swan had escaped from its cage and was bathing its wings in the dust of a gutter.

The allusion to Andromache is now clearer, for the "lying" Simoïs was a replica in Epirus of the small river that once flowed at the foot of the walls of Troy. In an attempt to make the widow happier, her captors had constructed this imitation, described by Baudelaire as "lying" because it is not only false but also actively and disappointingly deceitful. It can never replace the Simoïs but can only remind Andromache of the discrepancy between past and present. In the second part of the poem, Baudelaire explains the multiple analogy that had been left implicit in the first part. Returning to the present (the first part had been composed of three chronological layers: the legendary past of Andromache, the moment when the speaker saw the swan, and the approximate present in which he recollects the swan), he exclaims, "Paris changes! but nothing in my melancholy/ Has moved!"

What had seemed in the first part to be a comparison only between the widow and the swan now includes the speaker. Each of the three has an immovable memory on the inside—the speaker compares his to rocks—which cannot match the mutable outside world. This dissonance between mind and world is expressed not only in the image of the swan but also, more subtly and pathetically, in the temporal organization of the poem. Between the time he saw the swan and the time of the creation of the poem, the swan has vanished and the old carrousel has been changed into the new. The chronological layering of the text has the same function as the simile. Furthermore, the changes in Paris, composed of monumental constructions of carved stone, give the city an ironic and metaphoric significance. Monuments, like the palace of the Louvre near which the menagerie stood, are usually associated with memory. They are meant to last longer than individuals. Here, however, the city represents change. Baudelaire has thus united a commonplace of certain Romantic poets (the indifference of nature to humankind's suffering) with a classical poetry of cities (Troy, Epirus, Rome) to produce a thoroughly modern poetic idiom.

The conclusion of "The Swan" continues the interplay of literary allusion, for it opens still further the analogy involving Andromache, the swan, and the poet to include an African woman exiled in a northern climate, sailors, captives, and the conquered. There is a decidedly epic quality to this expansion of the analogy to include vast numbers of modern exiles. Baudelaire did not, unlike many Romantics, believe in long poems, and he seems here to be condensing the grandeur of the epic into the brevity of the personal lyric. The many components of this epic analogy, stretching from Andromache to the suggestively open-ended last line ("Of captives, of the conquered . . . of still others!"), are reminiscent of the multiple symbolic figures (the artists) of "Beacons." With this latter poem, "The Swan" also shares the vision of suffering as a defining characteristic of life, for exiles "Suck at the breast of Sorrow as if she were a good wolf." This image is a way of tying in the Roman epic of Romulus and Remus while emphasizing the voluntary or consoling aspect of pain and suffering.

SUFFERING

Suffering, inflicted on others or on oneself, is a frequent theme in *Flowers of Evil* and is linked to learning and self-awareness. In "Heautontimoroumenos" (a Greek term for "the executioner of oneself," borrowed from a comedy of Terence), the speaker declares himself a "dissonance in the divine symphony" on account of the irony that eats away at him. In the most remarkable stanza, he declares in part, "I am the wound and the knife!/ I am the blow and the cheek!" In the poem immediately following, "L'Irrémédiable" ("The Irreparable"), after briefly tracing the fall of an ideal being from Heaven into Hell, Baudelaire evokes a "Somber and clear tête-à-tête/ A heart become its own mirror!" This division of the self into two sides, each looking at the other, is then described metaphorically as a "Well of truth, clear and black/ Where a pale star trembles." Although, here, knowledge is stressed more than the pain that is so fiercely displayed in "Heautontimoroumenos," pain must be the outcome of self-examination in this "well of truth" because the inward discovery is the sentiment of a fall from a higher state, an "irreparable" decadence. However, there is a tension here between the claim to total clarity and the image of the well, for the latter promises depths that can never be coextensive with the mirroring surface. Working back from this tension, one can see that the whole poem is full of terms for depth, darkness, and entrapment. The lucidity toward which the poem tends will never be complete, for consciousness can only discover the extent, apparently infinite, of its deprivation.

"The Trip"

The concluding note of *Flowers of Evil*, the section called "Death," is a reminder of this perpetual quest for new discovery, even at the price of horror. In fact, the last stanza of the concluding poem, "Le Voyage" ("The Trip"), is based on the concept of depth that had already appeared in "The Irreparable": "Plunge into the deeps of the abyss, Hell or Heaven, that difference/ Into the depth of the Unknown to find something *new*!" Here the preoccupation with boredom as supreme evil in "To the Reader" appears coupled with the themes of knowledge and discovery that constitute much of the other sections. "The Trip" is a kind of summary in dialogue of *Flowers of Evil*, beginning with the childlike hope of discovery in the exploration of the real world. When asked later what they discovered, the travelers say that no city they discovered was ever as interesting as the cities they imagined in the shapes of clouds. Then, in passages that seem to recall the "Parisian Pictures," "Wine," and "Rebellion," the world of human sin is sketched out as a monotonous mirror in which humankind sees its own image, "An oasis of horror in a desert of boredom!" The only hope is in death itself, addressed in the last two stanzas as a ship's captain. He alone holds out a balm for people's boredom, which itself results from an unresolvable tension between the aspirations of the heart and the outside world, ostensibly a mirror but actually an incomplete reflection because it can capture only actions and not intentions.

Paris Spleen, 1869

Baudelaire's collection of prose poems, *Paris Spleen, 1869*, is thematically similar to *Flowers of Evil*. The prose pieces, however, have greater means to establish a situation for the poetic speaker and to accumulate aspects of life that seem "realistic" but serve ultimately to reveal figurative meanings in the most ordinary surroundings, a process sometimes called "correspondences" after the title of one of Baudelaire's verse poems. Frequently, as in "Le Gâteau" ("The Cake"), Baudelaire dramatically alters the situation of the poetic speaker so that he is not a representative of dissatisfaction with the world but an amazed spectator of the subjectivity of desire. In "The Cake," a traveler finds himself in a country where his plain bread is called "cake," unleashing a fratricidal war for its possession. In "Le Joujou du pauvre" ("The Poor Child's Plaything"), he discovers two children playing on opposite sides of a fence. One child is rich and has a meticulously crafted doll while the other holds his toy in a little cage. It is a living rat. Although these texts include elements of diction, characterization, and setting typical of fiction in the realist or naturalist vein, Baudelaire always suggests a larger significance that makes the scene or incident figurative. In "The Poor Child's Plaything," the fence between the children is referred to as a symbolic barrier, and the rat is described as a toy drawn from life itself. Baudelaire specifies the metaphoric meaning much less in the prose poems than in his verse. One can, however, easily view the rat as a synecdoche for Baudelaire's aesthetic, based on drawing beauty from those aspects of life that are most repulsive.

OTHER MAJOR WORKS
LONG FICTION: *La Fanfarlo*, 1847.
NONFICTION: *Les Paradis artificiels*, 1860 (partial translation as *Artificial Paradises: On Hashish and Wine as a Means of Expanding Individuality*, 1971; also as *Artificial Paradises*, 1996); *L'Art romantique*, 1868; *Curiosités esthétiques*, 1868; *Mon cœur mis à nu*, 1887 (*My Heart Laid Bare*, 1950); *The Letters of Baudelaire*, 1927; *My Heart Laid Bare, and Other Prose Writings*, 1951; *Baudelaire on Poe*, 1952; *The Mirror of Art*, 1955; *Intimate Journals*, 1957; *Beaudelaire as Literary Critic: Selected Essays*, 1964; *The Painter of Modern Life, and Other Essays*, 1964; *Art in Paris, 1845-1862: Salons and Other Exhibitions*, 1965.
TRANSLATIONS: *Histoires extraordinaires*, 1856 (of Edgar Allan Poe's short stories); *Nouvelles Histoires extraordinaires*, 1857 (of Poe's short stories); *Aventures d'Arthur Gordon Pym*, 1858 (of Poe's novel); *Eureka*, 1864 (of Poe's poem); *Histoires grotesques et sérieuses*, 1864 (of Poe's short stories).
MISCELLANEOUS: *Œuvres complètes*, 1868-1870, 1961.

BIBLIOGRAPHY
Blood, Susan. *Baudelaire and the Aesthetics of Bad Faith*. Stanford, Calif.: Stanford University Press, 1997. Examines the role of Baudelaire in the history of modernism and the development of the modernist consciousness. Detailed analysis of the poetry, especially its relationship to Baudelaire's writings on caricature and the prob-

lem of its "secret architecture." Also examines the nature of Baudelaire's symbolism.

Evans, Margery A. *Baudelaire and Intertextuality.* New York: Cambridge University Press, 1993. Study of *Paris Spleen, 1869* that validates its reassessment as a work that rivals the success of *Flowers of Evil.* Sees these prose poems as hybrid works that set themselves up for comparison with the novel as much as with lyric poetry.

Hyslop, Lois Boe. *Charles Baudelaire Revisited.* New York: Twayne, 1992. Useful and uncomplicated general introduction to the life and work of Baudelaire. Sees Baudelaire as transforming his emotional torment into aesthetic form, and as finding both beauty and spiritual revelations within the dark side of modernity. Discusses *Paris Spleen, 1869* and *Flowers of Evil* as major works and pays much attention to Baudelaire's theories of art. Includes a chronology and bibliography.

Leakey, F. W. *Baudelaire: "Les Fleurs du mal."* New York: Cambridge University Press, 1992. Thorough, appreciative, and thoughtful introduction to *Flowers of Evil*, with particular attention to the sociopolitical context in which the poems were written. Includes a detailed discussion of individual poems and a bibliography.

Lloyd, Rosemary. *Baudelaire's World.* Ithaca, N.Y.: Cornell University Press, 2002. A biography of the poet that examines the world in which he lived.

Thompson, William J., ed. *Understanding "Les Fleurs du mal."* Nashville: Vanderbilt University Press, 1997. Collection of sixteen essays on *Flowers of Evil*, with the purpose of giving students a clear, scholarly introduction to the poems. Each essay selects one particular poem for detailed discussion, and the analysis may be theoretical or textual. Essays represent a variety of critical perspectives, including feminist, Jungian, sociopolitical, and structuralist.

John D. Lyons

ANDRÉ BRETON

Born: Tinchebray, France; February 19, 1896
Died: Paris, France; September 28, 1966

PRINCIPAL POETRY
Mont de piété, 1919
Clair de terre, 1923
L'Union libre, 1931 (*Free Union*, 1982)
Le Revolver à cheveux blancs, 1932
L'Air de l'eau, 1934
Fata Morgana, 1941 (English translation, 1982)
Pleine marge, 1943
Young Cherry Trees Secured Against Hares, 1946
Ode à Charles Fourier, 1947 (*Ode to Charles Fourier*, 1970)
Poèmes, 1948
Poésie et autre, 1960
Selected Poems, 1969
Poems of André Breton, 1982 (includes *Free Union* and *Fata Morgana*, among other selected poems)

OTHER LITERARY FORMS

André Breton (bruh-TOHN) published many experimental works during his career, some of which were written in collaboration with friends. *Les Champs magnétiques* (1921; *The Magnetic Fields*, 1985), the first Surrealist text to employ the technique of what came to be called automatic writing, was done with Philippe Soupault. *L'Immaculée Conception* (1930; immaculate conception), an attempt to simulate the thought processes of various types of insanity, was written with Paul Éluard. Among the basic Surrealist documents were several works by Breton alone, such as *Poisson soluble* (1924; soluble fish) and *Les Vases communicants* (1932; *Communicating Vessels*, 1990), which mixed lyrical elements with philosophical speculations cast in the form of prose, as well as the numerous polemical manifestos such as *Manifeste du surréalisme* (1924; *Manifesto of Surrealism*, 1969) and *Second Manifeste du surréalisme* (1930; *Second Manifesto of Surrealism*, 1969). Breton's numerous essays were also collected in three volumes: *Les Pas perdus* (1924; the lost steps), *Point du jour* (1934; *Break of Day*, 1999), and *Perspective cavalière* (1970). Convenient selections from Breton's prose in English translation have appeared in *Les Manifestes du surréalisme* (1955; *Manifestoes of Surrealism*, 1969), translated by Richard Seaver and Helen R. Lane, and *What Is Surrealism? Selected Writings* (1978), edited by Franklin Rosemont.

Achievements

Above all, André Breton will be remembered as the founder and leader of the Surrealist movement. Of all the avant-garde movements that rocked the foundations of the arts at the beginning of the twentieth century, Surrealism has had perhaps the greatest and longest-lived impact. Surrealism, created in Paris in 1924 by Breton and a small group of friends, was the last inheritor of a long series of "isms," including Dadaism, German expressionism, French and Spanish cubism, Italian Futurism, and Anglo-American Imagism and Vorticism, which attempted to transform the conception of the world through artistic innovation. Under the leadership of Breton, Surrealism became the most mature expression of this developing sensibility, not only because of its relatively well developed underlying philosophy—which was both far-reaching and systematic in nature—but also because it eventually came to have the greatest international scope of all these movements and because it stimulated the production of a vast body of work of great diversity in all the major artistic genres—poetry, fiction, drama, philosophy, painting, sculpture, and film.

Biography

André Breton was born on February 19, 1896, in Tinchebray, a small inland town in the old French province of Normandy. The family soon moved, however, to the fishing port of Lorient, in Brittany, on the Atlantic coast of France. This seaside environment was particularly important later in the poet's life. When Breton first began to write in 1914, his highly imaginative lyrical poems expressed the wondrous abundance of nature and were often filled with images of sea life and other details evoking the maritime setting of his youth—which contrasted sharply with his life in Paris.

Breton was an only child, and his parents seemingly had an unusually strong influence on his personality. His father, who was a merchant, seems almost a prototype of the complacent, self-satisfied bourgeois that the Surrealists were later to attack as the epitome of the social conformity they rejected. Breton's mother, whom he described as straitlaced, puritanical, and harsh in her response to any suggestion of impropriety, must have also been responsible, to a large degree, for his later hatred of restraint and his provocative attitude toward anything he considered conventional.

Being the only child of a comfortably situated family, Breton had much attention lavished on him, and naturally, his parents had great ambitions for him. He attended school in Paris from 1907 until his graduation in 1912, entering the Sorbonne in 1913 to study medicine. This contact with medicine was also important for the later development of the poet and is reflected in Breton's diverse poetic vocabulary. Even more important, however, was the experience that resulted when Breton was sent to work at the neurological center of the hospital at Nantes during World War I instead of into combat. Breton's experiences as a medical assistant during the war—first at Nantes and later at the psychiatric center at Saint-Dizier, to which he was transferred in 1917—introduced the young, impressionable poet to the bizarre aberrations of mental illness.

During this period, Breton was exposed not only to the diverse forms of mental illness from which the soldiers suffered but also to the theories on which the practical measures used to treat them were based. Among the most important of these theories were those of Jean-Martin Charcot, Sigmund Freud, and Pierre Janet, each of which contributed an important element to the formulation of Breton's view of the operation, structure, and purpose of the human mind. From Charcot's work, Breton learned of the unlocking of the will through the use of hypnosis and saw some of the dramatic cures it was able to effect. From Freud's work, he learned about the existence of the unconscious, its role in determining mental health, and the method of dream interpretation by which one could reveal its secrets to the dreamer. From Janet's work, he learned about the existence of "psychic automatism" and the means by which it might be evoked—which eventually resulted in his own experiments with automatic writing.

These influences were reflected in three important ways in Breton's later work. First, they resulted in the two important prose experiments in automatic writing that he produced: *The Magnetic Fields*, written with Philippe Soupault, and *Poisson soluble*, which Breton created alone. The second product of his wartime experience was the novel *Nadja* (1928; English translation, 1960), which describes the encounter of an autobiographical persona with a mysterious woman who suffers a bizarre and debilitating psychosis. The third product of these influences was *L'Immaculée Conception*, a series of writings undertaken with Paul Éluard, with the purpose of simulating, in verbal form, the thought processes of various types of insanity.

Following the war, Breton came under the influence of Dadaism, which by then had moved its base of operation from Zurich to Paris. The heyday of Dada in Paris was brief, however, lasting from January of 1920 until July of 1923. In the meantime, beginning in May of 1921, Breton and some of his friends were forming a new group whose optimistic attitude toward life, experiments with new methods of literary composition, and increasingly systematic philosophical orientation was in marked contrast to Dada's attitude of nihilistic despair. Breton later called this period the intuitive phase of Surrealism, a phase that extended from May of 1921 until October of 1924, when the first *Manifesto of Surrealism* was published. The publication of this first manifesto established, in an explicit way, a new aesthetic and a profoundly optimistic, imaginative conception of the world which its author, Breton, named Surrealism. The intense period of Surrealist creative activity, which began at that time and continued unabated until the appearance of the *Second Manifesto of Surrealism* in 1930, Breton was later to call the reasoning phase of Surrealism. This period culminated in the appearance of *Communicating Vessels*, a series of lyrical philosophical discourses expressing in mature, fully developed form the central ideas of the Surrealist philosophy and aesthetic.

The period following 1930, the year of the second manifesto, was characterized by two developments. One of these was the Surrealists' increasing involvement with the

Communist International movement. The second development was, in a direct sense, an outgrowth of the first, for it was also during this period that Surrealism was disseminated on a worldwide scale and gained adherents outside Western Europe in many places where it was seen as the artistic concomitant of Marxist revolutionary philosophy. This period, which might be called, with some small injustice, the dogmatic phase of Surrealism, lasted until the outbreak of World War II. In 1941, Breton left France and lived for five years in New York. When he returned to Paris in 1946, Surrealism was effectively dead, although with those few friends of the original group who still remained, and with the growing support of countless other self-acknowledged "Surrealists" in many other countries where their dream had been carried, Breton lived on as the universally acknowledged magus of Surrealism until his death on September 28, 1966, in Paris.

Analysis

André Breton's poetry forms a relatively small though important part of his total literary output, being dwarfed in quantity by his lengthy experiments in prose and his numerous polemical writings. His poetry, from the first published collection, *Mont de piété* (mount of piety), to his last major poetic work, *Ode to Charles Fourier*, shows a remarkable consistency of style. As a poet, Breton is best known for his remarkable imagery—which, at its best, expresses the powerful ability of the imagination to reconcile basic human drives and desires with the material conditions of reality and, at its worst, lapses into bizarre forms of irrationality that are incomprehensible to all but the poet himself.

In general terms, Breton's poetic imagery is characterized by comparisons that yoke together extremely disparate objects; by the sudden, sometimes violent shifting of context as the poet moves from one image to the next; and by an extremely indirect method of expressing comparisons between objects. It is these three qualities, above all, that give his poetic imagery the appearance of being spontaneous rather than deliberate. As critics have shown, however, much to Breton's credit as a poet, this initial impression is a misleading one.

Breton's imagery is reinforced by other prominent aspects of his style, one of which might be called devices of syntactic derangement. These devices range from the use of simple paradoxes involving logical and semantic contradictions, to syntactic ambiguity involving multiple or imprecise grammatical modification, to much more unsettling contradictions of reference—where the referent of a speech act is left unidentified, is deliberately misidentified, or is made ambiguous.

One other important element of Breton's style that helps support the dramatic effect of his poetic images on his readers is his diction, which is characterized by two principal traits. The first of these is the extremely wide range of his vocabulary, which frequently includes the use of words from anatomical, zoological, botanical, and technical contexts that are unfamiliar to most readers of poetry. The second important trait of his diction is the tendency to use words in specialized, atypical ways that emphasize (and often create) their figurative meanings over their denotations. These qualities have two important effects on Breton's work: The first helps make possible his imagery of violent contrasts, and the second is, to a large degree, responsible for the great difficulty his readers and translators encounter searching for paraphrasable or translatable meaning in his work.

Another element of Breton's style is his use of recurring themes and symbolic motifs, such as the revolver as a synecdochic image for rebellion or revolt of any kind. These recurring thematic and symbolic elements in Breton's work can frequently be used as contextual clues for interpreting his most difficult works.

The poetry of Breton expresses three key ideas—the liberating power of the imagination, the transformation of the material world into a utopian state, and the exploration of human potentiality through love—which recur, with increasing elaboration, throughout the course of his work and constitute the essence of his Surrealist vision.

POWER OF IMAGINATION

Breton's faith in the liberating power of the human imagination, although suggested and influenced by his contact with modern psychoanalytic thought, especially that of Freud on the operations of the unconscious, goes far beyond the notion of simply releasing the bound or "repressed" energies that is the therapeutic basis of psychoanalytic practice. For Breton, the unconscious is not an enclosed inner space, or reservoir, of trapped energy; it is, rather, the way out of the everyday world of material reality into the realm of the surreal. According to the Surrealists, this realm—where human reason and imagination no longer struggle against each other but function in harmony—is the ultimate reality, and each person's goal in life is to seek out continually the signs of this reality, which, when directly experienced, is capable of transforming the life of the person. Although Breton envisioned the realm of the surreal as accessible to all men who seek it, it was especially important for the artist, whose goal was to capture the fleeting traces of *le merveilleux* (the marvelous) in his writing.

The Surrealists recommended a number of different methods for attaining this experience. Two, in particular, are frequently used and referred to in Breton's work: the surrendering of the person to the *hasard objectif* ("objective chance") of the universe, and the evocation of the "primary processes" of the unconscious through such procedures as automatic writing. The first of these methods is illustrated well in "Au regard des divinités" ("In the Eyes of the Gods"), one of Breton's early poems from *Clair de terre* (the light of Earth):

> Shortly before midnight near the landing-stage
> If a dishevelled woman follows you, pay no attention.
> It's the blue. You need fear nothing of the blue.
> There'll be a tall blonde vase in a tree.

> The spire of the village of melted colors
> Will be your landmark. Take it easy,
> Remember. The dark geyser that hurls fern-tips
> Towards the sky greet
> Greets you.

This poem reads like, and in fact is intended to be, a set of instructions for encountering the marvelous through the technique of objective chance.

Breton's other primary technique for evoking the marvelous—using the unfettered association of ideas in the unconscious to produce automatic writing—is illustrated by "Au beau demi-jour" ("In the Lovely Half-light"), a poem from *L'Air de l'eau* (air of the water):

> In the lovely half-light of 1934
> The air was a splendid rose the colour of red mullet
> And the forest when I made ready to enter it
> Began with a tree that had cigarette-paper leaves
> For I was waiting for you. . . .

UTOPIAN IDEAL

Breton believed not only in the power of the creative imagination to transform the life of individuals but also in the possibility of transforming society itself into a Socialist utopia, and he came to believe that the Communist International movement was a means to that end. Breton's association with the Communist Party, which began about 1930, was an increasingly divisive force among the French Surrealists. Many who were willing to accept Surrealism's aesthetic and philosophical premises did not believe that this view of life could ever transform the material world of nations and societies. Breton saw this resistance against political involvement as an indication of insufficient commitment, while those who resisted engagement countered by emphasizing the restrictive nature of the Communist Party, its repressive disciplinary practices, and its hostility to artistic activity that did not directly further the interests of the party itself. Regardless of the problems it created for him, Breton never gave up this utopian faith, as the choice of subject for his last major poetic work, *Ode to Charles Fourier*, makes clear.

TRANSFORMATIVE POWER OF LOVE

The third key idea that informs Breton's poetry is one that, like his belief in the liberating power of the imagination, was shared by many of the Surrealists: the belief that romantic love was the means by which humans might establish an enduring link between the mundane world of material reality and the limitless, eternal world of surreality. At times, the mere presence of the beloved is enough to evoke such a response, and some of Breton's most moving poetry deals with this experience. The idea is expressed in two principal forms in Breton's love poetry. The first is the belief in woman as muse: The beloved becomes the source of contact with the realm of surreality, where, Breton's friend Paul Éluard (the greatest of the Surrealist love poets) wrote, "all transformations are possible." This belief is clearly expressed in two of Breton's best poems: the famous "catalog-poem" "Free Union," which celebrates the magical connection between the poet's beloved and the unspoiled world of nature, and "Fata Morgana," which celebrates the ecstatic elation of the poet at the advent of a new love. The second form taken by this belief in the magical power of love is the equation of poetic creation itself with sexual love, as in "Sur la route de San Romano" ("On the Road to San Romano"): "Poetry is made in a bed like love/ Its rumpled sheets are the dawn of things."

It was these three ideas—together with the support of countless writers, scattered across the world, who identified themselves with the Surrealist ideal—that sustained Breton throughout a career that lasted more than fifty years. Although Breton died in 1966, the beliefs that he helped to formulate and that he expressed so brilliantly in his own poetry continue to exist.

OTHER MAJOR WORKS

LONG FICTION: *Nadja*, 1928 (English translation, 1960).

NONFICTION: *Les Champs magnétiques*, 1921 (with Philippe Soupault; *The Magnetic Fields*, 1985); *Manifeste du surréalisme*, 1924 (*Manifesto of Surrealism*, 1969); *Les Pas perdus*, 1924; *Poisson soluble*, 1924; *Légitime Défense*, 1926; *Le Surréalisme et la peinture*, 1928, 1945, 1965; *L'Immaculée Conception*, 1930 (with Paul Éluard); *Second Manifeste du surréalisme*, 1930 (*Second Manifesto of Surrealism*, 1969); *Les Vases communicants*, 1932 (*Communicating Vessels*, 1990); *Point du jour*, 1934 (*Break of Day*, 1999); *Qu'est-ce que le surréalisme?*, 1934 (*What Is Surrealism?*, 1936); *L'Amour fou*, 1937 (*Mad Love*, 1987); *Prolégomènes à un troisième manifeste du surréalisme ou non*, 1942 (*Prolegomena to a Third Surrealist Manifesto or Not*, 1969); *Arcane 17*, 1944 (*Arcanum*, 1994); *Situation du surréalisme entre les deux guerres*, 1945; *Les Manifestes du surréalisme*, 1955 (*Manifestoes of Surrealism*, 1969); *Perspective cavalière*, 1970; *What Is Surrealism? Selected Writings*, 1978.

BIBLIOGRAPHY

Aspley, Keith. *Surrealism: The Road to the Absolute*. 3d ed. Chicago: University of Chicago Press, 1986. Updated with a new introduction. A critical history of Surrealist literature.

Balakian, Anna. *André Breton: Magus of Surrealism*. New York: Oxford University Press, 1971. A biography by an expert in Surrealist art and literature.

Benedikt, Michael. *The Poetry of Surrealism: An Anthology*. Boston: Little, Brown, 1975. With introduction, critical notes, and translations.

Breton, André. *Conversations: The Autobiography of Surrealism*. Translated and with an introduction by Mark Polizzotti. New York: Paragon House, 1993. Collection of interviews with Breton.

Carrouges, Michel. *André Breton and the Basic Concepts of Surrealism*. Tuscaloosa: University of Alabama Press, 1974. Biography and an introduction to Surrealism with bibliographic references.

Caws, Mary Ann. *André Breton*. Rev. ed. New York: Twayne, 1996. Caws provides practical analysis of individual works. The French is ably translated into readable English.

Petterson, James. *Poetry Proscribed: Twentieth-Century (Re)visions of the Trials of Poetry in France*. Lewisburg, Pa.: Bucknell University Press, 2008. Examines the relationship among poetry, politics, and culture in France, with a chapter on Breton.

Polizzotti, Mark. *Revolution of the Mind: The Life of André Breton*. New York: Farrar, Straus and Giroux, 1995. A thorough biography of the artist and poet highlighting his lifelong adherence to Surrealist principles even at the expense of personal relationships. With an extensive bibliography and index.

Steven E. Colburn

PAUL CELAN
Paul Antschel

Born: Czernowitz, Romania (now Chernivtsi, Ukraine); November 23, 1920
Died: Paris, France; April, 1970
Also known as: Paul Ancel

PRINCIPAL POETRY
Der Sand aus den Urnen, 1948
Mohn und Gedächtnis, 1952
Von Schwelle zu Schwelle, 1955
Gedichte: Eine Auswahl, 1959
Sprachgitter, 1959 (*Speech-Grille*, 1971)
Die Niemandsrose, 1963
Gedichte, 1966
Atemwende, 1967 (*Breathturn*, 1995)
Ausgewählte Gedichte: Zwei Reden, 1968
Fadensonnen, 1968 (*Threadsuns*, 2000)
Lichtzwang, 1970 (*Lightduress*, 2005)
Schneepart, 1971 (*Snow Part*, 2007)
Speech-Grille, and Selected Poems, 1971
Nineteen Poems, 1972
Selected Poems, 1972
Gedichte: In zwei Bänden, 1975 (2 volumes)
Zeitgehöft: Späte Gedichte aus dem Nachlass, 1976
Paul Celan: Poems, 1980 (revised as *Poems of Paul Celan*, 1988)
Gedichte, 1938-1944, 1985
Sixty-five Poems, 1985
Last Poems, 1986
Das Frühwerk, 1989
Gesammelte Werke in sieben Bänden, 2000 (7 volumes)
Glottal Stop: 101 Poems, 2000

OTHER LITERARY FORMS

The literary reputation of Paul Celan (TSEHL-on) rests exclusively on his poetry. His only piece of prose fiction, if indeed it can be so described, is "Gespräch im Gebirg" (1959), a very short autobiographical story with a religious theme. Celan also wrote an introductory essay for a book containing works by the painter Edgar Jené; this essay, entitled *Edgar Jené und der Traum vom Traume*, (1948; *Edgar Jené and the Dream About the Dream*, 1986), is an important early statement of Celan's aesthetic theory. Another, more oblique, statement of Celan's poetic theory is contained in his famous speech, "Der Meridian" (1960), given on his acceptance of the prestigious Georg Büchner Prize. (An English translation of this speech, "The Meridian," was published in the Winter, 1978, issue of *Chicago Review*.)

Achievements

Paul Celan is considered an "inaccessible" poet by many critics and readers. This judgment, prompted by the difficulties Celan's poetry poses for would-be interpreters seeking traditional exegesis, is reinforced by the fact that Celan occupies an isolated position in modern German poetry. Sometimes aligned with Nelly Sachs, Ernst Meister, and the German Surrealists, Celan's work nevertheless stands apart from that of his contemporaries. A Jew whose outlook was shaped by his early experiences in Nazi-occupied Romania, Celan grew up virtually trilingual. The horror of his realization that he was, in spite of his childhood experiences and his later residence in France, a German poet was surely responsible in part for his almost obsessive concern with the possibilities and the limits of his poetic language. Celan's literary ancestors are Friedrich Hölderlin, Arthur Rimbaud, Stéphane Mallarmé, Rainer Maria Rilke, and the German expressionists, but even in his early poems his position as an outsider is manifest. Celan's poems, called Hermetic by some critics because of their resistance to traditional interpretation, can be viewed sometimes as intense and cryptic accounts of personal experience, sometimes as religious-philosophical discussions of Judaism, its tradition and its relation to Christianity. Many of his poems concern themselves with linguistic and poetic theory to the point where they cease to be poems in the traditional sense, losing all contact with the world of physical phenomena and turning into pure language, existing only for themselves. Such "pure" poems, increasingly frequent in Celan's later works, are largely responsible for the charge of inaccessibility that has been laid against him. Here the reader is faced with having to leave the dimension of conventional language use, where the poet uses language to communicate with his audience about subjects such as death or nature, and is forced to enter the dimension of metalanguage, as Harald Weinrich calls it, where language is used to discuss only language—that is, the *word* "death," and not death itself. Such poems are accessible only to readers who share with the poet the basic premises of an essentially linguistic poetic theory.

In spite of all this, much of Celan's poetry can be made accessible to the reader through focus on the personal elements in some poems, the Judaic themes in others, and by pointing out the biblical and literary references in yet another group.

Biography

Paul Celan was born Paul Ancel, or Antschel, the only child of Jewish parents, in Czernowitz, Romania (now Chernivtsi, Ukraine), in Bukovina, situated in the foothills of the Carpathian Mountains. This region had been under Austrian rule and thus contained a sizable German-speaking minority along with a mix of other nationalities and ethnic groups. In 1918, just two years before Celan's birth, following the collapse of the Austro-Hungarian Empire, Bukovina became part of Romania. Thus, Celan was reared in a region of great cultural and linguistic diversity, the tensions of which energized his poetry.

Little is known of Celan's early childhood, but he appears to have had a very close relationship with his mother and a less satisfying relationship with his father. Positive references to his mother abound in his poems, whereas his father is hardly mentioned. After receiving his high school diploma, the young Celan went to study medicine in France in 1938, but the war forced his return in the following year to Czernowitz, where he turned to the study of Romance languages and literature at the local university. In 1940, his hometown was annexed by the Soviet Union but was soon occupied by the Germans and their allies, who began to persecute and deport the Jewish population. Celan's parents were taken to a concentration camp, where they both died, while the young man remained hidden for some time and finally ended up in a forced-labor camp. These events left a permanent scar on Celan's memory, and it appears that he had strong feelings of guilt for having survived when his parents and so many of his friends and relatives were murdered. After Soviet troops reoccupied his hometown, he returned there for a short time and then moved to Bucharest, where he found work as an editor and a translator. In 1947, his first poems were published in a Romanian journal under the anagrammatic pen name Paul Celan. In the same year, he moved to Vienna, where he remained until 1948, when his first collection of poetry, *Der Sand aus den Urnen*, was published.

After moving to Paris in the same year, Celan began to frequent avant-garde circles and was received particularly well by the poet Yvan Goll and his wife. Unfortunately, this friendship soured after Goll's death in 1950, when Goll's wife, Claire, apparently jealous of Celan's growing reputation as a poet, accused him of having plagiarized from her husband. A bitter feud resulted, with many of the leading poets and critics in France and Germany taking sides. During this period, Celan also began his work as a literary translator, which was to be a major source of both income and poetic inspiration for the rest of his life. He translated from the French—notably the writings of Rimbaud, Paul Valéry, and Guillaume Apollinaire—as well as the poetry of William Shakespeare, Emily Dickinson, and Marianne Moore from the English and the works of Aleksandr Blok, Sergei Esenin, and Osip Mandelstam from the Russian.

In the following years, Celan married a French graphic artist, Gisèle Lestrange, and published his second volume of poetry, *Mohn und Gedächtnis* (poppy and memory), containing many poems from his first collection, *Der Sand aus den Urnen*, which he had withdrawn from circulation because of the large number of printing mistakes and editorial inaccuracies it contained. *Mohn und Gedächtnis* established his reputation as a poet, and most of his subsequent collections were awarded prestigious literary prizes.

Celan remained in Paris for the rest of his life, infrequently traveling to Germany. During his later years, he appears to have undergone many crises both in his personal and in his creative life (his feud with Claire Goll is only one such incident), and his friends agree that he became quarrelsome and felt persecuted by neo-Nazis, hostile publishers, and critics. His death in April of 1970, apparently by suicide—he drowned in the Seine—was the consequence of his having arrived, in his own judgment, at a personal and artistic dead end, although many critics have seen in his collections *Lightduress*, *Snow Part*, and *Zeitgehöft*, published post humously, the potential beginning of a new creative period.

Analysis

Paul Celan's poetry can be viewed as an expressive attempt to cope with the past—his personal past as well as that of the Jewish people. Close friends of the poet state that Celan was unable to forget anything and that trivial incidents and cataclysmic events of the past for him had the same order of importance. Many of his poems contain references to the death camps, to his dead parents (particularly his mother), and to his changing attitude toward the Jewish religion and toward God. In his early collections, these themes are shaped into traditional poetic form—long, often rhymed lines, genitive metaphors, sensuous images—and the individual poems are accessible to conventional methods of interpretation. In his later collections, Celan employs increasingly sparse poetic means, such as one-word lines, neologisms, and images that resist traditional interpretive sense; their significance can often be intuited only by considering Celan's complete poetic opus, a fact that has persuaded many critics and readers that Celan's poems are nonsense, pure games with language rather than codified expressions of thoughts and feelings that can be deciphered by applying the appropriate key.

Mohn und Gedächtnis

Mohn und Gedächtnis, Celan's first collection of poetry (discounting the withdrawn *Der Sand aus den Urnen*), was in many ways an attempt to break with the past. The title of the collection is an indication of the dominant theme of these poems, which stress the dichotomy of forgetting—one of the symbolic connotations of the poppy flower—and remembering, by which Celan expresses his wish to forget the past, both his own personal past and that of the Jewish race, and his painful inability to erase these experiences from his memory. Living in Paris, Celan believed that only by forgetting could he begin a new life—in a new country, with a non-Jewish French wife, and by a rejection of his past poetic efforts, as indicated by the withdrawal of his first collection.

Mohn und Gedächtnis is divided into four parts and contains a total of fifty-six poems. In the first part, "Der Sand aus den Urnen" ("Sand from the Urns"), Celan establishes the central theme of the collection: The poet "fills the urns of the past in the moldy-green house of oblivion" and is reminded by the white foliage of an aspen tree that his mother's hair was not allowed to turn white. Mixed with these reflections on personal losses are memories of sorrows and defeats inflicted on the Jewish people; references to the conquest of Judea by the Romans are meant to remind the reader of more recent atrocities committed by foreign conquerors.

The second part of *Mohn und Gedächtnis* is a single poem, "Todesfuge" ("Death Fugue"), Celan's most widely anthologized poem, responsible in no small part for establishing his reputation as one of the leading contemporary German poets. "Death Fugue" is a monologue by the victims of a concentration camp, evoking in vivid images the various atrocities associated with these camps. From the opening line, "Black milk of daybreak we drink it at sundown . . ."—one of the lines that Claire Goll suggested Celan had plagiarized from her husband—the poem passes on to descriptions of the cruel camp commander who plays with serpent-like whips, makes the inmates shovel their own graves, and sets his pack of dogs on them. From the resignation of the first lines, the poem builds to an emotional climax in the last stanza in which the horror of the cremation chambers is indicated by images such as "he grants us a grave in the air" and "death is a master from Germany." Although most critics have praised the poem, some have condemned Celan for what they interpret as an attempt at reconciliation between Germans and Jews in the last two lines of the poem. Others, however, notably Theodor Adorno, have attacked "Death Fugue" on the basis that it is "barbaric" to write beautiful poetry after, and particularly about, Auschwitz. A close reading of this long poem refutes the notion that Celan was inclined toward reconciliation with the Germans—his later work bears this out—and it is hard to imagine that any reader should feel anything but horror and pity for the anonymous speakers of the poem. The beautifully phrased images serve to increase the intensity of this horror rather than attempting to gloss it over. "Death Fugue" is both a great poem and one of the most impressive and lasting documents of the plight of the Jews.

"Auf Reisen" ("Travel"), the first poem of the third part of the collection, again indicates Celan's wish to leave the past behind and to start all over again in his "house in Paris." In other poems he makes reference to his wife, asking to be forgiven for having broken with his heritage and married a Gentile. As the title of the collection suggests, the poppy of oblivion is not strong enough to erase the memory of his dead mother, of his personal past, and of his racial heritage. In poems such as "Der Reisekamerad" ("The Traveling Companion") and "Zähle die Mandeln" ("Count the Almonds"), the optimistic view of "Travel" is retracted; in the former, the dead mother is evoked as the poet's constant travel companion, while in the latter, he acknowledges that he must always be counted among the "almonds." The almonds (*Mandeln*) represent the Jewish people and are an indirect reference also to the Russian Jewish poet Osip Mandelstam, whose work Celan had translated. The irreconcilable tension between the wish to forget and the inability to do so completely is further shown in "Corona," a poem referring to Rainer

Maria Rilke's "Herbsttag" ("Autumn Day"). Whereas the speaker of Rilke's poem resigns himself to the approaching hardships of winter, Celan converts Rilke's "Lord: it is time" into the rebellious "it is time that the stone condescended to bloom."

The poems in *Mohn und Gedächtnis* are not, for the most part, innovative in form or imagery, although the long dactylic lines and the flowery images of the first half begin to give way to greater economy of scope and metaphor in the later poems. There is a constant dialogue with a fictional "you" and repeated references to "night," "dream," "sleep," "wine," and "time," in keeping with the central theme of these poems. Celan's next collections show his continued attempts to break with the past, to move his life and his poetry to new levels.

Von Schwelle zu Schwelle

In *Von Schwelle zu Schwelle* (threshold to threshold), Celan abandoned his frequent references to the past; it is as if the poet—as the title, taken from a poem in *Mohn und Gedächtnis*, suggests—intended to cross over a threshold into a new realm. Images referring to his mother, to the persecution of the Jews, to his personal attitude toward God, and to his Jewish heritage are less frequent in this volume. Many German critics, reluctant to concentrate on Celan's treatment of the Holocaust, have remarked with some relief his turning away from this subject toward the problem of creativity, the possibilities of communication, and the limits of language. Indeed, if one follows most German critics, *Von Schwelle zu Schwelle* was the first step in the poet's development toward "metapoetry"—that is, poetry that no longer deals with traditional *materia poetica* but only with poetry itself. This new direction is demonstrated by the preponderance of terms such as "word" and "stone" (a symbol of speechlessness), replacing "dream," "autumn," and "time." For Celan, *Von Schwelle zu Schwelle* constituted a more radical attempt to start anew by no longer writing about—therefore no longer having to think about—experiences and memories that he had been unable to come to grips with in his earlier poems.

Speech-Grille

Speech-Grille is, as the title suggests, predominantly concerned with language. The thirty-three poems in this volume are among Celan's finest, as the enthusiastic critical reception confirmed. They are characterized by a remarkable discipline of expression, leading in many cases to a reduction of poetry to the bare essentials. Indeed, it is possible to see these poems as leading in the direction of complete silence. "Engführung" ("Stretto"), perhaps the finest poem in the collection and one of Celan's best, exemplifies this tendency even by its title, which is taken from musical theory and refers to the final section of a fugue. A long poem that alludes to "Death Fugue," it is stripped of the descriptive metaphors that characterized that masterpiece, such as the "grave in the air" and "the black milk of daybreak"; instead, experience is reduced to lines such as "Came,

came./ Came a word, came/ came through the night,/ wanted to shine, wanted to shine/ Ash./ Ash, ash./ Night."

DIE NIEMANDSROSE

Celan's attempt to leave the past behind in *Speech-Grille* was not completely successful; on the contrary, several poems in this collection express sorrow at the poet's detachment from his Jewish past and from his religion. It is therefore not surprising that Celan's next collection, *Die Niemandsrose* (the no-one's rose), was dedicated to Mandelstam, a victim of Joseph Stalin's persecutions in the 1930's. One of the first poems in this collection makes mention of the victims of the concentration camps: "There was earth inside them, and/they dug." Rather than concentrating on the horrors of camp existence, the poem discusses the possibility of believing in an omnipotent, benevolent God in the face of these atrocities; this theme is picked up again in "Zürich, zum Storchen" ("Zurich, the Stork Inn"), in which Celan reports on his meeting with the Jewish poet Nelly Sachs: "the talk was of your God, I spoke/ against him." Other poems contain references to his earlier work; the "house in Paris" is mentioned again, and autumn imagery, suggesting the memory of his mother, is used more frequently. Several other poems express Celan's renewed and final acceptance of his Jewish heritage but indicate his rejection of God, culminating in the blasphemous "Psalm," with its bitter tribute: "Praised be your name, no one."

LATER YEARS

Celan's poetry after *Die Niemandsrose* became almost inaccessible to the average reader. As the title *Breathturn* indicates, Celan wanted to go in entirely new directions. Most of the poems in Celan's last collections are very short; references to language and writing become more frequent, and striking, often grotesque, portmanteau words and other neologisms mix with images from his earlier poems. There are still references to Judaism, to an absent or cruel God, and—in a cryptic form—to personal experiences. In the posthumously published *Snow Part*, the reader can even detect allusions to the turbulent political events of 1968. The dominant feature of these last poems, however, is the almost obsessive attempt to make the language of poetry perform new, hitherto unimagined feats, to coerce words to yield truth that traditional poetic diction could not previously force through its "speech-grille." It appears that Celan finally despaired of ever being able to reach this new poetic dimension. The tone of his last poems was increasingly pessimistic, and his hopes, expressed in earlier poems, of finding "that ounce of truth deep inside delusion," gave way to silence in the face of the "obstructive tomorrow." It is the evidence of these last poems, more than any police reports, which make it a certainty that his drowning in the Seine in 1970 was not simply the result of an accident.

Celan's poetry can be understood only by grasping his existential dilemma after

World War II as a Jewish poet who had to create his poetry in the German language. Desperate to leave behind everything which would remind him of his own and his people's plight, he nevertheless discovered that the very use of the German language inevitably led him back to his past and made a new beginning impossible. Finally, the only escape he saw still open to him was to attempt to abandon completely the conventions of German lyric poetry and its language, to try to make his poetry express his innermost feelings and convictions without having to resort to traditional poetic diction and form. Weinrich suggests that Celan, like Mallarmé before him, was searching for the "absolute poem," a poem that the poet creates only as a rough sketch and that the reader then completes, using private experiences and ideas, possibly remembered pieces of other poems. If this is true, Celan must have ultimately considered his efforts a failure, both in terms of his poetic intentions and in his desire to come to terms with his personal and his Jewish past.

Other major works

SHORT FICTION: "Gespräch im Gebirg," 1959.

NONFICTION: *Edgar Jené und der Traum vom Traume*, 1948 (*Edgar Jené and the Dream About the Dream*, 1986); *Collected Prose*, 1986.

TRANSLATIONS: *Der goldene Vorhang*, 1949 (of Jean Cocteau); *Bateau ivre/Das trunkene Schiff*, 1958 (of Arthur Rimbaud); *Gedichte*, 1959 (of Osip Mandelstam); *Die junge Parzel/La jeune Parque*, 1964 (of Paul Valéry); *Einundzwanzig Sonette*, 1967 (of William Shakespeare).

MISCELLANEOUS: *Prose Writings and Selected Poems*, 1977; *Selected Poems and Prose of Paul Celan*, 2001.

Bibliography

Baer, Ulrich. *Remnants of Song: Trauma and the Experience of Modernity in Charles Baudelaire and Paul Celan*. Stanford, Calif.: Stanford University Press, 2000. Baer sees a basis for comparison of the nineteenth and the twentieth century poets. Bibliographical references, index.

Bernstein, Michael André. *Five Portraits: Modernity and the Imagination in Twentieth-Century German Writing*. Evanston, Ill.: Northwestern University Press, 2000. Compared with Celan are four other German poets and philosophers: Rainer Maria Rilke, Robert Musil, Martin Heidegger, and Walter Benjamin. Includes bibliographical references, index.

Chalfen, Israel. *Paul Celan*. New York: Persea Books, 1991. A biography of Celan's youth and early career. Includes bibliographical references.

Colin, Amy D. *Paul Celan: Holograms of Darkness*. Bloomington: Indiana University Press, 1991. An overview of Celan's cultural background as well as postmodernist textual analysis.

Del Caro, Adrian. *The Early Poetry of Paul Celan: In the Beginning Was the Word*. Baton Rouge: Louisiana State University Press, 1997. A detailed treatment of the early volumes *Mohn und Gedächtnis* (1952) and *Von Schwelle zu Schwelle* (1955).

Felstiner, John. *Paul Celan: Poet, Survivor, Jew*. 1995. Reprint. New Haven, Conn.: Yale University Press, 2001. Illuminates the rich biographical meaning behind much of Celan's spare, enigmatic verse. Includes bibliographical references, illustrations, map, index.

Hillard, Derek. *Poetry as Individuality: The Discourse of Observation in Paul Celan*. Lewisburg, Pa.: Bucknell University Press, 2009. An examination of individuality in the writings of Celan. Touches on philosophy and the psychology of knowledge.

Rosenthal, Bianca. *Pathways to Paul Celan*. New York: Peter Lang, 1995. An overview of the varied and often contradictory critical responses to the poet. Illustrated; includes bibliographical references, index.

Tobias, Rochelle. *The Discourse of Nature in the Poetry of Paul Celan: The Unnatural World*. Baltimore: The Johns Hopkins University Press, 2006. Provides critical analysis of Celan's poetry in terms of its relationship to the natural world.

Wolosky, Shira. *Language and Mysticism: The Negative Way of Language in Eliot, Beckett, and Celan*. Stanford, Calif.: Stanford University Press, 1995. A useful comparative study that helps to place Celan in context. Bibliographical references, index.

Franz G. Blaha

PAUL ÉLUARD
Eugène Grindel

Born: Saint-Denis, France; December 14, 1895
Died: Charenton-le-Pont, France; November 18, 1952

PRINCIPAL POETRY
Le Devoir et l'inquiétude, 1917
Poèmes pour la paix, 1918
Les Animaux et leurs hommes, les hommes et leurs animaux, 1920
Les Nécessités de la vie et les conséquences des rêves, 1921
Mourir de ne pas mourir, 1924
Capitale de la douleur, 1926 (*Capital of Pain*, 1973)
L'Amour la poésie, 1929
À toute épreuve, 1930
La Vie immédiate, 1932
La Rose publique, 1934
Faciles, 1935
Thorns of Thunder: Selected Poems, 1936
Les Yeux fertiles, 1936
Les Mains libres, 1937
Donner à voir, 1939
Médieuses, 1939
Le Livre ouvert I, 1938-1940, 1940
Choix de poèmes, 1914-1941, 1941
Le Livre ouvert II, 1939-1941, 1942
Poésie et vérité, 1942 (*Poetry and Truth, 1942*, 1944)
Au rendez-vous allemand, 1944
En avril 1944: Paris respirait encore!, 1945
Le Dur Désir de durer, 1946 (*The Dour Desire to Endure*, 1950)
Poésie ininterrompue, 1946
Corps mémorable, 1947
Dignes de vivre, 1947
Le Livre ouvert, 1938-1944, 1947
Marc Chagall, 1947
Poèmes politiques, 1948
Premiers Poèmes (1913-1921), 1948
Une Leçon de morale, 1949 (*A Moral Lesson*, 2007)
Le Phénix, 1951

Poèmes, 1951
Tout dire, 1951
Poèmes pour tous, 1952
Les Derniers Poèmes d'amour de Paul Éluard, 1962 (*Last Love Poems of Paul Éluard*, 1980)

Other Literary Forms

Paul Éluard (ay-LW AHR) wrote many critical essays explaining the theories of the Surrealist movement, in which he played so large a part, and delineating his personal aesthetic theories as well. These critical works include the various Surrealist manifestos (many coauthored with André Breton), *Avenir de la poésie* (1937), *Poésie involuntaire et poésie intentionelle* (1942), *À Pablo Picasso* (1944), *Picasso à Antibes* (1948), *Jacques Villon ou l'art glorieux* (1948), *La Poésie du passé* (1951), *Anthologie des écrits sur l'art* (1952), and *Les Sentiers et routes de la poésie* (1952). Because the Surrealists were little interested in the limitations of genre, much of Éluard's poetic work falls into the category of the prose poem. His complete works are published in *Œuvres complètes* (1968). Some of his letters are published in *Lettres à Joe Bousquet* (1973).

Achievements

Paul Éluard was, with Breton and Louis Aragon, a cofounder of Surrealism, one of the principal artistic movements of the twentieth century. Earlier, he had also been instrumental in the Dada movement. As one of the primary theoreticians of Surrealism, Éluard helped to outline its aesthetic concepts in a number of manifestos and illustrated its techniques in his huge output of poetry. He published more than seventy volumes of poetry in his lifetime, many of which reveal his ability to set aside Surrealist theories in favor of poetic effect. As a result, many critics have called him the most original of the Surrealist poets and the truest poet of the group. His love poetry in particular is singled out for praise. Éluard's *Capital of Pain*, *La Rose publique*, and *Les Yeux fertiles* are widely regarded as among the finest products of Surrealism in French poetry.

Biography

Paul Éluard was born Eugène Grindel on December 14, 1895, in Saint-Denis, a suburb of Paris. His background was strictly working-class—his father was a bookkeeper and his mother (from whom he took the name Éluard) a seamstress—and most of his early years were spent in the vicinity of factories in Saint-Denis and Aulnay-sous-Bois. Éluard was a good student at the École Communale, but later, when the Grindels moved to Paris and the boy was enrolled at the École Supérieure Colbert, his scholastic performance declined. His education was cut short by illness, and he was placed in a sanatorium in Davos, Switzerland, when he was sixteen. He returned to Paris two years later and almost immediately entered the army; his experiences in the trenches of World War

I crystallized his growing awareness of the suffering of humanity. Suffering from gangrene of the bronchi as a result of poison gas, Éluard spent more time in a sanatorium, reading much poetry, especially the works of Arthur Rimbaud, Lautréamont, and Charles Vildrac. He also read Percy Bysshe Shelley, Novalis, and Heraclitus of Ephesus, and he developed a special feeling for Walt Whitman, whose *Leaves of Grass* (1855) he read many times.

In 1917, Éluard published his first book of poetry, *Le Devoir et l'inquiétude*. The following year, his *Poèmes pour la paix* was published, and he met Jean Paulhan, "impresario of poets," who advanced his career. He also met Breton, Aragon, Tristan Tzara, Philippe Soupault, and Giorgio de Chirico—the writers and artists who would eventually become, with Éluard, the leading figures of the Surrealist movement. Surrealism, however, was preceded by Dada; Éluard, Breton, Aragon, Francis Picabia, Soupault, Marguerite Buffet, and others, according to Tzara, all took part in the public "debut" of Dada in January, 1920, at a matinee organized by *Littérature*, a Dadaist review. The spectacle caused an enormous uproar, and a week later, Éluard joined Breton, Soupault, and others in a public debate at the Université Populaire. Éluard began to publish a review called *Proverbe*, to which all the Dadaists contributed. Wrote Tzara, "It was chiefly a matter of contradicting logic and language."

As Dada moved toward the more rigorous Surrealism, Éluard's name appeared on various manifestos. His poetry changed as a result of his allegiance to Dada and Surrealism; under the influence of the Surrealists' enthusiasm for "automatic writing," his language became freer. He also developed friendships with some of the most influential artists of the time, including Pablo Picasso, Max Ernst, Salvador Dalí, and Joan Miró.

In 1917, Éluard married Gala (Elena Dimitievna Diakanova), whom he had met in Switzerland in 1912; they had a daughter, Cécile, in 1918. Gala turned her affections first toward the artist Max Ernst and later toward Salvador Dalì. Brokenhearted, Éluard disappeared without explanation in March, 1924. Rumors circulated that he had died. In fact, he had sailed on the first available ship out of Marseilles, beginning a mysterious seven-month voyage around the world. He was seen in Rome, Vienna, Prague, London, and Spain, and he visited such distant locales as Australia, New Zealand, the Antilles, Panama, Malaysia, Java, Sumatra, Ceylon, Indochina, and India.

On his return, Éluard once again enthusiastically threw himself into the Surrealist movement, becoming editor and director of the movement's reviews, *La Révolution surréaliste* and *La Surréalisme au service de la révolution*. Following Surrealist theories, he experimented in his poetry with verbal techniques, the free expression of the mind, and the relation between dream and reality. These inquiries led to *L'Immaculée Conception* (1930; *The Immaculate Conception*, 1990), which he wrote with Breton. That same year, he made a final break with Gala, having met Maria Benz (affectionately called Nusch), who was the subject of numerous works by Picasso. The publication of *Capital of Pain* had established Éluard as an important poet, and with *La Rose publique* and *Les Yeux fertiles*, he became the leading poet of Surrealism.

Éluard's world trip and his memories of proletarian life and of the war had made him sensitive to the political trends of the 1930's. These feelings came to the fore at the outbreak of the Spanish Civil War (1936-1939). The fascist armies in Spain seemed to Éluard the forerunners of a total destruction of the modern concept of freedom. In response, his poetry became more politically oriented. He wrote in *L'Évidence poétique* (1936) that "the time has come when poets have a right and a duty to maintain that they are profoundly involved in the lives of other men, in communal life." He became exasperated with the detachment of his Surrealist colleagues and separated from the group.

In 1939, Éluard once again found himself in the French army, and after the disastrous defeat, he courageously worked for the Resistance in Paris and Lozère, helping to found the weekly newspaper *Lettres Françaises*. He was constantly in danger of arrest, and he and Nusch, whom he had married in 1934, were forced to move every month to avoid the Gestapo. He joined the outlawed Communist Party in 1942 (he had been affiliated with it for nearly fifteen years). He used the pseudonyms Jean du Hault and Maurice Hervent, and the *maquis* circulated his poems underground. One poem, "Liberté," published in 1942 in the Nazi-denounced collection *Poetry and Truth, 1942*, which has been called one of the "consecrated texts of the Resistance." For a brief period, he was forced to hide in an asylum at Saint-Alban. He was deeply affected by the suffering of the inmates and the experience could be seen in his subsequent writings.

After the war, Éluard's life was shattered by the sudden death of Nusch. He sought a solution to his sorrow in his poetry and in extending his love to embrace all humankind. During this period, he was very active in the Communist Party, traveling to Italy, Yugoslavia, Greece, Poland, Switzerland, and the Soviet Union, which awarded him the International Peace Prize. In Mexico, attending the Congress of the World Council on Peace, he met Dominique Lemor, and his love for her did much to restore his moral vision. He married her in 1951, but a heart attack in September, 1952, weakened him, and he died of a stroke that November in his apartment overlooking the Bois de Vincennes, outside Paris.

Analysis

Paul Éluard is regarded by many critics as Surrealism's greatest poet. Dubbed the Nurse of the Stars by Soupault, he was central to the movement from the beginning. Breton once answered the question What is Surrealism? by saying, "It is a splinter of the sparkling glass of Paul Éluard." It is therefore ironic that when Éluard's work is praised, its "non-Surrealistic" elements are generally singled out as having made his work better than that of the poets around him. Critics point out his permanent and universal themes, present even before the birth of Surrealism. He continually explores the themes of love, human suffering, and the struggle of the masses against hunger, slavery, and deprivation. His avoidance of shock and violence, employed programmatically by many of the

Surrealists, is also pointed out as evidence of his internal distance from the movement in which he played such a central role. Finally, unlike many of his fellow Surrealists, who regarded the world of dreams as a higher reality, sufficient unto itself, Éluard used dreams to interpret his experience: In his poetry, the dreamworld helps make the "real" world more comprehensible.

Nevertheless, Éluard's poetry can be understood only in the context of Surrealism. His works strongly reflect the Surrealist rejection of nineteenth century values, which had led not to the paradise promised by progressives of that century but to the abject horror of World War I. It was necessary, therefore, to reject the worldview that brought about the enslavement of the human imagination. The enemy was not only order but also the belief in order. Religion and science are both inherently limiting, the Surrealists argued, and fail to take account of the most fundamental element of existence: disorder.

When Éluard found a mystical revelation in six consecutive lines beginning with the letter *p* in Tzara's *Grains et issues* (1935), he was expressing the Surrealist faith in a truth beyond the surface of things, a truth that could be explored only through absolute freedom. Naturally, this freedom must exist in the political sphere as well, that Éluard, like a number of Surrealists, embraced an idealistic vision of communism is not surprising, given the context of the times. Communism preached the destruction of religion and of the bourgeoisie, and it was an avowed enemy of the fascism taking hold all over Europe in the 1920's and 1930's.

Above all, however, the Surrealists turned inward. Love, a privileged theme in their works, is treated as a means of altering consciousness, analogous in its effects to hallucinogenic drugs. Love becomes, paradoxically, both a way of escaping the world and the profoundest way of knowing it. Éluard adamantly holds that all real knowledge comes from love, and his finest poems express a longing for transcendence through sexual love.

"Première du monde" and "A Woman in Love"

In Éluard's works, woman, as the object of love, is a mirror for which men reach; seeing themselves reflected there, they discover "surreality." Woman, in Éluard's poetry, is simultaneously a particular woman (Gala, Nusch, Dominique) and a universal woman, timeless, embodying womanhood and all women. She is a vision of light, and images of brightness, transcendence, and purity are associated with her. The poet, on the other hand, suffers in darkness, isolation, limitation, and impurity. He addresses her: "You who abolish forgetfulness, ignorance, and hope/ You who suppress absence and give me birth . . ./ You are pure, you are even purer than I." In "Première du monde" (from *Capital of Pain*), his woman is the first woman in the world. She is simultaneously held captive by the Earth and possessed by spirit. The light hides itself in her. She is a complex of wheels; she is grass in which one becomes lost; she resembles the stars; she takes upon herself a maze of fire. In another poem, he writes, "I love you for your wisdom that is not mine.../ For this immortal heart which I do not possess." In other poems, he relates the image of the mirror to the image of woman so that her eyes become mirrors and she plays a mirrorlike role. Woman is mirror is poetry is woman: Each reflects the other; each is the other. One sees this most strikingly in "L'Amoureuse" ("A Woman in Love," from *Mourir de ne pas mourir*), when the lover becomes one with the beloved: "She has the shape of my hands/ She has the color of my eyes/ She is swallowed in my shadow/ Like a stone against the sky."

SURREALIST INFLUENCES

Éluard's poetic vision of woman is representative of the constant shifting between opposites that characterizes his work. He moves between light and dark, despair and hope, mystery and knowledge. This subtle play between opposites is very much characteristic of Surrealism in general, but Éluard handles it with simple, direct language. Like many great writers dealing with enormously complex and difficult conceptions, Éluard simplifies his language, choosing ordinary words and rearranging them in extraordinary ways. One of his early short poems, "Enfermé, seul" (from *Les Nécessités de la vie et les conséquences des rêves*), illustrates his passionate simplicity: "Complete song/ The table to see, the chair to sit/ And the air to breathe./ To rest,/ Inevitable Idea,/ Complete song."

When Éluard is at his best, this plain language becomes exquisite, as in lines such as: "Dawn fallen like a shower"; "We were tired/ Of living in the ruins of sleep"; "The prism breathes with us"; "The fountain running and sweet and nude." Unlike traditional metaphors, which are based on logical resemblances between things, Éluard's metaphors come out of dreams, revealing the power of the mind to find meaning in "illogical" juxtapositions. The line "She is standing on my eyelids" from "A Woman in Love," for example, could be a literal transcription of a dream: Thus, the poet achieves expression of the previously inexpressible. Like Dalí's famous melting clocks, Éluard's images broaden the vision of the reader. This quality makes Éluard's poetry easy to grasp and yet extraordinarily difficult, immediately meaningful yet provoking endless reflection.

OTHER MAJOR WORKS

NONFICTION: *L'Immaculée Conception*, 1930 (with André Breton; *The Immaculate Conception*, 1990); *L'Évidence poétique*, 1936; *Avenir de la poésie*, 1937; *Poésie involuntaire et poésie intentionelle*, 1942; *À Pablo Picasso*, 1944; *Jacques Villon ou l'art glorieux*, 1948; *Picasso à Antibes*, 1948; *La Poésie du passé*, 1951; *Anthologie des écrits sur l'art*, 1952; *Les Sentiers et routes de la poésie*, 1952; *Lettres à Joe Bousquet*, 1973; *Letters to Gala*, 1989.

MISCELLANEOUS: *Œuvres complètes*, 1968.

Bibliography

Caws, Mary Ann. *The Poetry of Dada and Surrealism: Aragon, Breton, Tzara, Éluard, and Desnos*. Princeton, N.J.: Princeton University Press, 1970. The chapter on Éluard is a very good analysis of Éluard's views on love and death as they emerge from the poet's continuous fascination with the ineffable that transcends the world of appearances.

_____. *Surrealism*. New York: Phaidon, 2004. This art book format survey of Surrealism contains information on Éluard and other poets.

Gaitet, Pascale. "Éluard's Reactions, Poetic and Political to World War Two." *Literature and History* 2, no. 1 (1991): 24-43. Examines Éluard's shift from the destabilizing, antibourgeois doctrines espoused by the Surrealists toward a more conventional use of symbolism, reinforcing traditional values, and a unifying rhetoric during the Resistance era. Gaitet depicts Éluard's poetic output during this era as embracing a more utilitarian, propagandist function.

McNab, Robert. *Ghost Ships: A Surrealist Love Triangle*. New Haven, Conn.: Yale Press, 2004. Describes the love triangle among Max Ernst, Éluard, and Gala, as well as Éluard's disappearance and travels.

Meadwell, Kenneth W. "Paul Éluard." In *Modern French Poets*, edited by Jean-François Leroux. Vol. 258 in *Dictionary of Literary Biography*. Detroit: Gale, 2002. Provides an overview of the life and work of Éluard, with emphasis on collections and poems representing his literary evolution.

Montagu, Jemima. *The Surrealists: Revolutionaries in Art and Writing, 1919-1935*. London: Tate, 2002. This look at Surrealism in both literature and art contains a chapter on Éluard and Max Ernst.

Nugent, Robert. *Paul Éluard*. New York: Twayne, 1974. Approaches Éluard's poetry as the expression of the poet's solitude as well as humankind's solitude and includes a concise chronology and short bibliography of critical works.

Strauss, Jonathan. "Paul Éluard and the Origins of Visual Subjectivity." *Mosaic* 33, no. 2 (2000): 25-46. Offers close readings of passages taken from *Capital of Pain* to demonstrate Éluard's agile usage of the visual and his redefinition of subjectivity in terms of impossible images that can only be expressed through language. This tying of the sensuous to the abstract becomes the cornerstone of Éluard's attempt to create a new theory of subjectivity.

Watts, Philip. *Allegories of the Purge: How Literature Responded to the Postwar Trials of Writers and Intellectuals in France*. Stanford, Calif.: Stanford University Press, 1998. Chapter 4 examines Éluard's poetic output during the Occupation and the period of purge trials in France directly following the end of World War II to show that Éluard's shift from the linguistic and image play of his earlier writings to a strictly metered verse can be seen as a political act calling for the purge of collaborationist writers.

J. Madison Davis

VICTOR HUGO

Born: Besançon, France; February 26, 1802
Died: Paris, France; May 22, 1885

PRINCIPAL POETRY
 Odes et poésies diverses, 1822, 1823
 Nouvelles Odes, 1824
 Odes et ballades, 1826
 Les Orientales, 1829 (*Les Orientales: Or, Eastern Lyrics*, 1879)
 Les Feuilles d'automne, 1831
 Les Chants du crépuscule, 1835 (*Songs of Twilight*, 1836)
 Les Voix intérieures, 1837
 Les Rayons et les ombres, 1840
 Les Châtiments, 1853
 Les Contemplations, 1856
 La Légende des siècles, 1859-1883 (5 volumes; *The Legend of the Centuries*, 1894)
 Les Chansons des rues et des bois, 1865
 L'Année terrible, 1872
 L'Art d'être grand-père, 1877
 Le Pape, 1878
 La Pitié suprême, 1879
 L'Âne, 1880
 Les Quatre vents de l'esprit, 1881
 The Literary Life and Poetical Works of Victor Hugo, 1883
 La Fin de Satan, 1886
 Toute la lyre, 1888
 Dieu, 1891
 Les Années funestes, 1896
 Poems from Victor Hugo, 1901
 Dernière Gerbe, 1902
 Poems, 1902
 The Poems of Victor Hugo, 1906
 Océan, 1942

OTHER LITERARY FORMS

Besides his rather prolific output in the field of poetry, Victor Hugo (YEW-goh) achieved prominence in two other genres as well. His novels, for which he is best known in the United States, span most of his literary career and include such recognizable titles as *Le Dernier Jour d'un condamné* (1829; *The Last Day of a Condemned*, 1840), *Notre-Dame de Paris* (1831; *The Hunchback of Notre Dame*, 1833), and *Les Misérables* (1862; English translation, 1862). Hugo was a successful playwright in his time, but only *Hernani* (pr., pb. 1830; English translation, 1830) has received sustained attention. The preface to his play *Cromwell* (pb. 1827; English translation, 1896), however, is frequently studied by scholars because of its attack on the three unities, so long observed by French classical writers, and because of Hugo's elaboration on his theory of the union of the grotesque and the sublime. His other plays are a *mise en oeuvre* of the dramatic principles found in the *Cromwell* preface.

Although less well known as an essayist, Hugo did write in the genre. His better-known essay collections include *Le Rhin* (1842; *The Rhine*, 1843), *William Shakespeare* (1864; English translation, 1864), *Choses vues* (1887; *Things Seen*, 1887), and *En voyage: Alpes et Pyrénées* (1890; *The Alps and Pyrenees*, 1898). Hugo also wrote and delivered a number of political speeches in the Chambre des Pairs. Among these are the "Consolidation et défense du littoral," which was delivered in the summer of 1846, "La Famille Bonaparte," which was delivered the following spring, and "Le Pape Pie IX," which was presented in January, 1848.

Achievements

"Ego Hugo": This was the inscription emblazoned on the Gothic armchair that stood in the dining room in the Hugos' Guernsey home. Dubbed an ancestral chair by the poet, it remained conspicuously empty at mealtime. For Victor Hugo's critics, this motto became a symbol of an oversized ego. For his admirers, the empty chair symbolized the greatness of Hugo the poet, if not Hugo the man. Indeed, his place in literature is unquestioned, and no other French poet since has been able to match his production and influence.

Hugo excelled in a wide variety of verse forms: ode, lyric, epic, satire, and heroic narrative. His versatility in mode was matched by variations in tone, from the eloquence and rhetorical precision found in *Les Châtiments* (the chastisements), for example, to the simplicity and grace of *Les Contemplations*. Conventions that were in vogue at the time, such as the marvelous and the fantastic, the medieval and the Oriental, were translated by Hugo into verse. The poet also found inspiration in the imagery of dreams, spiritualism, and metempsychosis. His poetry set the tone and the style for Romantic verse; his choice of subjects and his novel uses of stylistic devices influenced the Parnassians and the Symbolists.

The sheer volume of Hugo's production would have assured him a place in literary history even if the strength and character of the man had not assured his celebrity. Hugo's resiliency allowed him to overcome personal tragedy and to express his grief in verse. He championed causes such as free, compulsory education, universal suffrage, the right to work, and the abolition of the death penalty, before such political postures were popular.

In all, Hugo was a man of deep convictions, of great sensibility, and of tremendous ego whose poetic creation reflected all these aspects of his complex personality.

Biography

Victor-Marie Hugo was born at Besançon, the third son of Joseph Léopold Sigisbert Hugo and Sophie Trébuchet. His father, a career military man, served with distinction in the postrevolutionary army. He later became a general and viscount, as well as a close associate of Joseph Bonaparte, Napoleon's brother. Though gifted with military tenacity, the elder Hugo unfortunately was not capable of such steadfastness on the home front. Madame Hugo soon tired of his lusty nature and infidelities, finding relief in the arms of General Victor Fanneau LaHorie, an opponent of Napoleon, who was Victor Hugo's godfather. Shortly after Hugo's birth, Madame Hugo moved her children to Paris to be near LaHorie. After LaHorie became an enemy of Napoleon's regime, she hid him in her quiet house with a large garden in the rue des Feuillantines. During those eighteen months, the gentle "M. le Courlandais" taught the eight-year-old Hugo to read and translate Tacitus, and he impressed the young boy with the ideal of liberty; indeed, Hugo was to have a lifelong sympathy for the oppressed. In later years, he would fondly remember those days spent playing in the garden with his brother and with a girl named Adèle Foucher. Madame Hugo somehow provided a tranquil environment for her children, unembittered by constant marital strife.

Though LaHorie had provided some formal training, the education of the Hugo brothers remained spotty because of the family's frequent moves. The family took two trips to visit the boys' father: to Italy in 1809 and to Spain in 1811-1812. During that last trip, the boys were enrolled at the Collège des Nobles in Madrid. The year in Spain was to provide Hugo with much material for his later works. The Spanish hero Ernani would become the hero of his play, with the Masserano palace as one of its settings; the hunchback Corcova at the seminary would become the inspiration for Quasimodo; the street Ortoleza reappears in the play *Ruy Blas* (pr., pb. 1838; English translation, 1890) .

In 1814, General Hugo insisted that his sons be enrolled at the Pension Cordier, where they spent four years studying the sciences. To relieve the drudgery, the brothers wrote poems and plays during their leisure hours. Soon, this pastime became a successful enterprise. At the age of fifteen, Hugo entered the French Academy's poetry contest, receiving an honorable mention . In 1819, he won two prizes from the Académie des Jeux Floraux of Toulouse. Hugo and his brother Eugène entered law school to please their father but spent most of their efforts in the founding of a magazine called *Le Conservateur littéraire*. Among the early contributors to the venture was Alfred de Vigny, who was to become one of Hugo's closest friends. In this magazine, Hugo published his "Ode sur la mort du duc de Berry" and the first version of what was to become his second novel, *Bug-Jargal* (1826; *The Noble Rival*, 1845). The ode placed Hugo in the favor of the Royalists, among them his idol François-René de Chateaubriand, in whose presence the poet was received shortly after the publication of his ode. Soon, the Hugo brothers were admitted into the Société des Bonnes Lettres, an ultra-Royalist group; by this time, Hugo had adopted his mother's Royalist views.

With the death of his mother in 1821, Hugo entered a period of extreme poverty. He abandoned *Le Conservateur littéraire* and strove to make a living. In 1822, Hugo published the *Odes et poésies diverses*. Conservative and Royalist in content, these odes earned for Hugo a royal pension. He was able to marry his childhood sweetheart, Adèle Foucher, and continue with his literary career.

The years between 1822 and 1828 were filled with creative and literary activities. In 1823, Hugo published the second edition of *Odes et poésies diverses* as well as his first novel, *Han d'Islande* (1823; *Hans of Iceland*, 1845). The following year, Hugo's *Nouvelles Odes* were published. In 1825, Hugo was named, along with Alphonse de Lamartine, to the Legion of Honor "for his noble efforts... to sustain the sacred cause of the altar and the throne." The year 1826 saw the publication of Hugo's *Odes et ballades*, as well as his second novel, *The Noble Rival*. The publication the following year of the bold preface to *Cromwell* established Hugo as the spokesperson for the new Romantic school. Hugo's father, Léopold, died in 1828, an event that greatly grieved the poet. Since the death of his mother, Hugo and his father had achieved a rapprochement. This friendship rendered the poet more sympathetic to the Bonapartist cause and served to counterbalance the Royalist fervor that he had received from his mother. In that same year, Hugo's play *Amy Robsart* (pr. 1828; English translation, 1895) was presented.

During these years, the Hugo home had become the focal point for the gathering of literary young men caught up in the Romantic revolution against the formalism of the seventeenth and eighteenth centuries, men such as Charles Augustin Sainte-Beuve, Alfred de Vigny, Alfred de Musset, Théophile Gautier, Gérard de Nerval, and Émile and Antoine Deschamps. This group, which became known as the *cénacle*, sought to break the bonds of the dramatic unities, of poetic versification, and of the choice of subject matter, and rallied to expand the imaginative and aesthetic field. Hugo was the unquestioned head of the group. From his ideas and from the discussions that took place in his home during those years sprang new branches of Romanticism, including the Parnassian school.

The next few years were emotionally difficult ones for Hugo. Though he continued to receive acclaim for his new collection of poems *Les Orientales*, striking because of their exoticism; for his play *Hernani*, which heralded a decisive victory for Romantic drama; and for *The Hunchback of Notre Dame*, which established Hugo as a great writer of the historical novel, the security of his home life had begun to crumble. In 1829, Hugo's best friend, Sainte-Beuve, had revealed to the poet his love for Hugo's wife, Adèle. In spite of this revelation, Hugo tried to maintain the friendship, made more difficult by Sainte-Beuve's assertion that his love was reciprocated. In his distress, Hugo found comfort in a relationship with an actress, Juliette Drouet. It was an affair that would last fifty years and that was eventually accepted by Adèle Hugo. Drouet was transformed through her love for the poet into a devoted companion who remained virtually cloistered in her quarters, content to read and to copy his books.

These personal afflictions and affections found expression in the poetic works that followed: *Les Feuilles d'automne* (the leaves of autumn), *Songs of Twilight, Les Voix intérieures* (the interior voices), and *Les Rayons et les ombres* (the rays and shadows). These collections contrasted markedly with Hugo's previous poetic works in both tone and style. Unlike the exotic and colorful *Les Orientales*, for example, these poems sought to express the more intimate relationships found in love, childhood, and friendship, as well as in humankind's association with nature. In 1843, two other disasters, the death of his daughter Léopoldine and the failure of his play *Les Burgraves* (pr., pb. 1843; *The Burgraves*, 1896) caused Hugo to put down his pen for some time. As always, tragedy accompanied success in the poet's life.

Meanwhile, Hugo's political involvement intensified. In 1841, he was elected to the French Academy. As his prominence grew, it followed that he should be raised to peerage, and this indeed occurred in 1845. From this position, Hugo addressed the parliament on such matters as capital punishment and the plight of the poor, subjects on which he had already written in *The Last Day of a Condemned* and *Claude Gueux* (1834), and which would be fully exploited in a work already in progress at this time, *Les Misérables*. Because of his concern for the ordinary man and the unfortunates, he was elected a "representative of the people" in 1848 and a year later became a Parisian delegate to the Assemblée Nationale. During the 1848 Revolution, Hugo published his opinions in his journal *L'Événement*, and though he was aligned with no particular political party, the periodical was suppressed. He grew increasingly suspicious of Louis Napoleon's ambitions, and though Hugo had originally supported him for the presidency, he delivered a scathing address before the Assemblée in July of 1851 in which he called the president "Napoleon the Little." As a consequence of this attack, Hugo fled France shortly after the coup d'état of December, 1851. This event marked another change in the poet's political stance: Having been a Royalist and then a Bonapartist, Hugo next became a Republican.

Hugo went first to Belgium, where he stayed only for a short time, then moved to the Channel Islands of Jersey and then Guernsey, where he finally settled with his family and with Juliette Drouet from 1855 to 1870. These were to be very productive years for Hugo. After a long silence, the poet's voice was again heard in 1853 with the publication of *Les Châtiments*, in which he vehemently denounced Louis Napoleon and his empire. In 1856, Hugo published *Les Contemplations*, in which he integrated lyrics, meditative poems on his daughter's death, and more visionary and mystical verses. In large measure, these poems would influence the Symbolists. With the publication of the first *The Legend of the Centuries* in 1859, an extensive epic that detailed humankind's progress from slavery to freedom, Hugo achieved the unquestioned reputation of "poet-seer."

It was as if Hugo's long silence had caused him to relish his renewed literary voice, for his productivity during the 1860's remained substantial. In 1862, his great novel *Les Misérables* appeared, succeeded by *Les Chansons des rues et des bois* (the songs of the streets and the woods) in 1865. These were followed in 1866 by another novel, *Les Travailleurs de la mer* (1866; *The Toilers of the Sea*, 1866). As always, his literary acclaim was accompanied by personal sorrow. Adèle Hugo died in 1868 in Brussels of apoplexy. Her wish had been to be buried beside her daughter Léopoldine. Hugo accompanied her body as far as the French frontier. The following year, Hugo's next novel, *L'Homme qui rit* (1869; *The Man Who Laughs*, 1869), was published. It received little acclaim at the time, and it has been only rarely studied since.

The fall of the Second Empire on September 3, 1870, ended Hugo's long exile from France. He returned during turbulent times: The war with Prussia and the civil war that ensued left Hugo disillusioned. During this time, his son Charles died, his daughter Adèle was confined to an asylum, and his son François became gravely ill. Once more, the poet returned to Guernsey, this time not so much to escape political forces as to seek solace. He recorded his feelings in *L'Année terrible* (terrible year).

Hugo returned to Paris in 1873 after finishing his novel *Quatre-vingt-treize* (1874; *Ninety-three*, 1874), which was published the following year. Then seventy-one years old, he found great consolation in his grandchildren, spending long hours with them and sharing childhood delights. For his age, his productivity was amazingly constant. In 1877, there appeared the second volume of *The Legend of the Centuries*, as well as *L'Art d'être grand-père* (the art of being a grandfather). These were followed by *Le Pape* (the pope), *La Pitié suprême* (the supreme pity), *Religions et religion* (1880), *L'Âne* (the ass) and a play, *Torquemada* (pb. 1882; English translation, 1896). On May 11, 1883, Juliette Drouet died of stomach cancer; her death was a terrible blow to Hugo. He published nothing else during his lifetime except the final volume of *The Legend of the Centuries* in 1883. His health steadily declined, and he died of pneumonia on May 22, 1885. He was buried in the Panthéon beside Voltaire and Jean-Jacques Rousseau.

In 1875, Hugo had written his literary will, which specified that after his death all his manuscripts without exception should be published. This testament was faithfully executed, allowing for the appearance of the following posthumous publications: *Théâtre en liberté* (pb. 1886), *La Fin de Satan* (the end of satan), *Toute la lyre* (all of the lyre), *Dieu* (God), *Les Années funestes* (the fatal years), and *Dernière Gerbe* (last sheaf). A portion of his letters, *Correspondence* (1896-1898), and his travel books, *The Alps and Pyrenees* and *Things Seen*, were also published.

Analysis

Victor Hugo's poetry took many forms, from the lyric to the epic to the elegiac. Along with this variety of form, the range of the poet's ideas expanded during his long career. From poems with political overtones, Hugo's poetry grew to exhibit the tenets of

Romanticism. He wrote of more personal and intimate subjects, such as family and love. He also wrote about humankind's relationship with nature and with the Creator. As Hugo matured, his themes became more philosophical and humanitarian, and his self-appointed role became that of a poet-seer attempting to understand the mysteries of life and creation.

ODES ET BALLADES

Hugo's shift toward Romanticism and away from political themes first became apparent in *Odes et ballades*. In this collection, the poet makes copious use of the fantastic, the uncanny, and the horrifying, a popular style of the time, exemplified by the German ballads of Gottfried Burger, Christoph Wieland, and Johann Wolfgang von Goethe. Hugo's inspiration was drawn also from contemporary translations of Spanish, English, and French ballads, a diversity of sources that infused his own ballads with eclecticism.

In the preface to *Odes et ballades*, Hugo compares the sculptured gardens of Versailles with the primitive forests of the New World. The artificiality of the former, Hugo claims, stands in opposition to the laws of nature, whereas in the untouched forests, "everything obeys an invariable law." The true poet, then, must look to nature as his model, forsaking the contrived in favor of the natural. This was the new precept that Hugo sought to follow in this work.

Hugo received praise from his contemporaries for his imaginative use of his subject matter and for his great technical versatility. He used not only the classical Alexandrine but also other forms of versification, such as the octosyllabic line in the poem "La Fiancée du timbalier" ("The Cymbaleer's Bride") and the little-used Renaissance seven-syllable line in "À Trilby." Though original and clever, these poems are devoid of the philosophical intent that characterizes the poet's later work. They were pronounced excellent, however, by a young critic for *Le Globe* by the name of Charles-Augustin Sainte-Beuve.

LES ORIENTALES

Les Orientales marks Hugo's departure from neoclassical rhetorical forms and inaugurates his bolder, more colorful style. Hugo's use of metaphor gains precision and originality; he employs verse forms drawn from the Renaissance Pléiade, to which he had been led by Sainte-Beuve.

The most famous poem of *Les Orientales* is "Les Djinns" ("The Djinns"), which exhibits Hugo's technical virtuosity. There is exoticism in the choice of both subject and form; in this, the poem is representative of the entire collection. The djinns are identified as evil spirits who sweep into a town and leave just as quickly. Their anticipated arrival is marked by a mounting from a two-syllable line to a decasyllabic line, while their departure is signaled by a parallel decrescendo. In this manner, Hugo is able to create an atmosphere of mystery and terror, with a contrasting feeling of relief. The poem won the plaudits not only of Hugo's contemporaries, but also of later poets and critics; Algernon Charles Swinburne was to comment that no other poet had "left a more exquisite piece or one more filled with delicate lyricism."

LES FEUILLES D'AUTOMNE

In *Les Feuilles d'automne*, Hugo's lyrical voice achieves maturity. The central themes are those of childhood, nature, and love. Although the style is less spectacular than that of *Les Orientales*, Hugo achieves a profound poetic effect through greater simplicity. His treatment of domestic themes is reminiscent of William Wordsworth, whose works Hugo may have known through the influence of Sainte-Beuve.

The opening poem is a tribute to the poet's mother's love and devotion. This is followed by a warm acknowledgment of his father, in which Hugo recalls the General's house at Blois and mourns his father's death. These panegyrics to his parents set the tone for the entire collection.

Less than a handful of poems deal with the topic of childhood, yet Hugo was the first to introduce this subject into French verse. The masterpiece of the collection is one such poem, "Lorsque l'enfant paraît" ("Infantile Influence"), touching in its description of the young child whose presence signifies a blessed household. Hugo concludes with a prayer imploring God to preserve family and friends from a home without a child. Such a sentimental ending would not have been found in *Les Orientales*, and it manifests a further development in the poet's style.

Another development, but on a different plane, establishes the poet's concern for the correspondences between people and nature, as in the poem "Ce qu'on entend sur la montagne" ("What Is Heard on the Mountain"). The role of the poet becomes significant in such an interchange; he becomes an interpreter in this dialogue, as Hugo announces in "Pan." These assertions were manifest again in later poetic works.

LES RAYONS ET LES OMBRES

In *Les Rayons et les ombres*, Hugo conceives of a social mission for the poet. The poet becomes a sacred dreamer, an impartial observer of his time, seeking inspiration from humankind, nature, and God. This collection is, therefore, rather diverse in its subject matter. There are love poems, poems devoted to nature, verses inspired by a search for religious significance, childhood memories, and poems with greater social content.

Two celebrated poems are to be found in *Les Rayons et les ombres*. The first is "Tristesse d' Olympio," in which the poet is presented as a keeper of the secrets of the universe. The tone of sadness that pervades the piece is in large measure a reflection of the unhappy events of 1837, the year it was written. Sainte-Beuve had published a story titled "Mme de Pontivy," in which he described a love affair similar to his alleged affair with Adèle Hugo. Hugo's daughter Léopoldine had been seriously ill that year. At the same time, the poet himself had been afflicted with an eye disorder. In that same year also, Hugo's brother Eugène died after spending many years in an asylum, his illness caused in large part by Hugo's marriage with Adèle, whom he had also loved. The inspiration for the poem is, therefore, overwhelmingly personal. The mood of the poem reflects Hugo's disillusionment with the mutability of nature. In striking contrast with poems of this same genre, such as Alphonse de Lamartine's "Le Lac" ("The Lake"), Hugo asserts that, though nature may forget, humankind will not.

The second important poem in this collection is "Oceano Nox." Though it is much shorter and less complicated than "Tristesse d'Olympio," it nevertheless successfully introduces the sea into Hugo's poetic corpus. The poet chose the elegiac form to describe the force of the ocean and the tragedy of men who are engulfed in the sea, remembered only for a short time by their loved ones. The final stanza is powerful in its description of the desperate voices contained in the roar of the sea at night.

"L'EXPIATION"

It was during his stay in Jersey in 1853 that Hugo published *Les Châtiments*, a volume of satiric poetry. The work is a ceaseless diatribe against the Second Empire and Louis Napoleon. Hugo's indignation against the emperor was inexhaustible. He believed Napoleon to be a tyrant, a ruler who had compromised the liberty of the French people. Hugo evokes every imaginable vituperative image in his denunciation of "Napoleon the Dwarf." Though these pages are replete with a succession of ingenious epithets and metaphors, one poem in this collection is particularly noteworthy, "L'Expiation."

The poem combines both epic and satiric styles; its structure is particularly ingenious. Opening with an account of the glorious reign of Napoleon I, it develops the concept of the crime that the poet must expiate: the coup d'état on the *Dix-huit Brumaire* of the revolutionary calendar. Hugo then details the emperor's retreat from Moscow, his army's struggle in the blinding snow, the loss of countless men to the elements. Napoleon wonders at this point whether this is his punishment. A voice replies: *No*.

The second part of the poem recounts the Battle of Waterloo. Hugo describes the conflict at its height. Napoleon witnesses the fall of the French army, and this time he knows that his defeat will be total. Once more the question is asked: Is this the punishment? Once more, the voice answers: *No*.

The third segment of the poem concerns Napoleon's exile on Saint Helena. Hugo ably contrasts the prisoner Napoleon with the formerly glorious emperor. The latter is now preoccupied with the memories of Moscow, with his wife's infidelity, and with the constant surveillance of his jailer, Sir Hudson Lowe. As the fallen emperor lies dying, he once more raises the question: Is this the punishment? This time, the voice replies: *Not yet*.

Thirty years later, Napoleon I is awakened in his tomb by a familiar voice. It is the voice of his nephew, who has debased the name of Napoleon. Now the punishment is clear: The name of Napoleon is to be remembered not in glory but in ignominy.

Though it is known that Hugo researched his subject carefully, the tension and the concentration of events that make this poem so remarkable are his own distinctive contributions. The ingenuity of the threefold intervention of the voice sustains the dramatic movement, while the portrait of Napoleon is a powerful study in contrast.

LES CONTEMPLATIONS

Published in two volumes, titled *Autrefois* (former times) and *Aujourd'hui* (today), *Les Contemplations* has been called by the critic Ferdinand Brunetière "the most lyrical collection in the French language." The dividing line between the two volumes was the death of Hugo's daughter Léopoldine, in 1843. Consequently, the poems in this collection are very personal, yet the poet generalizes his experiences to include the experiences of all people. Central to the work is the relationship of God and humankind, of humankind and external nature, and of life and death.

In this collection, there are two groups of poems that are particularly significant. The first is "Pauca meae," comprising seventeen poems composed between 1841 and 1855. They were inspired by Hugo's daughter, Léopoldine. The best-known poem in this series is "A Villequier," which expresses the poet's deep despair at the loss of his beloved daughter. It treats the poet's attempt to submit to the will of God and to resign himself to a life without his child. Though he is able to achieve the former, complete resignation is something that eludes him. Unable to restrain his emotion, he claims the right to weep. The grief of a father dominates the rest of the poem, which concludes on a note of extreme sadness.

The second important series in *Les Contemplations*, "Au bord de l'infini," comprises twenty-six poems containing a statement of Hugo's philosophical ideas. The poet aspires to penetrate the unknown, perhaps through prayer. His search for truth will be as a winged dreamer or as a startled wise man. The crowning piece of this series, "Ce que dit la bouche d'ombre" ("What the Mouth of the Shadow Says"), deals with such concepts as Pythagoreanism (in particular, the metempsychosis of souls), Platonism, and pantheism.

"What the Mouth of the Shadow Says" is set at the dolmen of Rozel. There the poet meets a specter with whom he discusses the unity of the universe and the essential vitality of all that is in it. Everything in creation has a soul and a consciousness, but how is this universe to be explained? If God is in everything and everything is in God, then how can one reconcile the imperfections of the world with the perfection that is God? It is here that Hugo introduces the notion of evil. If evil is caused by the absence of light, then the resulting darkness and heaviness can only be associated with matter. Because humans are conscious of the difference between darkness and light, then humans choose to do evil by their own free will. Moreover, humans choose their own punishment. An evildoer's soul will be metamorphosed into something degrading; the soul of Judas, for example, is to be found in the spit of men. Ultimately, however, there is hope for humankind, a hope that the dualism between light and darkness, between goodness and evil, will be reconciled. It is on this thought that the poem ends.

THE LEGEND OF THE CENTURIES

Considered by many to be the greatest epic poem since the Middle Ages, *The Legend of the Centuries* differs from other epics in its humanitarian concerns. Hugo states in the preface that he is interested in showing the human profile "from Eve, the mother of men, to the Revolution, the mother of peoples." This is to be accomplished with the notion of progress foremost in his mind. This is not a historical collection, but rather, as Charles Baudelaire put it, a collection of those things that are poetic, that is, legend, myth, and fable, those things that tap the deep reservoirs of humanity.

Among the many subjects presented are the following: "Le Sacre de la femme" ("The Crowning of Women"), which opens the volume and which treats the story of Eve, not from the perspective of Original Sin, but from the perception of idyllic beauty; "La Conscience" ("Conscience"), which is the story of Cain's attempt to flee from the Eye that follows him everywhere, even to his grave; "Booz endormi" ("Boaz Asleep"), which was inspired by the Book of Ruth and in which Hugo attributes to the patriarch Boaz a dream in which he sees a great oak leading from himself to David and finally to Christ; "Le Mariage de Roland," which is considered by critics to be the prototype of the little epic and which presents the four-day struggle between Roland and Olivier, ending with the proposal that Roland marry Olivier's sister; "La Rose de l'infante" ("The Infanta's Rose"), which deals with the destruction in 1588 of the Spanish Armada and describes a great gust of wind that scatters the fleet and simultaneously arrives in the royal garden of Aranjuez, stripping the petals of the rose held by the infanta and scattering them in the nearby fountain; "Le Satyr" ("The Satyr"), which is considered to be the most important philosophical poem of the collection and treats the double nature of humankind, beings at once allied with the gods because of their spirit, but who now have their feet in the mud; and two poems, "Pleine mer" ("Out at Sea") and "Plein ciel" ("Up in the Sky"), which together constitute "Vingtième siècle," contrasting the evils of old-world war symbolized by the steamship Leviathan with the vision of goodness symbolized by the airship.

LA FIN DE SATAN

Although *La Fin de Satan* was not published until after Hugo's death, it was conceived of during his stay in Guernsey. Hugo's treatment of the fallen angel differs greatly from the Miltonic version. Whereas the fall of Satan in Milton's work is precipitous, in Hugo's version Satan's fall takes thousands of years, while the feathers from his wings fall even more slowly. Furthermore, while Milton's Satan reigns over a host of other devils, Hugo's Satan is alone until he is able to engender a daughter, the veiled

Isis-Lilith. It is she who brings evil into the world. After the great Flood, she returns to Earth the three weapons with which Cain had slain Abel: a bronze nail, a wooden club, and a stone. For Hugo, these instruments symbolically represent war, capital punishment, and imprisonment. These thre e representations determine the structure of the work.

In the first section, "Le Glaive," Hugo illustrates the evils of war through the symbolic character of Nimrod. Hugo's Nimrod is arrogant and bellicose, and his attack on the kingdom of God is doomed to failure. The most remarkable section of this first part concerns another Hugoesque creation. One of the feathers from Lucifer's wings had not fallen into the abyss, landing instead on the edge of a precipice. The angel, Liberty, engendered from this feather is a creation of God rather than of Satan, and together with Lilith, she represents the dual nature of Lucifer-Satan.

The second section, centering on an earthly drama, is titled "Le Gibet" ("The Cross"). It is divided into three parts: "La Judée," "Jésus-Christ," and "Le Crucifix." Hugo's attack on capital punishment takes the form of a contrast between the innocent Christ, who is crucified, and the guilty Barabbas, who is set free. Hugo adds an effective scene not found in the biblical narration, wherein Barabbas comes to the foot of the Cross after the Crucifixion.

In the meantime, Liberty beseeches God to allow Lucifer to return to the light. Before putting Lucifer into a peaceful sleep, she receives his blessing to undo the work of Lilith on Earth. The final section of the poem, dealing with imprisonment, was not complete at Hugo's death. Hugo, however, did write a conclusion to the work, titled "Satan pardonnée" ("Satan Pardoned"). Liberty is able to gain the salvation of both humankind and Lucifer.

Dieu

Composed in large part during Hugo's stay in Guernsey in 1855, *Dieu* was left unfinished for many years. Hugo returned to it in 1875, and it was published posthumously in 1891. The poem concerns Hugo's search for God. Twenty-one voices warn the poet of the futility of his search for a complete understanding of God; nevertheless, the poet continues on his journey. He meets a series of symbolic birds, for he himself is winged. These birds are emblems of various understandings of the godhead: atheism, skepticism, Manichaeanism, paganism, Judaism, and Christianity. Finally, the poet achieves the light in "La Lumière" ("The Light"), although he is denied complete understanding, for a veil falls before him. Humankind is to know the secrets of the infinite only in death.

Together with *La Fin de Satan*, *Dieu* represents a synthesis of Hugo's religious and philosophical ideas, revealing the poet as a privileged seeker of truth. Hugo shows himself to be not only a master of versification but also a man consumed by the desire to comprehend the deeper mysteries of existence and of the universe.

OTHER MAJOR WORKS

LONG FICTION: *Han d'Islande*, 1823 (*Hans of Iceland*, 1845); *Bug-Jargal*, 1826 (*The Noble Rival*, 1845); *Le Dernier Jour d'un condamné*, 1829 (*The Last Day of a Condemned*, 1840); *Notre-Dame de Paris*, 1831 (*The Hunchback of Notre Dame*, 1833); *Claude Gueux*, 1834; *Les Misérables*, 1862 (English translation, 1862); *Les Travailleurs de la mer*, 1866 (*The Toilers of the Sea*, 1866); *L'Homme qui rit*, 1869 (*The Man Who Laughs*, 1869); *Quatre-vingt-treize*, 1874 (*Ninety-three*, 1874).

PLAYS: *Cromwell*, pb. 1827 (verse drama; English translation, 1896); *Amy Robsart*, pr. 1828 (English translation, 1895); *Hernani*, pr., pb. 1830 (verse drama; English translation, 1830); *Marion de Lorme*, pr., pb. 1831 (verse drama; English translation, 1895); *Le Roi s'amuse*, pr., pb. 1832 (verse drama; *The King's Fool*, 1842; also known as *The King Amuses Himself*, 1964); *Lucrèce Borgia*, pr., pb. 1833 (*Lucretia Borgia*, 1842); *Marie Tudor*, pr., pb. 1833 (English translation, 1895); *Angelo, tyran de Padoue*, pr., pb. 1835 (*Angelo, Tyrant of Padua*, 1880); *Ruy Blas*, pr., pb. 1838 (verse drama; English translation, 1890); *Les Burgraves*, pr., pb. 1843 (*The Burgraves*, 1896); *Inez de Castro*, pb. 1863 (wr. c. 1818; verse drama); *La Grand-mère*, pb. 1865, pr. 1898; *Mille Francs de Recompense*, pb. 1866; *Les Deux Trouvailles de Gallus*, pb. 1881; *Torquemada*, pb. 1882 (wr. 1869; English translation, 1896); *Théâtre en liberté*, pb. 1886 (includes *Mangeront-ils?*); *The Dramatic Works*, 1887; *The Dramatic Works of Victor Hugo*, 1895-1896 (4 volumes); *Irtamène*, pb. 1934 (wr. 1816; verse drama).

NONFICTION: *La Préface de Cromwell*, 1827 (English translation, 1896); *Littérature et philosophie mêlées*, 1834; *Le Rhin*, 1842 (*The Rhine*, 1843); *Napoléon le petit*, 1852 (*Napoleon the Little*, 1852); *William Shakespeare*, 1864 (English translation, 1864); *Actes et paroles*, 1875-1876; *Histoire d'un crime*, 1877 (*The History of a Crime*, 1877-1878); *Religions et religion*, 1880; *Le Théâtre en liberté*, 1886; *Choses vues*, 1887 (*Things Seen*, 1887); *En voyage: Alpes et Pyrénées*, 1890 (*The Alps and Pyrenees*, 1898); *France et Belgique*, 1892; *Correspondance*, 1896-1898.

MISCELLANEOUS: *Oeuvres complètes*, 1880-1892 (57 volumes); *Victor Hugo's Works*, 1892 (30 volumes); *Works*, 1907 (10 volumes).

BIBLIOGRAPHY

Bloom, Harold, ed. *Victor Hugo*. New York: Chelsea House, 1988. Essays on all aspects of Hugo's career. Includes introduction, chronology, and bibliography.

Frey, John Andrew. *A Victor Hugo Encyclopedia*. Westport, Conn.: Greenwood Press, 1999. A comprehensive guide in English to the works of Victor Hugo. Includes a foreword, a biography, and a bibliography. Frey addresses Hugo as a leading poet, novelist, artist, and religious and revolutionary thinker of France. The balance of the volume contains alphabetically arranged entries discussing his works, characters, and themes as well as historical persons and places. Includes a general bibliography.

Ionesco, Eugène. *Hugoliad: Or, The Grotesque and Tragic Life of Victor Hugo*. New

York: Grove Press, 1987. This uncompleted work of Ionesco's youth—written in the 1930's in Romanian—is a sort of polemical antibiography, intended to dethrone its subject. The reader must take responsibility for separating fact from fiction, to say nothing of judging the aptness of the playwright's cheerless embellishments of anecdotal material. Postscript by Gelu Ionescu.

Ireson, J. C. *Victor Hugo: A Companion Guide to His Poetry*. New York: Clarendon Press, 1997. A detailed critical study dealing with Victor Hugo's verse in its totality, showing how each work was composed, how the themes evolved, and the considerations that dictated the sequence of his publications. Includes bibliographic references.

Maurois, André. *Olympio: The Life of Victor Hugo*. Translated by Gerard Hopkins. New York: Harper & Row, 1956. Originally published in French in 1954. This is probably as close an approach as possible to an ideal one-volume biography dealing with both the life and the work of a monumental figure such as Hugo. Of the sparse illustrations, several are superb; the bibliography, principally of sources in French, provides a sense of Hugo's celebrity and influence, which persisted well into the twentieth century.

———. *Victor Hugo and His World*. London: Thames & Hudson, 1966. The 1956 English translation of Maurois' text noted above was edited to conform to the format of a series of illustrated books. The result is interesting and intelligible, but rather schematic. In compensation for the vast cuts in text, a chronology and dozens of well-annotated illustrations have been added.

Peyre, Henri. *Victor Hugo: Philosophy and Poetry*. Translated by Roda P. Roberts. University: University of Alabama Press, 1980. A study of Hugo's philosophy as evidenced by his poetry. Contains translations of selected poems with an index and bibliography.

Porter, Laurence M. *Victor Hugo*. New York: Twayne, 1999. A basic biography of Hugo that covers his life and works. Bibliography and index.

Richardson, Joanna. *Victor Hugo*. New York: St. Martin's Press, 1976. A well-written, scholarly biography divided into three sections, "The Man," "The Prophet," "The Legend." With detailed notes and extensive bibliography.

Robb, Graham. *Victor Hugo*. New York: W. W. Norton, 1998. Thorough biography of Victor Hugo reveals many previously unknown aspects of his long life and literary career. Includes detailed notes and bibliography.

Sylvie L. F. Richards

JEAN DE LA FONTAINE

Born: Château-Thierry, Champagne, France; July 8, 1621
Died: Paris, France; April 13, 1695

PRINCIPAL POETRY
 Adonis, 1658 (English translation, 1957)
 Le Songe de Vaux, 1659
 Contes et nouvelles en vers, 1665 (*Tales and Short Stories in Verse*, 1735)
 Deuxième partie des "Contes et nouvelles en vers," 1666 (*Part Two of "Tales and Short Stories in Verse,"* 1735)
 Fables choisies, mises en vers, 1668-1694 (*Fables Written in Verse*, 1735)
 Troisième partie des "Contes et nouvelles en vers," 1671 (*Part Three of "Tales and Short Stories in Verse,"* 1735)
 Nouveaux Contes, 1674 (*New Tales*, 1735)
 Poèmes et poésies diverses, 1697

OTHER LITERARY FORMS

The verse fable has attracted numerous writers over the centuries extending as far back as Aesop. The success of Jean de La Fontaine (lah fohn-TEHN) in the genre, however, surpassed them all. Though his verse novel *Les Amours de Psyché et Cupidon* (1669; *The Loves of Cupid and Psyche*, 1744) may be considered a major work and he wrote plays, librettos, translations, and letters, La Fontaine's name has become, for young and old, inseparably linked with the fable, a genre that he brought to its ultimate fruition.

ACHIEVEMENTS

Jean de La Fontaine is unquestionably one of France's most beloved poets. He is a classical writer in the true meaning of the word. For centuries, French schoolchildren have learned his fables by heart. He is so important in France that he has often been compared with Dante and William Shakespeare as a national literary monument. The poet's universal fame derives primarily from his verse fables; La Fontaine developed this literary genre to perfection, and there have been no great fabulists after him (with the possible exception of the Russian writer Ivan Krylov). The fables of La Fontaine culminated a long tradition in Western literature that began in antiquity with Aesop and Phaedrus. His works have been printed and reprinted in magnificent editions. They have been translated into many languages and have been illustrated by great artists down through the centuries: the *Fables* by Alphonse Oudry, Gustave Doré, and Marc Chagall; *Tales and Short Stories in Verse* by Charles-Dominique Joseph Eisen, Jean-Honoré Fragonard, and others.

Jean de La Fontaine
(Library of Congress)

La Fontaine unites the two major contrasting aesthetics found in the literature of seventeenth century France: artistic exuberance and classical restraint. Of the two, the former is best represented in poetry by the libertine poets, the so-called free spirits, such as Théophile de Viau and Marc-Antoine Saint-Amant. Temperamentally and in his general approach to life, La Fontaine belonged to this group of poets. His early works reveal a strain of playful sensuality and outspoken humor that are more representative of a hedonistic school of thought than one would normally expect from a renowned classical poet. Unlike other poets of his day, however, he was able to temper this natural tendency. One of La Fontaine's cardinal rules was that poetry should first of all give pleasure. He understood that pleasure is not an end in itself, that it must be deep and rich rather than facile or superficial. Wishing to please his readers, he hoped and believed that they would like what he himself liked.

Accordingly, he accepted the tenets of a classical doctrine that was very influential during this period. The influence of classical restraint is apparent in his mature works, especially the fables. In matters of style (he strove for simplicity, clarity, brevity), choice of language (a restrained vocabulary), versification, and the insertion of old materials among new, La Fontaine showed himself to be a genuine classical author. Moreover, the meter of classical French poetry, with the ubiquitous Alexandrine, was at times threatened with monotony and stiffness. Through his writings, La Fontaine managed to infuse new life in French versification. He achieved a melodic depth unsurpassed by his contemporaries and proved to be a superb craftsman. The quick movement of his verse, with those sudden short lines and that frequent suddenness of feminine rhyme that can create surprise, fun, or intimacy, has been emulated by generations of French poets. Above all, he had the gift of being sincere, personal, and completely natural in his finest poetry, at a time when it was not at all fashionable to be so.

BIOGRAPHY

Jean de La Fontaine was born in the province of Champagne at Château-Thierry in 1621. In spite of his name, he was not of noble birth. His father held a government post as an administrator of forest and water resources. It was in the lush, green countryside of Château-Thierry that the poet spent his first twenty years. He loved the surrounding neighborhood with its woods, waters, and meadows. He admired the natural world during a century when it went mostly unappreciated; indeed, to most of his contemporaries the term "nature" meant primarily human nature. Thus, his early upbringing set him apart from the other great classical writers of France's Golden Age, and the influence of nature and of country people is apparent in many of his tales and fables.

It is well documented that as a boy, La Fontaine was dreamy and absent-minded. He was also cheerful and lively, possessing an amiable disposition that remained with him throughout his life. In 1641, at the age of twenty, La Fontaine decided to study for the priesthood at the Oratoire in Paris, but he abandoned this pursuit after eighteen months and turned to the study of law. In 1647, his father transferred his official post to La Fontaine and married him off to a girl from an affluent family. The match proved to be a disaster, and the couple formally separated after eleven years of marriage. During this period, La Fontaine lived the life of a dilettante. He showed a disinclination for steady work and was content to spend much of his time in idleness; he was a voracious reader. He eventually sold his father's post and took up permanent residence in Paris.

La Fontaine began writing comparatively late in life, in his middle thirties. Throughout his career as a man of letters, he relied on generous patrons for his support and well-being. His first patron was also his most important—the wealthy finance minister Nicolas Fouquet. La Fontaine became a pensioner of Fouquet in 1656 and wrote for him such early major works as *Adonis* and *Le Songe de Vaux* (the dream of Vaux). Unfortunately for La Fontaine, Fouquet soon fell into disgrace. His opulent lifestyle aroused the envy and anger of the young King Louis XIV. Fouquet was accused of appropriating state funds and spent the rest of his life in prison. During Fouquet's ordeal, La Fontaine exhibited that particular virtue that would always be characteristic of him as pensioner—a deep sense of loyalty. He did not abandon Fouquet as did so many others, and he even wrote poems, including the "Elégie aux nymphes de Vaux," begging the king to be lenient. For this display of allegiance, he incurred the king's lasting enmity. He thus never received a pension from the government, as did many other writers and artists, and his election to the prestigious French Academy was delayed on the king's order.

After Fouquet's downfall, La Fontaine was aided for a short time by the powerful Bouillon family and later by a royal patron, the dowager duchess of Orléans. He was by then forty years old, well into middle age for the times, and he was not a popular or well-known author. He realized that writing idyllic works such as *Adonis* would no longer be financially rewarding for him. Accordingly, he turned to more popular genres, such as tales and fables. He published *Tales and Short Stories in Verse* in 1665. They were written in the tradition of Giovanni Boccaccio and Ludovico Ariosto, among others, and they became an immediate success. A second collection appeared a year later, in 1666; a third collection was published in 1671; and the final collection appeared in 1674. At that time, La Fontaine also began to publish those works on which his fame rests—the *Fables Written in Verse*. The first collection appeared in 1668, when he was forty-seven years old; the second, ten years later; and the last collection, in 1694, one year before his death.

The success of the *Fables Written in Verse* placed La Fontaine at the forefront of French writers. In 1669, he published *The Loves of Cupid and Psyche*, taken from the tale of Cupid and Psyche in Lucius Apuleius's *The Golden Ass* (second century). La Fontaine continued writing many occasional verses of small importance for various patrons. In 1684, despite earlier opposition by the king, he was finally elected to the French Academy. In 1692, a serious illness occasioned a spiritual renewal, which, in turn, caused him to disavow publicly his earlier tales. In that same year, some of La Fontaine's fables were translated into English for the first time, by Sir Roger L'Estrange. In 1695, while attending a play, La Fontaine was struck ill and taken to the house of friends, the Haberts, where he died several days later. He is buried in the cemetery of the Saints-Innocents in Paris.

Analysis

Jean de La Fontaine's poetic output mirrors the two major styles of seventeenth century French literature—that is to say, it lies between artistic exuberance, on one hand, and classical restraint, on the other. This has not always been apparent, however, since the fame of his *Fables Written in Verse* was such as to put his other poetic works in partial eclipse for a long period. Later scholarship has attempted to redress this imbalance. Such works as *Adonis*, *Le Songe de Vaux*, and *The Loves of Cupid and Psyche* reflect the grandiose splendor and fantasy characteristic of the Baroque style of the period. Conversely, the brevity, clarity, and logic of the *Fables Written in Verse* are more typical of the classical style associated with the authors of France's "grand siècle."

Adonis

La Fontaine presented his first major poetic endeavor, *Adonis*, to his new patron, Fouquet, in June, 1658. It was a fine example of calligraphy by Nicolas Jarvey, with the title page illustrated by François Chauveau. The poem was a long pastoral work whose subject was borrowed from Ovid. It relates the legend of the goddess Venus's love for a youth, Adonis, and of his untimely death. La Fontaine's work is only half the length of William Shakespeare's better-known version, *Venus and Adonis* (1593). Furthermore, La Fontaine's Adonis is not a cold and reluctant character, as is Shakespeare's. Instead, La Fontaine chose to emphasize the theme of youth cut off in the flower of strength and beauty. For La Fontaine, Adonis symbolizes the agony of helpless strength, a paradoxical antithesis characteristic of the Baroque. The poet's vivid and enjoyable descriptions of nature create a self-contained poetic world. It is not the real world, yet La Fontaine, a true lover of nature, has managed to make the setting of his poem so directly appealing to the senses and simple instincts of his readers that the illusion is all but complete.

On the other hand, his amorous poetry is too artificial and conventional. He composed his idyll in the Alexandrines typical of French poetry: lines of twelve syllables, with four stresses to the line and rhyming in couplets. The stately Alexandrine was not well adapted to the subject matter of the poem. Even in the most tender passages, there is some monotony of cadence. A shorter verse line with its rapid movement would have smoothed the transitions between episodes in the narrative. Nevertheless, this first major poetic undertaking taught La Fontaine much about the writing of Alexandrines. For a long period unfairly neglected, *Adonis* deserves the recognition it has received during the past few decades. The poem contains verse worthy of La Fontaine at his best, and one can discern in it many of the traits that find fuller expression in his subsequent writings: skillful assimilation of source material, a refined musical style, close observation of human or animal life in a mythological setting, and, above all, an ability to infuse humor without compromising the decorous mood of the poem.

Le Songe de Vaux

Fouquet was pleased with *Adonis* and asked La Fontaine to undertake a new work in praise of Vaux, the magnificent white-stone palace that the finance minister was engaged in creating for himself with the help of the best architects, garden designers, and artists in France. La Fontaine accommodated his patron with *Le Songe de Vaux*, a work that, as a result of the disgrace of Fouquet, was never completed. Nine fragments have survived, written in a mixture of verse and prose. The poem fits marvelously into the parklike landscape of Vaux in which La Fontaine places it. It is enveloped in a world of fantasy. Artificial as it may be, there is enough imagination to give a touch of fairyland to the scene. Wishing to give posterity a picture of Vaux as it would appear in all the beauty of its maturity, the poet used his imagination in describing Fouquet's magnificent estate. He proposed to describe—in lyrical, allegorical, and mythological terms—what the Vaux gardens, newly planted and only shrub-high, would be like in years to come.

The plot of *Le Songe de Vaux* revolves around the discovery of some imagined buried treasure on the palace grounds. A mysterious inscription on a jewel case leads to a kind of beauty contest in which the four nymphs representing architecture, painting, gardening, and poetry contest the honor of being responsible for the chief beauties of Vaux. The poem evokes an ideal world from which all ugliness is banished. La Fontaine had the rare gift, unique in seventeenth century France, of communicating in poetry the sensations aroused by colors and forms. This is particularly apparent in *Le Songe de Vaux*, a work permeated with poetic feeling for beauty, peace, and sensual pleasure akin to one of Charles Le Brun's paintings, which it celebrates. The verse, more smooth and melodious than in *Adonis*, seems to have developed effortlessly. The limpid simplicity of the shorter, octosyllabic lines assures a more flowing rhythm. The precious imagery and the choice of vocabulary help sustain the quiet enjoyment of varying moods.

THE LOVES OF CUPID AND PSYCHE

La Fontaine continued the practice of interweaving prose and poetry with *The Loves of Cupid and Psyche,* based on the classical tale of a jealous Venus who sends Cupid to make the beautiful maiden Psyche fall in love with an ugly creature, only to have Cupid fall in love with Psyche instead. This long novel-poem is set within the framework of a conversation in the park of Versailles among four friends—Polyphile, Acante, Ariste, and Gélaste. The gardens of Versailles and the surrounding area provide an atmosphere of fantasy similar in tone and style to the one depicted in *Le Songe de Vaux.* Indeed, La Fontaine transposed materials from the latter into this work. Once again, it is interesting to note the changes wrought by the poet on his source material—changes that enabled him to achieve effects unmatched by writers such as Vergil, Torquato Tasso, and Ariosto who had treated this myth before him. His Psyche is a much more complex character than any of her prototypes. She is sensual, tender, and open-minded, vain at times but always charming. Rather than portray her in bleak, isolated settings, as did his predecessors, La Fontaine shows her in beautiful surroundings. The joining of sensuous love and bucolic descriptions of nature bathe this work in an aura of voluptuous, Epicurean delight. *The Loves of Cupid and Psyche* is important as a transitional work in La Fontaine's oeuvre; it draws the curtain on the period of youthful ardor, of love and beauty, of preciosity and gallantry associated with the works of the Vaux period.

TALES AND SHORT STORIES IN VERSE

Second only to the *Fables Written in Verse* in their popularity, the *Tales and Short Stories in Verse* were first published in 1665. Three more collections of similar material appeared in 1666, 1671, and 1674. These tales belong to the Western literary tradition of stock ribald stories told and retold during the Middle Ages and the Renaissance by Boccaccio, Geoffrey Chaucer, Marguerite de Navarre, and many others. The predominant theme of these tales is illicit love: the frolicsome comedy of marital infidelity, the sexual prowess of men or lack of it, the frailty of women, the lustful desires of priests and nuns, and so forth. A total of thirty-five tales appeared over the years, of which "Joconde" and "Le Cocu battu et content" ("The Cudgelled and Contented Cuckold") are perhaps the most popular. In the later tales, the subjects include not only the illicit affairs of typically crafty women, paramours, and cuckolds but also the daily tribulations of ordinary people: a poor shoemaker, a cynical judge, a peasant and his master, among others. Like the fables, these tales first circulated in manuscript, soon winning favorable response from La Fontaine's friends. Licentious tales became extremely popular during the early reign of young Louis XIV; La Fontaine was aware of this trend and sought to cater to the salacious taste of the public. Nevertheless, the tales caused him enormous difficulties. Each collection was more licentious than its predecessors until the final published tales were ordered suppressed by the police. In his old age, La Fontaine publicly repudiated these tales, expressing regret at ever having written them; it should be noted, however, that this recantation was made during a period when strict moral severity prevailed at the court of Versailles.

NARRATIVE TECHNIQUE AND POETIC EXPRESSION

The fact that La Fontaine did not invent his plots—he borrowed freely from his precursors—enabled him to focus all his talents on details of narrative technique and poetic expression. It is in these two areas that he made his greatest contribution as a writer of tales. La Fontaine always had a flair for the dramatic, and in his tales he shows himself to be a master storyteller. His skill at creating action without impeding the progress of the plot (effected primarily by means of alteration in the rhythm of the poetry), his penchant for producing situations that shock or surprise, his ability to vary and freshen the treatment of old, banal themes—in brief, his talent for adroit handling of the strictly narrative aspects of the art—is his major appeal. Whatever plots he chose, his own special genius gave them new life.

In his tales, La Fontaine adopted a free-flowing conversational style. In fact, he seems to have gone to great lengths to ensure that the graceful, chatty style of these stories would appear as natural as possible to the reader. Toward that end, he employed an irregular and loose sort of verse, known as *vers libre* (not to be confused with modern free verse), consisting of lines in two or more meters without a fixed rhyme scheme. La Fontaine's two favorite verse forms were the eight-syllable line of the old French fabliaux and the ten-syllable line. These two verse lines, along with the lack of any clear-cut rhyme scheme, gave the tales a colloquial tone that one would normally expect to find only in prose. Such verse had greater flexibility than anything previously written in French. It allowed the poet to tell his stories in a familiar, relaxed style, addressing himself directly to the reader. Curiously enough, he frequently felt a need to justify his use of this form, declaring that it was the most suitable and that it had given him as much trouble as the writing of regular verse or prose. In truth, it must be said that La Fontaine employed *vers libre* with great restraint. He introduced other rhythmic patterns as well, but only on rare occasions. His poetic expertise was to be found elsewhere: in the subtle interplay of rhymes, in evocative combinations of sounds, in complex rhythmic gradations and contrasts, in the joining of heterogeneous stanza forms, in the interplay of thought patterns with metrical patterns—all the stylistic characteristics that became asso ciated with his masterpiece, the *Fables Written in Verse*.

FABLES WRITTEN IN VERSE

In the *Fables Written in Verse*, as in his tales, La Fontaine was reviving a genre that had been popular throughout the Middle Ages and the Renaissance. The *Fables Written in Verse* is a work of maturity, nourished by wide reading and a long apprenticeship in poetic technique. They were published in three cycles spanning twenty-five years. The first cycle, containing 125 fables, appeared in 1668. Ten years later, La Fontaine added nearly one hundred more, and the 1694 edition—the last edition published during his lifetime—included two dozen new fables. Thus, he wrote nearly 250 fables in all. The early fables owe a great deal to classical sources, in particular Aesop and Phaedrus; the later ones find their inspiration in Asian stories.

These fables are the work of a man who had an intimate acquaintance with nature and an instinctive understanding of animals and country things. La Fontaine's *Fables Written in Verse* has always appealed to three distinct audiences: to children, because of the vividness and freshness of the stories; to literary students, because of their accomplished artistry; and to people of the world, because of their penetrating psychological observation of human behavior. Of these three disparate audiences, La Fontaine sought in particular the third category of readers, for he himself often said that his fables would be fully appreciated only by those who had had a long experience of life and people.

A comparison of La Fontaine's fables with others in the genre reveals the importance of his achievement. Traditional materials are handled with shades of feelings not to be found in earlier fables. In particular, his approach to the depiction of animals in the *Fables Written in Verse* is at variance with that of practically all the previous writers of fables who had found favor with the public. Like all fabulists, La Fontaine treats animals in anthropomorphic terms: They are used to depict certain human foibles. Moving beyond his predecessors artistically, La Fontaine's portrayals of the human as well as the animal aspects of his characters have not been surpassed by his followers and imitators. Strange, clumsy little creatures wander about, fiercely acting their parts to what is, at times, a merciless finish. These animals show the desires, appetites, and fears that are humankind's brutish inheritance. The dominant ones among them are forceful, secretive, cunning, and sharp-witted, and their ends are as elemental as their means are ingenious. Their victims are like those in the human world: muddleheaded, cringing before their masters, into whose maws they are ever ready to drop. The weak countenances of these victims remain plaintive, frightened, and pitiful—revealing the essential cruelty of existence.

What the *Fables Written in Verse* reveals, above all, is La Fontaine's conception of power (the first edition was dedicated to the future king of France). Animal hierarchies provided him with an opportunity to examine certain types of formal relations among control, resistance, and violence so that he could uncover, by implication, the same relationships in human society. In fact, the *Fables Written in Verse* constitute a survey of the struggle for power among men. La Fontaine views the political world as an arena in which the strong seek to defend and extend their powers and privileges. He posits a view of humankind that sees conflict as the only mode of action and insists that no moral considerations should be taken into account, the political aims justifying any means.

The prevalence of such motifs clearly indicates a substratum of belief that La Fontaine could not have derived from his learned sources alone. Themes such as these illustrate the extent to which he appropriated the idiom of the fable for his own wholly different ends. To study La Fontaine's fables is to investigate power *in extremis*. In the *Fables Written in Verse*, power must be exercised rather than merely possessed. It must be seized and maintained even at the cost of a progressive enslavement to its instinctive violence. The traditional concept of power as a societal mechanism that lays down the law for everyone alike no longer applies. Animals, men, and institutions are treated and studied mainly as objects of domination. There is no reason to doubt that La Fontaine's contemporaries understood perfectly the "message" of this important work—one that has become obfuscated down through the centuries by the rote memorizations of schoolchildren and the musty compilations of scholars. One can also understand better why Jean-Jacques Rousseau denounced the use of such texts to shape young sensibilities.

Each generation takes a different approach to La Fontaine's individual vision. Certain past generations saw him as a detached observer of the human comedy, while others have seen him as a dissatisfied man with a gift for caricature, as a poet of the picturesque in nature and in rural life, as a dilettante with dregs of smug morality, or merely as a pleasant storyteller. No subsequent writer of fables has sustained such an intense emotional vision of man and of the forces that dominate and shape the world in which he lives as did La Fontaine. Above all, his fables repay study because of their poetic beauty and simplicity; they are a deeply felt artistic manifestation of the human condition, derived mostly from the bitter truth of experience.

OTHER MAJOR WORKS
LONG FICTION: *Les Amours de Psyché et Cupidon*, 1669 (*The Loves of Cupid and Psyche*, 1744).
PLAYS: *L'Eunuque*, pb. 1654; *Clymène*, pb. 1671; *Daphné*, pb. 1682 (libretto); *Galatée*, pb. 1682 (libretto); *L'Astrée*, pb. 1692 (libretto).
NONFICTION: *Relation d'un voyage en Limousin*, 1663; *Discours à Mme de La Sablière*, 1679; *Épître à Huet*, 1687.

MISCELLANEOUS: *Œuvres complètes*, 1933 (2 volumes); *Œuvres diverses*, 1942; *Œuvres, sources, et postérité d'Ésope à l'Oulipo*, 1995.

BIBLIOGRAPHY

Birberick, Anne L. *Reading Undercover: Audience and Authority in Jean de La Fontaine*. London: Associated University Presses, 1998. In her readings of La Fontaine's major poetic works, Birberick proposes the possibility of a "circular writing" resulting from the multiplicity of author/audience relationships in the poet's works, which allows La Fontaine room to criticize court patronage and tyranny, while nonetheless winning the necessary approbation of the Sun King.

———. *Refiguring La Fontaine: Tercentenary Essays*. Charlottesville, Va.: Bookwood Press, 1996. In addition to Birberick's introductory summary of La Fontaine's critical reception since his death, this volume contains nine essays (three in French, six in English) that explore La Fontaine's adaptations of and challenges to literary structure, questions of discourse in the *Fables Written in Verse*, and new treatments of other, more neglected works by the poet. Of particular interest to an audience obliged to rely on translations from French is the last essay by David Lee Rubin, which examines three English translations of one fable in order to discuss how each translator's different approach informs, or distorts, the image of La Fontaine and his poetry.

Calder, Andrew. *The Fables of La Fontaine: Wisdom Brought Down to Earth*. Geneva: Droz, 2001. Arguing that it is essential to consider La Fontaine's *Fables Written in Verse* from a perspective both of utility and pleasure in some sixteen, self-contained chapters that look to the fables as lessons in life, Calder's book is also of interest in that it explores La Fontaine's philosophical similarities with schools of thought in antiquity and with his Renaissance predecessors, such as Erasmus, François Rabelais, and Michel Eyquem de Montaigne.

Fumaroli, Marc. *The Poet and the King: Jean de La Fontaine and His Century*. Translated by Jane Marie Todd. Notre Dame, Ind.: University of Notre Dame Press, 2002. A biography of La Fontaine that details his relations with Louis XIV.

Guiton, Margaret. *La Fontaine: Poet and Counterpoet*. New Brunswick, N.J.: Rutgers University Press, 1961. Examines La Fontaine's competing visions of comedy and imaginative poetry. French passages translated. Contains chronological table of La Fontaine's life and works.

Lapp, John C. *The Esthetics of Negligence: La Fontaine's "Contes."* New York: Cambridge University Press, 1971. Refutes previous disparaging studies by demonstrating how La Fontaine's wit, eroticism, lyricism, and charm make the *Tales and Short Stories in Verse* superior to their sources.

Mackay, Agnes Ethel. *La Fontaine and His Friends: A Biography*. London: Garnstone Press, 1972. Examination of La Fontaine's relationship with intimate friends and influential patrons. French passages translated in chapter endnotes.

Sweetser, Marie-Odile. *La Fontaine*. Boston: Twayne, 1987. In this very approachable critical biography of La Fontaine, Sweetser organizes her chapters by the chronological appearance of each of the poet's major works. Her volume is also useful in that it makes available to a non-francophone readership a concise, well-documented synthesis of continental scholarship concerning La Fontaine.

Wadsworth, Philip A. *Young La Fontaine*. Evanston, Ill.: Northwestern University Press, 1952. A detailed study of La Fontaine's growth as a poet up to publication of his first fables in 1668. Good discussion of influences that shaped his early works.

Raymond LePage

JULES LAFORGUE

Born: Montevideo, Uruguay; August 16, 1860
Died: Paris, France; August 20, 1887

PRINCIPAL POETRY
Les Complaintes, 1885
L'Imitation de Notre-Dame la lune, 1886
Des fleurs de bonne volonté, 1888
Les Derniers Vers de Jules Laforgue, 1890
Poésies complètes, 1894, 1970
Œuvres complètes de Jules Laforgue, 1902-1903 (4 volumes; 1922-1930, 6 volumes)
Poems, 1975
Selected Poems, 1998

OTHER LITERARY FORMS

In the short but prolific writing career of Jules Laforgue (lah-FAWRG), he produced more than two hundred poems and many works in other literary forms, only some of which have been rescued from the papers left at his death. His surviving verse dramas include "Tessa," written in 1877, existing in a manuscript only recently discovered; *Pierrot fumiste*, composed in 1882, first published in 1892; and *Le Concile féerique*, published in 1886, compiled from five poems originally written for *Des fleurs de bonne volonté* (poems that Laforgue composed between 1883 and 1886 and that first appeared in 1888). These three cabaret farces command the attention of scholars eager to explore Laforgue's developing themes and ironic dialogue; they are not major contributions to theatrical literature.

Masterpieces of an original genre are Laforgue's six fanciful prose tales, *Moralités légendaires* (1887; *Six Moral Tales from Jules Laforgue*, 1928), retelling myths in details both mundane and psychologically plausible. Among these, "Hamlet" and "Persée et Andromède" ("Perseus and Andromeda: Or, The Happiest One of the Triangle") have provoked considerable admiring commentary. The actor and mime Jean-Louis Barrault performed a memorable adaptation of "Hamlet" in 1939. Several works of fiction have apparently been lost, but there survive a short autobiographical novel, *Stéphane Vassiliew*, written in 1881, first published in 1946, and a short autobiographical story, "Amours de la quinzième année," written about 1879, first published in 1887.

Laforgue's selected letters, especially those to his sister, created the legend of the poet as a self-conscious, sensitive, starving aesthete, but his letters to various other friends reveal his humor, his broad interests in philosophy, art, and music, and his acute observations of society. A fuller portrait of Laforgue's intellectual range emerges from his critical essays on Impressionist aesthetics, on the Symbolist poets Charles Baudelaire and Tristan Corbière, and on life in the German imperial court. Laforgue's translations of Walt Whitman's verse were published in 1886.

Among his other essays and drafts published posthumously are some provocative comments on the cultural definitions constricting the roles of women, including "La Femme—la légende féminine," among many others. Simone de Beauvoir, in *Le Deuxième Sexe* (1949; *The Second Sex*, 1953), and Léon Guichard, in his critical study of Laforgue, have evaluated these comments on feminine roles.

Achievements

Jules Laforgue's poetry published in 1885 and 1886 earned for him praise from contemporary critics and established him as one of the leading innovators of poetic form at the time. The literary circle within which he moved made his classification as a Symbolist poet inevitable. His sudden death in 1887 gave his career a tragic plot, especially for literary historians eager to contribute to the mythology of doomed poets.

Laforgue's most significant contributions to the development of modern poetry are his rhymed free verse, his verbal playfulness, his juxtaposition of melancholy and gaiety in his ironic tone, and his psychologically complex monologues and dialogues, which give voice to the unconscious and to dream states, as well as to masks consciously assumed.

Although Laforgue has often been dismissed as a minor poet, his philosophical sophistication may deserve as much praise as his technical innovations. In his poetry, Laforgue explored the conflicts between the conscious and the unconscious, exposed the illusions of rational pessimism, and exploited the literary consequences of an idealist philosophy against those of determinism (as practiced by the naturalists), but he set all these metaphysical confrontations in the real, familiar world of trivial remarks and superficial gestures.

Biography

Born in Uruguay, Jules Laforgue was sent at the age of six to a boarding school in Tarbes, France, where he remained until he was fifteen. Laforgue felt isolated and persecuted at school; he left an account of his childhood and adolescence in the autobiographical novel *Stéphane Vassiliew*. His family returned from Uruguay in his sixteenth year, and the eleven children and two parents crowded into an apartment in Paris. That spring, his mother died after a twelfth pregnancy; she was thirty-seven. In "Avertissement," Laforgue wrote that he hardly knew his mother, but his awareness of her situation may be glimpsed in "Complainte du fœtus de poète," in which an unsympathetic and egotistic voice describes his birth, blithely unconcerned with any feelings but his own.

Laforgue attended the Lycée Fontanes (now Condorcet) but twice failed his oral examination for the *baccalauréat*. A paralyzing fear of failure afflicts many of Laforgue's poetic alter egos. After failing his examinations, Laforgue continued to study independently, reading omnivorously and attending lectures on the philosophy of art by the determinist Hippolyte Taine, whose assertions that art is completely determined by milieu, race, and historical moment Laforgue rejected.

In 1880, the twenty-year-old Laforgue met several influential men whose friendship helped launch his career. Gustave Kahn became a good friend, confidant, and literary editor. Kahn introduced Laforgue to the regular Tuesday readings by Stéphane Mallarmé and also to Charles Henry, an intellectual equally brilliant on scientific and literary topics. That same year, Laforgue also met the literary critic Paul Bourget, who generously criticized his writing and who arranged a job for Laforgue assisting the art critic Charles Ephrussi. He introduced Laforgue to the paintings of the Impressionists, and evidence from Laforgue's poems and essays indicates that the Impressionist aesthetic reflected his conviction that art aims at fusing a sensual and intellectual apprehension of life.

Late in 1881, Laforgue's father, who was dying from tuberculosis, moved the rest of the family to Tarbes, leaving Laforgue behind. Although he took a cheap room to remain in Paris, Laforgue was employed by Ephrussi, was writing poems, and was enjoying his literary life; ironically, a self-pitying letter written to his sister during this period, exaggerating his timidity and his loneliness and appealing for sympathy, later contributed to the legend of the starving poet.

That year, with the recommendations of Bourget and Ephrussi, Laforgue was appointed the French reader to the German Empress Augusta, a job that paid well, gave him leisure to write, introduced him to rich food and luxurious apartments, and required his residence in Germany. From November, 1881, through September, 1886, Laforgue lived with the peripatetic German imperial court for ten months of the year; he spent his long vacations of 1883, 1884, and 1885 in Paris, and his constant correspondence kept him in touch with contemporary literary developments in France.

Although he complained of his boredom in the German court, Laforgue worked steadily on his poems, and during the court's residence in Berlin, he enjoyed the company of musicians and artists (especially his friends the brothers Théophile and Eugène Ysaÿe, a pianist and a violinist) and amused himself at the aquarium, circuses, music halls, museums, the opera, the ballet, and orchestral concerts. His experience of Berlin's cultural life influenced the imagery of his poems, in which one finds clowns, harlequins, underwater creatures, sublime music, and playfully improper cabaret patter.

On New Year's Day, 1886, Laforgue, who identified his anguished self-consciousness with Hamlet's character, visited the castle of Elsinore; he later reworked his experience of Hamlet's haunt into his *Des fleurs de bonne volonté* and his prose fantasy about the indecisive Dane. Back in Berlin, late in January, Laforgue met an English woman,

Leah Lee, who had chosen to live independently from her family and who was supporting herself by teaching English. As he fell in love with her, he was reaching his decision to leave the German court position. He spent three weeks in Paris in late June and early July, then returned to the German court, and by August, in the resort at Schlagenbad, he was writing his first poems in free verse.

Laforgue returned to Berlin with the German court on September 1, 1886, Lee accepted his marriage proposal on September 6, and he left the employ of the Empress Augusta that month. By October, Laforgue was living in Paris, waiting for his own wedding, reworking and finishing his poems in free verse, completing his *Six Moral Tales from Jules Laforgue*, and discussing the movement newly named "Symbolist" with Édouard Dujardin and Teodor de Wyzewa (editors of *La Revue indépendante*) and his old friends Kahn (later editor of *La Vogue*) and Félix Fénéon (who edited and reshaped Laforgue's new poems in free verse). Laforgue's moral tales and his new poems were published in various issues of *La Vogue* and *La Revue indépendante*, so that by the autumn of 1886, Laforgue's star had burst onto the Parisian literary scene, with the publication of his tales, his free verse, *L'Imitation de Notre-Dame la lune*, and *Le Concile féerique*. Laforgue was being hailed as a leader in the avant-garde.

On the last day of that wonderful year, Laforgue and Leah married, in London (at St. Barnabas, where T. S. Eliot and Valerie Fletcher were married in 1957). Laforgue returned to Paris with a bad cough, which, as it developed, was a symptom of tuberculosis. For eight months, he was too ill to write much poetry, and he died on August 20, 1887.

Analysis

Although the legend of his short, tragic life shaped the initial critical response to his work, Jules Laforgue is now recognized as one of the first modernist poets. Laforgue is notable for his technical innovations, for his ironic voices and psychologically complex personas, for his verbal and syntactic playfulness, and for his fusion of sublimely serious philosophical questions with the plainly vulgar language and concerns of ordinary life.

Laforgue developed the poetic form known as *vers libre*, or free verse, in which he used lines of varying length, subtle rhyming patterns, and diverse rhythms to correspond, flexibly, to shifts in mood and subject. Although Arthur Rimbaud also has been credited with inventing free verse (with his "Marine" and "Mouvement," poems written earlier than *Les Derniers Vers de Jules Laforgue*), Laforgue's innovative verse forms were published in periodicals before Rimbaud's examples, and his *Les Derniers Vers de Jules Laforgue* more directly influenced the free verse of modernist poets.

Most English and American readers know Laforgue through his influence on Eliot, Ezra Pound, Hart Crane, and Wallace Stevens. In 1908, Eliot read about Laforgue in *The Symbolist Movement in Literature*, by Arthur Symons; in 1909, Eliot read Laforgue's poems and letters selected in *Œuvres complètes de Jules Laforgue*. Eliot's poems influenced by Laforgue's irony, dialogues, and verse forms include the 1909 "Nocturne," "Humouresque," and "Spleen," and the more famous "The Love Song of J. Alfred Prufrock," "Conversation Galante," "Portrait of a Lady," and "La Figlia che Piange," as well as sections of *The Waste Land* (1922). Pound and Crane both published translations of Laforgue's work, and Pound praised Laforgue's intellect dancing playfully among words. Laforguian irony and wordplay may be found in Pound's "Hugh Selwyn Mauberley" and in Crane's "Chaplinesque," among other poems. Stevens transformed Laforgue's Impressionist images and his verse forms extensively, but the French poet's diffused influence may be traced in such works of Stevens as "The Comedian as the Letter C," "Sea Surface Full of Clouds," "Peter Quince at the Clavier," and "Notes Toward a Supreme Fiction."

Laforgue anticipated the psychological narratives of both James Joyce and Marcel Proust in the interior monologue he developed in such poems as "Complainte de Lord Pierrot" and "Dimanches." He split his monologues and dialogues into multiple voices that are wittily self-aware and self-mocking. Although the contrapuntal dialogue of his "Complainte du soir des comices agricoles" was inspired by Gustave Flaubert (in a notorious scene in *Madame Bovary*, 1856, the overblown romantic language of a seduction is undercut by the vulgar realism of an animal auction at a country fair), Laforgue neither relied on simple antithesis nor assumed a superior moral stance; rather, his ironic conversations and monologues offer multiple perspectives that remain irreconcilable.

Pound and Joyce delighted in Laforgue's demolition and recombination of language. The amusing colloquialisms and revolutionary neologisms that appear in Laforgue's verse violated poetic etiquette but revealed the psychology of his speakers. They wittily or ignorantly combine two words from different realms to disclose an unexpected association. Examples include "sangsuelles," "éternullité," "violuptés," "spleenuosité," and "crucifige" (these neologisms are derived, respectively, from blood plus sensual, eternal plus nullity, violation or violence plus voluptuous, spleen plus sinuosity, and crucify plus to clot). Laforgue often fused common words, but he also correctly employed arcane, archaic, and slang words in lines of impeccably sublime diction. The shock of contrast, with the implied assertion of the validity and significance of these verbal intrusions, radically changes the poet's relationship to language.

In his images and subjects, Laforgue, like the Impressionists and the Symbolists in painting and literature, claimed for his art both a psychological and a physical definition of reality and envisioned correlations between the sublime and the ordinary, between the spiritual and the objective worlds. Eliot, in his celebrated definition of the "objective correlative," drew on Laforgue's example.

Laforgue's literary legacy also includes his black humor. In poems such as "Excuse macabre," "Guitare," and "Complainte des blackboulés" ("Lament of the Blackballs"), his ironic but not pompous stance treated the grim themes of death, frustration, self-doubt, boredom, melancholy, alienation, nihilism, and the failure of passion with a racy wit, slipping often into gaiety. In this, Samuel Beckett is one of Laforgue's heirs.

The bathetic, self-centered misery of the gloomy poems Laforgue wrote from 1880 to 1882, for *Le Sanglot de la terre* (first pb. in *Œuvres complètes de Jules Laforgue*), has provoked speculation about a period of depression he suffered, but these metrically conventional and sentimental verses, laboriously exploring correlations between an adolescent's passionate psyche and the world's turbulence, have a literary antecedent in the splenetic poems of Baudelaire, and they also betray the influence of the moral and metaphysical idealism of Arthur Schopenhauer. Recognizing the inadequacy of these early poems, Laforgue chose not to publish them.

From 1882 through 1884, Laforgue worked on a group of comic poems based on popular street ballads. In them, he experimented with unconventional metric forms and broken syntax, and introduced slang, puns, and vulgar words into poems that also played with liturgical images. In a letter, he described these poems as "psychology in the form of dream," and they contain free associations of words and sudden juxtapositions of sublime and tawdry images. These poems were written after Laforgue had immersed himself in the philosophy of Eduard von Hartmann, whose emphasis on the unconscious profoundly shaped the poet's definition of identity. The conflicting voices and shifting tones within Laforgue's poetry reflect his belief in the multiple selves that coexist in any personality. Consequently, his narrative verse seems to leap between dream states and waking; among past, present, and future experiences; and from unquestioning sympathy to biting mockery, while continuing to portray one persona. Publishing delays kept these poems from appearing until 1885, but, when *Les Complaintes* finally appeared, the volume was enthusiastically reviewed.

Les Complaintes

Les Complaintes consists of two preliminary poems and fifty laments titled "Complainte de . . ."—with the titles playing upon the subjective-objective ambiguity of the genitive. The ambiguous titles reflect the multiple voices speaking within these dramatic poems and also the poems' themes. For example, "Complainte de Lord Pierrot" is a divided interior monologue spoken by Pierrot, and his lament also defines his identity; "Complainte du soir des comices agricoles" is set during the night of the country fair and may also be heard as the lament of that night; "Complainte des pianos qu'on entend dans les quartiers aisés" is both a lament of a man walking in well-to-do neighborhoods, who hears and is aroused by the sounds of girls' piano practice, and an imaginary dialogue between the man and the pianos concerning the girls' inarticulate, romantic illusions, and their sexuality.

In "Complainte de Lord Pierrot," the individual is divided in time and in space, with Pierrot singing a self-mocking version of the ballad "Au clair de la lune," then commenting in rhymed couplets on his sexual timidity and inexperience, then in irregularly rhymed ten-syllable lines imagining himself under the influence of Venus, dressed as a swan, boldly coupling with Leda, then abruptly shifting to a mocking couplet, "—Tout cela vous honore,/ Lord Pierrot, mais encore?" ("All that pays you tribute,/ Lord Pierrot, but what next?"), which becomes a two-line refrain as it is repeated later in the poem. Similarly, in "Complainte des pianos qu'on entend dans les quartiers aisés," the lonely speaker meditates on desirable young girls who provoke his sexual longing, but a two-line refrain, echoing a popular song, seems to tease and mock him: "Tu t'en vas et tu nous quittes,/ Tu nous quitt's et tu t'en vas!" ("You depart and you leave us/ You leave us and you depart!"). As readers familiar with "The Love Song of J. Alfred Prufrock" will recognize, Eliot adopted Laforgue's device, the ironic couplet refrain, in his lines rhyming "come and go" with "Michelangelo."

Just as Pierrot's various moods are expressed in different verse forms, so the sexual longing, the self-doubting mockery, the erotic curiosity, and the contemptuous cynicism of a lonely man are represented in the shifting forms of "Complainte des pianos qu'on entend dans les quartiers aisés," in which the syllabic length of the lines changes with each stanza. The basic group of four verse forms, recurring five times in the same order, comprises a quatrain of irregular Alexandrines rhymed *abab*, followed by a rhymed couplet of seven-syllable lines, followed by a rhymed couplet of four-syllable lines, and concluded by a quatrain of seven-syllable lines rhymed *abab*, the first two lines being some version of the refrain, "Tu t'en vas et tu nous laisses,/ Tu nous laiss's et tu t'en vas." Although these shifts create the impression, on a first reading, of the free-flowing and disparate lines of thought within the lonely man's mind, the larger formal pattern is quite elaborate. The poem seems a patchwork of quatrains and couplets, in which the significant pattern of the whole shifts as one focuses on different combinations of the parts. Are the girls singing to the man? Is he imagining their mockery? The deliberate ambiguity reflects the psychological complexity of Laforgue's portrait and also the inevitability of change: from innocence to experience, from the sublimity of imaginary voyeurism to the vulgar reality of physical sexuality, from spiritual eroticism to the ordinary, routine materialism of life—embodied in the ludicrous exclamations on the month, the underclothes, and the routine meal of the final line: "Ô mois, ô linges, ô repas!"

L'IMITATION DE NOTRE-DAME LA LUNE

The twenty-two poems for *L'Imitation de Notre-Dame la lune* were written at lightning speed, in six weeks of 1885, and dedicated to Laforgue's friend Kahn and to Salammbô, Flaubert's fictional pagan priestess. These litanies in praise of the moon ridicule the excessive zeal and overstated piety that characterize both Salammbô's behavior and most public professions of idolatrous worship. Utilizing the literary conventions associating the moon and the cultural archetype "woman," Laforgue mocks the lunatic lover who throws himself at the feet of the woman ("aux pieds de la femme," in the poem "Guitare"), and his obsessive myth defining woman as mysterious, cruel, changeable, and purely sensual is exposed in the allusions to Delilah, Eve, the Sphinx, and La Joconde (the Mona Lisa).

The eminent lunologist in *L'Imitation de Notre-Dame la lune* is Pierrot, whose ancestor is Pagliacco, of the commedia dell'arte, but who, in the French tradition, became fused with Harlequin. The Pierrot figure in Laforgue's poetry has contradictory characteristics: He is both a disappointed lover, melancholy and vulnerable, and a deceiving lover, frivolous and cynical. In either mode, Pierrot avoids the entangling responsibilities of love. This clown, in whiteface, with his long skinny neck, dilated eyes, reddened mouth, and black skullcap, both longs for a woman and fears passion. He closely resembles Eliot's Prufrock.

DES FLEURS DE BONNE VOLONTÉ

Des fleurs de bonne volonté is, in part, a response to Charles Baudelaire's *Les Fleurs du mal* (1857, 1861, 1868; *Flowers of Evil*, 1909). Written in 1886, these fifty-six poems reflect Laforgue's fascination with Hamlet's indecisiveness. Throughout these poems, he sprinkled epigraphs from Hamlet's and Ophelia's verbal duels, and his persona agonizes over his own inability to marry. Like Hamlet, this character cannot allow himself to trust a woman. Unlike Baudelaire, who treats the infidelity of woman as a cosmic truth, Laforgue focuses on the psychology of the lover whose fear of betrayal paralyzes him. Like Jaques in William Shakespeare's *As You Like It* (pr. c. 1599-1600), this character's cynicism makes him miserable. His assertion in "Célibat, célibat, tout n'est que célibat" that human history is the history of one unmarried man at first seems ridiculous, a product of his obsession, but one may read the dramatic situation of these poems, the prolonged hesitation before risking a commitment, as an extended metaphor for human history.

Twelve different poems in this collection bear the title "Dimanches" (Sundays), and each portrays a profoundly melancholic state of mind; images of rain, gray skies, and the haunting refrain of a piano recur throughout. As Laforgue dissects ennui in these Impressionistic poems, it is self-generated and circles from dissatisfaction to longing for release, to fearing change, to resigning oneself to the misery of inaction.

"Dimanches" is representative. It consists of four stanzas, with the second and the fourth in parentheses. The first, invoking autumn, associates the fall of leaves with death and love's suffering; the second, replying parenthetically, pleads that the speaker can believe in himself only in moments when he is lost; the third raises the possibility of marriage; and the fourth replies with a hypothesis—what if he could believe in himself and then marry?—followed by a renunciation expressed in a self-wounding comparison: "C'est Galatée aveuglant Pygmalion!" (it is Galatea blinding Pygmalion!). Laforgue's use of myth here suggests that the artist, by dedicating himself to the abstract ideal of incorruptible beauty, comes to be transfixed by his own artifice; similarly, the woman, imprisoned in the statuesque role of perfect physical beauty, becomes a seductress as she embraces the one who created that role. The circular dialogue this speaker conducts with himself imprisons him in his own unhappiness.

When Laforgue decided to marry, he decided not to publish *Des fleurs de bonne volonté*, but he did rework several of the poems into his new poems in free verse. Laforgue's final poems develop his earlier themes with greater technical and psychological sophistication.

LES DERNIERS VERS DE JULES LAFORGUE

The twelve free-verse poems of *Les Derniers Vers de Jules Laforgue* cohere as twelve movements of one long symphony might; their interrelated themes and recapitulated forms reward close reading extended to the structure of the whole. Laforgue's extraordinary technical and thematic control reveals itself in the illusion of free-flowing lines, which, although irregular in length and grouped in no conventional stanzas, are linked by careful alliteration, internal harmonies, and end rhymes. The lines are grouped thematically, developing a mood, or symbol, or idea, in verse paragraphs, thus creating a verbal image of the memories, free associations, recurrent dreams, and self-conscious observations that compose an individual's interior universe.

Laforgue again treats the theme of an overly sensitive man, agonizing about the extent and the limits of his self-knowledge, who seeks release in a loving companion, but, associating sexuality with death, despairs of love. The personal tragedy, finally, is given broad cultural significance by Laforgue's allusions to historical events, to literary antecedents, to musical revolutions, to paintings, and to powerful myths. These poems, like Impressionist paintings, take into account the sensibility of the viewer and appeal to the imagination through associated sensual memories. Unlike Mallarmé, Laforgue does not invoke the poet as sole symbol for humankind; moreover, the ivory tower of abstract thought and artifice does not confine Laforgue's persona, whose feelings and sensual impressions reflect factory smoke as well as fog, spittle as well as the sun's blinding white disk, the pettiness of objects consumed daily as well as the tragic grandeur of human mortality glimpsed in a sunset or in the coming of winter.

"L'Hiver qui vient," the first poem of the collection, illustrates the broader references and more radical techniques. Laforgue breaks poetic convention with his first line: "Blocus sentimental! Messageries du Levant!" ("emotional blockade! Levantine carrier ships!"). The line nullifies syntax by exclamation and alludes by echo to the glory and grim cost of the Napoleonic War's Continental System (known as the "blocus continental") and the eastern packet ships running the blockade. Neither national history nor seasonal change is the subject; rather, both are employed as correlatives of the persona's mood, a complex mixture of self-indulgent pity, rage against frustration, and ironic mockery. Facing the coming of winter yet again, the persona recalls associated feelings, images, and events: a child's loneliness at the *lycée*, the ennui of rainy Sundays, the end of a love affair, the suffering of soldiers far from home, the end of a foxhunt, each day's death of the sun, and the misery of urban life. From the music of Richard Wagner, Laforgue had learned to interweave distinctive themes representing complex passions. The weeping and sighing of autumnal rain and wind, the miserable coughing of a consumptive, the sad tones of hunting horns (imitated in "Ton ton, ton taine, ton ton!") resound in the poem, evoking compassion for the cornered creature, nostalgia for a lost social order, and the longing for an unattainable happiness. Laforgue's aim in these musical, free-verse poems may be understood in his last line of "L'Hiver qui vient": "J'essaierai en choeur d'en donner la note" ("I will try, in this choir, to give it its note").

Perceiving the human situation as essentially hopeless and feeling the tragic disparity between glorious aspirations and sordid or merely ordinary lives, Laforgue nevertheless rejects the Romantic poet's uncontrolled sentimentalism, undercutting self-pity by vulgar language, tawdry details, and the wry commentary of a rhymed couplet. His characteristic fusion of sensitivity and ironic distance, his representation of divided psychological states, his masterful exploitation of free verse to evoke shifting moods and associated ideas, his consciously comic treatment of serious subjects, and his playful re-creation of language mark Laforgue as one of the first modernist poets.

Other major works

LONG FICTION: *Stéphane Vassiliew*, 1946.

SHORT FICTION: *Moralités légendaires*, 1887 (*Six Moral Tales from Jules Laforgue*, 1928).

PLAYS: *Le Concile féerique*, pb. 1886; *Pierrot fumiste*, pb. 1892.

NONFICTION: *Berlin: La Cour et la ville*, 1922 (*Berlin: The City and the Court*, 1996); *Lettres à un ami, 1880-1886*, 1941.

Bibliography

Arkell, David. *Looking for Laforgue: An Informal Biography*. New York: Persea Books, 1979. A biographical study of Laforgue with a bibliography and index.

Dale, Peter, trans. Introduction to *Poems of Jules Laforgue*. London: Anvil Press Poetry, 2001. Dale's twenty-page introduction provides a solid overview of the poet, his body of work, and the history of the texts. This bilingual English-French edition also offers notes on the text, a brief bibliography, and indexes of both French and English titles.

Franklin, Ursula. *Exiles and Ironists: Essays on the Kinship of Heine and Laforgue*. New York: Peter Lang, 1988. Critical analysis considering the influence of Heinrich Heine on Laforgue's work. Includes a bibliography.

Holmes, Anne. "'De Nouveaux Rhythmes': The Free Verse of Laforgue's 'Solo de Lune.'" *French Studies* 62, no. 2 (April, 2008): 162. Holmes argues that Larforgue's interest in music influenced the structure and detail of his free verse.

_____. *Jules LaForgue and Poetic Innovation*. New York: Oxford University Press, 1993. A critical analysis focusing on Laforgue's innovations in technique. Includes bibliographical references and index.

Howe, Elisabeth A. *Stages of Self: The Dramatic Monologues of Laforgue, Valéry, and Mallarmé*. Athens: Ohio University Press, 1990. A study of the representations of the self in three nineteenth century French poets. Includes bibliographic references and an index.

Ramsey, Warren, ed. *Jules Laforgue: Essays on a Poet's Life and Work*. Carbondale: Southern Illinois University Press, 1969. A collection of critical and biographical essays with bibliographic references.

Watson, Lawrence J. *Jules Laforgue: Poet of His Age*. Rev. ed. Mahwah, N.J.: Ramapo College of New Jersey, 1980. A short introduction to Laforgue and his work.

Judith L. Johnston

ALPHONSE DE LAMARTINE

Born: Mâcon, France; October 21, 1790
Died: Paris, France; February 28, 1869

PRINCIPAL POETRY
Méditations poétiques, 1820 (*Poetical Meditations*, 1839)
La Mort de Socrate, 1823 (*The Death of Socrates*, 1829)
Nouvelles méditations poétiques, 1823
Chant du sacre, 1825
Le Dernier Chant du pèleringe d'Harold, 1825 (*The Last Canto of Childe Harold's Pilgrimage*, 1827)
Harmonies poétiques et religieuses, 1830
Œuvres complètes, 1834
Jocelyn, 1836 (English translation, 1837)
La Chute d'un ange, 1838
Recueillements poétiques, 1839
Œuvres poétiques complètes, 1963

OTHER LITERARY FORMS

The attempts at drama of Alphonse de Lamartine (lah-mahr-TEEN) are poor, often embarrassing, imitations of the works of Jean Racine, Pierre Corneille, and Voltaire, as well as William Shakespeare. Lamartine was somewhat more successful in the realm of prose fiction. He wrote two semiautobiographical novels, *Graziella* (1849; English translation, 1871) and *Raphaël* (1849; English translation, 1849); the former was the more popular, while the latter is the better of the two. *Raphaël*, which is based on the poet's love affair with Julie Charles, has been criticized as a novel that was outmoded even in its time, as well as being excessively sentimental. Certainly, *Raphaël* bears the imprint of Jean-Jacques Rousseau's *La Nouvelle Héloïse* (1761; *Julia, or the New Eloisa*, 1773) but it is nevertheless an impressive treatment of Lamartine's favorite themes: religion, love, politics, and nature.

In the course of a long political career, Lamartine delivered some exceptionally eloquent and often politically perspicacious speeches before the French Chamber of Deputies. On the eve of the February Revolution of 1848, he published in eight volumes a fearless glorification of the French Revolution, *Histoire des Girondins* (1847; *History of the Girondists*, 1847-1848). While not a historian's history, it offers such a colorful and sweeping vision of a period that in many ways it is really a historical novel in the guise of nonfiction. Among many other works, Lamartine also wrote popular histories of the 1848 Revolution in France, the Restoration, Turkey, and Russia.

Achievements

The critic Henri Peyre has observed that among the great French Romantics, Alphonse de Lamartine demonstrated "the keenest political insight." His work in politics was as important as the politics in his works, but his formal, aesthetic accomplishments in poetry were strong, too. He made his first and his most lasting mark in poetry with *Poetical Meditations*. This collection, which enjoyed tremendous success with the readers of its day, has been hailed as the first masterpiece of the Romantic movement in French poetry. Lamartine, seen by his contemporaries as an innovator, is often condemned by modern critics for his neoclassical diction, for his rhetorical flourishes, and for his sentimentalism. If one takes Lamartine's poetry on its own terms, however, and particularly if one appreciates its musical prosody, it will be clear why a handful of his poems have a permanent place in anthologies of French literature.

Biography

Alphonse de Lamartine's life can be schematized as a pattern that shifts among four points: political commitments, a sentimental intermixture of women and natural scenery, a personalized and heretical form of Catholicism, and a semiautobiographical approach to poetry. Each, either through circumstance or through the poet's whims, was allowed periodically to reach an ascendancy over the others and to dominate his time and energy. To give emphasis to one over the other is to understand none of them; all must be considered in due course. If one is to understand Lamartine's heavily autobiographical poetry, one must consider his politics, his religion, and his love of women and nature.

Given his family and the events of his early years, it is no surprise that the adult Lamartine was to demonstrate an active interest in politics—although the leftward direction of that interest could hardly have been predicted. On October 21, 1790, in the opening years of the French Revolution, Lamartine was born into a gentry family that was staunchly Royalist. His father was imprisoned for a long while during the Terror but was not executed. Lamartine's mother, a deeply religious woman who combined the ideas of Rousseau with Catholicism, gave Lamartine his early religious training and had a deep influence on him. At the Jesuit college at Belley, Lamartine again was exposed to liberal Catholic attitudes as well as to a broad range of world literature. It is a tribute to Lamartine's capacity for development that throughout his life he carried this liberalism in religion, as well as in politics, to points just short of radicalism, so much so that by old age he had evolved far beyond the paradigms of his youth.

An early and deep interest in nature and in love was to initiate Lamartine's metamorphosis. In 1811 and 1812, he visited Italy, which, as in the case of Johann Wolfgang von Goethe several decades before, proved a great impetus to Lamartine's development as a poet. An affair with an Italian cigar maker of loose morals named Antoniella (the probable model for Graziella) had the effect of loosening those of the poet. The scenery, particularly that of the Bay of Naples, left a strong impression on several of his lyrics.

The real turning point, however, came during the autumn of 1816. While convalescing at a fashionable bath in Savoy, Lamartine met Charles, who had all the requisite qualities for attracting the affections of a romantic poet: She was beautiful, consumptive, and married. They carried on an affair amid splendid alpine scenery, which helped to set the tone of pantheism in Lamartine's religious development. In spite of periodic separations, an amorous but perhaps unconsummated relationship continued until Charles finally died of tuberculosis in December, 1817. This affair left a permanent mark on Lamartine. Other affairs and even his marriage in 1820 to Marianne Birch, a wealthy Englishwoman, had no effect on his feelings for Charles and did not disperse the aura of melancholy that her death had imposed on him. Indeed, two further sorrows resulted from his marriage: the deaths of a son and a daughter.

Lamartine's career in the Chamber of Deputies, the elective legislative body of France during the first half of the nineteenth century and in the governments of the 1848 Revolution and the Second Republic is important historically and biographically. A consideration of this career is crucial to an understanding of Lamartine's political poetry. Charles-Maurice de Talleyrand-Périgord said of Lamartine that he had the acumen to penetrate to the heart of his country. He foresaw the dangers of military dictatorships—one of which was soon to materialize under Napoleon III. Lamartine also read an important message in the unsuccessful workers' riots in Lyons and in Paris (1831-1832). He foresaw the necessity for the political education of the working class, who he believed would initiate all future revolutions. (The events of 1848 and 1878 proved him, in great part, correct.)

Above all, Lamartine demonstrated an ability to adapt to a changing political climate—so much so that he was often a bit ahead of his time. Lamartine discovered to his sorrow that flexibility, no matter how logical, can be a fatal flaw in politics. What through twentieth century hindsight seems a sincere, if gradual, move from bourgeois liberalism to a moderately leftist stance seemed to his contemporaries to be inconsistency. Lamartine's sorrow was to have been a statesman in a time of political conservatives and opportunists, the worst and most formidable among whom was Napoleon III. Lamartine could easily have set himself up as a dictator, thereby gaining the support of the Right, but he decided instead to share his power as the head of the 1848 Provisional Government with the leader of the Left, A. A. Ledru-Rollin; this decision lost him the support of the wealthy ruling class.

Lamartine ran unsuccessfully for public office in 1848. Much of the remainder of his life was spent writing popular histories, biographies, and similar works to produce needed income. Lamartine's wife died in 1863; in 1867, the government of Napoleon III, acknowledging the relative poverty of the former statesman, granted Lamartine a substantial sum. Lamartine died in Paris on February 28, 1869.

Analysis

Alphonse de Lamartine's poetry developed, as did everything in his life, by degrees, with no marked departures from the past. Rarely have life and art been so closely intertwined. All his passions became the stuff of his art, to be woven into complex patterns of alliteration and assonance. Perhaps he created only a handful of enduring works, but few poets can claim to have done more.

Lamartine's ability to accept and assimilate change as a Christian, a politician, and a poet demonstrates, more than any of his other qualities, his Romantic worldview. He did not merely accept nineteenth century historicism; he lived it. Change is the dominant theme of his poetry.

Poetical Meditations

It is no surprise, then, that Lamartine's first collection of poems had a profound effect on the evolution of French poetry. Indeed, *Poetical Meditations* demonstrates the same gradual development that characterized Lamartine the statesman. The work at the time seemed a radical departure from the neoclassical sensibility that continued to dominate French poetry under the directorate, the empire, and the early Restoration—indeed, it seemed so radical a departure that it was refused by the publisher to whom Lamartine first submitted it in 1817. What was acceptable in the prose of Vicomte François-René de Chateaubriand was, until 1820, not palatable in the more formalized realm of poetry. Lamartine took the first, appropriately cautious, step.

"The Lake"

The most famous and enduring work of this collection is "Le Lac" ("The Lake"); this lyric is also Lamartine's most frequently anthologized poem. The essential theme of the poem, mutability in the light of the permanence of nature, is introduced in the first stanza. Here, the natural world is treated metaphorically—"eternal night," "time's sea"—to suggest the uncertainty of human fate in the eternal flux. In short, the first stanza maintains a tradition that is at least as old as the first century Greek critic Longinus. Beginning with the second stanza, however, a new, albeit tentative, tone is struck. Natural objects, ceasing to be metaphors, have an existence all their own and are conveyed to the reader with a directness that had not been heard in French poetry for a long time. Although nature in Lamartine certainly lacks the concrete immediacy that it had already found in the poetry of William Wordsworth or Goethe, the lake, addressed as it is by the persona, is a natural object and not an imaginary shepherdess or an actual patron of the poet; thus, a new directness is gained. Stanzas 2 and 3 picture a time when the persona sat by an alpine lake with his beloved—a figure not individualized in the poem but based on Charles.

The fourth stanza deals with a third Wordsworthian "spot in time": The persona recalls a night when Charles and he were rowing on the lake. This complex layering of three events is characteristic of Lamartine's obsession with time. Stanza 5 introduces the motif of a nature sympathetically resonant with human relations. The persona's beloved begins to speak, causing the shore to be spellbound and drawing the attention of the waves. The beloved's reply in stanzas 6 through 9 is still in the eighteenth century tradition; personified time is now addressed far more conventionally than in the persona's earlier address to the lake. Stanza 9 is a twofold culmination of the beloved's address. First, it gives clear expression to the carpe diem theme to which it has all been leading: "So let us love, so let us love! let us hasten, let us enjoy the fleeting hour" ("Aimons donc, aimons donc! de l'heure fugitive,/ Hâtonsnous, jouissons!"). Second, the stanza returns to the opening image of the lyric, time as an expanse of water without a harbor: "Man has no harbor, time has no shore:/ It flows and we pass on."

In stanza 10, "jealous time" is addressed by the persona, who asks how time can take away the same "moments of intoxication" that it gives. In the last four stanzas, the persona addresses the "lake! mute rocks, grottos! dark forest!" asking them to keep alive the memory of the young couple's night on the lake. With measured rhythms, the poet appeals to all the different sounds of nature, "everything that is heard, seen, or breathed,/ Let all say: 'They loved!'" This musical voice of nature is a poetic credo that Lamartine repeats often in his poetry; the limpid rhythm and assonance that embody this natural music account for the great popularity of the poem.

"THE VALLEY"

A quick glance at another poem in the collection, "Le Vallon" ("The Valley"), indicates the unity of the *Poetical Meditations*. The theme and many of the motifs of "The Lake" are also found in "The Valley." Here, the persona again laments the brevity of life's pleasures, but the added motif of the anonymity of death sounds a new note. The waves and murmuring of the lake are replaced by those of two hidden streams, which meet to form one. The streams flow from their respective sources only to lose their individual identities by merging with each other. These natural images become metaphors for the persona's lost youth: "The source of my days like the streams has flowed away,/ It has passed without a sound, without a name, and without any hope of return."

In "The Valley," the poet employs one of his favorite metaphors: the capacity of sounds in nature to lull the senses and to heal hurts. These effects he sought, often with great success, in his lyrics: The persona says that, "Like an infant rocked by a simple chant,/ My soul is assuaged by the murmur of the waters" ("Comme un enfant bercé par un chant monotone,/ Mon âme s'assoupit au murmure des eaux"). The music of these lines, with their *n* and *m* sounds, creates precisely the soothing effect that they describe. The water of the brooks and other images taken from nature are used to symbolize the transience of human life; paradoxically, for the poet, nature has the ability to console humans because, although subject to change in its parts, it is permanent in its totality: "While everything changes for you, nature is the same." Behind nature is the quintessential permanence of God. For Lamartine, there is no consolation in change as manifested in natural phenomena such as water except in the thought that it is a part of some greater mystical whole.

Nouvelles méditations poétiques

It is both the strength and the weakness of *Nouvelles méditations poétiques* that Lamartine continues to explore the themes of the *Poetical Meditations*. "Tristesse" (sorrow) is a poem that draws on Lamartine's experiences in Naples with Antoniella. As he often does in this volume, the poet draws on images found in the earlier collection. For example, the "laughing slopes" of "The Lake" appear again in "Tristesse." The lake is now a bay, but it is still an expanse of water that provides a place for lovers to listen "to the gentle noise of the waves or the murmuring wind" ("Au doux bruit de la vague ou du vent qui murmure"); indeed, any hasty glance at Lamartine's poetry will demonstrate the poet's predilection for the word *murmure*—whether it is the murmur of the waves, wind, or foliage. The persona of "Tristesse," as the title implies, suffers in a state of melancholy and nostalgia for a happy past that is lost, never to return. Life and death are joined, a final paradox in which the poet wishes "to die in the place where he has tasted life." There are, however, some new elements in "Tristesse": There is a growing specificity both in the poet's description of the locus of Vergil's tomb and as he conveys his youthful passion with images of "enflamed Vesuvius once again arising from the bosom of the waves."

Harmonies poétiques et religieuses

Harmonies poétiques et religieuses reflects the concerns of Lamartine the political figure. Indeed, even the religious aspects of this work can best be understood in a political context, for the separation of church and state was a crucial issue in the politics of nineteenth century France. This relationship between politics and religion must be kept in mind if the reader of *Harmonies poétiques et religieuses* is to comprehend Lamartine's merging of Christianity with the secular historicism of eighteenth and nineteenth century France.

"Les Revolutions" (the revolutions) was first published in a review and later incorporated into *Harmonies poétiques et religieuses*. Inspired by the workers' uprisings in Paris and Lyon, which helped to provoke the turn left in Lamartine's politics, it demonstrates the concept of historical relativism that was to culminate in the works of Georg Wilhelm Friedrich Hegel, Charles Darwin, and Karl Marx. Lamartine shared a growing awareness that, in the evolution of social structures, whether religious or political, there are no absolute values. In this eloquent lyric, the poet expresses a genuine contempt for the backward-looking conservatism of the majority of his European contemporaries. He contrasts them metaphorically with the nomadic peoples of Arabia, who physically (if certainly not religiously or socially) packed up their belongings and passed on to new horizons. By contrast, the European conservatives are, as Lamartine tells them, "men petrified in [their] timid pride." Lamartine's preoccupation with change, previously applied to nature and to human relationships, is here applied to politics and religion; these human institutions are subject to the mutability that is part of a divine plan: "all things/ Change, fall, perish, flee, die, decompose" ("et toute chose/ Change, tombe, périt, fuit, meurt, se décompose") and all creation is subject to "divine evolutions."

Lamartine goes on, in a second section of "Les Revolutions," to say that the history of humankind is a course of changes, of rises and falls of empires: "All the course [of history] is marked out only/ By the debris of nations." The poet catalogs a variety of both religious and political forms that have been invented and discarded along the roadway of human history: "Thrones, altars, temples, porches, cultures, kingdoms, republics/ Are the powder covering the roadway." In this portion of the poem, Lamartine presents one of his comprehensive, universal visions of the history of Western civilization since ancient Egypt.

The final section of "Les Revolutions" gives perfect expression to Lamartine's conception of an evolutionary progression of human ethics and social structures—each valid only for a single day: "'Advance!' Humanity does not live by a single idea!/ Each night it extinguishes the candle that has guided it,/ it lights another from the eternal torch." Even religion evolves—even the sacred revelation of the Bible. Each generation reads its structures into the seemingly fixed text: "Page by page your epochs spell out the Gospel:/ Therein you have read but a single word, and you shall read a thousand;/ Therein your more venturesome children will read even more still!" God's revelation to humankind, for Lamartine, is not something fixed in time but is, rather, a dynamic, winged phenomenon: "In thunder and lightning your Word soars" ("Dans la foudre et l'éclair votre Verbe aussi vole"). Although many modern theologians share, in general outline at least, this notion of revelation, in Lamartine's day, it represented a clearly heretical conception of the relationship between humankind and God.

JOCELYN

According to Peyre, such a conception, which offers a new basis for Christianity, is also embodied in Lamartine's *Jocelyn*. The Church of Rome took such exception to the heretical nature of this work that it immediately placed it on the Index. *Jocelyn* is an epic work that was to be a part of an even larger, projected work, "The Epic of the Ages," never completed. A rather melodramatic narrative poem about a priest hiding in the Savoy Alps during the Terror, *Jocelyn* was nevertheless important in Lamartine's development, for in it he broke decisively with neoclassical norms of poetic diction, coloring his verse with real human speech.

LA CHUTE D'UN ANGE

Another work that was to form a part of "The Epic of the Ages," *La Chute d'un ange* (the fall of an angel) is little read today, but it contains an often anthologized passage,

"Chœur des cèdres du Liban" (chorus of the Cedars of Lebanon), in which the poet reiterates his theme of the passage of time.

The ageless cedars are symbols for the continuity of nature and the transience of humanity: They have stood since before the Flood; they provided the wood for the Ark; they have witnessed the passage of sacred and profane history in the Levantine. Holy men, philosophers, and poets come to do homage to these trees; Lamartine himself saw them on his voyage to the Orient. They are emblems of the creation, the making, the *poesis* that is nature itself—"the great vital chorus" ("le grand chœur végétal"). Nature is the inspiration for poetry: "And under our prophetic shadows/ They compose their most beautiful hymns out of the murmurs of our branches" ("Et sous nos ombres prophétiques/ Formeront leur plus beaux cantiques/ Des murmure de nos rameaux"). As Geoffrey Brereton has observed, this murmur of the cedars in the wind is an apt image for Lamartine's poetry, underlaid as it is with an all-important rhythm. The poet himself says that the trees roar "in glorious harmonies,/ Without articulated works, without precise language" ("en grandes harmonies/ Sans mots articulés, sans langues définies"). The emphasis on music over meaning that is found in Lamartine's most enduring lyrics foreshadows the verbal magic of Paul Verlaine and Stéphane Mallarmé.

OTHER MAJOR WORKS

LONG FICTION: *Graziella*, 1849 (English translation, 1871); *Raphaël*, 1849 (English translation, 1849); *Geneviève*, 1850 (English translation, 1850); *La Tailleur de pierres de Saint-Point*, 1851 (*The Stonesman of Saint-Point*, 1851).

PLAYS: *Toussaint Louverture*, pr., pb. 1850; *Saül*, pb. 1861; *Medée*, pb. 1873; *Zoraide*, pb. 1873.

NONFICTION: *Sur la politique rationelle*, 1831 (*The Polity of Reason*, 1848); *Voyage en Orient*, 1835 (*Travels in the East*, 1835); *Histoire des Girondins*, 1847 (*History of the Girondists*, 1847-1848); *Histoire de la révolution de 1848*, 1849 (*History of the French Revolution of 1848*, 1849); *Histoire de la Restauration*, 1851-1852 (*The History of the Restoration of Monarchy in France*, 1851-1853); *Histoire de la Turquie*, 1855; *Histoire des constituants*, 1855 (*History of the Constituent Assembly*, 1858); *Vie des grands hommes*, 1855-1856 (*Biographies and Portraits of Some Celebrated People*, 1866); *Correspondance inédite d'Alphonse de Lamartine*, 1994-1996 (2 volumes).

MISCELLANEOUS: *Œuvres complètes*, 1860-1866 (41 volumes).

BIBLIOGRAPHY

Barbin, Judith. "Liszt and Lamartine: Poetic and Religious Harmonies." *Comparatist: Journal of the Southern Comparative Literature Association* 16 (1992): 115-122. Compares religious elements and musicality in Lamartine's poems in his 1829 book with selected works by the great Polish Romantic composer Franz Liszt.

Betz, Dorothy M. "*Poetical Meditations*." In *Masterplots*, edited by Laurence W.

Mazzeno. 4th ed. Pasadena, Calif.: Salem Press, 2011. A plot summary and an indepth analysis of *Poetical Meditations*.

Birkett, Mary Ellen. *Lamartine and the Poetics of Landscape*. Lexington, Ky.: French Forum, 1982. Explores relationships between the representation of natural beauty in Romantic landscape painting and Lamartine's poetry. Examines the intimate connections between literature and the other arts that were so important during the Romantic period in France.

Bishop, Lloyd. "'Le Lac' as Exemplar of the Greater Romantic Lyric." *Romance Quarterly* 34, no. 4 (November, 1987): 403-413. This close reading of Lamartine's most famous poem explains how the poet's solitary meditation on the beauty of a lake reminds him of his deceased lover, with whom he often walked around the same lake. Argues that nature and death are important themes in Romantic lyric poetry.

Boutin, Aimeé. *Maternal Echoes: The Poetry of Marceline Desbordes-Valmore and Alphonse de Lamartine*. Newark: University of Delaware Press, 2001. Compares and contrasts the work of Desbordes-Valmore and Lamartine. Desbordes-Valmore published a similar work before Lamartine's *Poetical Meditations*, but her work did not receive the acclaim that Lamartine's did.

Fortescue, William. *Alphonse de Lamartine: A Political Biography*. New York: St. Martin's Press, 1983. Despite its title, this biography does not simply treat Lamartine's unsuccessful run for the French presidency and his opposition to the overthrow of the French Republic by Emperor Napoleon III in 1851. It also examines Lamartine's gradual evolution from a conservative Royalist to a fervent defender of democratic freedoms.

Lombard, Charles. *Lamartine*. New York: Twayne, 1973. Remains a clear introduction in English to Lamartine's lyric and epic poetry. Contains an annotated bibliography of important critical studies on the poetry.

Rodney Farnsworth

STÉPHANE MALLARMÉ

Born: Paris, France; March 18, 1842
Died: Valvins, France; September 9, 1898

PRINCIPAL POETRY
L'Après-midi d'un faune, 1876 (*The Afternoon of a Faun*, 1936)
Les Poésies de Stéphane Mallarmé, 1887
Un Coup de dés jamais n'abolira le hasard, 1897 (*A Dice-Throw*, 1958; also as *Dice Thrown Never Will Annul Chance*, 1965)
Igitur, 1925 (English translation, 1974)
Poems by Mallarmé, 1936 (Roger Fry, translator)
Herodias, 1940 (Clark Mills, translator)
Selected Poems, 1957
Les Noces d'Hérodiade, 1959
Pour un "Tombeau d'Anatole," 1961 (*A Tomb for Anatole*, 1983)
Poésies, 1970 (*The Poems*, 1977)
Collected Poems, 1994

OTHER LITERARY FORMS

Stéphane Mallarmé (mah-lahr-MAY) is known chiefly for his poetry. A selection from his numerous critical essays and reviews, including some important theoretical statements, was published in *Divagations* (1897; English translation, 2007). Following the example of Charles Baudelaire, Mallarmé translated Edgar Allan Poe. He also published an idiosyncratic introduction to English philology, *Petite Philologie à l'usage des classes et du monde: Les Mots anglais* (1878; little philology for classroom use and for society: English words). It should be noted that Mallarmé wrote a number of prose poems, treated by some critics as prose works. The best edition of Mallarmé's poetry and essays is the Pléiade *Œuvres complètes de Stéphane Mallarmé* (1945), prepared by Henri Mondor and G. Jean-Aubry, although it is not a complete collection.

ACHIEVEMENTS

Stéphane Mallarmé's work is both the culmination of French Romanticism and the harbinger of the more hermetic poetry of the twentieth century. His vision of poetry as a sacred art, created with considerable sacrifice by an elite, derives from the Romantic image of the poet as prophet, typical of Victor Hugo. Mallarmé's "pure poetry," without reference to history or to social reality and characterized by a dense and elliptical style, however, deliberately abandons the attempt of many Romantics to bring poetry closer to life and to make it a social force. Very early in his career, Mallarmé said that it was heresy to try to make poetry understandable to a large audience. He sought instead to give expression to a higher form of intellectual experience in a language that is suggestive and indirect. Mallarmé's disciples, notably Paul Valéry, used the term "symbolism" to describe the new poetry. Mallarmé exerted a great personal influence on the theories developed in modernist artistic circles through his Tuesday receptions in his apartment on the rue de Rome in Paris.

Biography

Stéphane Mallarmé was born Etienne Mallarmé into a middle-class Parisian family of government administrators. His mother died when he was five. He was taken in by his maternal grandparents, who placed him in a series of boarding schools from the time he was ten. This forcible separation from a family environment was particularly painful because it deprived him of the company of his only sibling, his sister, Maria, who was younger by two years. He continued to write to her until her death at the age of thirteen. This disappearance of mother and sister, both idealized figures strongly linked in Mallarmé's mind to the religious life, seems to have caused Mallarmé to abandon conventional religious beliefs and to seek in his adolescent poetry a way of preserving the memory of these beloved presences. At the same time, Mallarmé's active sexual life seems to have left him disappointed and perhaps guilty about physical pleasure.

In 1860, Mallarmé took a position with the French administration, then went to London in 1862 with a young German woman, Maria Gerhard, whom he married in 1863. At the end of that year, he took his first position as a teacher of English. His entire professional career consisted of a series of appointments in secondary schools, first in the provinces and then, after 1871, in Paris. He retired in 1894. During the 1870's, Mallarmé published translations, textbooks, a women's fashion magazine, and his own poetry.

His period of great celebrity began around 1884, when Paul Verlaine and Joris-Karl Huysmans acclaimed him in their own works. During the last fifteen years of his life, Mallarmé exercised enormous influence on the younger poets, who hailed him as the prophetic exemplar of Symbolism. Mallarmé himself did not seek honor or public attention. He left the publication of manifestos to his followers and preferred to devote his time to research for his oeuvre, his great "work," which he never finished. His poetic works, considerable as they are, did not live up to his ambition, although his manuscripts give evidence of intense labor.

Analysis

"Everything in the world exists to end up in a book," wrote Stéphane Mallarmé in 1895. It is this attitude toward reality and toward the importance of the book that makes Mallarmé the preeminent Symbolist poet. For him, reality exists only in the symbol, which, in poetry, is constructed out of language. This position, apparently influenced by Hegelian idealism, does not mean that poetry is necessarily about language—although a number of Mallarmé's poems are about language and poetry themselves—but rather that language provides the only systematic and rational framework, the only escape from randomness, in a world in which there is no sign of a personal God. Mallarmé's poetry is a kind of metaphysical poetry, in that it aspires to go beyond the physical reality of everyday life to uncover the mysterious world of a pure ideal that can exist nowhere except in the mind and in language.

Even though many of Mallarmé's poems seem at first to be completely obscure, in most cases careful reading will reveal that a kernel drawn from everyday life has been transformed into a spare, unsentimental, timeless formal variation (in the way that a composer makes a variation on a musical theme). The effect is neither an enshrinement of a particular moment, place, or picturesque character nor an appeal to emotional sympathy. It is still less a moral or political message. Instead, such poems invite the reader to experience the power of the mind and of language.

For Mallarmé, the most important experience is the experience of the poem itself, and if such a statement seems commonplace and even trite, it is because Mallarmé's influence has been so pervasive. For him, however, the experience of the poem was particularly concrete and precise, and he frequently wrote about acts and objects connected with writing and reading with a kind of religious awe. The word *livre* (book) and such kindred terms as *grimoire* (book of magic incantations) and *bouquin* (old book) have in his vocabulary an importance rarely found in other bodies of poetry except in religious texts, where "the book" is the sacred scripture explaining and justifying the world. Mallarmé attempted during his life to create a nonreligious scripture.

Most of his poems, however, are playful occasional pieces such as "Eventail de Madame Mallarmé" ("Madam Mallarmé's Fan"); brief poems written in honor of other artists, such as the "Hommage" to Richard Wagner and "Le Tombeau d'Edgar Poe" ("The Tomb of Edgar Poe"); erotic poetry based on elliptical sexual fantasy, such as *The Afternoon of a Faun* and "Victorieusement fui le suicide beau" ("The Beautiful Suicide Victoriously Escaped"); or the long series of poems lamenting the difficulty of escaping from the base material world and of writing the higher kind of poetry. The last category includes the well-known "L'Azur," sometimes called the "Swan Sonnet," "Les Fenêtres" ("The Windows"), and "Le Pître châtié" ("The Clown's Punishment"). Only the three longer poems, *Herodias, Igitur* (read to friends in unfinished form and published posthumously), and *Dice Thrown Never Will Annul Chance* (published in the magazine *Cosmopolis* in May, 1897, but not published in book form until 1914) give some idea of the form of Mallarmé's more ambitious projects.

There is nevertheless a stylistic and thematic coherence in Mallarmé's work, which proceeds by a kind of condensation and subtraction. The extremely difficult but logical grammar absorbs the reader in the enigmatic possibilities of meaning, thus fixing attention on the poem's language. Objects and persons named in the poems are described as absent or "abolished."

"ALL THE SOUL INDRAWN..."

A good way to begin with Mallarmé's poetry is to look at his brief poem "Toute l'âme résumée..." ("All the Soul Indrawn..."), which is a witty response to a survey on free verse. Mallarmé compares making poetry to smoking a cigar. The successive rings of smoke are "abolished" by those that follow, and the ash keeps falling away from the "bright kiss of fire." Poetry is not what is left behind, Mallarmé implies; it is rather the process itself, momentary but renewed. Because the word *âme* can mean both "soul" and, with some etymological delving, "breath," and *résumée* means both "summed up" and "drawn in," Mallarmé has put into play a metaphor for the content of poetry that eludes the traditional distinction between form and content, vehicle and tenor. The breath is what permits the cigar to keep burning; it is also the proof that one is alive. Yet this thing, which is so essential to smoking and to life, is empty. Similarly, the burning tip of the cigar, the thing showing that the cigar is "alive," is the fire that can survive only by emptying itself of the ash. Like smoking, Mallarmé suggests, poetry should be regarded as pure activity, without product and without connection with any external reality. After making this comparison explicit in the third quatrain, which advises writers to exclude vile reality, Mallarmé concludes with a distich that pointedly inverts the usual literary and rhetorical values of his day: "A too precise meaning scratches out/ Your vague literature." The more definite and specific the reference a poem makes to reality, the less it can be considered precisely literary.

"MY OLD BOOKS CLOSED AT THE NAME OF PAPHOS"

Another celebrated poem centered on the powers of literature, considered this time from the point of view of the reader, is "Mes bouquins refermés sur le nom de Paphos" ("My Old Books Closed at the Name of Paphos"). The speaker of the poem tells of closing his book and looking out on a snowy landscape where he imagines a Mediterranean scene. There is a parallel between the foam of the sea splashing against a ruin in the first quatrain and the white snow presented as part of the reader's material reality in the second quatrain. The speaker makes clear, however, that he will not wail a funereal lament (*nénie*) if the snowy reality does not coincide with his imagined seascape. The tercets make clear why the speaker so calmly accepts the divorce of dream from reality. The absence of things, which one notices because literature draws one's attention to such lacunae, is presented as a superior value. Mallarmé's negative approach, his preference for hollowing out a dream world by "abolishing" elements of the everyday world, appears in the speaker's claim: "My hunger, which is satisfied here by no fruits/ Finds in their learned lack an equal savor." To be satisfied by "no fruits" is not the same as being unsatisfied. It is a state in which the learned vision imposes a preference for the dream.

The second tercet goes even further, recalling that absence is not merely in the speaker's present world but in the scene imagined as well. Apparently addressing a lover, he confesses: "I think longer, perhaps desperately,/ Of the other, with the seared breast of an ancient Amazon." The scene is not only absent but also organized around an absence, the missing breast of one of the legendary warrior-women who founded the city of Paphos. Even these two absences are not all one can find here. The adverb translated as "desperately" or "distractedly" to describe the speaker's preoccupation with the Amazon is *éperdument*, which contains the word *perdu* (lost). The speaker, as reader, is thus also in some way lost to the everyday world and to ordinary love.

"Her Pure Fingernails on High Offering Their Onyx"

The procedure of creating a scene by "abolishing" is taken closer to Mallarmé's project of a great magical work in the sonnet "Ses purs ongles trés haut dédiant leur onyx" ("Her Pure Fingernails on High Offering Their Onyx"), known as the "Sonnet in yx" because of its unusual rhymes. This sonnet apparently describes a deserted parlor belonging to a magician, the "Master," who has gone to get tears in the underworld from the river Styx. The vessel the Master will use is a *ptyx*. This is a word that has a meaning in Greek but none in French. Mallarmé may have meant it to remain meaningless, for the *ptyx* is called "this unique object of which Nothingness is proud." Furthermore, the *ptyx* is designated in the poem only as an absence: "in the empty parlor: no ptyx,/ Abolished trinket of sonorous inanity."

Scholars have studied the problem of the *ptyx* at length with reference to its ancient meanings, ranging from "book" to "seashell." As one scholar has noted, however, the more meanings that are proposed for the word, the less it actually signifies. It has become an empty form that traps the reader into deep and repeated investigations of semantic, phonetic, and etymological networks in the sonnet in the hope of finding some meaning. This sonnet certainly follows the precepts of "All the Soul Indrawn . . ." in avoiding a "too precise sense." It also exemplifies the kind of dream to which Mallarmé wanted to lead his readers. Although psychoanalytic readings of Mallarmé have been among the most interesting, Mallarmé himself did not use the word *rêve* (dream) to designate a person's unconscious. For Mallarmé, "dream" suggested both the aspiration to a world of pure thought without material limitation (this is particularly clear in "The Windows") and the realm in which language unfolds in all its ambiguity. The Master's absence from this parlor could be interpreted as the author's desire to absent himself from the scene within which the reader can experience the possibilities of language, including the possibility that the most important words exist anagrammatically within the evident ones.

Herodias

Of Mallarmé's longer poems, those that seem to be part of his "great work," only *Herodias* and *Dice Thrown Never Will Annul Chance* gave the public some idea of the synthesis of poetic research of which he often spoke. Those works and the posthumous publications are all extremely difficult to interpret, but they seem to have at their core a struggle between the magic of the poetic symbol and the Nothingness (*le Néant*) that, for Mallarmé, constituted the universe. Because he rejected the physically present world for an ideal one and yet did not believe in religious spirituality, the magic of the great work would be to create a place where the ideal could exist. The language of the great work would have to be a special one, not the "unrefined and immediate" but the "essential" word free from the "chance" of usage, as he wrote in a preface to a work by René Ghil.

Herodias, a verse drama with little of the apparatus of a theater script, unites the themes of incantation, abolition, cerebral eroticism, and the preservation of the memory of the beloved dead. In most editions of Mallarmé, *Herodias* is divided into an "overture," in which the nurse of Princess Herodias describes the imaginary setting; a "scene," consisting of a dialogue between Herodias and her nurse; and a "canticle," in which the voice of John the Baptist sings at the moment of his decapitation. In the overture, the palace is evoked as empty and abandoned, like the parlor of the "Sonnet in yx." The king is long absent, the basin deserted by its swan, the sun rising red for the last time.

Even if one could create such a setting on the stage, the words of the overture make it clear that the real stage for these words is in the mind. The nurse, for example, speaks of a voice that evokes the past and then asks, "Is it my voice ready for the incantation?" If the speaker responsible for the exposition is not sure whether she has spoken, this suggests that she has merely thought the words. Moreover, the words that her voice may be ready to pronounce are an evocation of the past. Future and past thus join to create a situation in which imminent doom, nostalgia, and uncertainty about time coexist in a paradoxical equilibrium. The abstract quality of this setting is further emphasized by such metaphors as "the bed with pages of velum." The princess's bed is thus characterized as entirely chaste, while the whole drama takes on the aura of something entirely within a book.

In "Scene," the nurse tries to persuade Herodias to satisfy her awakening sexuality, while the princess insists that she loves the "horror" of being a virgin and that she cannot tolerate any touch. In place of touch, sight becomes the only sense through which Herodias can open herself to sexuality or even to consciousness. The scene is full of mirrors, described as cold and distant like "water frozen from boredom." All the mirrors serve to reflect the princess's image, excluding the menacing outside world. In the last lines, Herodias, at the departure of the nurse, announces that she is waiting for an unknown thing and that she has lied to her nurse about her voluntary solitude.

The connection between "Scene" and "Canticle," which follows it, is not clear, although the fragments edited by Gardner Davies in *Les Noces d'Hérodiade* permit some conjectures. Several critics have advanced the idea that John the Baptist has seen Heriodas, who then feels that only his death can restore her sense of intactness. The saint is what the fragment calls the "somber pretext" for the princess's full achievement of self-consciousness. His crime is to be different from a mirror, which offers a neutral image without judgment. According to "Canticle," there is a tension between the ideal and the physical in John as well, and this tension is released by the decapitation, in which the saint sees salvation. Mallarmé, however, avoids religious statement by concluding with the word *salut*, which can mean both "salvation" and "salute." The word describes both the movement of the head as it follows its trajectory up and then down and the hope expressed by baptism. In the unfinished version of this drama, Herodias seems to have captured the dying glance of John and to consider herself united to the prophet in a wedding that is both sexual and ideal. She addresses the head, saying "I reason for you, head, not about you."

Herodias's hope to snatch consciousness from death was apparently the long-term result of Mal larmé's adolescent poetic meditations on death. It is also a hope that appears in the fragmentary *A Tomb for Anatole* (edited by Jean-Pierre Richard), in which the poet tried to re-create the life of his dead son through imagination. In a passage similar to that in which Herodias declares that she will think for John, Mallarmé tells his dead son that the poet will *be* the son hereafter. The question of the apparent futility of such a project is addressed by two other long poems by Mallarmé, *Igitur* and *Dice Thrown Never Will Annul Chance*.

IGITUR

Igitur, a prose poem written between 1867 and 1870 and left unfinished at Mallarmé's death, was edited by the scholar Edmond Bonniot, the poet's son-in-law, who discovered the manuscript in 1900. The poem relates the adventures of Igitur, a prince haunted by a supreme "Idea" and by the destiny imposed by his race, which has somehow projected Igitur outside time. The next-to-last section is titled "A Roll of Dice" and takes place in the family tomb. There, Igitur confronts the problem of the relationship among personal action, necessity, and chance. Understanding that action is absurd except as a return to infinity, which is a form of the pure absolute, he throws the dice before laying himself on the ashes of his ancestors. This metaphysical hero, described by critics as a Hamlet stripped of psychology, confronts the problems of individual time-bound existence (versus a timeless ideal) and of the tradition of a nation or race. This can be considered as Mallarmé's own problem, for the poet is both haunted by the literary and scriptural tradition and faced with the apparent randomness of his own efforts. Mallarmé's flight from a psychological and emotional poetry toward an intellectual and apparently impersonal one corresponds to the desire to escape from chance into a pure rationality in which everything would be determined and necessary, although not foreseeable to the human mind.

DICE THROWN NEVER WILL ANNUL CHANCE

Dice Thrown Never Will Annul Chance follows from *Igitur* and seems to be the work that most closely approaches Mallarmé's ambition for "pure poetry." This work has had a wide influence on such twentieth century movements as Dada, Surrealism, and Lettrism, not because of its theme but because of its innovative typographical form. Mallarmé had the text set in type of various sizes and specified the exact location of each word on the double-page layouts. Some pages have as few as four words, while others have nearly a hundred. The poet can control more than the verbal aspect of the poem by dealing directly with the visual domain usually left to the printer. Mallarmé here manifests his obsessive concern for the concrete aspects of the book, for the obliteration of the distinction between form and content, and for the reduction of chance in the production of a literary work. The title of the poem runs in the largest type through the poem in such a way that the last word, "Chance," appears only on the ninth double-page unit (out of a total of eleven). Interrupting the title sentence are qualifications expressed in subordinate clauses and in various forms of apposition in various smaller type sizes. The effect is one of suspense, like that which attends a throw of the dice. The last small line of the poem reveals an application of the metaphor of the dice: "Every thought makes a roll of the dice."

Even though Mallarmé eschewed appeals to a broad public, and despite the fact that, aside from a half-dozen shorter poems frequently taught in *lycées* and colleges, his work does not have a wide readership, he has had an enormous influence on twentieth century poets, artists, and critics.

OTHER MAJOR WORKS

NONFICTION: *Petite Philologie à l'usage des classes et du monde: Les Mots anglais*, 1878; *Les Dieux antiques*, 1880; *Divagations*, 1897 (English translation, 2007); *Correspondance*, 1959-1984 (10 volumes); *Documents Mallarmé*, 1968-1971 (3 volumes); *Mallarmé in Prose*, 2001 (Mary Ann Caws, editor).

TRANSLATION: *Les Poémes d'Edgar Poe*, 1888.

MISCELLANEOUS: *Album de vers et de prose*, 1887; *Pages*, 1891; *Vers et prose*, 1893; *Œuvres complètes de Stéphane Mallarmé*, 1945; *Selected Prose Poems, Essays, and Letters*, 1956; *Mallarmé*, 1965; *Selected Poetry and Prose*, 1982; *Divagations: The Author's 1897 Arrangement, Together with "Autobiography" and "Music and Letters,"* 2007.

BIBLIOGRAPHY

Cohn, Robert Greer, ed. *Mallarmé in the Twentieth Century*. London: Associated University Presses, 1998. A collection of essays by many of the most eminent figures in the study of Mallarmé, including Julia Kristeva, Mary Ann Caws, Albert Cook, Anna Balakian, and Robert Cohn. An important summary of the state of scholarship on the poet.

Lloyd, Rosemary. *Mallarmé: The Poet and His Circle*. Ithaca, N.Y.: Cornell University Press, 1999. A literary biography of the poet and his period. Mallarmé hosted gatherings attended by writers, artists, thinkers, and musicians in France, England, and Belgium. Through these gatherings and voluminous correspondence Mallarmé developed and recorded his friendships with Paul Valéry, André Gide, Berthe Morisot, and many others. Includes bibliographical references and index.

Millan, Gordan. *A Throw of the Dice: The Life of Stéphane Mallarmé*. New York: Farrar, Straus and Giroux, 1994. This biography of Mallarmé, who has a reputation for difficulty and obscurity, proves equally valuable to students and specialists. The narrative is aimed at the general reader while the ample footnotes provide material for the specialist. The text draws on previously unpublished correspondence and new documentation and includes bibliographical references and an index.

Pearson, Roger. *Unfolding Mallarmé: The Development of a Poetic Art*. New York: Oxford University Press, 1996. An account of the development of Mallarmé's poetry from his earliest verse to his final masterpiece. Close readings demonstrate the intricate linguistic and formal play to be found in many of his major poems.

Sartre, Jean Paul. *Mallarmé: Or, The Poet of Nothingness*. Translated by Ernest Sturm. University Park: State University of Pennsylvania Press, 1988. A leading existentialist's view of Mallarmé.

Sugano, Marian Zwerling. *The Poetics of the Occasion: Mallarmé and the Poetry of Circumstance*. Stanford, Calif.: Stanford University Press, 1992. Focuses on Mallarmé's occasional poems.

Takeda, Noriko. *The Modernist Human: The Configuration of Humanness in Stéphane Mallarmé's "Hérodiade," T. S. Eliot's "Cats," and Modernist Lyrical Poetry*. New York: Peter Lang, 2008. Takeda examines modernist humanity as evidence in the poetry of Mallarmé and Eliot. Contains a general discussion of Mallarmé's poetry.

Temple, Michael. *The Name of the Poet: Onomastics and Anonymity in the Works of Stéphane Mallarmé*. Exeter, England: University of Exeter Press, 1995. Study of the use of place-names versus personal anonymity in Mallarmé's work.

———, ed. *Meetings with Mallarmé*. Exeter, England: University of Exeter Press, 1998. Critical interpretation of Mallarmé's major works. Includes bibliographical references and index.

John D. Lyons

MARIE DE FRANCE

Born: Île de France; c. 1150
Died: England(?); c. 1215

PRINCIPAL POETRY

Lais, c. 1167 (*Lays of Marie de France*, 1911; better known as *The Lais of Marie de France*, 1978)
Ysopet, after 1170 (*Medieval Fables*, 1983; also known as *Fables*)
La Vie seinte Audrée, after 1179 (*The Life of Saint Audrey*, 2006)
Espurgatoire Saint Patriz, 1208-1215 (translation of *Tractatus de purgatorio Sancti Patricii*, attributed to Henry of Saltrey)

OTHER LITERARY FORMS

In addition to two collections of short narrative poems, *The Lais of Marie de France* and *Fables*, Marie de France (mah-REE duh FRAHNS) translated a long poem, the *Espurgatoire Saint Patriz* (purgatory of Saint Patrick). The Latin original, *Tractatus de purgatorio Sancti Patricii* (1208), has been attributed to Henry of Saltrey. Although the particular version Marie translated is no longer extant, virtually all its lines are to be found in surviving manuscripts. The translation is a faithful one, to which a brief prologue and epilogue (and only a few "asides" or editorial comments) have been added. Because it is a translation and not an original work, its chief interest—if it is properly attributed to Marie de France—is in the testimony it bears to the poet's thorough knowledge of Latin and to her concern, expressed in the epilogue, that the treatise be accessible to the layperson. The narrative also bears some resemblance in form to the genre of the *roman* (romance), which was becoming increasingly popular in this period. Saint Patrick's "purgatory" is a cave on an island in Lough Derg, Donegal, which to this day still draws pilgrims; it was said to have been revealed to Saint Patrick in answer to a prayer, and those who enter it hope to witness or experience the sufferings of the souls in purgatory. The treatise translated by Marie describes the adventures of a particular knight, Owein, who entered the cave and was tempted by demons but was saved by invoking the name of Christ. One motif is of particular interest to students of medieval romance: To cross the river of Hell, Owein must resort to a high and dangerously narrow bridge, which widens as soon as he has the courage to start across. Lancelot, the hero of Chrétien de Troyes's romance *Lancelot: Ou, Le Chevalier à la charrette* (c. 1168; *Lancelot: Or, The Knight of the Cart*, 1913), must cross a similarly narrow bridge in order to rescue the abducted Queen Guinevere; once he has crossed it, the lions who seemed to be guarding the farther end have disappeared. In contrast to most romances, however (and in contrast to Marie's own *The Lais of Marie de France*), the *Espurgatoire Saint*

Patriz involves no profane love story; its inspiration is purely religious.

Other works have been attributed to Marie de France. The current scholarly consensus, however, is that none of them is hers, with the possible exception of another translation, *The Life of Saint Audrey*, which would confirm her interest in religious themes.

ACHIEVEMENTS

Marie de France was probably not the first woman to write poetry in the French vernacular. She is, however, the earliest whose name has been recorded. In fact, she is one of the few twelfth century poets, male or female, whose names are known. This is partly because she wished to be remembered; thus, she "signed" her works by naming herself in their opening or closing lines. It is almost certain that she is also the Marie mentioned by a contemporary, Denis Piramus; if so, she was already well known and "much praised" in the aristocratic circles of her day, where her lays were often read aloud. (Piramus's further observation that her stories were "not at all true" may even indicate some jealousy of her popularity.)

Marie's originality is harder to gauge, for although she claims to retell "Breton lays," there are no direct parallels to her tales in extant Celtic literature. She gives Celtic names to most characters and places and uses recognizable Celtic motifs (such as the fairy lover, the magic boat, and the hunt for a white animal), but her plots hinge on affairs of the heart, and her characters bear a closer resemblance to those of twelfth century romances than to the heroes and heroines of Celtic folk literature. One critic, Lucien Foulet, has gone so far as to argue that Marie herself invented the genre of the narrative lay. Though scholarly debate in this area is still lively, most would reject Foulet's hypothesis as too extreme; there are courtly lays not by Marie, and even relative dates are difficult to establish for this period. Nevertheless, few modern critics would argue with Foulet's emphasis on the conscious art with which Marie shaped her material, wherever she may have found it. Each of the twelve lays is a carefully constructed whole; the tales are told with great economy of means, yet they include nuances of feeling and of moral character that can be quite delicate. Some critics, notably Edgar Sienaert, have seen a structure in the collection as a whole, and most will grant it a thematic unity, though there is disagreement on the nature and import of this unity. Because of the uncertainty about Marie's originality, nineteenth century critics tended to give her less than her due, but no contemporary scholar will deny that she was one of the major poets of her age.

BIOGRAPHY

Of the life of Marie de France, nothing can be said with certainty; her name is known because she included it in her works, but her identity is otherwise obscure. It is probable that she was born in France, in Île de France (the region of which Paris was the capital), and that she lived much of her life in England. She wrote in the Anglo-Norman dialect of Old French, which was spoken by the ruling class in twelfth century England, and knew

English as well (she translated her *Fables* from an English original, now lost). It is unlikely that she would have identified herself by her place of origin if she had still been living there; moreover, the best manuscripts of *The Lais of Marie de France* and *Fables* were found in England. It is also probable that she was a woman of noble birth, for she had noble patrons and even dedicated *The Lais of Marie de France* to a king; she may also have been a nun, for she knew Latin well (as can be seen from her translation of the teatise on Saint Patrick's purgatory) and was better educated than most laywomen would have had occasion to be.

Beyond this, all is speculation, and as Philippe Ménard has observed, the very number of proposed identifications indicates the tenuous character of the evidence. An attractive possibility—but only a possibility—is that she was Mary, abbess of Shaftesbury, an illegitimate daughter of Geoffrey Plantagenet and half sister to Henry II of England. This would account for her apparent familiarity with members of noble circles and with the courtly literature of which Henry's queen, Eleanor of Aquitaine, was an important patron.

Analysis

Despite the volume of critical writing on Marie de France, and despite the limpidity of her own style, there is yet no clear scholarly consensus on how *The Lais of Marie de France* should be read. The age of the poems is undoubtedly one source of difficulty: Not only do they belong to a vanished cultural and intellectual milieu, but also much external evidence (such as sources and the means of accurate dating) that might have made their interpretation easier has been lost.

Two further difficulties recur in all discussions of *The Lais of Marie de France*. The first is a question of genre. The genre of the narrative lay is represented in surviving literature by only thirty-odd poems, and these are too diverse to suggest a clear-cut definition. What is more, Marie's own collection of twelve lays contains pieces that are quite disparate in theme and plot structure. The critic must thus seek unifying elements, and while most would agree that the theme of love runs through all the tales like a connecting thread, few agree on Marie's understanding of love or on her intention in portraying it.

The second major difficulty, which individual critics fail to acknowledge but which is evident from a review of the literature, is that the theme of love necessarily evokes subjective responses in readers, even when those readers are scrupulously "objective" critics. This is, of course, a danger in all criticism; it is exacerbated in Marie's case by the dearth of external evidence and by the intimate, almost seductive quality of some of her tales. Though it is important to consider the whole range of such responses, because each may have something to contribute to a full appreciation of the work, the most fruitful lines of research have been a new approach to the issue of genre and various efforts to see the lays in their original cultural and poetic context.

Thanks to important work by Sienaert, real progress has been made on the genre question; the unique and often puzzling emotional effects of the lays may plausibly be attributed to the ways in which they combine elements of two well-known genres, the fairy tale and the realistic *nouvelle*, or short story. At the same time, the lays have been shown to include didactic, courtly, and religious elements that reflect distinct tendencies of the age in which they were written. Marie is not content merely to entertain or "seduce" her readers; she has much to say about the real world and about the moral choices her characters are called upon to make in it.

Marie's concept of love

She also puts forward a conception of love that has at least something in common with the courtly love celebrated by her contemporaries the troubadours and trouvères. (Here it may be helpful to recall that Marie may have spent some time at the court of Henry II, whose wife, Eleanor of Aquitaine, was herself a French woman and the granddaughter of a troubadour.) As Emanuel Mickel has observed, Marie approves of love when it is elevated above concupiscence and self-seeking by a freely given pledge of loyalty. She differs from those courtly authors who celebrate one-sided love; in nearly every lay, the love portrayed is mutual. Though she often depicts such love as triumphing over obstacles, she also acknowledges that it may result in great suffering for the lovers. Her appeals to explicitly Christian values can be unorthodox, and she combines romantic love with Christian charity in unexpected ways, but she does not hesitate to condemn those who betray trusting spouses—or feudal lords or vassals—out of calculated self-interest. The concluding lay of the collection also suggests that romantic love can serve as a bridge to the more complete love of God. Marie's chief interest, however, is unquestionably in the depiction of mutual romantic attachment and its various outcomes.

If there is still disagreement about Marie's thematic focus, her stylistic gifts are scarcely in doubt. In a reversal of earlier assessments, later critics have seen in her an accomplished storyteller and poet, suiting the length of each tale to its content, using dialogue to great effect, and endowing key objects with symbolic value so that they epitomize the themes of individual tales. The shortest of the tales—"Laüstic" ("The Nightingale") and "Chèvrefeuille" ("The Honeysuckle")—have even been seen as essentially lyric poems, so dominated are they by the central symbols of the nightingale and the honeysuckle entwined with the hazel. However, even these lays have plots, as Sienaert does well to recall. Though Marie translated her *Fables* from an English original that has been lost, these, too, display poetic and narrative skill (especially in the phrasing of dialogue) that must be attributed, at least in part, to the translator.

The lay as genre

Sienaert's description of the lay as a mixed or intermediary genre is based on the work of folklorists, notably Vladimir Propp and Max Lüthi, who have identified (independently of one another) the basic structure of the European folktale. One of the most striking features of the folktale, or fairy tale (Sienaert's term for the genre is *conte merveilleux*: a tale with a happy ending, in which the "marvelous" is paramount) is that the identities and motivations of characters may be freely altered from one version to another, whereas the plot sequence, and the roles characters may fill in it, are rigidly maintained. The mainspring of the fairy-tale plot is not the motivated action of its characters but rather the intrusion of the marvelous, and although the working out of the plot satisfies deep human desires, its conclusion is not attained by human effort but by magic (a potion, a ring) or by a deus ex machina (a fairy, a speaking animal). It has long been recognized that there were affinities between the fairy tale and *The Lais of Marie de France*, but these affinities had remained somewhat vague, limited to the happy ending (which does not apply to a number of lays) and an ill-defined "charm." As Sienaert has shown, however, the lays sometimes follow the fairy-tale pattern in which motivation is not linked to plot. Thus, the knight Eliduc, for example, scarcely earns his happiness; it comes to him in spite of the bad faith he has shown his wife and his young lover. At the same time, though, and in the same tales, the motivation of Marie's characters can be essential to the outcome; thus, Eliduc's wife, by her unexampled generosity, makes possible for her husband the happy ending he had deserved to forfeit. Sometimes it even happens that a realistically motivated character *forestalls* the expected happy ending, as does the young man in "Les Dues Amanz" ("The Two Loves"), who refuses to drink the magic potion that would restore his strength. Finally, there are a few stories from which the fairy-tale plot is completely missing. "Equitan" has been compared to a fabliau (a more consistently realistic, generally coarse and cynical, short narrative genre contemporary to the lay) because of its realistic and cautionary plot of betrayal, attempted crime, and punishment; while falling within the scope of the medieval exemplum, or tale with a moral, it resembles the modern short story in linking the outcome to the character and actions of the central figures. Sienaert argues that Marie deliberately placed it second in her collection, after a tale that has many affinities with the fairy tale, to mark the two poles between that her pieces would move.

As will become apparent from a closer look at several lays, this approach to the genre question can be extremely useful. Its chief drawback is its degree of abstraction—it cannot account for the thematic content of the collection.

"LANVAL"

"Lanval" is a good example of a lay using a straightforward fairy-tale plot. Lanval, a "foreign" knight at King Arthur's court, is slighted by the King until a beautiful fairy maiden approaches him, offering both her love and riches if he will keep her existence secret. This he does, until one day the Queen likewise offers him her love, and he reveals the fact that he already loves another, whose least handmaiden surpasses the Queen in beauty and accomplishments. At this, the Queen denounces him to the King as having accosted her, nor will the fairy-lover come at his call, since he has revealed her existence. When he is put on trial, however—more for insulting the Queen's beauty than for allegedly accosting her—the fairy relents, first sending her handmaidens and then arriving in person so that all can see the truth of Lanval's boast. The tale ends as Lanval rides off with her to the otherworldly Avalon, to live happily ever after.

This lay epitomizes a tendency of many of Marie's tales to fuse Celtic folk motifs with the courtly love theme. As Jean Frappier has observed, there is an analogy between the "otherworld" of Celtic mythology, to which the "marvelous" properly belongs, and the privileged condition of courtly lovers, whose experience of love (open only to a small, elect group), gives them a taste of paradise on earth. Avalon thus becomes an allegory for the state of mutual love, where the "foreigner" Lanval finds his true home after rejecting, and being rejected by, the flawed world of Arthur's court (where the king has slighted him and the queen accused him of her own infidelity). As Sienaert would add, however, the motivations of the characters—even of the fairy, who relents in her punishment of Lanval—are fully humanized and linked to the outcome. The lay is thus emotionally satisfying, not only for its fairy-tale ending but also for its vindication of mutual love—though it should also be noted that the "real world" is seen as hostile to that love, which can flourish only in a land of its own. In this respect, "Lanval" is perhaps the most frankly escapist of the lays.

"THE TWO LOVERS"

"The Two Lovers," by contrast, creates the expectation of a fairy-tale ending only to reverse it at the last moment. A widowed king, unwilling to part with his sole daughter, invents a trial in which he thinks no suitor can succeed: To win her hand in marriage, the suitor must carry her to the top of a mountain without pausing to rest. To help a young man whom she favors, the girl sends him to her aunt in Salerno, who provides him with a potion that can restore strength. During the trial, however, the young man feels strong enough to do without the potion; he resists the girl's repeated pleas that he drink it and reaches the summit only to collapse—his heart has given out. The distraught girl spills the potion, which causes medicinal herbs to spring up on the mountainside, and herself dies of grief on the spot, where the two are buried together.

Of all the lays, this one has perhaps evoked the greatest diversity of interpretation. It has been seen as a tragedy, a cautionary tale, even a satire. Here, Sienaert's insights are especially helpful, accounting for the diversity of critical (and emotional) response without explaining it away. The story is indeed tragic insofar as it reverses the carefully created expectation of a happy ending, and it is cautionary insofar as Marie stresses the *démesure* (lack of moderation) that leads to the boy's death. However, there is also something positive about the ending: After rejecting the magical means to success, the boy accomplishes the feat (though none of his predecessors had come close), and the girl's love, because it equals his, unites them in death. The boy's decision is flawed, as

Marie herself observes: "I fear [the potion] will do him little good/ For he had in him no moderation." As Emanuel Mickel points out, the potion is not merely a magical expedient but a symbol of the potential strength and fruition to which the couple's love might have come; thus, the good herbs it causes to flourish on the mountainside might have been the couple's good deeds (as in "Eliduc") or those of their heirs. Nevertheless, it is hard not to sympathize with the boy's desire to prove himself or with the girl's anguished sense of what she has lost. Both characters are brought to vivid life in the scene on the mountain, as Marie endows them with fully human motives.

"Equitan"

"Equitan," the "realistic" lay mentioned above, offers yet another perspective on love; it is also one of the most carefully structured of the lays, making expert use of dialogue, symbolism, and irony. Equitan is a king who seems to possess all the knightly virtues. It soon emerges, though, that, like the boy in "The Two Lovers," he has no sense of moderation in love; what is more, he prefers pleasure to his responsibilities and often leaves the administration of justice to his seneschal while he goes hunting—literally and metaphorically, for he is fond of the ladies. (The hunt was frequently used by medieval authors as a metaphor for the pursuit of a woman's favors.) As it happens, the seneschal has a wife who is among the most beautiful women of the realm; hearing her praised, Equitan goes to hunt on the seneschal's lands, succeeds in meeting her, and falls passionately in love with her. Though he recognizes (in a soliloquy) that it means breaking faith with his loyal deputy, the king persuades himself by specious arguments to pursue the woman. At first she objects, but only on the grounds that his rank will make for inequality in their love; he assures her that—in accordance with the courtly convention—he will be her servant and she his lady. As Marie makes plain, this is what literally happens. Urged by his subjects to marry, Equitan refuses, assuring his lover that he would marry her if she were free; she then proposes that they murder her husband, and the king agrees to every detail of her plan. The hunt has become lethal, but this time Equitan is destined to become the quarry. Caught by the seneschal in his lady's arms, Equitan leaps into the boiling bath prepared for the murder. The irony is complete as the seneschal, to whom Equitan had delegated his own judicial responsibilities, proceeds to complete the punishment by throwing his wife in the bath after her lover. As might have been expected, those nineteenth century critics who were chiefly impressed by the "charm" of lays ike "Lanval" found "Equitan" shockingly sordid; it seemed, moreover, to give a different and unfavorable account of the courtly love celebrated in many of the lays. Clearly, Marie does not disapprove of courtly love per se. As the ending of "Lanval" indicates, however, it is not always possible to reconcile the state of love—that "otherworld" to which Lanval and his mistress retreat—and the "real world," which makes claims of its own on the lovers. The fidelity of Equitan and his lady might in itself be admirable, but because it is grounded in the infidelity of both to the seneschal, it leads them to crime. Because it is also characterized by *démesure*, it also leads to death. In contrast to the *démesure* of the boy in "The Two Lovers," which is excusable because of his youth and which has a dimension that may be considered heroic, the *démesure* of Equitan is a form of slavery to appetite, which is all the more demeaning in the light of Equitan's rank as well as his responsibilities.

As Sienaert observes, "Equitan" is an extreme case—a worst case, in *The Lais of Marie de France*, where adulterous love is concerned. Marie frequently treats of courtly love that is also adulterous, and she is often sympathetic to the lovers. This is especially true of the three lays "Guigemar," "Yonec," and "The Nightingale," in which the female protagonist is a *mal mariée*—a woman married against her will, usually to a much older man who treats her as his property and shows her no love. Though the protagonist's love for another is portrayed sympathetically in each case, the stories end in very disparate ways: In the most realistic, "The Nightingale," the husband succeeds in separating the lovers by an act of cruelty (killing the bird that gave the wife an excuse to stand at the window from which she could see her lover); in the most fairy-tale-like, "Guigemar," the husband simply disappears from the story as the wife escapes and rejoins her lover in his distant homeland.

"Eliduc"

The most complex case of adulterous love, however, is that seen in "Eliduc," the longest of the lays and the last in the manuscript that Sienaert takes to reflect Marie's own ordering of the tales. When the story opens, Eliduc has been happily married for some time; he decides to leave home because envious men have slandered him to the Breton king whom he faithfully serves. Crossing to England, he offers his services to the king of Exeter, who is hard-pressed by enemies, and wins a signal victory. The king's daughter, Guilliadun, hearing only good spoken of Eliduc, asks to meet him, and the two fall in love. Though Eliduc restrains himself to the extent that he does not sleep with the girl, he accepts her gifts and kisses and does not tell her of his wife. When his original sovereign, hard-pressed in turn, sends for him, he feels duty-bound to go and refuses to abduct the princess (who wants to go with him) on the grounds that he would be showing disloyalty to her father; yet he promises to return for her when his contract with her father will have expired. He does so—still without telling her of his wife—and during a storm on the channel, she learns the truth from a frightened sailor who thinks Eliduc's adulterous love has caused the storm. At the news, Guilliadun falls in a faint, and thinking she is dead, Eliduc throws the sailor overboard. The ship reaches land safely, and Eliduc, who cannot yet bring himself to bury the girl, hides her in a chapel on his estate. Worried by his obvious grief, his wife, Guildeluec, has him followed and discovers the girl's body; far from showing envy or hatred, she revives Guilliadun with the aid of a magic herb and says she wishes to enter a convent so that Eliduc can marry the girl. After living for some time in "perfect love," the couple in turn enter religious life, and

Guildeluec, now an abbess, welcomes Guilliadun "as her sister."

Once again, Sienaert's observations offer a useful line of approach to this puzzling tale. Like other courtly lovers in *The Lais of Marie de France*, Eliduc would like to keep his love in a world apart, safe from the interference of real life; when the sailor tries to call him back to reality, he blindly kills the man. (It should be noted, however, that the sailor scarcely speaks for Marie; he wants to do away with the innocent Guilliadun.) Unable to resolve his own dilemma, Eliduc is saved by the action of his wife, whose unparalleled generosity takes the place of the magical resolution one would expect in a fairy tale. What this approach cannot account for, however, is the care and the sheer length devoted to the developing love between Eliduc and Guilliadun. If, as Sienaert claims, Guilliadun's swoon represents the impotence of the courtly ethic (and even of a "fairy-tale princess") to deal with the moral dilemmas of the real world, why is such care devoted to the portrayal of her love for Eliduc, and above all, why does she and not Guildeluec win him back?

Mickel has observed that there is a correspondence between the lengths of individual lays and their plot structures: The shorter lays all end unhappily, whereas the longer ones end with the reunion of the lovers (or, as in "Yonec," with their vindication). Mickel attributes this characteristic to Marie's preference for faithful love, which must develop and be tested over time, yet it is Guildeluec who has loved Eliduc longest. Given the care with which Marie describes the growth of the adulterous love (it occupies 431 of 1,184 lines, or more than a third of the poem), it seems hard to avoid the conclusion that Marie meant her audience to be caught up in it. Though Eliduc is clearly acting in bad faith at some level, he never allows this to reach his awareness in his dealings with Guilliadun; he is a confused man, but not a bad one at heart. Because both lovers are essentially good, and can see the good in each other, their mutual love (in which they manage to observe some *mesure*) is more than mere concupiscence. This is why it can lead them to a life of shared good works, and ultimately to the love of God. Despite the decisive role of Guildeluec's selfless love and the fact that all three protagonists learn to love in her way, it seems wrong to read the entire lay as an exemplum. There is a real difference between romantic and Christian love, and Guildeluec is the first to recognize it. Romantic love must be mutual and cannot be learned; it is, as has been observed, akin to the "marvelous." Thus, Guildeluec makes her decision on the basis of Guilliadun's exquisite beauty, whose power she herself feels. Though Marie admits, in "Equitan," that such love can lead the partners to evil, she prefers stories in which it ennobles them, whether through shared happiness or shared suffering. She is thus both a didactic and a thoroughly courtly poet.

Marie as storyteller

Because Marie is a narrative poet, her literary art is primarily that of the storyteller; thus, critical studies have emphasized her choice of significant detail, her use of dialogue, and above all, her skill in the ordering and pacing of plots. It is important to remember, however, especially if one reads her in a prose translation (and there are no verse translations in English), that she is also a poet, writing in rhymed octosyllabic couplets. Far from interrupting the flow of her narrative, this form contributes to its spare and vigorous quality. In contrast to the romances being written by her contemporaries in the same meter, the lays are anything but digressive. This is especially striking in the shorter lays, where not a line is wasted. *Fables*, though not an original work, deserves to be mentioned in this context because it demonstrates the same skill of compression to an even greater degree: The longer of the fables are of the same length as the shorter of the lays. The moral with which each fable concludes is particularly compressed (between four and eight lines long), and the rhymes are carefully chosen to bring home the point with special force.

IMAGERY AND SYMBOLISM

The other specifically poetic skill Marie displays is in the use of controlling images, which in her narrative context are usually symbolic objects (although she can also use metaphor, as in the tale of Equitan, "the hunter hunted"). Such objects loom especially large in two of the shortest lays, "The Nightingale" and "The Honeysuckle"; in both cases, they are related to the love theme central to the collection. Though the nightingale is on one level a pretext that the woman uses to see her lover, it also symbolizes mutual love as something alive and beautiful. Though the husband can kill it and thus prevent the lovers from seeing each other, he cannot obliterate its memory; thus, the lover, to whom the woman sends the bird's body, has it encased in a jeweled box, which he carries about with him always.

The honeysuckle, which twines itself about the hazel until neither can stand alone, is a related symbol of love as a beautiful living thing. Though the bird and the plant are themselves vulnerable, the fidelity of the lovers in each case holds out a hope that human love may be more durable. In "The Honeysuckle," which describes a meeting between Tristan and Iseult, Tristan himself uses the symbol in this sense. In a passage that is a true lyric fragment (and that may be the message, inscribed on a hazel stick, alerting Iseult to her lover's presence), he exclaims, "Fair love, so it is with us:/ Neither you without me, nor I without you." Deservedly one of Marie's most famous couplets, it captures both her spare, direct style and the ideal of mutual fidelity embodied in so many of her lays.

BIBLIOGRAPHY
Bloch, R. Howard. *The Anonymous Marie de France*. Chicago: University of Chicago Press, 2003. Argues that Marie de France was a writer of profound importance and significance, a "[James] Joyce of the twelfth century." Includes notes and an index.
Burgess, Glyn S. *The "Lais" of Marie de France: Text and Context*. Athens: University of Georgia Press, 1987. A detailed study of the twelve lays contained in the British

Library. The study notes thematic and textual parallels in the lays, with the author's hope that they will help scholars in future evaluations of the authorship of these works. Burgess discusses the problem of internal chronology and focuses attention on key terms in Marie's use of language. Includes extensive notes for further study, a bibliography, and an index.

_____. *Marie de France: An Analytical Bibliography.* Supplement no. 3. Woolbridge, Suffolk, England: Tamesis, 2007. A bibliography of the works by and about Marie de France, with critical analysis.

McCash, June Hall. "The Swan and the Nightingale: Natural Unity in a Hostile World in the *Lais* of Marie de France." *French Studies* 49 (October, 1995): 385-396. Discusses Marie's symbolic and mimetic depiction of nature in *The Lais of Marie de France*. Notes that although she uses a wealth of symbolic associations of birds, she does not alter their natural functions.

Maréchal, Chantal, ed. *In Quest of Marie de France: A Twelfth-Century Poet.* Lewiston, N.Y.: Edwin Mellen Press, 1992. Contains fifteen articles by established medievalists: three articles on the *Fables*, six general articles on *The Lais of Marie de France*, and six with a narrower focus. Of special interest is the editor's introduction, which offers a chronological approach to critical assessment of Marie through the centuries.

_____. *The Reception and Transmission of the Works of Marie de France, 1774-1974.* Lewiston, N.Y.: Edwin Mellen Press, 2003. A collection of essays that look at how Marie de France's works have been received and transmitted through time.

Mickel, Emanuel J. *Marie de France.* New York: Twayne, 1974. A good, full-length study of Marie, her works, and the intellectual background of the twelfth century for the general reader and for the student of medieval literature. Contains individual chapters on Marie's identity, the narrative lays, sources and plot summaries for the various lays, an interpretation, and the structure and style of *The Lais of Marie de France*. Includes a chronology of the time period, useful notes and references for further study, a select bibliography, and an index.

Semple, Benjamin. "The Male Psyche and the Female Sacred Body in Marie de France and Christine de Pizan." *Yale French Studies*, no. 86 (1994): 164-186. Discusses the first of Marie's lays, "Guigemar," and Christine de Pizan's *Livre de la cité des dames*; argues that the image of humanity that emerges from the texts, like the mystical vision, invites us to contemplate the essential paradox of a body that is at once sexual, intellectual, and ethical.

Sethurman, Jayshree. "Tale-Type and Motif Indexes to the *Fables* of Marie de France." *Le Cygne: Bulletin of the International Marie de France Society* 5 (Spring, 1999): 19-35. A table of folktale types linking Marie's *Fables* to the compilations of universal folktale motifs classified and cataloged by Antti Arne and revised and expanded by Stith Thompson.

Whalen, Logan E. *Marie de France and the Poetics of Memory*. Washington, D.C.: Catholic University of America Press, 2008. This study of Marie's poetry looks at all works ascribed to her and analyzes them. Also provides a table of extant medieval manuscripts.

Lillian Doherty

GÉRARD DE NERVAL

Born: Paris, France; May 22, 1808
Died: Paris, France; January 26, 1855

PRINCIPAL POETRY
Elégies nationales, 1826
Poésies allemandes, 1830 (translation)
Petits Châteaux de Bohême, 1853 (includes poetry and prose)
Les Chimères, 1854 (English translation, 1965; also known as *Chimeras*, 1966; best known as *The Chimeras*, 1982)
Fortune's Fool: Selected Poems, 1959

OTHER LITERARY FORMS

Gérard de Nerval (nehr-VAHL) tried his hand at drama, short fiction, and nonfiction. He wrote two dramas in collaboration with Alexandre Dumas, *père*. They are *Piquillo* (pb. 1837) and *Alchimiste* (pb. 1839). His other dramas include *Chariot d'enfant* (1850, with Joseph Méry), *L'Imagier de Harlem* (pr. 1851), and a translation of Johann Wolfgang von Goethe's *Faust: Eine Tragödie* (pb. 1808; *The Tragedy of Faust*, 1823) and *Faust: Eine Tragödie, zweiter Teil* (pb. 1833; *The Tragedy of Faust, Part Two*, 1838) in 1827 and 1840. Among his nonfiction prose works are *Voyage en Orient* (1851; *Journey to the Orient*, 1972); *Les Illuminés* (1852), and *Aurélia* (1855; English translation, 1932). A collection of his stories came out as *Les Filles du feu* (1854; *Daughters of Fire*, 1922).

ACHIEVEMENTS

During his lifetime, Gérard de Nerval was generally regarded as an enthusiastic but harmless eccentric, a writer of some genius whose best and freshest productions were marred by occasional lapses into obscurity. Because of his bouts with madness—both manic-depressive psychosis (or, in modern psychological language, cyclothymic depression) and schizophrenia—he struck most of his contemporaries as an oddity, a poet sometimes pathetic yet never dangerous except to his own well-being. Around him numerous legends accumulated, most of them ludicrous. Some of the more absurd stories were given wider circulation by Jules Champfleury in *Grandes Figures d'hier et d'aujourd'hui: Balzac, Gérard de Nerval, Wagner, Courbet* (1861) and by Arsène Houssaye in *Les Confessions: Souvenirs d'un demi-siècle* (1885, 6 vols.). In part as a result of such droll anecdotes, Nerval's reputation during the first half of the nineteenth century was that of a minor figure: a poet with close affinities with German Romanticism, a distinguished translator of Johann Wolfgang von Goethe's *Faust*, a moderately

Gérard de Nerval
(Library of Congress)

popular playwright and the author of sumptuously exotic travel literature, and a lyricist whose originality and vigor were evident but whose interests were too often attached to the curious and the extravagant. Later during the century, critics compared Nerval with Charles Baudelaire, treating both as psychologists of the aberrant. After the beginning of the twentieth century, commentators judged Nerval favorably in relation to the Symbolists, especially to Stéphane Mallarmé and Arthur Rimbaud. Still later, Nerval was appreciated as a forerunner of Guillaume Apollinaire and modernist experimentation. Since the 1920's, Nerval's achievements have been viewed independently of their connections with other writers or movements. Treated not as a precursor of greater talents but as a towering genius in his own right, Nerval has been examined as a seer, a mystic, a student of Hermetic doctrine and of alchemy, a poet of extraordinary complexit, resonance, and power. His most important works in prose and poetry—*Petits Châteaux de Bohême*, *Aurélia*, and *Daughters of Fire*— are among the glories of French literature.

Biography

Gérard de Nerval was born Gérard Labrunie, the son of Étienne Labrunie, a medical doctor, and of Marie-Antoinette Marguerite Laurent, daughter of a Paris draper. Nerval did not change his name until 1831, when he signed a letter "G. la Brunie de Nerval," taking the name from a property, Le Clos de Nerval, belonging to his mother's family. The name is also an anagram of his mother's maiden name, Laurent. It is known that Nerval hated his father, who served with Napoleon's Grande Armée as a field surgeon and who was, throughout the poet's life, an aloof, insensitive parent. Nerval's mother died when the boy was only two years old, and Nerval was sent to live with his great-uncle, Antoine Boucher, at Mortefontaine. Nerval later described these early years as the happiest of his life. He had free range of a library of occult books and discussed philosophy with his great-uncle, who may have served as a model for Père Dodu in Nerval's short story "Sylvie" (1853; English translation, 1922). When Nerval's father returned from the front in 1814, the boy joined him in Paris. In 1820, Nerval entered the Collège Charlemagne, where he began to exhibit a fondness for literary pursuits and began his lifelong friendship with the poet Théophile Gautier.

In November, 1827, Nerval published his translation of Goethe's *The Tragedy of Faust*, but under the publication date of 1828. This work was well received in Parisian literary circles, and Nerval became a disciple of Victor Hugo and joined his *cénacle romantique*. In the notorious dispute that followed the disruptive theatrical opening (February 25, 1830) of Hugo's play *Hernani* (pr., pb. 1830; English translation, 1830) however, Nerval sided with Gautier, and thereafter Nerval frequented Gautier's *petit cénacle*.

An inheritance from his maternal grandfather in 1834 allowed Nerval to give up his medical studies and pursue a literary career, much to his father's disapproval. In the fall of that year, Nerval visited Italy (Florence, Rome, and Naples), a trip that later proved invaluable to his writing. Upon his return to Paris in 1834, he met and fell in love with the actress Jenny Colon. In May of 1834, he founded the theatrical review *Le Monde dramatique*, dedicated to the glorification of Colon. For a brief time, Nerval enjoyed a life of prosperity, identifying himself with the "Bohème galante." When the review failed in 1836, however, financial difficulties forced Nerval to become a journalist, writing articles for *Le Figaro* and *La Presse*. He visited Belgium with Gautier in 1836 in an effort to forget his personal struggles for a time.

On October 31, 1837, Nerval's play *Piquillo* premiered in Paris with Colon in the lead role as Silvia. The play was a success, and Nerval was encouraged to declare his love for her. On April 11, 1838, however, Colon married the flutist Louis-Gabriel Leplus, an event that left the poet bitterly disillusioned. During the summer of that year, he traveled to Germany with Dumas, *père*, and from that time the two writers began a series of theatrical collaborations.

The next two years were ones of increasing mental instability and depression for

Nerval. Though he published his translation of *The Tragedy of Faust, Part Two* in 1840, the strain of the work took its toll, and Nerval was hospitalized as a result of a nervous breakdown. The death of Colon in 1842 did nothing to restore his ailing spirits. In ill health and overcome with grief, he embarked in 1843 on a trip to Malta, Egypt, Syria, Cyprus, Constantinople, and Naples. He later published an account of his travels in *Journey to the Orient*. Nerval had discovered his psychological need to wander, a theme found in his major works.

Though his mental and physical health continued to deteriorate, Nerval struggled to support himself with his writing. Still hoping to establish himself in the theater, he wrote *Chariot d'enfant* with Méry, a production which premiered on May 13, 1850. In September, 1851, Nerval suffered an accident, followed by a serious nervous breakdown. Nerval believed that he would soon become incurably insane, a realization which made him increase his literary efforts. In 1852, he published *Les Illuminés*, a series of biographies on historical figures interested in mysteries of the occult and of alchemy. In 1853, he published a volume of nostalgic poems recalling a happier youth, *Petits Châteaux de Bohême*. In the summer of that year, Nerval published his best-known story, "Sylvie," followed by two other great works, *Daughters of Fire* and *The Chimeras*, in 1854. *Aurélia*, an account of his madness, appeared in 1855. Alone and destitute, Nerval hanged himself in an alley on January 26, 1855.

Analysis

Gautier, who perhaps appreciated the fine qualities of Gérard de Nerval's character and art more than any other contemporary, once described his friend as an "apodal swallow." To Gautier, Nerval was

> all wings and no feet: At most he had perceptible claws; these enabled him to alight, at least momentarily, just long enough to catch his breath, then go on . . . to soar and move about in fluid realms with the joy and abandon of a being in his element.

Gautier's idealization of Nerval as an ethereal figure—a Percy Bysshe Shelley-like bird in flight who abjured the common terrestrial condition of humanity—is a valid judgment only to a limited degree. To be sure, a reader may approach Nerval on a superficial level as a poet of intense, vivid, direct intuition; a poet of dreams and visions; a creator of myths and fantastic personal symbolic constructs that reach into the archetypal imagination.

Certainly, most of Nerval's poetry, much of his prose poetry, and a portion of his dramatic work can be appreciated according to the qualities of Impressionism. His work has, on a simple level of perception, an evocative, dreamy, otherworldly, melancholy vein that resembles the Impressionism of otherwise dissimilar poets such as Edgar Allan Poe and Paul Verlaine. One can enjoy the seemingly imprecise but hauntingly evocative imagery of a familiar Nerval poem such as "Le Point noir" ("The Dark

Smudge") as though the writer were merely inducing an impression of malign fate. Reading Nerval for his surface characteristics of hauntingly sonorous music, vague but unsettling imagery, and technically perfect mastery of verse forms, one can accept Gautier's early evaluation of the poet as a kind of birdlike spirit—or, to use Baudelaire's image of a poet idealized as an albatross ("L'Albatros"), a creature free in the air but confined and crippled on the crass Earth.

Moreover, a reader who approaches Nerval's basic themes without first investigating their intellectual context is likely to appreciate their surface qualities of authentic feeling and simplicity of expression. Nerval is always concerned with human values, no matter that he may choose exotic subjects or complex methods to express them. His work is nearly always confessional. Although he rarely tends to be self-dramatizing in his poetry, he often places his persona—his other self—at the center of the theme in order to examine the psychological insights of a human life. An early verse, "Épître première" (first epistle), at once expresses his artistic philosophy and predicts his fate; he will, despite madness under the aegis of the moon, serve humanity with a generous desire. In his poems as well as in much of his prose and drama, Nerval appeals directly—without a reader's need for critical exegesis—to the human heart: to its courage, its idealism, its love. Although Nerval's subjects often appear to be odd, exotic, or perverse, the poet treats the flowers of his imagination not as "evil," as does the great poet of the next generation, Baudelaire, but as fragrant symbols of a mysterious, arcane harmony in the universe.

Indeed, Nerval is best appreciated as a mystic and a seer, a poet whose surface qualities of vague dreaminess conceal an interior precision of image and ideas. Reading a popularly anthologized lyric such as "Fantaisie" ("Fantasy"), for example, one tends to dismiss the poem as a piece influenced by German Romanticism, especially by the *Märchen*-like songs of Heinrich Heine or Goethe. A closer reading, however, will show that the seemingly vague images are not merely decorative; they are rendered with precision, although their precise significance as personal symbol is not clear. Nevertheless, the "green slope gilded by the setting sun" and the stone castle are objects, not atmosphere, and the mysterious theme of déjà vu is intended to be psychological truth, not fairy tale.

GERMAN ROMANTICISM

To appreciate Nerval fully, one should understand the poet's relationship to German Romanticism without treating him exclusively as a Romantic—or, indeed, exclusively as a pre-Impressionist, pre-Symbolist, or pre-modernist. Although his affinities to poets such as Heine and Goethe (Romantics), Poe and Verlaine (Impressionists), and Mallarmé and Rimbaud (Symbolists) are obvious—as are his temperamental affinities to Baudelaire—Nerval is best compared to two poets whose productions are similarly visionary and, in some respects, arcane: William Blake and William Butler Yeats. Like

Blake, Nerval was a seer who searched into the heart of mysteries to discover the correspondence of opposites; a follower of the eighteenth century mystic Emanuel Swedenborg; and an originator of complex myths and symbolic systems. Like Yeats, Nerval was a student of theosophy and an adept of the religions of the East. He believed in magic and the occult, communicated with revealers of the spirit world, and—using the phases of the moon and similar cosmic symbols—created a complex system of psychological and historical types of personalities.

Archetypal imagery

In addition, Nerval cultivated dream visions, experimented with drugs such as hashish, and was a student of the Kabbalah, alchemy, ancient mystery religions, Illuminism, Orphism, Sabbean astral worship, and the secrets of the Egyptian pyramids. If his abstruse researches were merely incidental to his work, much of his thinking might be safely ignored as burdensome, esoteric, or irrelevant. Nerval, however, uses a great deal of his learning in his prose and poetry. An extremely careful writer, he placed layer upon layer of meaning, often mixing different systems that are not related historically into a single new system, within the texture of his poetic prose and his poetry. To ignore these layers of meaning is to neglect as well a great deal of Nerval's subtlety as an artist.

In *Aurélia*, for example, he used archetypal images that appear to emanate from the collective unconscious—among them the image of the *magna mater* (great mother). Included are manifestations of woman as loving, gentle, compassionate, noble-hearted; as vain, dissembling, inconstant; or as the dangerous fury who terrorizes a dreamer; or finally, as the temptress, the coquette. Also he includes, in various manifestations, the father archetype. In *Journey to the Orient*, the poet transmutes the legend of Solomon and Sheba from a biblical tale into a personal vision centering on the character of Adoniram, a "double" for the artist, the creator. In this book, Nerval exposes themes involving the story of Cain as well as the secrets of Hermetic lore and of the pyramids (Nerval actually visited the site of the Great Pyramid of Khufu, or Cheops, and descended into its depths).

Symbolism and Hermeticism

Nerval's poetry is less obviously arcane than much of his symbolic prose; nevertheless, a careful student should understand that the poet uses language in a very special way. His constant endeavor was to express through symbolic language a unity that he perceived in the spiritual and the material elements of the universe. To grasp this language, a reader needs to know several concepts basic to Swedenborgian correspondence and Hermetic alchemy.

Nerval's research into these abstruse subjects began early in his life, notably from his interest in a tradition of thought known as Illuminism. This tradition affected writers from the middle of the eighteenth century until the end of the nineteenth century.

Illuminists were fascinated with ancient Oriental manuscripts and with the tenets of Middle Eastern thinkers. Among the manuscripts that they studied were the *Corpus Hermeticum*, a collection of forty-two books attributed to Hermes Trismegistus, perhaps the most important source of alchemical knowledge of the period. To these books were added the works of Paracelsus and his disciples.

These doctrines were cultivated by members of various secret societies (Rosicrucians, Freemasons, Martinists) which flourished at the end of the eighteenth century, particularly in France and in Germany. By means of such secret societies, Nerval came to acquire knowledge and appreciation of alchemy, while his visionary application of alchemical principles can be traced to the works of Swedenborg. In his study of the *Corpus Hermeticum* and of the Kabbala, Swedenborg had reached two conclusions that were to have a tremendous influence upon the literary world of the nineteenth century. The first of these conclusions was his idea of correspondence, the notion that every visible phenomenon has a direct opposite—upon which it depends—in the invisible and spiritual world. The second conclusion was his conception of a universal language in which these correspondences can best be expressed.

The Chimeras

Nerval's poetry reveals his obsession with creating a new language, one that will allow for a communication between the visible and the invisible, the sensible and the spiritual. Such a language would permit a correspondence between the two orders. A corollary of this belief is the principle of the identity of contraries or opposites. Thus, in *The Chimeras*, Nerval establishes a syncretism of religious beliefs based upon compatibilities. His object is to demonstrate the oneness of religious thought; to achieve this high purpose, he selects a special language, using the metaphors of alchemy principally but not exclusively, as a vehicle to redeem humanity.

A reader may wonder whether a poet so learned as Nerval actually believed in the esoteric doctrines of alchemy. Certainly he used these doctrines, extracting from their classical and medieval origins a philosophical rather than pseudoscientific content, in order to construct his metaphors. In this sense, Nerval believed in alchemy as Blake believed in his visions and as Yeats believed in the symbolic constructs of his spiritual communicators. Nerval's poetry incorporates four basic alchemical principles: first, the theory of correspondence; second, the act of imagining, which can bring about corporeal transformations; third, meditation, or an inner dialogue with the invisible, which requires a "new language"; and finally, the identity of opposites, whereby every image elicits by definition its contrary. In this complex scheme, Mercury (quicksilver) becomes the symbol of alchemy: liquid metal, or the embodiment of a contradiction.

To appreciate how deeply interfused with the surface dreaminess of Nerval's verse are his symbolic constructs of alchemy, one can examine the cycle of twelve sonnets titled *The Chimeras*. The number twelve is crucial in the alchemical system, since it represents the *coniunctio tetraptiva*, or the dilemma of three and four—the chimera being the archetype of the triad. It should also be noted that the structure of the sonnet itself is representative of the problem of three and four, but in reverse. If the chimera represents the triad in the *coniunctio tetraptiva*, the four symbolizes the union of persons, and this is the underlying matrix of *The Chimeras*. By a process known as *henosis*, a tetrasomia or synthesis of opposites is produced to create a unity.

"El desdichado"

The first sonnet of *The Chimeras* is probably Nerval's best-known poem, "El desdichado" (the title, meaning "the unhappy one," was borrowed from Sir Walter Scott's *Ivanhoe*, 1819). It focuses upon the descent into the abyss, the *nigredo* of the alchemist, or the opening stage of the process. The images used to describe this phase are all somber: images of death and of caves, and even of Hell (the Achéron and the evocation of Orpheus). More important, however, is Nerval's linking of these dark, demoniac images with traditionally positive images—the union of contraries being the functional principle in such expressions as *soleil noir* ("black sun"). The most powerful character in the poem, one who is there by implication and not by name, is Melusina, the absent-but-present feminine principle. Melusina also embodies the identity of contraries, possessing either the tail of a fish or that of a snake; sometimes she appears only as a snake. Her ability to metamorphose as well as to heal diseases and injuries makes her—in the mind of the alchemist and of the poet-seer—the feminine counterpart to Mercury. Thus, in "El desdichado," Nerval posits a synthesis of the medieval duality with the Greco-Roman duality, Hermes-Mercury.

"Myrtho"

In the succeeding sonnet, "Myrtho," Nerval assesses the descent into the abyss. It is in this manner that one can achieve the light. Moreover, it is here that the black is an essential component of the gold: "Aux raisins noirs mêlés avec l'or de ta tresse" ("and black grapes mingled in your golden tresses"). In this descent into the interior world of the light, the poet-seer necessarily meets the sovereign of the underworld, Bacchus-Dionysus-Osiris. The final two lines announce the reconciliation of certain poetic visions: that of Vergil's neopaganism with the Illuminism of the eighteenth century. Like "El desdichado," then, "Myrtho" presents a unification of various systems of thought.

"Horus"

The sonnet "Horus" concerns the Egyptian deity considered by the syncretists to be a prefiguration of Christ. Horus also symbolizes Hellenistic mysticism, providing a direct link with Hermes and, by association, with Hermes Trismegistus, the alchemist. Isis, Horus's mother, the symbol of nature's mysteries, is identified with Venus in the same manner that Hermes is linked with Osiris, leading to a form of Greco-Egyptian religious syncretism. In this system is to be found the "esprit nouveau," the result of which is a rainbow or the vision of colors, a necessary stage which precedes the appearance of gold in alchemy.

"Antéros"

"Antéros" presents a vision of Hell, with Semitic overtones. To be of the race of Antéros (Antaeus) means to gather strength from the earth from which one has sprouted. This agrarian subtext is consistent with references to Cain, the keeper of the fields, and to Dagon, the Philistine agrarian god. The Satanic aspect is sustained in the mark of Cain and in the thrice-dipping into the Cocyte, one of the rivers of Tartarus. The sonnet projects the archetypal struggle of the vanquished giant who refuses defeat—here represented by the Amalekites, a nomadic tribe which was virtually exterminated by the Israelites during the time of David. These pagans are associated with the race of Satan and Cain. "Antéros" ends with a metaphor of rebirth, that of sowing the dragon's teeth in order to create a new race of giants. In alchemical terms, the sowing of the divine seed (*germinis divi*) provides the continuity necessary for the continual process of transformation which involves death and rebirth, descent and resurrection. The baptism of Hell is the equivalent of the baptism at the holy font.

"Delfica"

In "Delfica," Nerval includes the trees most often discussed by alchemists as symbols for the human body . Daphne, who was transformed into a tree, is the personification par excellence of the desired synthesis of humanity and nature. The lemons which carry the imprint of her teeth are the natural equivalents in tree code to the metallic gold. Just as the *lapis philosophorum* (the philosopher's stone) holds the key to the mysteries at its center, so too the grotto holds the dragon, sign of the danger of the penetration into the mysteries and also carrier of the all-important seed, or seminal material, which now lies dormant. Ancient beliefs, Nerval suggests, have been overcome by Christianity, yet like the anima of Daphne in the tree, they remain essentially intact, awaiting a revival.

"Artémis"

"Artémis" begins with an invocation to the mysteries: the number thirteen, an indivisible number, joining the basis of oneness and of the Trinity (which is always One). Thirteen is also the symbol of death in the Tarot (Arcane XIII). The sonnet centers upon the alchemical mystique of the rose; Nerval follows the tradition whereby the rose symbolizes the relationship between king and queen. More important, the rose provides the essential alchemical link with Christ. As such, the rose must be blood-colored in order to be identified with the Redeemer and the Cross. The final line indicates that the descent into the abyss is a necessary step in the making of a saint.

In alchemical writings, the philosopher's stone represents the *homo totus*, which will shed a bloody sweat. In this way, the stone prefigures the agony of Christ. Indeed, the Evangelist Luke says of Christ: "and His sweat was as it were great drops falling down to the ground" (Luke 22:44). It should therefore come as no surprise that Nerval would follow "Artémis" with five sonnets dealing with Christ in the Garden of Gethsemene. In his final hours of agony, Nerval's Christ is truly human, doubting the existence of a supreme power. In the fifth sonnet of the series, he recalls the necessity of descent in order to ascend, the necessity of death in order to give life. Christ's death gives life to a new belief which spells death to the old gods, yet Nerval poses an interesting question: "Quel est ce nouveau dieu qu'on impose à la terre?" ("who is this new god who is being imposed on Earth?"). The answer is reserved for the Almighty, who blessed the children of Adam ("les enfants du limon"). As already noted, the lemon is symbolic of the alchemical gold—that is, the quest for perfection and transcendence that Christ represents.

"VERS DORÉS"

In "Vers dorés" ("Golden Verses"), Nerval not only states his theory of correspondences but also offers his most compact statement concerning the role of alchemy in poetry. A new language is to be found—"À la matière même un verbe est attaché" ("even with matter there's a built-in word")—and a Divine Spirit is present in the darkness, waiting to shed his light. The last two lines describe the poet-seer as having opened his third eye; thus, he is able to strip away the layers of stone (the *lapis*) and finally attain the "gold" of the alchemist. Nerval's *The Chimeras*, therefore, achieves a synthesis of various manifestations of contrary elements, each time through the use of personification. "Vers dorés" symbolizes the achievement of the *coniunctio*, the realization of a new form of poetic inspiration and performance.

OTHER MAJOR WORKS

SHORT FICTION: *Les Illuminés*, 1852; "Sylvie," 1853 (English translation, 1922); *Les Filles du feu*, 1854 (*Daughters of Fire*, 1922).

PLAYS: *Faust*, pb. 1827, 1840 (translation of Johann Wolfgang von Goethe's play); *Piquillo*, pb. 1837 (with Alexandre Dumas, *père*); *Alchimiste*, pb. 1839 (with Dumas, *père*); *Léo Burckart*, pr., pb. 1839 (with Dumas, *père*); *Chariot d'enfant*, pb. 1850 (with Joseph Méry); *L'Imagier de Harlem*, pr. 1851.

NONFICTION: *Voyage en Orient*, 1851 (*Journey to the Orient*, 1972); *Promenades et souvenirs*, 1854-1856; *Aurélia*, 1855 (English translation, 1932).

MISCELLANEOUS: *Selected Writings*, 1957 (Geoffrey Wagner, translator); *Selected Writings*, 1999 (Richard Sieburth, translator).

BIBLIOGRAPHY

Behdad, Ali. "Orientalist Desire, Desire of the Orient." *French Forum* 15, no. 1 (January, 1990): 37-51. Useful background on the psychological implications of Nerval's fascination with the East. The story of Adoniram is discussed in relationship to its context in the storytelling tradition of Constantinople. The veiled women of the East symbolize another aspect of the separation between Nerval and the woman who represents his ideal, and the author sees this concealment as increasing desire.

Dubruck, Alfred. *Gérard de Nerval and the German Heritage*. The Hague, the Netherlands: Mouton, 1965. This study of German influences in Nerval's work cites E. T. A. Hoffmann, Johann Wolfgang von Goethe, and Heinrich Heine.

Ender, Evelyne. "A Case of Nostalgia: Gérard de Nerval." In *Architexts of Memory: Literature, Science, and Autobiography*. Ann Arbor: University of Michigan Press, 2005. In this chapter, Ender argues that the main theme in Nerval's writing is nostalgia, and that his writing predominantly involves memory.

Jones, Robert Emmet. *Gérard de Nerval*. New York: Twayne, 1974. This volume situates Nerval within the Romantic movement in France. Discusses his life and work.

Knapp, Bettina L. *Gérard de Nerval: The Mystic's Dilemma*. Tuscaloosa: University of Alabama Press, 1980. Knapp's study is organized as a biography and looks at mysticism in his works.

Lokke, Kari. *Gérard de Nerval: The Poet as Social Visionary*. Lexington, Ky.: French Forum, 1987. This thematic study uses Nerval's works to define the nature of his hallucinations and his concept of "the other."

MacLennan, George. *Lucid Interval: Subjective Writing and Madness in History*. Rutherford, N.J.: Fairleigh Dickinson University Press, 1992. A history of literature and mental illness with particular attention to the work of Nerval. Includes bibliographical references and index.

Rhodes, S. A. *Gérard de Nerval, 1808-1855: Poet, Traveler, Dreamer*. New York: Philosophical Library, 1951. This biography offers useful background on Jenny Colon and how Nerval linked her to the Queen of Sheba.

Rinsler, Norma. *Gérard de Nerval*. London: Athlone Press, 1973. This volume begins with a brief biography and goes on to cover his works.

Strauss, Jonathan. "Death-Based Subjectivity in the Creation of Nerval's Lyric Self." *Espirit Créateur* 35, no. 4 (Winter, 1995): 83-94. Focuses on Nerval's lyric poetry, specifically his most famous sonnet, "El desdichado," in the context of the influence of Georg Wilhelm Friedrich Hegel. This discussion raises issues of the author's alienation from himself that illuminate the use of doubled characters in the short stories.

_____. *Subjects of Terror: Nerval, Hegel, and the Modern Self*. Stanford, Calif.: Stanford University Press, 1998. Despite the mention of Georg Wilhelm Friedrich Hegel in the title, this is a book about Nerval. The first two chapters deal with Hegel and other influences in order to put Nerval's madness in context in chapter 3, ending with an overview of *Daughters of Fire*. Chapter 4 focuses on "Les Faux Saulniers," an extract from "L'Abbé de Bucquoy" from *Les Illuminés*.

Leslie B. Mittleman

SAINT-JOHN PERSE
Alexis Saint-Léger Léger

Born: Guadeloupe, French Antilles; May 31, 1887
Died: Giens, France; September 20, 1975

PRINCIPAL POETRY
Éloges, 1911 (English translation, 1944)
Amitié du prince, 1924 (*Friendship of the Prince*, 1944)
Anabase, 1924 (*Anabasis*, 1930)
Exil, 1942 (*Exile*, 1949)
Pluies, 1943 (*Rains*, 1949)
Éloges, and Other Poems, 1944 (includes *Éloges* and *Friendship of the Prince*)
Neiges, 1944 (*Snows*, 1949)
Vents, 1946 (*Winds*, 1953)
Exile, and Other Poems, 1949 (includes *Exile*, *Rains*, and *Snows*)
Amers, 1957 (*Seamarks*, 1958)
Chronique, 1960 (English translation, 1961)
Oiseaux, 1962 (*Birds*, 1966)
St.-John Perse: Collected Poems, 1971, 1982

OTHER LITERARY FORMS

Some 440 pages of the Pléiade edition of the *Œuvres complètes* (1972) of Saint-John Perse (pehrs), which was supervised by the poet himself, are given to letters. Perse's letters provide the reader not only with a wealth of details about his life but also with comments about his poems and political and cultural events during more than half a century. In Perse's letters to his family and to literary figures such as André Gide, Paul Claudel, Jacques Rivière, Archibald MacLeish, Allen Tate, and T. S. Eliot, one can find clues to the duality of Saint-John Perse the poet and Alexis Saint-Léger Léger the diplomat. An English translation of these letters by Arthur Knodel, *St.-John Perse: Letters* (1979), gives them the same emphasis as Gide's or Claudel's journals.

Perse's Nobel Prize acceptance speech, "Poésie" ("On Poetry"), delivered in Stockholm on December 10, 1960, and his address "Pour Dante" ("Dante"), delivered in Florence on April 20, 1965, to mark the seventh centenary of Dante's birth, are available in *St.-John Perse: Collected Poems*, a bilingual edition. Perse's manuscripts, his annotated personal library, his notebooks on ornithology, several scrapbooks with clippings, and other documents have all been gathered by the Saint-John Perse Foundation in Aix-en-Provence, France.

Saint-John Perse
(©The Nobel Foundation)

ACHIEVEMENTS

Saint-John Perse is a "poet's poet." Although he won international recognition with the Nobel Prize in Literature in 1960, preceded by the Grand Prix National des Lettres and the Grand Prix International de Poésie in 1959, his readership has remained small. Poets as diverse as Eliot and Czesław Miłosz have paid him tribute; it is in the tributes of Perse's fellow poets that one finds the measure of his work, rather than in the standard literary histories of his age, for he remained aloof from fashionable movements of the century.

Indeed, Perse is characterized above all by a self-conscious detachment. During his diplomatic career, from 1914 to 1940, he maintained a sharp division between his public and his poetic persona. In these years, he published only two works, *Anabasis* and *Friendship of the Prince*. His choice of a partly English pseudonym emphasized his aloof stance.

Perse's exile to the United States in 1941 marked the end of his political career but the revival of his poetic creation. *Exile*, his first poem written in the United States, was first published in French in *Poetry* magazine in 1941. Although Perse never wrote in English, his poems were always published in the United States in bilingual editions and followed by numerous articles and reviews by American critics. Perse disdained literary factions and did not give public readings of his works. He twice refused the Norton Chair of Poetry at Harvard, in 1946 and 1952, but he was officially recognized by the American Academy of Arts and Letters in 1950, when he received the Award of Merit Medal for poetry.

In his poetry, Perse maintained distance by seldom including place-names or markers of any kind that would locate his work in a specific place or time. In Perse's conception, the poet's task, like the scientist's, is to explore the universe, the elements, and human consciousness. The distinguishing quality of Perse's poetry is its universality, its endeavor to celebrate the cosmos and humankind beyond the limits of the personal, beyond the literary currents of the time. In this conception, poetry is not a re-creation or a transcription of reality; rather, poetry is reality, continually in flux, with all its tensions and its complexity. Perse's long poems, free from a specific form or traditional meter, and his symphonic compositions, with echoes and variations of the same phrase, achieve a musical quality seldom surpassed by his contemporaries.

Biography

Alexis Saint-Léger Léger (who wrote using the pseudonym Saint-John Perse) was born on May 31, 1887, on a small island near Pointe-à-Pitre in Guadeloupe. His parents were both of French descent and came from families of plantation owners and naval officers established in the islands since the seventeenth and eighteenth centuries. Perse spent his childhood in Guadeloupe, where his father was a lawyer. The young poet and his sisters were brought up on family plantations among servants, private tutors, and plantation workers. It was not until the age of nine that Perse started school. In 1899, a few years later, earthquakes, the Spanish-American War, and an economic crisis compelled the family to leave for France, where they settled in Pau. In 1904, Perse began studying law, science, literature, and medicine at the University of Bordeaux. He wrote his first poems there, and between 1904 and 1914, he met a number of writers, among them Francis Jammes, Claudel, Paul Valéry, Gide, and Rivière. After his military service in 1905 and 1906, Perse divided his time between traveling and studying political science, music, and philosophy; he soon extended his circle of friends to include Erik Satie and Igor Stravinsky.

Perse spent the years from 1916 to 1921 in Peking, where he wrote *Anabasis*. After serving in the Ministry of Foreign Affairs, he was promoted in 1933 to secretary general, a position that he held until 1940, when the war and the Vichy government forced him to leave for England and, shortly after, for the United States. It was MacLeish who encouraged him to accept an appointment at the Library of Congress. In 1942, Perse published *Exile* and became known officially as Saint-John Perse. He spent the following seventeen years in the United States, where his voluntary exile provided him with an endless array of new scenery, including rare species of birds and plants that he painstakingly detailed in his notebooks. In 1946, he published *Winds*, followed by *Seamarks* in 1957; in the latter year, he returned to France, where he continued to spend most of his summers. In 1958, he married Dorothy Milburn Russell in Washington, D.C. Limited editions of his last two major works, *Chronique* and *Birds*, were illustrated with color etchings by Georges Braque. Although the years that followed his Nobel Prize in 1960 were rich in translations, new editions, and tributes, Perse's publications after *Birds* were limited to a few short poems. He spent his last years in France at the Presqu'île de Giens, where he died in 1975 at the age of eighty-eight.

ANALYSIS

When asked why he wrote, Saint-John Perse always had the same answer: "to live better." For him, poetry was a way of life, not self-centered but open to the world. In his work, the universe predominates over the self, and very little space is left in the texts for the poet's own life and feelings. Perse recorded details of travels and carefully described the flora and fauna that he encountered; these details constitute the only "autobiographical" elements in his *Œuvres complètes*. Perse was a close observer of nature, often compared to the Swedish botanist Carolus Linnaeus, Henry David Thoreau, and Walt Whitman. He was not only a scientist who named things but also a thinker and wanderer. The constant tension between the microcosm and the macrocosm, the precise words for small details, provided Perse with a means to stop, to reverse, or to capture what the Romantics cried for: the passage of time. Few poets have been so at ease with the concept of time and space; for Perse, these concepts are not limited by nihilism or religion. Perse rejected the alternatives represented by Jean-Paul Sartre and Claudel: Neither humanity nor God is the center of his vision. There is only the universe and the beyond, the symbiosis of humanity and the elements. Perse goes beyond traditional spatiotemporal limits. He is everywhere and nowhere in particular; in his sweeping vision, time and space merge in one eternal movement.

This universality was recognized by the Swedish Academy, which awarded Perse the Nobel Prize for "the soaring flight and the evocative imagery of his poetry, which in a visionary fashion reflects the conditions of our time." Perse's oeuvre leaves an impression of wholeness. He saw his poems as "one long uninterrupted phrase," as if they belonged to the same mold or flow.

ÉLOGES

In Perse's first collection, *Éloges*, one can find the roots of his later, more solemn, longer poems: the mysterious forces of the elements, the insistent presence of the sea, the celebration of life as well as the yearning for other shores, for a place *outre-mer* (beyond the sea) and *outre-songe* (beyond the dream). The figure dominating Perse's works has no proper name; "Navigator" and "Poet" together provide enigmatic suggestions of anonymity and leadership.

Perse's manuscripts, with their lists of variations and echoes of other poems or lines, sometimes more than half a century apart, show that the final version of a given poem was often highly condensed, frequently a synthesis of passages written at different times. His oeuvre is characterized by an unusual consistency of style and vision; a complex network of recurring motifs provides an inner structure that belies the prosaic "formlessness" of his verse.

ANABASIS

Anabasis, Perse's first major poem, recounts an expedition through the desert, the symbol of humankind's march through time and space and through consciousness. Although it was written in China in a Daoist temple in the Gobi Desert, it echoes the *Kyrou anabasis* (n.d.; *Anabasis*, 1623; also known as *Expedition of Cyrus*, and *The March Up Country*) of the Greek historian Xenophon, describing the retreat of a mercenary force of ten thousand Greeks after the failure of an expedition organized by Cyrus the Younger against his older brother Artaxerxes. Emphasizing the literal meaning of "anabasis," an expedition beyond geographical boundaries (in this case, both inland and inward, toward the essence of Being), Perse sets his poem outside a particular time and place. In addition to the narrative and epic aspects of the poem, it is perhaps this very movement of the expedition and march that has inspired composers such as Alan Hovhaness and Paul Bowles in their musical transcriptions of passages from *Anabasis*. They were preceded by the Swedish composer Karl-Birger Blomdahl, a disciple of Paul Hindemith and Béla Bartók, who composed an oratorio using the original French version of the poem. Blomdahl saw *Anabasis* as an "uninterrupted dialogue" and compared the work to a Byzantine mosaic. This fragmented aspect of some of the more elliptical and condensed passages in *Anabasis* perhaps results from the fact that the published poem was the condensed version of an original poem four times as long.

This epic poem has ten cantos framed by two songs in which the birth of a colt, the passage of a stranger, and the "feminine" soul are related parts of Perse's main network of motifs. In the first group of cantos, the stranger reappears, contemplating his land. Through the figure of the stranger, Perse explores the conflict between the restless urge to conquer new lands and the civilizing impulse to build a city. Tracing a cycle of exploration, achievement, and renewed restlessness, the poem conveys the movement of human history.

SEAMARKS

Seamarks, Perse's longest poem, recalls classical Greek drama with its imagery, its chorus and altar, and the sea being the theatrical arena where man and woman celebrate life. In French, the title *Amers* also suggests a fusion of "sea" (*mer*) and "love" (*amour*).

The poem's four parts are divided in turn into cantos of uneven length. In the first part, "Invocation," ritual preparation for the celebration of the sea is accompanied by ritual preparation for the poem, unifying reality and poetry. The second part, "Strophe," or "movement of the chorus around the altar," introduces the different groups and individuals confronting the sea for "questioning, entreaty, imprecation, initiation, appeal, or celebration." The second part ends with a very long canto, "Étroits sont les vaisseaux . . ." ("Narrow Are the Vessels . . ."), the high point of the poem, which celebrates the physical and psychological union of man and woman. They are navigating on a ship as narrow as a couch, and the woman's body has the shape of a vessel; thus, the sea, which seems to protect and "bear" the lovers, becomes feminine and a synonym for love.

In the third part, "Choeur" ("Chorus"), one collective voice exalts the sea on behalf of humankind, and the procession from the city to the shore led by the poet is, according to Perse, the "image of humanity marching towards its highest destiny." In the concluding fourth part, "Dédicace" ("Dedication"), it is noon; the drama is over, and the poet removes his mask, after having brought his people to the highest point in time and space, where humanity is immortal. One finds the same ascension and defiance of death in Perse's next poem, *Chronique*, which is the "chronicle" of the earth, of humanity, and of the poet himself in pursuit of nomadism toward higher elevations and a "higher sea," beyond death.

BIRDS

Perse's last major poem, *Birds*, is more a meditation on art and on poetry than a continuation of the cosmic cycle of *Anabasis*, *Seamarks*, and *Chronique*. The limited first edition of the poem was illustrated with twelve lithographs by Braque; the references to Braque's birds were added after Perse had already written most of the poem. They add a new dimension to the bird in flight, now caught on the canvas, where it continues to live, not as a visual image but as a living part of reality. The descriptive, the technical, and the metaphysical passages of the poem, although very different from one another, all convey the movement of the bird in flight—on the canvas, in the air, and in poetry.

The poem is divided into thirteen parts, the first part introducing the migratory bird, which searches for "an uninterrupted summer," as do the painter and the poet. The asceticism and the "combustion" of his flight have a symbolic import, reinforced in the last part, in which the bird's wings are like a cross. Part 2 presents a very technical description of the anatomy of the bird compared to the structure of a ship, as was the woman in *Seamarks*. It is followed in parts 3 through 7 by the description of the bird perceived by Braque's eye, like the eye of a bird of prey, and painted on the canvas, where it continues to live and fly in its metamorphoses throughout the successive stages of the painting. The finished painting is like the launching of a ship, and the needle of the nautical compass, shaped as a bird, now becomes the symbol for direction and equilibrium. In parts 8 through 10, the bird, defying the seasons, night, and gravity, continues its migration, searching for eternity and "the expanse of Being." In parts 11 and 12, Perse returns to Braque, but only to give a long list of legendary or historical birds that are different from Braque's anonymous birds on the canvas. Thus, the bird becomes the poet's sacred messenger and a symbol for the nomadism of his poetic creation.

Perse's epic vision of the universe informs his entire oeuvre—a timeless vision that will endure when many celebrated poems, tied too closely to their time and place, have faded into oblivion.

OTHER MAJOR WORKS

NONFICTION: *St.-John Perse: Letters*, 1979; *The Poet and the Diplomat: The Correspondence of Dag Hammarskjöld and Alexis Leger*, 2001 (Marie-Noëlle Little, editor).
MISCELLANEOUS: *Œuvres complètes*, 1972 (includes poetry and letters).

BIBLIOGRAPHY

Baker, Peter. *Obdurate Brilliance: Exteriority and the Modern Long Poem*. Gainesville: University Press of Florida, 1991. Critical interpretation of some of Perse's works with an introduction to the history of American poetry in the twentieth century. Includes bibliographical references and index.

Galand, René. *Saint-John Léger*. Boston: Twayne, 1972. A standard critical biography of Perse.

Knodel, Arthur. *Saint-John Perse*. Edinburgh: Edinburgh University Press, 1966. Critical analysis of selected works by Perse. Includes bibliographic references.

Kopenhagen-Urian, Judith. "Delicious Abyss: The Bib lical Darkness in the Poetry of Saint-John Perse." *Comparative Literature Studies* 36, no. 3 (1999): 195-208. Kopenhagen-Urian examines Saint-John Perse's oxymoron "delicious abyss" in relation to four functions observed in Perse's use of the Bible: the contrasting perspective, the structured allusion, the repeated motif, and the "collage."

Loichot, Valérie. *Orphan Narratives: The Postplantation Literature of Faulkner, Glissant, Morrison, and Saint-John Perse*. Charlottesville: University of Virginia Press, 2007. Loichot compares and contrasts Perse's *Éloges* with works by William Faulkner, Édouard Glissant, and Toni Morrison.

Ostrovsky, Erika. *Under the Sign of Ambiguity: Saint-John Perse/Alexis Léger*. New York: New York University Press, 1984. A thorough biography, with aesthetic and psychological insights into Perse's life and accomplishments.

Poiana, Peter. "The Order of *Mimesis* in Saint-John Perse's *Vents*." *Neophilologus* 91 (2007): 33-49. This extensive examination of how mimesis functions in Perse's *Winds* sheds light on many aspects of his poetic vision.

Rigolot, Carol. *Forged Genealogies: Saint-John Perse's Conversations with Culture*. Chapel Hill: University of North Carolina Press, 2002. Analyzes Perse's multiple strategies of dialogue within his poems.

Sterling, Richard L. *The Prose Works of Saint-John Perse: Towards an Understanding of His Poetry*. New York: Peter Lang, 1994. A critical study of the prose works of Perse that is intended to give a fuller understanding of his poetry. Includes bibliographical references and index.

Marie-Noëlle D. Little

JACQUES PRÉVERT

Born: Neuilly-sur-Seine, France; February 4, 1900
Died: Omonville-la-Petite, France; April 11, 1977

PRINCIPAL POETRY
Paroles, 1945
Histoires, 1946 (with André Verdet)
Poèmes, 1946
Contes pour enfants pas sages, 1947
La Pluie et le beau temps, 1955
Selections from "Paroles," 1958 (Lawrence Ferlinghetti, translator)
Carmina burana, 1965 (translation)
Fatras, 1966
Prévert, 1967
Arbres, 1976
Words for All Seasons, 1979
Soleil de nuit, 1980
Blood and Feathers: Selected Poems of Jacques Prévert, 1988 (includes selections from *Paroles*, *Spectacle*, *Soleil de nuit*, and more)

OTHER LITERARY FORMS

Outside France, Jacques Prévert (pray-VEHR) is best known as a screenwriter; among his credits are a number of films that have become classics of the French cinema. His first screenplay was written for his brother, Pierre Prévert, the director of *L'Affaire est dans le sac* (1932). The success of his dialogue in Jean Renoir's *Le Crime de Monsieur Lange* (1935) led to more such scripts, marked by Prévert's sparkling wit and poetic repartee. His long collaboration with director Marcel Carné produced eight major films by 1950, including such masterpieces as *Jenny* (1936), *Drôle de drame* (1937), and *Les Enfants du paradis* (1945; *Children of Paradise*, 1968). Many film historians credit Carné's success to Prévert's scripts, although it must be pointed out that the highly successful *Le Jour se lève* (1939) was simply adapted by Prévert from an existing script, and that Prévert also adapted the unsuccessful 1956 version of *Notre Dame de Paris*. Carné regards Prévert as "the one and only poet of the French cinema," one whose contribution "reflects the soul of the people."

Prévert's cabaret-style songs and stage pieces for the group Octobre are often overlooked in his oeuvre. Although they predate his major film successes and seem minor in comparison, these verses contain the seeds of both Prévert's screen dialogue and his later poetry. Most screenwriters of Prévert's time came to the new art burdened with

Jacques Prévert

preconceptions from the theater or literature, but Prévert simply wrote scenarios that he thought would appeal to moviegoers, and he succeeded. Many of his scripts have been published and today provide texts for students writing screenplays.

Prévert also produced several charming books for children, including *Le Petit Lion* (1947; the little lion) and *Des bêtes...* (1950; the beasts...). In 1953, he wrote lyrics for Christiane Verger's *Tour de chant* and *L'Opéra de la lune*. His translation into French of the medieval *Carmina burana*, set to the music of Carl Orff, was published in 1965 and achieved high critical esteem. In the United States, Prévert is known as the lyricist of such popular songs as "Les Feuilles mortes" ("Autumn Leaves") and "Ne me quitte pas" ("Don't Leave Me").

Achievements

Despite his sweeping success, Jacques Prévert received no major literary awards. For his work as a filmmaker, he received the Grand Prix from Societé des Auteurs et Compositeurs Dramatiques in 1973 and the Grand Prix National from *Cinéma* in 1975.

The appellation "the most popular poet" (in this case, of postwar France) carries a stigma in the world of poetry, where popularity is not usually a mark of quality. The

French writer Guy Jacob good-naturedly referred to Prévert's "easy-going muse," who had "lent him in place of a lyre a barrel-organ." His apparent simplicity of expression, his concern with the emotions and things of everyday life, and his singsong rhythms and insistent rhymes combined to create a poetry at once accessible and self-explanatory. Prévert restored the popular validity of poetry to a literature that had been rarefied and intellectualized by movements such as Surrealism, Dadaism, and Symbolism. He refused to permit poetry to remain the means of expression of the privileged, helping himself freely to the argot of the streets for his verses.

Free of allegiance to any literary clique, Prévert reinforced the very idea of individuality at a time when the historical and political developments of World War II had necessitated conformity. A Marxist without theoretical pretensions and an anarchist at heart, he mocked pomposity and unmasked exploitation wherever he found them, all the while maintaining an aloof attitude toward partisan politics. His poetry demonstrates the charm, wit, and humanistic goals of popular poetry as well as its limitations.

Biography

The son of working-class parents, Jacques Prévert was born February 4, 1900, in Neuilly-sur-Seine. At the age of fifteen, having completed his primary education—a process he obviously did not enjoy—he left school and began to earn his living. He once, in a radio interview, confessed that, had the label "juvenile delinquent" been part of the vocabulary of the early twentieth century, it would have been applied to him.

Despite his distaste for school, Prévert read a great deal and was particularly interested in the authors of the Enlightenment and their ideas about the natural rights of humankind, as well as such distinctions as natural evil as opposed to human evil. Nevertheless, he quickly developed a distrust of great intellectual constructs and philosophical debate. His friendship with the Surrealist painter Yves Tanguy began in the regiment in which they both served in 1920, as part of the occupation army of Thessaloníki, Greece. There he also made the acquaintance of Marcel Duhamel, who would later become a film director. The three young men went to Paris upon their demobilization and established what they jokingly called a phalanstery (after the Fourierist communes known by that name) in the no longer extant rue de Château. Raymond Queneau, who thirty years later would write critical works on Prévert, soon joined them, and their house became a gathering point for the young writers and artists of the Surrealist movement.

A shared passion for the cinema prompted them to attend films daily, sometimes three or four in a single day. Prévert and his friends, including his brother, Pierre, later attested the significant impact of these cinematic experiences upon their later work. Prévert fondly recalled long walks in the middle of the night through the streets of Paris, from which he returned to the rue de Château full of life and impatient with the intellectual turmoil of the Surrealists. His disdainful attitude toward the dogmatism of the movement ultimately led to his being excluded by its leader, André Breton.

Prévert circulated his poems in handwritten form, a habit that led to the existence of numerous textual variations. Between 1930 and 1936, three long poems appeared in reviews. "Souvenirs de famille, ou l'Ange garde-chiourme" (family souvenirs or the Martinet angel), published in *Bifur* in 1930, appealed to an extremely refined literary audience. In 1931, the magazine *Commerce* at first hesitated to publish "Tentative de description d'un diner de têtes à Paris-France" ("An Endeavor to Describe a Dinner of Heads at Paris, France"), but it conceded at the insistence of Saint-John Perse. The third poem, "La Crosse en l'air" (the crook in the air), appeared in *Soutes* in 1936, a communist tract more dedicated to politics than to literature. Such beginnings reflect the diversity of Prévert's appeal as well as his difficulty in getting his poetry published.

In 1933, with the theater group Octobre, Prévert visited Moscow to perform on the occasion of the International Olympiad of Theater. In 1938, he spent a year in the United States, returning home in time to be called up in the French mobilization in 1939. An attack of appendicitis prevented his military service in the war.

After the war, the Hungarian-born composer Joseph Kosma, who had worked on films with the Prévert-Carné team, began to set Prévert's verses to music, and the songs were every bit as popular as Prévert's volumes of poetry, which had also begun to appear after the war. Prévert carried his celebrity quite modestly and was regarded as a man of the people. He was, for example, a figure of interest for the most popular magazines in France, which celebrated him in interviews and profiles.

Other artistic inclinations found expression in Prévert's collages. He enjoyed two exhibitions, one in Paris in 1957 and one in 1963 in Antibes on the Riviera. In 1977, Prévert died after a long illness and was buried in a quiet, simple ceremony in his village of Omonville-la-Petite near the English Channel.

Analysis

The poetry of Jacques Prévert is pervaded by an innocence that allows him to cultivate a world in which animals, plants, and objects speak or are metamorphosed at will. There is in his verse no development of a self-contained world of fable or faerie with symbolic weight; rather, the Surrealist influence manifests itself in vignettes or episodes within individual poems. Prévert brought an unaccustomedly cheerful mien to Surrealism, employing its devices not to frighten or to dwell on the victimization of people but to portray the imagination as an escape route from the dreariness of life's minor burdens.

In his less childlike or innocent verses, Prévert expresses outraged indignation at social and political injustice and is capable of piercing the affectations of those whom he considers unworthy of respect. There is a remarkable consistency of tone and outlook throughout Prévert's work, and whether one draws examples from early volumes or later ones, one finds an unchanging *Weltanschauung*. In part, this consistency can be attributed to Prévert's comparatively late success at a time when stylistic experiment was behind him.

Poems about Children

From Prévert's poems about children to his antiwar utterances, there persists a naïveté that seems to challenge the values of the adult world and its rationalizations of people's inhumane acts toward others. Children, according to Prévert, are blessed with an innocence and a capacity to dream that can be corrupted only by growing up. One of his oft-cited poems, "Page d'écriture" (page of writing), from *Paroles* (words), depicts a math lesson during which a child, seeing a lyrebird fly by, asks it for help. The bird's help is forthcoming but causes something of an insurrection in the classroom before the entire scenario is metamorphosed in the final lines into a scene from nature.

In "En sortant de l'école" (upon leaving school), from *Histoires* (stories), Prévert portrays the gentle fantasies of a group of children, who, upon coming out of school, discover a train with a gilded wagon to take them through the world, where the sea promenades with all her seashells. From the same volume comes "Jour de fête" (day of the party), a heartfelt expression of the disappointment of a child who wants to celebrate a holiday dedicated to the frog, an animal that is not only a friend but that also sings to him nightly. The adults, who cannot comprehend this liaison, will not let the child go out in the rain. In the opening line, Prévert captures the parents' inhibiting concern: "Ou va-tu mon enfant avec ces fleurs/ Sous la pluie/ Il pleut il mouille/ Aujourd'hui c'est la fête à la grenouille" ("Where are you going my child with these flowers/ in the rain/ it's raining it's pouring/ Today is a holiday in honor of the frog"). The difference between the child's world and the world of adults is expressed in another way in "Arbres" (trees, from *Arbres*), in which a child understands when trees "speak tree"; only later, when he learns to speak "arboriculture," does he not understand the voice of the trees, the song of the wind. The dreamworld of the child is that of the poet. In "Dehors" (outside of), from *La Pluie et le beau temps* (rain and nice weather), Prévert describes a child who, dreaming, follows his dream smiling, for the dream is hilarious and almost alive. In "Encore une fois sur le fleuve" (along the river once more, from *Histoires*), Prévert advises: "alors fais comme moi . . ./ parle seulement des choses heureuses/ des choses merveilleuses rêvées et arrivées . . ." ("Then do as I . . ./ speak only of happy things/ of marvelous things dreamed and come to pass . . .").

Animals

Some of Prévert's most charming poems are addressed, in fact, to children by way of amusing descriptions of animals. *Contes pour enfants pas sages* (tales for misbehaving children) contains a dialogue between Tom Thumb and an ostrich who rescues him; the latter complains that the child's mother sports ostrich feathers in her hat and that his father, upon seeing an ostrich egg, thinks: "That would make a great omelette!" Another dialogue, "L'Opéra des girafes" (the giraffe's opera), is written as an opera. A dromedary, antelopes, elephants, a horse on an island, a young lion in a cage, and a good-natured donkey are all subjects of brief fables, unburdened by any higher mythology.

Throughout, Prévert's sympathies lie with the beasts, who are maltreated or misunderstood by humans.

The bird achieves a special status in Prévert's poems—sometimes representing liberation, as in "Quartier libre" ("Free Sector," from *Paroles*), sometimes as a symbol of sorrow, as in "Les Oiseaux du souci" ("Birds of Sorrow"), where the first line, "Pluie des plumes, plume de pluie" ("Rain of feathers, feather of rain"), reflects the indifference of the lonely poet in an atmosphere of despair and boredom to some birds who are trying to console him. One of Prévert's best-known poems, featuring a consummate demonstration of his technique of repetition, is "Chanson de l'oiseleur" (the bird-catcher's song), a poem of thirteen brief lines, the first twelve of which begin with the words "L'Oiseau," followed by descriptive characteristics. In the thirteenth and final line, the bird becomes a woman's heart beating its wings pathetically in her hard, white breast.

In "Au hasard des oiseaux" (the randomness of birds, from *Paroles*), the poet opens by regretting that he learned to love the birds too late, then continues with a diatribe against a certain Monsieur Glacis, who is ironically portrayed as having fought courageously in the war against young Paul, a character described as poor, handsome, and decent, who later becomes old Paul, rich, aged, honorable, and stingy but masquerading as philanthropic and pious. Prévert adds that Paul had a servant who led an exemplary life, because she never quarreled with her master or mentioned the unmentionable question of wages. The poem concludes by contrasting again the bestial nature of humans with the humane nature of the birds: "La lumière des oiseaux" (the light of the birds), in the final line, carries the implication of enlightenment.

JUSTICE AND PACIFISM

Prévert's sense of justice finds metaphoric expression in "Les Prodiges de la liberté" (the wonders of life, from *Histoires*), which opens with the pathetic picture of the paw of a white fox caught in the teeth of a trap in the snow. The fox holds between its teeth a rabbit, still alive. Prévert seems to be able to reconcile himself to the natural order but continually objects to the evil that originates with humankind. For example, in the poem "La Pêche à la baleine" ("Whaling," from *Paroles*), a father is astounded that his son does not want to go whaling with him. "Why," asks the son, "should I hunt a beast who has done nothing to me, Papa?"

Prévert's antiwar sentiments were perhaps best formulated in "Barbara" (*Paroles*), in which a tender and tragic tone is established in his comparison between the fate of a young girl and that of the city of Brest. The individual experiences pain in the loss of life, love, hope, and happiness, while the collective loss is shown in the destruction of the town, the ruins, and the fire raining down on one and all.

In 1952, Prévert took up his pen against the colonial war in "Entendez-vous gens du Viet-Nam" (do you hear people of Vietnam, from *La Pluie et le beau temps*), in which he denounces the French use of sophisticated tactics against the unarmed peasants. He notes that with the arrival of Admiral Thierry d'Argenlieu came a recrudescence of terror and suffering.

"FAMILIALE"

One of Prévert's best-known pacifist poems is "Familiale" (family, from *Paroles*), which is characteristic of his ability to paint in a brief scene a moral dilemma:

> La mère fait du tricot
> Le fils fait la guerre
> Elle trouveça tout naturel la mère
> Et le père qu'est-ce qu'il fait le père?
> Il fait des affaires. . . .
>
> (A mother makes a sweater,
> a son makes war,
> which she finds quite natural,
> but the father—what is he doing?
> Business.)

The rhymes and the singsong rhythm lend the poem the aspect of a children's chant, but the content grows grim after the innocent opening of a mother knitting. The reduction of each life to its most typical activity shows the isolation in which people play out their roles, unconscious of the interdependence of their activities.

LOVE

Prévert championed love as passionately as he railed against war. Human happiness recognizes its most profound expression in love, and Prévert's contribution to erotic poetry has the simplicity of the classical Greek lyric poets. "Fiesta" (*Histoires*) describes a seduction over empty glasses and a shattered bottle; the bed is wide open and the door closed; the poet is drunk and his lover is likewise drunk but lively and naked in his arms. The image of a woman "naked from head to toe" occurs frequently in Prévert's poems, but his physical descriptions rarely go further. In "Les Chiens ont soif" (the dogs are thirsty, from *Fatras*), the poet describes two lovers he has seen naked and entwined; he then assumes the point of view of the man: "He looks at her and knows without saying it that there is nothing more . . . indispensable, more simple and more inexplicable than love on a bed, than love on this earth."

The lighter side or more ephemeral aspect of love does not escape Prévert's wit. A character in *Fatras* exclaims how happy she is because her lover has said that he loves her, but she is even happier because she is still free, since he did not say he would love her forever. The lover in "Les Chansons les plus courtes . . ." (the shortest songs, from *Histoires*) complains of the bird in his head repeating the refrain "I love you" so insistently that he will have to kill him the next morning. In "Le Lézard" (the lizard, from *Histoires*), the poet declares: "The lizard of love has fled once again and left his tail between my fingers and that's all right/ I wanted to keep something for myself."

Many critics find the mechanics of Prévert's poetry too obtrusive, arguing that his rhymes and his wordplay, the adroit twists with which he frequently concluded his poems, lack the depth and resonance of great poetry. That he was a genuinely popular poet, however, is denied by none. The natural quality of his verse had an appeal that revived the spirit of France after World War II, and his can be called a poetry of recovery.

OTHER MAJOR WORKS

SCREENPLAYS: *L'Affaire est dans le sac*, 1932; *Le Crime de Monsieur Lange*, 1935; *Jenny*, 1936; *Drôle de drame*, 1937 (with Marcel Carné); *Le Jour se lève*, 1939; *Les Visiteurs du soir*, 1942 (with Carné and Pierre Laroche); *Les Enfants du paradis*, 1945 (with Carné; *Children of Paradise*, 1968); *Notre Dame de Paris*, 1956.

TRANSLATION: *Carmina burana*, 1965.

CHILDREN'S LITERATURE: *Le Petit Lion*, 1947; *Des bêtes...*, 1950; *Bim, le petit âne*, 1952 (*Bim, the Little Donkey*, 1973).

MISCELLANEOUS: *Spectacle*, 1949, 1951 (includes poetry, plays, and prose); *L'Opéra de la lune*, 1953 (song lyrics); *Tour de chant*, 1953 (songs for piano and voice).

BIBLIOGRAPHY

Baker, William E. *Jacques Prévert*. New York: Twayne, 1967. An overview that is fair and balanced in its assessment and limited only by its date. Prévert's work is discussed as antipoetry, as the poetry of plain talk, and as an expression of both romanticism and stark political views. A good annotated bibliography in both French and English is included.

Bishop, Michael. *Jacques Prévert: From Film and Theater to Poetry, Art, and Song*. New York: Rodopi, 2002. Examines Prévert's life and the many genres in which he worked, including poetry.

_____. *Jacques Prévert Revisited*. New York: Twayne, 2000. A general biography of Prévert that looks at his life and works.

Blakeway, Claire. *Jacques Prévert: Popular French Theatre and Cinema*. Cranbury, N.J.: Associated University Presses, 1990. Although the focus is on Prévert's work in cinema and theater, especially his collaborations with Marcel Carné, the discussions of politics and Surrealism apply to the poetry as well. Of special interest are the abundant black-and-white photographs.

Greet, Anne. *Jacques Prévert's Word Games*. Berkeley: University of California Press, 1968. A brief examination of Prévert's wordplay. Includes bibliographical footnotes.

Karen Jaehne

PIERRE REVERDY

Born: Narbonne, France; September 13, 1889
Died: Solesmes, France; June 17, 1960

PRINCIPAL POETRY

Poèmes en prose, 1915 (*Prose Poems*, 2007)
La Lucarne ovale, 1916
Quelques poèmes, 1916
Les Ardoises du toit, 1918 (*Roof Slates*, 1981)
Les Jockeys camouflés, 1918
La Guitare endormie, 1919
Cœur de chêne, 1921
Étoiles peintes, 1921
Cravates de chanvre, 1922
Grande Nature, 1925
La Balle au bond, 1928
Sources du vent, 1929
Pierres blanches, 1930
Ferraille, 1937
Plein verre, 1940
Plupart du temps, 1945 (collected volume, 1913-1922)
Le Chant des morts, 1948
Main d'œuvre: Poèmes, 1913-1949, 1949
Pierre Reverdy: Selected Poems, 1969
Roof Slates, and Other Poems of Pierre Reverdy, 1981
Selected Poems, 1991

OTHER LITERARY FORMS

Pierre Reverdy (ruh-VEHR-dee) worked extensively in other forms besides poetry. He wrote two novels and many stories and published collections of prose poems. Most of these are in a Surrealist vein, mixing experimentation in language with personal and unconscious reflection. As an editor of an avant-garde review, Reverdy also contributed important theoretical statements on cubism and avant-garde literary practice. Later in his career, he published several volumes of reminiscences, including sensitive reevaluations of the work of his near contemporaries, including Guillaume Apollinaire.

ACHIEVEMENTS

Pierre Reverdy is one of the most central and influential writers in the tradition of twentieth century avant-garde poetry. Already well established in terms of both his

Pierre Reverdy

work and his theoretical stance by the mid-1910's, Reverdy exerted considerable influence over the Dada and Surrealist movements, with which he was both officially and informally affiliated.

Reverdy's firm conviction was in a nonmimetic, nontraditional form of artistic expression. The art he championed and practiced would create a reality of its own rather than mirror a preexisting reality. In this way, the language of poetry would be cut loose from restraining conventions of meter, syntax, and punctuation in order to be able to explore the emotion generated by the poetic image.

In connection with the avant-garde artists of cubism, Dada, and Surrealism, Reverdy's formulations helped to break down the traditional models of artistic creation that then held firm sway in France. Reverdy's firm conviction was that artistic creation precedes aesthetic theory. All the concrete means at an artist's disposal constitute his aesthetic formation.

Along with Apollinaire, his slightly older contemporary, Reverdy became a central figure and example for a whole generation of French poets generally grouped under the Surrealist heading. His having been translated into English by a range of American poets from Kenneth Rexroth to John Ashbery shows the importance of his work to the modern American tradition as well.

Biography

Pierre Reverdy was born on September 13, 1889, in Narbonne, France, a city in the Languedoc region. The son and grandson of sculptors and artisans in wood carving, he grew up with this practical skill in addition to his formal studies. The Languedoc region at the turn of the century was an especially volatile region, witnessing the last major peasant uprising in modern French history.

After completing his schooling in Narbonne and nearby Toulouse, Reverdy moved to Paris in 1910, where he lived on and off for the rest of his life. Although exempted from military service, he volunteered at the outbreak of World War I, saw combat service, and was discharged in 1916. By profession a typesetter, Reverdy also worked as the director of the review *Nord-Sud*, which he founded in 1917.

From 1910 to 1926, Reverdy worked in close contact with almost all the important artists of his time. He had especially close relationships with Pablo Picasso and Juan Gris, both of whom contributed illustrations to collections of his verse. As the editor of an influential review, he had close contact with and strong influence on the writers who were to form the Dada and Surrealist movements. Already an avant-garde poet and theorist of some prominence by the late 1910's, Reverdy was often invoked along with Apollinaire as one of the precursors of Surrealism. He collaborated with the early Surrealist efforts and continued his loose affiliation even after a formal break in 1926.

That year saw Reverdy's conversion to a mystic Catholicism. From then until his death in 1960, his life became more detached from the quotidian, and he spent much of his time at the Abbey of Solesmes, where he died.

Analysis

In an early statement on cubism, Pierre Reverdy declaimed that a new epoch was beginning, one in which "one creates works that, by detaching themselves from life, enter back into it because they have an existence of their own." In addition to attacking mimetic standards of reproduction, or representation of reality, he also called for a renunciation of punctuation and a freeing of syntax in the writing of poetry. Rather than being something fixed according to rules, for Reverdy, syntax was "a medium of literary creation." Changing the rules of literary expression carried with it a change in ideas of representation. For Reverdy, the poetic image was solely responsible to the discovery of emotional truth.

From 1915 to 1922, Reverdy produced many volumes of poetry. The avant-garde called for an overturning of literary conventions, and Reverdy contributed with his own explosion of creative activity. In addition to editing the influential review *Nord-Sud*, he used his experience as an engraver and typesetter to publish books, including his own. The list of artists who contributed the illustrations to these volumes of poetry by Reverdy reads like a Who's Who of the art world of the time: Gris, Picasso, André Derain, Henri Matisse, Georges Braque, among others. Reverdy's work, along with that of Apollinaire, was cited as the guiding force for Surrealism by André Breton in his

Manifestes du surréalisme (1962; *Manifestoes of Surrealism*, 1969).

Reverdy's early work achieves an extreme detachment from mimetic standards and literary conventions that allows for the images to stand forth as though seen shockingly for the first time. The last two lines from "Sur le Talus" (on the talus), published in 1918, show this extreme detachment: "L'eau monte comme une poussière/ Le silence ferme la nuit" (The water rises like dust/ Silence shuts the night). There can be no question here of establishing a realistic context for these images. Rather, one is cast back on the weight of emotion that they carry and that must thus guide their interpretation. Reflections off water may appear to rise in various settings, though perhaps particularly at twilight. The dust points to a particular kind of aridity that may be primarily an emotional state. The sudden transition from an (implied) twilight to an abrupt nightfall undercuts any kind of conventional emotional presentation. The quick cut is a measure perhaps of the individual's lack of control over external phenomena and, by extension, inner feelings as well.

"Carrefour"

Much of Reverdy's early work is based on just such an imagistic depiction of interior states, with a strong element of detachment from reality and a certain resulting confusion or overlapping. The force of emotion is clearly there, but to pin it down to a particular situation or persona proves difficult because any such certainty is constantly being undercut by the quick transitions between images. The complete suppression of punctuation as well as a certain freedom of syntax as one moves from line to line are clearly tools that Reverdy developed to increase the level of logical disjunction in his poetry. At times, however, this disjunction in the logical progression of word and image gives way to a resolution. The short poem "Carrefour" (crossroad) sets up a surreal image sequence:

> De l'air
> De la lumière
> Un rayon sur le bord du verre
> Ma main déçue n'attrape rien
>
> Air
> Light
> A ray on the edge of the glass
> My disappointed hand holds nothing

Here the elements are invoked, and then two images, one of an inanimate object and one the hand of the speaker. From this atmosphere of mystery and disjunction, the poem's conclusion moves to a fairly well-defined emotional statement:

> Enfin tout seul j'aurai vécu
> Jusqu'au dernier matin
> Sans qu'un mot m'indiquât quel fut le bon chemin

> After all I will have lived all alone
> Until the last morning
> Without a single word that might have shown me
> which was the right way

Here, as in many of Reverdy's poems, the emotion evoked is a kind of diffused sadness. The solitary individual is probably meant to stand for an aspect of the human condition, alone in a confrontation with an unknown destiny.

It was Reverdy's fate to see actual military duty during World War I, and it may well be that the magnitude of human tragedy he witnessed at the front lines served to mute the youthful enthusiasm that pervades his earliest works. It may also be the case that Reverdy, while espousing radical measures in literary practice, still was caught in the kind of bittersweet ethos that characterizes fin de siècle writers generally.

"Guerre"

Whatever the case may be, there is no question that Reverdy wrote some of the most affecting war poems in the French language. One of the most direct is titled simply "Guerre" (war). Running through a series of disjointed, if coherent, images, Reverdy toward the end of the poem approaches direct statement, when the speaker says:

> Et la figure attristée
> Visage des visages
> La mort passe sur le chemin
>
> And the saddened figure
> Visage of visages
> Death passes along the road

Close to a medieval allegorizing of death, this figure also incorporates a fascination with the effect of the gaze. One's face is revealing of one's emotion because of the way one looks—the distillation of the phenomenon into a general characteristic is a strong term to describe death. If this image is strong, the poem's ending is more forceful still:

> Mais quel autre poids que celui de ton corps
> as-tu jeté dans la balance
> Tout froid dans le fossé
> Il dort sans plus rêver
>
> But what other weight than that of your body
> have you thrown in the balance
> All cold in the ditch
> He sleeps no longer to dream

Philosophers have questioned whether the idea of death is properly an idea, since strictly speaking, it has no content. Caught between viewing another's death from the outside and facing one's own death, which one can never know, death is a supreme mystery of human existence. Reverdy in these lines seems to cross the line between the exterior, objective view of another's death and the unknowable, subjective experience of the individual. This is what he means by the emotion communicated through the poetic image.

Despite a continued tendency toward the surreal image in Reverdy's work, these poems in *Sources du vent* (sources of the wind) also represent the first major collection of poems after Reverdy's conversion to a mystic Catholicism in 1926. Increasingly, his poetry of the postconversion period tends toward an introjection of the conflicts raised through the poetic image. While a tone of lingering sadness had always been present from the earliest work, in these poems, the atmosphere of sadness and loss moves to the center of the poet's concerns. Unlike the conservative Christian poets Charles-Pierre Péguy and Paul Claudel, the content of the poems is never directly religious. Rather, a mood of quietism seems to become more prominent in the collections of poems after the conversion. A concurrent falling off in the level of production also takes place. After 1930, Reverdy publishes only two more individual collections of verse, along with two collected volumes and works in other forms. After 1949, for the last twelve years of his life, the heretofore prolific Reverdy apparently ceased to write altogether.

"Mémoire"

The poem "Mémoire" (memory) from *Pierres blanches* (white stones), shows this mood of increasing resignation in the face of worldly events. The poem invokes a "she," someone who has left or is going to leave, but then, in apparent reference to the title, says there will still be someone:

> Quand nous serons partis là-bas derrière
> Il y aura encore ici quelqu'un
> Pour nous attendre
> Et nous entendre
>
> When we will have gone over there behind
> There will still be someone
> To wait for us
> And to understand us

The positive mood of these lines, however, is undercut by the poem's ending: "Un seul ami/ L'ombre que nous avons laissée sous l'arbre et qui s'ennuie" ("A single friend/ The shadow we have left beneath a tree and who's getting bored"). The impersonality tending toward a universal statement that was present in Reverdy's early work here seems to work toward an effacement of the individual personality. If memory can be imaged as a bored shadow left beneath a tree, the significance of the individual seems tenuous at best. The emotion generated through the poetic image here seems to be one of sadness and extreme resignation.

The interpretation of a poet's work through biography must always be a hazy enterprise, all the more so in a poet such as Reverdy, whose life directly enters into his work not at all. In a general sense, then, the course of his poetic life and production might be said to mirror the course of French literary life generally. The enthusiasm of the avant-garde literary and artistic movements in Europe generally in the early years of the twentieth century saw a reaction in the post-World War I years toward an art that questioned societal assumptions. Dada and Surrealism can be seen in terms of this large movement, and Reverdy's work as an example. The coherence of the Surrealist movement in turn breaks down in the late 1920's and early 1930's with the split coming over what political allegiance the Surrealist artists should take, according to its leaders. Reverdy's personal religious convictions cause him to cease active involvement with the movement altogether. It is a measure of his status as a strong precursor to the movement that he is not attacked directly by the more politically motivated leaders of Surrealism.

"MAIN-MORTE"

With the extreme politicization of the Surrealist movement in the late 1930's, even some of the most dedicated younger adherents to Surrealism cut their formal ties with the movement. René Char is an example. The young Yves Bonnefoy is an example of a poet with early leanings toward Surrealism who in the late 1940's moved more in the direction of a poetry expressive of essential philosophical and human truths. It might be possible, in like manner, to trace Reverdy's increasing distance from Surrealism as a movement to some kind of similar feelings that have been more openly expressed by his younger contemporaries. His collection *Plein Verre* (full glass) does indeed move more toward the mode of longer, contemplative poems, still in the atmosphere of sadness and resignation to life. The end of "Main-Morte" (dead-hand) shows this well:

> Entre l'aveu confus et le lien du mystère
> Les mots silencieux qui tendent leur filet
> Dans tous les coins de cette chambre noire
> Où ton ombre ni moi n'aurons jamais dormi
>
> Between the confused vow and the tie of mystery
> The silent words which offer their net
> In every corner of this black room
> Where your shadow nor I will have ever slept

Even the highly suggestive early lyrics do not contain quite the level of hovering mystery and intricate emotional states offered in these lines. One may well wonder if the "you" invoked here even refers to a person or whether it might be a quasi-human interior presence such as that invoked in the later poems of Wallace Stevens (such as "Final Soliloquy of the Interior Paramour"). The weight of the images in the direction of silence lends to this whole utterance an aura of high seriousness.

"Enfin"

The last poem in *Plein Verre*, titled "Enfin" (at last), also ends with a statement hinting at a highly serious attitude. The speaker states:

> À travers la poitrine nue
> Là
> Ma clarière
> Avec tout ce qui descend du ciel
> Devenir un autre
> À ras de terre
>
> By means of the naked breast
> There
> My clearing
> Along with all that descends from the sky
> To become an other
> At earth level

More and more in the later poems, a level of ethical statement seems to emerge. Whereas the early poems introduce strange and startling images in an apparently almost random fashion, the images here seem to be coordinated by an overall hierarchy of values, personal and religious. The naked breast at the beginning of this passage thus could refer to the lone individual, perhaps alone with his or her conscience. This is in contrast to something which descends from the sky, an almost unavoidably religious image. The wish "To become an other/ At earth level" might then be interpreted as the fervent desire of an extremely devoted individual to attain a higher level of piety here on earth.

Le Chant des morts

The extended sequence, *Le Chant des morts* (the song of the dead), composed in 1944-1948 and published in 1948 as part of the collected volume *Main d'œuvre* (work made by hand), presents an extended meditation on the emotional inner scene of war-devastated France. In this sequence, as in his earlier poems on World War I that drew on his direct experience of the horrors of war, Reverdy uses a diction stripped bare of rhetoric, preferring instead the direct, poignant images of death and suffering. Death in these poems is both inescapable and horrible, or as he calls it: "la mort entêtée/ La mort vorace" ("stubborn death/ Voracious death"). As a strong countermovement to the implacable march of death, there is also a tenacious clinging to life. As the poet says: "C'est la faim/ C'est l'ardeur de vivre qui dirigent/ La peur de perdre" ("It is hunger/ It is the ardor to live that guide/ The fear of losing"). The poet of the inner conscience in these poems confronts the essential subject of his deepest meditations: the conscious adoption of his authentic attitude toward death.

The ultimate renunciation of poetry that characterizes the last years of Reverdy's life is preceded by an exploration of the subject most suited to representing death (remembering Sigmund Freud)—that is, silence.

"ET MAINTENANT"

The poem that Reverdy seems to have chosen to come at the end of his collected poems, titled "Et Maintenant" (and now), ends with a poignant image of silence: "Tous les fils dénoués au delà des saisons reprennent leur tour et leur ton sur le fond sombre du silence" ("All the unknotted threads beyond the seasons regain their trace and their tone against the somber background of silence"). Reverdy here seems to hint at what lies beyond poetic expression in several senses. His entire ethos of poetic creation has been consistently based on an act of communication with the reader. Thus, the threads he refers to here could well represent the threads of intention and emotion that his readers follow in his poetry to achieve an experience of that emotion themselves, or to discover an analogous emotional experience in their own memory or personal background. He might also be hinting at those threads of intention and emotion that led beyond the limitations of individual life in a reunification with a divine creator. In the former interpretation, the background of silence would be that silence which precedes the poetic utterance or act of communication, as well as the silence after the act of communication or once the poet has ceased to write. In the religious interpretation, the background of silence would be that nothingness or nonbeing out of which the divine creation takes place and which, in turn, has the capability of incorporating silence or nonbeing into self, a religious attitude of a return to the creator even in the face of one's own personal death.

LEGACY

Reverdy is a complex and fascinating figure in the history of French poetry in the first half of the twentieth century. He was a committed avant-garde artist in the years directly preceding, during, and following World War I; his outpouring of poetry and aesthetic statements made him one of the most significant precursors to the movements of Dada and Surrealism. Though his formal affiliation with the Surrealist movement was of brief duration, his example of using the poetic image to communicate emotion is central to everything for which Surrealism stood. The extreme respect shown to his work by other poets and artists confirms his importance as a creative innovator. Reverdy, in turn, paid respectful homage to his poet and artist contemporaries a stance that shows his ongoing intellectual commitment to the importance of art and literature in human terms, despite his personal isolation and quietism toward the end of his life. The poems from the end of his career that bear the weight of a continued meditation on death are a moving commentary on that from which language emerges and into which it returns: silence.

OTHER MAJOR WORKS
LONG FICTION: *Le Voleur de Talan*, 1917; *La Peau de l'homme*, 1926.
SHORT FICTION: *Risques et périls*, 1930.
NONFICTION: *Self Defence*, 1919; *Le Gant de crin*, 1927; *Le Livre de mon bord*, 1948; *Cette émotion appellée poésie: Écrits sur la poésie, 1932-1960*, 1975; *Nord-Sud, Self Defence, et autres écrits sur l'art et la poésie*, 1975; *Note éternelle du présent*, 1975.

BIBLIOGRAPHY
Greene, Robert W. *The Poetic Theory of Pierre Reverdy*. 1967. Reprint. San Bernardino, Calif.: Borgo Press, 1990. An analysis of Reverdy's work in poetic theory.
Pap, Jennifer. "Transforming the Horizon: Reverdy's World War I." *Modern Language Review* 101, no. 4 (October, 2006): 966-978. Pap examines the theme of war in Reverdy's works, noting that although he favored an art that followed its own aims, he did treat the war in his poetry.
Rizzuto, Anthony. *Style and Theme in Reverdy's "Les Ardoises du toit."* Tuscaloosa: University of Alabama Press, 1971. Rizzuto's critical study of one of Reverdy's poetic works. Includes bibliographic references.
Rothwell, Andrew. *Textual Spaces: The Poetry of Pierre Reverdy*. Atlanta: Rodopi, 1989. A critical analysis of Reverdy's works. Includes bibliographic references.
Schroeder, Jean. *Pierre Reverdy*. Boston: Twayne, 1981. An introductory biography and critical study of selected works by Reverdy. Includes an index and bibliographic references.
Sweet, David LeHardy. *Savage Sight/Constructed Noise: Poetic Adaptations of Painterly Techniques in the French and American Avant-gardes*. Chapel Hill: Department of Romance Languages, University of North Carolina, 2003. The poetry of experimental poets Reverdy, Guillaume Apollinaire, André Breton, Frank O'Hara, and John Ashbery is examined for the poets' use of painterly techniques.

Peter Baker

RAINER MARIA RILKE

Born: Prague, Bohemia, Austro-Hungarian Empire; December 4, 1875
Died: Valmont, Switzerland; December 29, 1926

PRINCIPAL POETRY
Leben und Lieder, 1894
Larenopfer, 1896
Wegwarten, 1896
Traumgekrönt, 1897
Advent, 1898
Mir zur Feier, 1899
Das Buch der Bilder, 1902, 1906 (*The Book of Images*, 1994)
Das Stundenbuch, 1905 (*Poems from the Book of Hours*, 1941)
Neue Gedichte, 1907-1908 (2 volumes; *New Poems*, 1964)
Die frühen Gedichte, 1909
Requiem, 1909 (*Requiem, and Other Poems*, 1935)
Das Marienleben, 1913 (*The Life of the Virgin Mary*, 1951)
Duineser Elegien, 1923 (*Duinese Elegies*, 1931; better known as *Duino Elegies*)
Die Sonette an Orpheus, 1923 (*Sonnets to Orpheus*, 1936)
Vergers, suivi des Quatrains Valaisans, 1926 (*Orchards*, 1982)
Gesammelte Werke, 1927
Les Fenêtres, 1927 ("The Windows" in *The Roses and the Windows*, 1979)
Les Roses, 1927 ("The Roses" in *The Roses and the Windows*, 1979)
Verse und Prosa aus dem Nachlass, 1929
Späte Gedichte, 1934 (*Late Poems*, 1938)
Poèmes français, 1935
Aus dem Nachlass des Grafen C. W.: Ein Gedichtkreis, 1950
Christus—Visionen, pb. 1950 (wr. 1896-1898)
Poems, 1906 to 1926, 1957
Poems, 1965
Uncollected Poems, 1996

OTHER LITERARY FORMS

The rich symbolic content and specific themes that characterize the famous lyrics of Rainer Maria Rilke (RIHL-kuh) also inform his narrative prose. Recollections of his boyhood and youth are given romantic, fairy-tale coloring in *Vom lieben Gott und Anderes* (1900; republished as *Geschichten vom lieben Gott*, 1904; *Stories of God*, 1931, 1963), a cycle of short tales that replace traditional Christian perceptions of God with depictions of a finically careful artist. *Die Weise von Liebe und Tod des Cornets Christoph Rilke* (1906; *The Tale of the Love and Death of Cornet Christoph Rilke*, 1932), a terse yet beautifully written story, is more like an epic poem than a prose work, especially in its emphasis on the power of the individual word and its intensely rhythmic language. The psychologically intricate novel *Die Aufzeichnungen des Malte Laurids Brigge* (1910; *The Notebooks of Malte Laurids Brigge*, 1930; also known as *The Journal of My Other Self*) is one of Rilke's most profound creations. Written from the point of view of a young Danish nobleman living in exile in Paris, it offers in random sketches a peculiar summation of the central concerns of the author's literary art.

Between 1894 and 1904, Rilke wrote more than twenty plays, many of which were lost and never published. The most important of his remaining theatrical works are either pessimistically Naturalistic or intense dramas of the soul. *Jetzt und in der Stunde unseres Absterbens* (pr., pb. 1896; *Now and in the Hour of Our Death*, 1979) and *Im Frühfrost* (pr., pb. 1897; *Early Frost*, 1979) reflect the influence of Rudolf Christoph Jenny in their materialistic determinism, while later pieces such as *Höhenluft* (pr. 1969; *Air at High Altitude*, 1979) and *Ohne Gegenwart* (pb. 1898; *Not Present*, 1979) document a development in the direction of Symbolism, motivated especially by the dramatic theories of Maurice Maeterlinck. Rilke's best-remembered play is *Die weisse Fürstin* (pb. 1929; *The White Princess*, 1979), which in its lyric depth and power illustrates his view that drama and poetry have similar goals.

Apart from his writings in other genres, Rilke also produced a few works of nonfiction. Most notable among these are the biographical study *Auguste Rodin* (1903; English translation, 1919) and the descriptive lyric essays of *Worpswede* (1903). Much of his extensive correspondence has been collected and published. Especially important for what they reveal of his artistic personality and poetic process are volumes of letters exchanged with Lou Andreas-Salomé and Princess Marie von Thurn und Taxis.

Achievements

Commonly ranked alongside Hugo von Hofmannsthal and Stefan George as a giant of twentieth century German poetry, Rainer Maria Rilke is perhaps the most controversial of the three in point of critical and popular reception of his works. Although his substantial collections published soon after the turn of the century, especially *The Book of Hours* and *New Poems*, were greeted with uniformly favorable recognition, there is wide disagreement among critics concerning the literary value of both his early poems and those of his final, major creative period. A significant key to the divided viewpoints is his boldly daring, uniquely creative use of language in strange new relationships, his peculiar departures from traditional grammar and syntax, and his unusual forms of subjective and objective expression. The pure individuality of his poetic utterances often makes them difficult to understand and repels the reader who approaches Rilke's art with anything less than full and active concentration. As a result, the most problematic of Rilke's mature poems, especially the *Duino Elegies*, are regarded by some scholars as the most important German lyric creations of the first half of the twentieth century, whereas others dismiss them as lacking substance. Regardless of these disagreements, Rilke's influence on the development of German verse is unrivaled by that of any other German-language poet of his time. His most lasting and important contribution remains the concept of the *Dinggedicht* (thing poem) introduced in *New Poems*.

Biography

The life of René Karl Wilhelm Johann Josef Maria Rilke can be described in its entirety as a productive, if not always successful, search for fulfillment in reaction to an inhibiting, psychologically destructive childhood. Critical elements of Rilke's early experience contributed to his development as a hypersensitive individual unsuited to the demands of practical existence. They include the rapid failure of his parents' marriage; the rape of his personality by a mother who dressed him in feminine clothing and reared him for a time as a replacement for a lost daughter; a partial education in military academies and a school of commerce to which he could never adapt; and a brief exposure to the university world in Prague. The young Rilke responded to a continuing feeling of being out of place by trying diligently to become part of active cultural and artistic circles. While still a student, he published his first lyric anthology, composed naturalistic plays, contributed literary reviews to newspapers and journals, and founded his own periodical. He also participated in cultural organizations, lecture presentations, readings of drama and poetry, and similar activities.

When Rilke left the university in 1896, he went to Munich. An incurable restlessness dictated his lifestyle from that time forward. His serious evolution as a writer began under the influence of significant figures whom he encountered in Munich; friendships with Jacob Wassermann and Wilhelm von Scholz were especially productive. Wassermann acquainted him with the writings of Jens Peter Jacobsen, which Rilke soon learned to treasure. Still more important was the relationship that he formed with Andreas-Salomé, whom he met in 1897. It was she who persuaded him to change his name from René to Rainer. After she became his mistress, she exposed him to contemporary philosophical trends and the ideas of the Italian Renaissance. He quickly followed her to Berlin and later traveled with her and her husband twice to Russia, where he was introduced to Leo Tolstoy and other authors. The vast Russian landscape and the Russian people impressed him as examples of original, elemental nature. From them, he drew ideas and perceptions that informed his verse long afterward.

Rilke's only attempt to establish a permanent family situation ended in failure. In 1902, he dissolved his household in the Worpswede artists' colony, left his wife, the sculptress Clara Westhoff, and their daughter, and moved to Paris, where he intended to write a book about Auguste Rodin. His friendship with the famous sculptor was extremely significant for the direction of his poetic development in the years between

1902 and the beginning of World War I. Rodin provided Rilke with an example of strict artistic discipline that had profound impact on his maturation as a poet.

Even more critical to his literary growth during this time was Rilke's association with Impressionist painter Paul Cézanne, whose painting technique contributed much to the evolving visual orientation of Rilke's verse. Not only special individuals but also Paris itself, the French people, and even the French language indelibly marked Rilke's subsequent creations, giving them substance and eventually, during his final years, their very medium of expression.

The atmosphere of two other locales gave peculiar flavor to Rilke's most powerful, most complex masterworks. The first was Duino Castle near Trieste; the second, the Château de Muzot in Valais. After visiting North Africa and Egypt in 1910 and 1911, he went to Duino Castle at the invitation of Princess Marie von Thurn und Taxis. There, he wrote the first two of the *Duino Elegies* before moving on to Spain and then back to Germany. The war years, which he spent primarily in Munich, constituted an unproductive interlude that was inwardly devastating to him. He found it exceedingly difficult to begin writing again when hostilities ceased. Only after moving to Switzerland and his secluded refuge at the Château de Muzot did he find inner peace sufficient to complete his finest lyric cycles. He spent most of the remainder of his life in the Rhône Valley, where he died of leukemia.

Analysis

During the course of his development as a poet, the creative task became for Rainer Maria Rilke a process of objectification and externalization of his own inner world. Couched in language that is notable for its musicality and its frequently playful moods are the peculiarities of a unique spiritual life that emerged from special responses to outside stimuli. The melody of lyrics rich in alliteration, assonance, consonance, and rhyme provides a naturally flowing framework for the presentation of the poet's feelings and reflections. Especially typical components of his verse are encounters with sorrow and pain, powerful absorption in specific objects, a strange blending of the experiences of death and love, and an overwhelming sense of isolation.

The landscape of these revelations of self is transformed and varied in direct relationship to new outward contacts with people, things, and places. Russia, Paris, Duino, and Valais provide for different works, shaping influence and substance, timeless symbols and concrete reality, worldview and microcosmic conception. Taken in sequence, Rilke's cycles and poems document his endeavors to purify the portrayal of the scenes within him, to clarify obscurities and nail down uncertainties. By its very nature, this act of poetic refinement was deeply religious, reflecting a sincere humility in the face of creation's vast mysteries. Rilke's entire oeuvre proclaims a consciousness of an artistic calling that had its basis in an existential anxiety that was translated into joyful, almost rapturous affirmation of mortality.

Early poems

Rilke's earliest published poems, which appeared in the collections *Leben und Lieder* (life and songs), *Larenopfer* (offering to the household gods), *Wegwarten* (watch posts), and *Traumgekrönt* (dream-crowned), are marked by a naïve simplicity and a degree of sentimentality that are absent from his more mature writings. Under the influence of Jens Peter Jacobsen, he created particularly sensitive lyrics centered on nature, as well as penetrating psychological portraits of people. Among his favorite subjects were women and children. Even in these youthful creations, there is already a strong emphasis on visual imagery, although the artistic focus of attention is frequently not the object that is described, but rather the spiritual stirrings that occur within the poet because of what he sees.

Mir zur Feier

In *Mir zur Feier* (celebrating me), Rilke began to move from the lyric forms and approaches of his student years, adopting in the transition techniques that he later perfected in his first broadly successful cycle, *The Book of Hours*. The poems of *Mir zur Feier* present in precise detail their creator's innermost personal concerns, describing in tones of religious fervor his yearnings, prayers, and self-perceptions. Framed in language that is rich in texture yet soft in tone, the poems glorify things that cannot be comprehended through human volition. These verse productions represent a calculated justification of the poet's art as a means of celebrating that which can be revealed in its essence and fullness in no other manner.

The Book of Images

The Book of Images, a collection written at about the same time as *The Book of Hours*, is in some respects poetically stronger. Under the influence of Rodin, Rilke made the transition from a poetry informed by blurred feeling to precise, objective, carefully formed verse characterized by the complete sacrifice of the poet's immanence to an emphasis upon things in themselves. The creations of *The Book of Images* reveal the writer's progress toward the establishment of a literary integration of visual impressions with sight-oriented components of language. The artistic process becomes a perfecting of the act of seeing, in which the poet organizes the elements of the visual image through subjective cognition of his external world. Although these lyrics do not attain to the plastic monumentality of Rilke's later writings, they are forerunners of the *Dinggedichte* that are collectively the most important product of Rilke's years in Paris.

The Book of Hours

The commemoration of self is a significant aspect of *The Book of Hours*, divided into three sections that were the product of diverse influences and experiences: Rilke's impressions of Russia and Paris, his love affair with Andreas-Salomé, the dramatic writings of Maurice Maeterlinck and Henrik Ibsen, Friedrich Nietzsche's philosophical ideas, and the cultural legacy of the Italian Renaissance. The work as a whole portrays the author's movement toward an internalization of external phenomena in a poetic act of preservation and redemption. There is evident within the individual poems a new kind of friendly relationship between the poet and God's handiwork that surrounds him. Nevertheless, what is presented is definitely not a traditional Christian attitude toward life. These lyrics are the product of an aggressively demanding mind; in them, a strongly individual interpretation of the religious dimension of experience is advanced without equivocation. The thrust of *The Book of Hours* is to refine the notion that God is not static, a complete and perfect being, but rather a continually evolving artistic creation. Rilke insists that the reader accept this idea on faith, equating his poetic message with spiritual revelation. The result is a celebration of "this world" that the poet continued to elaborate and modify until his death.

The three parts of *The Book of Hours* are discrete sets of deeply intimate confessions that arose out of special relationships and encounters that shaped Rilke's artistic outlook. "Das Buch vom mönchischen Leben" ("Of the Monastic Life"), written in 1899, reflects the strong influence of the poet's attachment to Andreas-Salomé and the cultural, historical, and philosophical ideas to which she introduced him. His ecstatic love for Andreas-Salomé and their visits to Russia are the key elements that give "Das Buch von der Pilgerschaft" ("Of Pilgrimage") its specific flavor, while "Das Buch von der Armut und vom Tod" ("Of Poverty and Death") was a product of Rilke's impressions during his first year in Paris. The individual poems of the three cycles are experiments in which Rilke tested various symbols and metaphors, metric and rhythmic possibilities, and rhyme schemes in documenting a deep worship of life as a sacred motivating force.

"Of the Monastic Life" is a series of prayerful outpourings of the spirit in which a young monk addresses God. In this context, prayer is an elemental religious act with two goals: self-discovery in the process of establishing and expanding personal modes of expression, and the "creation" of God and the growth of a sense of brotherhood with him in one's relationship to nature. The fictive prayer situations provide the setting for a portrayal of the innermost stirrings of the soul in an endless reaching outward to illuminate the divine. Melodic language and strength of visual image are brought together with rich imagination to reveal the lyricist's almost Franciscan sympathy with the world.

Specific items of the cycle "Of Pilgrimage" attain peaks of religious rapture in the glorification of the mystical union between man and woman, offered in newly intensified homage to Andreas-Salomé. Thematically, however, this portion of *The Book of Hours* focuses primarily on key aspects of the poet's Russian experience. It emphasizes especially the idea that the pious Russian people are the embodiment of humility and spirituality within a topographical frame that is the archetype of God's creation. Spatial relationships are particularly important as the vastness of the Russian countryside melts into the author's inner landscape. A few of the lyrics reveal an inclination toward things that need humans, presenting them in impressionistic trappings that show a predilection for that which is most immediate and intricate.

"Of Poverty and Death," the final segment of *The Book of Hours*, anticipates the negative, sometimes melancholy tone of Rilke's later collections. Its substance is human misery presented in variations that expose in stark coloration the world of the homeless, the infirm, the abandoned, and the afraid. Christian motifs and themes are employed to accentuate Rilke's rejection of the Christian God, while rich images establish a substantial tie to "Of the Monastic Life" in the affirmation of God as an original poetic creation.

DINGGEDICHTE

Rilke's most lasting legacy and most important contribution to German poesy is the *Dinggedicht*, an originally conceived interpretation of inner experience generated in response to encounters with external objects and phenomena that the poet transformed into symbols for the elements of human life. With *New Poems*, in which he perfected this particular form, Rilke made a breakthrough that was immeasurably far-reaching in its implications for the expansion of German poetry's expressive domain.

A reflection of Rilke's attention to impulses from Rodin's sculpture and Cézanne's paintings, the *Dinggedicht* is the product of disciplined and thorough scrutinization of its model. Outwardly, it seeks to offer the character and intrinsic constitution of an object that is described for its own sake in painstakingly refined language. On another level, however, it documents the acquisition of external things for the poet's inner domain, thereby transforming the physical phenomenon into a precise and specifically calculated symbol for a portion of his re-creation of the world for himself. Some of the poems analyze people, buildings, natural and artificial scenes, plants, animals, and even motifs from mythology and the Bible; others are lyric translations of statues and paintings. Each provides a segment of Rilke's new interpretation and clarification of existence. Unlike the earlier forms, the *Dinggedicht* renounces the commitment to melodic sound relationships and connected imagery chains. The exacting identification of the poem's external object and its reduction to its fundamental nature permitted the poet to place it into an absolute domain of pure symbol.

NEW POEMS

Rilke achieved his most representative mastery of the *Dinggedicht* in *New Poems*, a collection in which heavy stress is placed on negative moods in the explication of the view that God is the direction and not the object of love. In their extreme subtlety and refinement of language, their worldly elegance, and their moral and emotional engagement, the most representative poems of Rilke's Paris period form the center of his work as a whole. The *Dinggedichte* of *New Poems* are a detailed reflection of his view that his poetic task was the interpretation and clarification of existence for the purpose of healing the world. By accepting, recognizing, and loving things for themselves, the poet places himself in a position to trace animals, plants, works of art, human figures, and other objects back to their true nature and substance. Precise seeing and artistic transformation enable him to project in symbols the content and meaning both of his surroundings and of that which is within him.

Divided into two loosely chronological parts, the poems in *New Poems* examine in objectively plastic, precisely disciplined structures representative manifestations and individuals that belong to the world of nature and to humanity's most important cultural attainments, from the Bible to classical antiquity, from the Middle Ages to the Renaissance. Mystical inwardness is projected in carefully defined symbols that objectively externalize the events within the poet that are stimulated by the process of seeing. Gloom, absurdity, and disintegration are common moods in poems that question the possibility for everything, including humanity, to exist and thereby to become the subject of literature.

"THE PANTHER"

The symbolic portraits of *New Poems* focus on a broad variety of models. Among the most successful are those based on impressions from the Jardin des Plantes. "Der Panther" ("The Panther"), the earliest and most famous of the *Dinggedichte*, transforms its object into a symbol of heroic existence. By the very power of its seeing, the panther, like the poet, is able to create its own inner landscape, absorbing the visual impressions of external objects into itself, where it may modify, penetrate, or even destroy them. One of Rilke's most vivid depictions of rapport with an object, achieved in the act of intense observation, is given in "Archaïscher Torso Apollos" ("Archaic Torso of Apollo"), the first work in the second volume of *New Poems*. The headless statue becomes a kind of spiritual mirror that directs the onlooker's gaze back into the self, enabling him to recognize the need for change in his own life.

DUINO ELEGIES AND SONNETS TO ORPHEUS

An important consequence of Rilke's Paris experience was a reevaluation of his literary existence that led ultimately to a significant turning point in his career. The problem of an irreconcilable conflict between the demands of practicality and art was compounded by a philosophical crisis involving the tensions that he felt in his need to make a definitive break with Christianity and in his loathing of modern technology. Against this background, an encounter with Søren Kierkegaard's existential philosophy led eventually to Rilke's production of the mythologically exaggerated *Duino Elegies* and *Sonnets to Orpheus* as the peak of his literary endeavor. In these mature lyrics, the creative attitudes and symbolic devices of *New Poems* were refined and perfected. Rilke responded to many different stimuli—World War I, the works of Friedrich Gottlieb Klopstock, Johann Wolfgang von Goethe, and Heinrich von Kleist, Sigmund Freud's psychology, among others—in creating a culminating synthesis of his own poetic view of human life and destiny. Dactylic and iambic meters, free rhythms, questions, and exclamations provide the frame for bold images that pinpoint once again the fundamental directions of Rilke's work as a whole.

Between 1912 and 1922, Rilke created the ten Duino elegies in monumental celebration of humanity as the final, most extreme possibility of existence. The ultimate refinement of the delineation of his own calling focuses no longer on the artist as interpreter and clarifier of his surroundings, but rather ordains the poet as a prophet and savior whose task is to preserve everything that has being. He thus becomes the protagonist and representative of humanity in a new religion of life that is an expression of unchecked aestheticism. By saving the world from a collapse that seems unavoidable, the poet engages in an act of self-purification and follows the only possible course of personal redemption.

Taken together, the elegies offer a mural of Rilke's inner landscape. Internalization of travel experiences, the lonely scenery at Duino Castle, the flight of birds, mythological constructs, and other phenomena create a background of timeless "inner space" against which the author projects his coming to grips with the existential polarities of life and death. Progressing from lament to profound affirmation of mortality, the poems glorify the fulfillment of humanity's promise to maintain all things of value through a process of transformation that rescues external nature by placing it in the protected realm of the spirit. The power by which this is accomplished is love, supremely manifested by lovers, people who die young, heroes, children, and animals. By bringing together earth and space, life and death, all dimensions of reality and time into a single inward hierarchical unity, Rilke sought to ensure the continuation of humanity's outward existence.

In the first elegy, the poet states his view of the human condition: imperfection, the questionable status of humanity, the experience of transience, the pain of love. On this basis, he builds a new mythology of life. Its center is the non-Christian angel who appears in the second elegy as a symbol for the absolute and unattainable, the norm from which humans in their limitations deviate. In a valid transformation of psychoanalysis into images, Rilke pinpoints the threat that exists within the human self in the power of natural drives. Illumination of the brokenness, ambiguity, superficiality, and mechanical senselessness of human pursuits is followed in the sixth elegy by identification of the hero as a symbolic concept that contrasts with average life. The seventh poem of the cycle breaks away from the lament of human insufficiency, suddenly glorifying the here and now in hymnic language that moves to a confessional peak. Renewed expression of the idea that the difference between humans and the natural creature cannot be resolved is followed by an attempt to show that life must be accepted and made fruitful despite its limitations. The culminating elegy creates a balance between mourning and celebration that unites the antithetical problems in a grand, affirmative vision of pain and death as the destiny of humanity and the only true evidence of his existence.

Late poems in French

The verse written in French after *Duino Elegies* and *Sonnets to Orpheus* was anticlimactic for Rilke's career. It lacks the depth and profundity of earlier works, although individual poems achieve lightness and sparkle in their reflection of a new rejoicing in mortal existence.

Other major works

LONG FICTION: *Am Leben hin*, 1889; *Die Letzten*, 1902; *Die Weise von Liebe und Tod des Cornets Christoph Rilke*, 1906 (*The Tale of the Love and Death of Cornet Christopher Rilke*, 1932); *Die Aufzeichnungen des Malte Laurids Brigge*, 1910 (*The Notebooks of Malte Laurids Brigge*, 1930; also known as *The Journal of My Other Self*).

SHORT FICTION: *Zwei Prager Geschichten*, 1899 (*Two Stories of Prague*, 1994); *Vom lieben Gott und Anderes*, 1900 (republished as *Geschichten vom lieben Gott*, 1904; *Stories of God*, 1931, 1963); *Erzählungen und Skizzen aus der Frühzeit*, 1928.

PLAYS: *Murillo*, pb. 1895 (English translation, 1979); *Jetzt und in der Stunde unseres Absterbens*, pr., pb. 1896 (*Now and in the Hour of Our Death*, 1979); *Im Frühfrost*, pr., pb. 1897 (*Early Frost*, 1979); *Vigilien*, wr. 1897 (*Vigils*, 1979); *Ohne Gegenwart*, pb. 1898 (*Not Present*, 1979); *Das tägliche Leben*, pr. 1901 (*Everyday Life*, 1979); *Waisenkinder*, pb. 1901 (*Orphans*, 1979); *Die weisse Fürstin*, pb. 1929 (*The White Princess*, 1979); *Höhenluft*, pr. 1969 (wr. 1897; *Air at High Altitude*, 1979); *Nine Plays*, 1979.

NONFICTION: *Auguste Rodin*, 1903 (English translation, 1919); *Worpswede*, 1903; *Briefe an einen jungen Dichter*, 1929 (*Letters to a Young Poet*, 1934); *Wartime Letters of Rainer Maria Rilke, 1914-1921*, 1940; *Tagebücher aus der Frühzeit*, 1942 (*Diaries of a Young Poet*, 1997); *Letters of Rainer Maria Rilke*, 1945-1948 (2 volumes); *Selected Letters of Rainer Maria Rilke, 1902-1926*, 1947; *Briefwechsel [zwischen] Rainer Maria Rilke und Marie von Thurn und Taxis*, 1951 (*The Letters of Rainer Maria Rilke and Princess Marie von Thurn und Taxis*, 1958); *Rainer Maria Rilke, Lou Andreas-Salomé: Briefwechsel*, 1952; *Rainer Maria Rilke and Lou Andreas-Salomé: The Correspondence*, 2006.

MISCELLANEOUS: *The Poet's Guide to Life: The Wisdom of Rilke*, 2005 (Ulrich Baer, editor).

Bibliography

Andreas-Salomé, Lou. *You Alone Are Real to Me: Remembering Rainer Maria Rilke*. Translated by Angela von der Lippe. New York: BOA Editions, 2003. In her memoir, Andreas-Salomé describes her relationship with Rilke.

Bernstein, Michael André. *Five Portraits: Modernity and the Imagination in Twentieth-Century German Writing*. Edited by Gary Saul Morson. Evanston, Ill.: Northwestern University Press, 2000. Presents Rilke's poetry in the context of the shift among

German writers from Romanticism and aestheticism to twentieth century modernism.

Freedman, Ralph. *Life of a Poet: Rainer Maria Rilke*. New York: Farrar, Straus and Giroux, 1996. A helpful complement to Donald Prater's definitive biography, this work draws extensive parallels between Rilke's life and the content of his poetry. Also contains several photographs of Rilke and his family.

Kleinbard, David. *The Beginning of Terror: A Psychological Study of Rainer Maria Rilke's Life and Work*. New York: New York University Press, 1993. A critical rather than comprehensive biography, attempting a psychoanalysis of Rilke and his published writing. Examines issues such as Rilke's childhood, his relationships with his parents (both biological and surrogate), and his debilitating blood disorder and its effect on his work.

Prater, Donald. *A Ringing Glass: The Life of Rainer Maria Rilke*. New York: Clarendon Press, 1993. A definitive biography of Rilke that concentrates on his European travels and correspondence with friends. Also, the bibliography is highly helpful for those who need a comprehensive, expert guide to Rilke criticism. Illustrated.

Ryan, Judith. *Rilke, Modernism, and Poetic Tradition*. New York: Cambridge University Press, 1999. Although Rilke saw himself as a more or less self-created writer, who needed extended periods of solitude in which to work, Ryan shows him in his relationship to other writers and even painters in the European culture of his day. Traces his movement from the art-for-art's-sake school of writing into modernism.

Schoolfield, George C. *Young Rilke and His Time*. Rochester, N.Y.: Camden House, 2009. A biography of Rilke that focuses on the writer as a youth and how the circumstances of his youth affected his writing.

Lowell A. Bangerter

ARTHUR RIMBAUD

Born: Charleville, France; October 20, 1854
Died: Marseilles, France; November 10, 1891

PRINCIPAL POETRY
Une Saison en enfer, 1873 (*A Season in Hell*, 1932)
Les Illuminations, 1886 (*Illuminations*, 1932)

OTHER LITERARY FORMS

The impact of Arthur Rimbaud (ram-BOH) on the literary world stems entirely from his poetry.

ACHIEVEMENTS

Arthur Rimbaud's meteoric career has forever earned for him a place as the brilliant *enfant terrible* of French verse. Since his death, he has attracted more critical attention than any French poet save Stéphane Mallarmé. A revolutionary both in his life and in his art, Rimbaud exerted a radical influence on the scope and direction of French poetry. He has been credited with introducing *vers libre* (free verse), which would come to dominate modern poetry, and his systematic cultivation of dreams, hallucinations, and madness anticipated modern interest in the irrational side of the human mind. He became, for a time, the patron saint of André Breton and the Surrealists. Rimbaud's conception of the poetical "I" as "other" ("Je est un autre") has been acclaimed as an intuitive perception of the unconscious that predated its mapping by Sigmund Freud. Finally, Rimbaud was the first French literary figure to sound a distinctly feminist note in his writings, condemning the cultural repression of women and looking forward to a future day of liberation when they would assume their rightful place in society and art. Faithful to his own precept, "Il faut être absolument moderne" ("We must be absolutely modern"), he prefigured key trends in modern art and thought.

BIOGRAPHY

Jean-Nicolas-Arthur Rimbaud was born in the provincial town of Charleville on the Franco-Prussian border. His mother, Vitalie Cuif, was of peasant stock and a devout Jansenist; his father, Captain Frédéric Rimbaud, was an itinerant army officer who abandoned the family when Rimbaud was only six years old. A brilliant student, Rimbaud completed nine years of schooling in eight, earning numerous literary prizes in the course of his studies. His earliest attempts at verse were in Latin, followed by his first poem in French, "Les Étrennes des orphelins" ("The Orphans' New Year's Day Gifts"), published in January, 1870. Encouraged by his teacher, Georges Izambard,

Arthur Rimbaud
(Library of Congress)

Rimbaud sent off three poems to the Parnassian poet Théodore de Banville, who, however, failed to express any interest.

The outbreak of the Franco-Prussian War in July, 1870, put an end to Rimbaud's formal schooling. Alienated by the hypocrisy of provincial society, which he satirized in various poems composed in the early months of 1870, he ran away from home three times: first to Paris, then to Belgium, and again to Paris. He was back in Charleville when the Paris Commune was declared on March 18, 1871. Although much critical attention has been devoted to Rimbaud's possible ties with the Commune, there is no clear evidence that he ever left Charleville during the crucial period of the Paris uprising. On May 15, Rimbaud composed his celebrated "Lettre du voyant" ("Seer Letter"), addressed to a friend, Paul Demeny. Rimbaud's break with traditional poetry was by this time already complete, and on August 15, he again wrote to Banville, enclosing a new poem, "Ce qu'on dit au poète à propos de fleurs" ("What One Says to the Poet in Regard to Flowers"), a vitriolic attack on Parnassian poetics. Shortly thereafter, Rimbaud also sent off eight new poems, in two installments, to Paul Verlaine, who responded with the famous phrase "Venez, chère grande âme, on vous appelle, on vous attend" ("Come, dear great soul, we call to you, we await you").

Rimbaud arrived in the capital with a copy of his newly composed poem, "Le Bateau ivre" ("The Drunken Boat"), which brought him some notoriety among the Parisian literary crowd. The young poet's obnoxious behavior soon alienated him, however, both from Verlaine's family and his fellow artists, and March, 1872, found him back in Charleville. Rimbaud returned to Paris in May and there began a series of escapades with Verlaine that some have characterized as simply youthful exuberance and others as an unhappy love affair. The pair fled first to Brussels, then to London, where a quarrel erupted. Verlaine returned to Brussels, where he was soon followed by Rimbaud.

In Brussels, events soon took a tragic turn. In a moment of drunken rage, Verlaine fired on Rimbaud, wounding him slightly in the hand. The incident might have ended there, but Verlaine later accosted Rimbaud in the street, and the frightened youth sought help from a passing police officer. The authorities intervened, and Verlaine was sentenced to two years in prison. Rimbaud returned to his mother's family farm at Roche, where he completed *A Season in Hell*, begun in April. In late 1873, Rimbaud again visited Paris, where he made the acquaintance of the young poet Germain Nouveau, with whom he traveled to London in the early months of 1874. Almost nothing is known of this second friendship beyond the fact that it ended with Nouveau's abrupt return to Paris in June of that year.

In 1875, Rimbaud embarked on a new series of travels that led him to Stuttgart, across the Swiss Alps on foot into Italy, and back to Charleville via Paris. After visiting Vienna in April, 1876, he enlisted in the Dutch colonial army on May 19 and set sail for Java. He deserted ship in Batavia (modern Djakarta) and returned to Charleville. In May, 1877, Rimbaud was in Bremen, where he attempted (in vain) to enlist in the American Marines. Subsequent travels the same year took him to Stockholm, Copenhagen, Marseilles, Rome, and back to Charleville. In early 1878, he visited Hamburg, returning during the summer to work on the family farm at Roche. In October, he again traversed Switzerland on foot, crossing the Alps into Italy. There he took the train to Genoa and embarked for Alexandria, later departing for Cyprus, where he worked as a foreman in a marble quarry. Stricken with typhoid, he returned to Charleville in May, 1879, once again spending the summer at Roche. In March, 1880, he was back in Cyprus, where he found work as a construction foreman. An intemperate climate and a salary dispute soon forced him to resign his position and to seek employment elsewhere.

Rimbaud spent the remaining eleven years of his life as the business agent of a French colonial trading company in the remote wilds of Abyssinia (modern-day Ethiopia) and Aden. At the end of this time, he had amassed, through agonizing labor and in the face of constant adversity, the modest sum of 150,000 francs (approximately 30,000 dollars). In February, 1891, intense pain in his right knee forced him to return to France for medical treatment. Doctors in Marseilles diagnosed his illness as cancer and ordered the immediate amputation of the infected right leg. The cancer proved too widespread to check, however, and Rimbaud died in a state of delirium on November 10, 1891. According to a tradition spawned by his devout sister, Isabelle, who was with the poet in his final moments, Rimbaud returned to Catholicism on his deathbed. Since Isabelle is, however, known to have tampered with her brother's personal letters, critics have given little credence to her testimony.

Analysis

Arthur Rimbaud's early verse (of which he published only three short pieces in various academic bulletins) falls into two general categories. First, there is his satiric verse, exemplified by such poems as "Les Premières Communions" ("First Communions") and "Les Assis" ("The Seated Ones"), which attacks religious hypocrisy and the sterility of bourgeois society. Second, there is his erotic verse, typified by such poems as "Vénus anadyomène" ("Venus Emerging from the Waves") and "Le Coeur volé" ("The Stolen Heart"), which speaks of the trauma of sexual coming-of-age. A pastiche of traditional styles and forms, these initial works nevertheless evidence a brilliant gift for verbal expression and announce the theme of revolt which informs all Rimbaud's writings.

"Seer Letter"

On May 15, 1871, Rimbaud declared his emancipation from traditional poetics in his celebrated "Seer Letter," addressed to his friend Paul Demeny. This letter, Rimbaud's *ars poetica*, begins with a contemptuous denunciation of all previous poetry as nothing more than rhymed prose. Only Charles Baudelaire, "un vrai dieu" ("a true god"), is spared and, even then, only partially—he frequented a self-consciously artistic milieu, and he failed to find new forms of expression. Rimbaud then calls for a radically new conception of the poet's mission: "Car je est un autre" ("For I is an other"). It is the essential task of the poet to give voice to the repressed, unconscious "other" that lies concealed behind the mask of the rational, Cartesian "I"—the "other" that societal restrictions have condemned to silence. This can be accomplished only by "un long, immense et raisonné dérèglement de tous les sens" ("a long, immense and reasoned derangement of all the senses"). Unlike his Romantic predecessors and such Symbolist contemporaries as Mallarmé, who passively awaited the return of the muse, Rimbaud insists on the active role the poet must take: "Le Poète se fait voyant" ("The poet makes himself a seer"). The poet must actively cultivate dreams, hallucinations, and madness. In so doing, he becomes the great liberator of humanity, a Prometheus who steals fire from the gods, the spokesperson for all those whom society has ostracized: "Il devient entre tous le grand malade, le grand criminel, le grand maudit—et le grand Savant!" ("He becomes, more than anyone, the great sick one, the great criminal, the great accursed one—and the great Learned One!"). Such a poet will be "un multiplicateur de progrès" whose genius, unrestrained by societal taboos and the limitations of rational thought, will lead humankind into a new golden age.

Throughout the remaining months of 1871 and the following year, Rimbaud endeavored to give form to this poetic vision in a new series of songs and verse that are best exemplified by two poems that critics have universally acclaimed as masterpieces: "Le Bateau ivre" ("The Drunken Boat") and "Voyelles" ("Vowels").

"THE DRUNKEN BOAT"

Perhaps the best known of Rimbaud's works, "The Drunken Boat" was composed during the summer of 1871 and presented to Verlaine in September of that same year. Although the work borrows from a wide variety of sources (Victor Hugo, Baudelaire, Jules Verne, and Vicomte Chateaubriand, to name but a few), it remains a stunning and original tour de force—particularly for a young poet of sixteen. The poem, composed of twenty-five quatrains in classical Alexandrines and narrated in the first person, is a symbolic drama in three acts. In the first act (quatrains 1 through 4), set on a vast river in the New World, the boat recounts its escape from its haulers, who are massacred by screaming natives, and its subsequent descent toward the sea. There follows a brief, transitional interlude (quatrain 5) in which the boat passes through a ritual purification: Its wooden shell is permeated by the seawater that cleanses it of wine stains and vomit and bears off the boat's rudder and anchor.

The second and central act (quatrains 6 through 22) tells of the boat's intoxicating maritime adventures and its fantastic, hallucinatory vision of a transcendental reality that ordinary mortals have only glimpsed in passing. Yet, the boat's long and frenetic voyage of discovery ultimately begins to turn sour. After braving whirlpools, hurricanes, raging seas, and Leviathans from the deep, the boat unexpectedly declares its nostalgia for the ancient parapets of Europe.

In the third and final act (quatrains 23 through 25), the boat's delirious optimism turns to anguished despair. Its quest for the absolute has at length proved futile, and the boat now seeks dissolution in death. If it desires a return to European waters, it is to the cold, black puddle into which a sad, impoverished child releases a boat as frail as a May butterfly. At the same time, the boat realizes the impossibility of any turning back to its previous mode of existence. It can no longer follow in the wake of the merchant ships, nor bear the haughty pride of the military gunboats, nor swim beneath the horrible eyes of the prison ships that lie at anchor in the harbor.

"The Drunken Boat" reflects both Rimbaud's new conception of the poet as "seer" and the influence of the French Symbolists, such as Verlaine and Baudelaire, who sought to replace the effusive, personalized verse of the Romantics with a symbolic, impersonal mode of expression. Critics have generally equated the work's "protagonist," the boat, with the poet himself, reading the poem as a symbolic account of Rimbaud's own efforts to transcend reality through language. Most critics are also agreed that the poem's final two stanzas, while they suggest the advent of a new self-awareness, evince a disillusionment with the "seer" experiment and prefigure Rimbaud's later renunciation of poetry.

"Vowels"

Rimbaud's celebrated sonnet "Vowels," written in decasyllabic verse, dates from the same period as "The Drunken Boat" and was similarly presented to Verlaine in September, 1871. Another of Rimbaud's "seer" poems, the work postulates a mystic correspondence between vowels and colors: "A noir, E blanc, I rouge, U vert, O bleu" ("A black, E white, I red, U green, O blue"). The poem has its literary source in Baudelaire's famous sonnet "Correspondences," which had asserted an underlying connection between sounds, perfumes, and colors and had popularized the concept of synesthesia. Another probable source for the work has been found in an illustrated alphabet primer that Rimbaud may have read as a child and that has served to elucidate some of the sonnet's enigmatic imagery.

Perhaps the most ingenious interpretation of the poem is that of the critic Lucien Sausy, who argued that the work exploits correspondences not between sound and color (there are, in fact, few traces of such matching within the phonetic content of the poem) but rather between the visual form of the vowels themselves and the images to which the latter are linked: *A*, if inverted, thus suggests the delta-shaped body of a fly; *E* (written as a Greek epsilon in the manuscript), if turned on its side, suggests vapors, tents, and glaciers; and so on. (Sausy's interpretation, first advanced in *Les Nouvelles Littéraires*, September 2, 1933, is available in the notes to the Pléiade edition of Rimbaud's works.) As a counterbalance, however, one might mention Verlaine's explanation of the sonnet: "Rimbaud saw things that way and that's all there is to it."

A Season in Hell

By his own account, Rimbaud composed *A Season in Hell* during the period from April to August of 1873. Rimbaud supervised the book's publication, and it was printed in Brussels in the fall of 1873 in an edition of five hundred copies. Rimbaud was unable, however, to pay the printing costs, and this first edition, save for six author's copies that circulated among his friends, remained in the attic of a Brussels publishing house until discovered in 1901 by a Belgian bibliophile, who did not make his discovery public until 1914.

The text, which Rimbaud had originally intended to entitle "Livre païen" (pagan book) or "Livre nègre" (Negro book—the French adjective is pejorative), consists of nine prose poems and seven poems in verse, the latter all contained within the section "Délires II" ("Deliria II"). The work has been variously acclaimed by critics for its original and stunning verbal display, its fantastic, visionary imagery, and its prophetic pronouncements concerning Rimbaud's own future. As the title indicates, *A Season in Hell* is Rimbaud's poetic attempt to come to grips with his recent "dark night of the soul"—his unhappy adventure with Verlaine and his anguished experience as "seer." Viewed from the perspective of Rimbaud's own metaphysical dictum—"I is an other"—the work, narrated in the first person, recounts a confrontation between the rational, conscious "I" and the irrational, unconscious "other" which the poet had systematically worked to cultivate.

The text opens with a brief introductory section (untitled) in which the poet evokes with longing his lost state of childhood innocence. He recalls his frenzied flight from reason, his revolt against traditional concepts of beauty and morality, his pursuit of crime, and his cultivation of madness. He momentarily dreams of regaining his former state of innocence through a return to Christian charity but immediately rejects the latter as an empty illusion. Inescapably condemned to death and damnation, he dedicates his opus not to the traditional poetic Muse but rather to Satan. This introductory segment serves to announce the key themes that the body of the work will subsequently develop: the abandonment of the "seer" experiment, the nostalgia for the comfort afforded by traditional Christian values, and the attainment of a new self-awareness that, however, prevents any naïve return to the past.

"Bad Blood"

In the following prose poem, "Mauvais Sang" ("Bad Blood"), the poet attributes his failure to transcend the vulgar world or reality to some inherited defect that now condemns him to a life of manual toil. Nor does he envision any hope in the progress promised by Cartesian rationalism and the advent of science. The world may yet be headed toward total destruction. Disillusioned with Western civilization, he seeks imaginative shelter in what he perceives as the savage freedom of black African society. His amoral utopia is, however, destroyed by the arrival of the white colonialists, who impose their debilitating Christian ethics by force of arms. Momentarily seduced by Christianity, the poet ultimately rejects it as an infringement on human freedom and refuses to embark on a honeymoon with Jesus Christ as father-in-law. Rather than remain enslaved, he hurls himself to his death beneath the horses of the conquering Europeans.

"Night in Hell"

The conflict between Christianity and paganism is further developed in "Nuit de l'enfer" ("Night in Hell"). Here, the poet is engulfed in the fires of Hell, to which his parents have condemned him through baptism and catechism lessons. His suffering derives from his inability to choose between the absolute but terrible freedom offered by Satan and the serene but limited freedom promised by the Christian God. Hell, in short, is a state of eternal and lucid alienation.

"Deliria I"

"Délires I" ("Deliria I") introduces a "Vièrge folle" ("Foolish Virgin") who recounts her difficult life with "l'Époux infernal" ("The Infernal Spouse") who seduced her with the false promise of an amoral and transcendent Paradise. Numerous critics have found in this passage a mythic retelling of Verlaine's intellectual and erotic seduction by Rimbaud; other critics have preferred to read the passage as emblematic of the seduction of the poet's rational and moral self by his own irrational and amoral unconscious. In either case, the poem is a bitter indictment of Rimbaud's failed efforts to transform reality.

"Deliria II"

In "Délires II" ("Deliria II"), subtitled "L'Alchimie du verbe" ("Verbal Alchemy"), the poet looks back on what he now views as an act of folly: his attempt to transcend reality through the systematic cultivation of the irrational and the invention of a new language that would draw in all the human senses and give voice to everything in humans that had previously been barred from expression. He gives as tangible examples of this enterprise six verse poems, the visionary imagery of which speaks symbolically of his hunger and thirst for the absolute, his frustration with past theology and future technology, and his fervent conviction that he has indeed found the mystic line of juncture between sea and sky, body and soul, the known and unknown. This metaphysical quest has ultimately failed, the poet says, for he has been damned by the rainbow—an ironic allusion to the rainbow sent by God to Noah as a sign of future redemption. As his dream-filled night draws to a close, and morning approaches, the poet awakes to hear the strains of the hymn "Christus venit" (Christ has come) resounding through the somber cities of the world. His career as "seer" has ended with the bleak dawn of reality.

"The Impossible," "Lightning," "Morning," and "Farewell"

The four remaining prose poems, all of them brief, further expand on major themes in the work. In "L'Impossible" ("The Impossible"), the poet tells of his futile efforts to reconcile Christianity and Eastern mysticism and his ultimate rejection of both. In "Éclair" ("Lightning"), the poet finds momentary comfort in the dignity of work but cannot avoid perceiving the vanity of all human efforts in the face of death and dissolution. "Matin" ("Morning") announces the end of the poet's night in Hell. In spite of the limitations imposed by the human condition, he chooses life over death. Although all men are slaves, they should not curse life. In the final passage, "Adieu" ("Farewell"), the poet renounces his unsuccessful career as "seer" in favor of a newfound divine clarity, the anguished self-knowledge that his experience has brought him. There will be no turning back to the past for solace, nor any attempt to seek oblivion in the love of a woman. Humans must be absolutely modern, the poet declares; for himself, he is content to possess the truth that humans are both body and soul.

ILLUMINATIONS

Illuminations was published in 1886, without Rimbaud's knowledge. Some years earlier, he had left a manuscript of the work with Verlaine, whence it passed through several hands before it was published in the Symbolist periodical *La Vogue*, appearing in book form (edited and with a preface by Verlaine) later in the same year.

Although a century has passed since the first appearance of *Illuminations*, a number of fundamental questions concerning the collection remain to be resolved and perhaps will never be definitely resolved. First there is the matter of the title. The manuscript itself is untitled, and the only evidence for the title by which the collection is known is the statement of Paul Verlaine, a notoriously unreliable witness. In a letter written in 1878 to his brother-in-law, Charles de Sivry, Verlaine says: "Have re-read *Illuminations* (painted plates). . . ." Later, in the preface to the first edition of *Illuminations*, he adds that "the word [that is, "illuminations"] is English and means *gravures coloriées*, colored plates," claiming that this was the subtitle that Rimbaud had chosen for the work.

The question of the title and subtitle may seem a mere scholarly quibble, but it is more than that, for at issue is the significance that Rimbaud himself attached to the title and, by extension, the spirit in which he intended the work to be read. Some critics, accepting Verlaine's testimony without qualification, suggest that by "painted plates" or "colored plates," Rimbaud meant the cheap colored prints that had recently become widely available. The tone of the title, then, would be highly ironic. Other critics suggest that Verlaine garbled Rimbaud's meaning—that Rimbaud had in mind the illuminated manuscripts of the Middle Ages. Still others reject Verlaine's testimony on this matter as another of his fabrications, arguing that by "illuminations" Rimbaud meant moments of spiritual insight; some readers have seen in the title a reference to the occult doctrines of Illuminism.

Another important debate concerns the date of composition. It was long believed that *Illuminations* preceded *A Season in Hell*, but later this assumption was seriously challenged. Again, the question of dating may appear to be of interest only to specialists, but such is not the case. The conclusion to *A Season in Hell* has been widely regarded as Rimbaud's farewell to poetry. If, in fact, he wrote *Illuminations* after *A Season in Hell*, many existing critical interpretations are invalid or in need of substantial revision.

This argument for dating *Illuminations* after *A Season in Hell* is primarily based on the pioneering research of Henri de Bouillane de Lacoste. Bouillane de Lacoste's graphological analysis of the manuscript, in conjunction with other, more subjective, arguments, has persuaded many scholars to accept Verlaine's once-rejected assertion that the work was written during the period from 1873 to 1875 in the course of Rimbaud's European travels. On the other hand, there are a number of reputable Rimbaud scholars who find Bouillane de Lacoste's analysis inconclusive at best and who thus retain the old chronology. In any case, one cannot know with certainty the date of composition of the individual poems themselves, nor is there any clear indication of the final order in which Rimbaud intended them to appear. The reason for Rimbaud's prolongation of his poetic career beyond his abdication from poetry in *A Season in Hell* seems destined to remain a mystery.

Illuminations is regarded by many critics as Rimbaud's most original work and his consummate contribution to French poetry. Although it represents a continuation of the "seer" experiment conducted in his earlier verse, it also marks a radical departure from the narrative, anecdotal, and descriptive modes of expression to be found in his previous poetry and in that of his contemporaries. The poems in *Illuminations* are strikingly modern in that each forms a self-contained, self-referential unit that stands independent of the collection as a whole and remains detached from any clear point of reference in the world of reality. They do not purport to convey any didactic, moral, or philosophical message to the reader. Ephemeral and dreamlike, each emerges from the void as a spontaneous flow of images generated by free association. They are works in which the rational "I" allows the unconscious "other" to speak . As manifestations of the unconscious, they reveal an almost infinitely rich condensation of meaning that defies any linear attempts at interpretation. They thus elucidate Rimbaud's earlier remark in *A Season in Hell* that he "reserved all translation rights." They are, again in the poet's own words, "accessible to all meanings." If they are coherent, it is in the way dreams are coherent, and like dreams, they speak from the hidden recesses of the mind. Hermetic in form, they lead down a different path from that charted by the Symbolist verse of Rimbaud's contemporary, Mallarmé: They reflect not an aesthetic obsession with the problematics of language but a perpetual striving to give voice to all that reason and social mores have condemned to silence.

Although *Illuminations* consists of a discontinuous series of pieces devoid of any central narrative plot, critics have drawn attention to a number of major recurring themes to be found within the text. Given the work's dreamlike qualities and its close affinity with the unconscious, it is not surprising that the theme most often cited by critics is that of childhood. Numerous passages in the work evoke the blissful innocence of childhood, Rimbaud's "paradise lost," irrevocably destroyed by the advent of civilization and Christianity. The theme is developed at particular length in the two prose poems "Enfance" ("Childhood") and "Après le déluge" ("After the Deluge"). In the first, the child-poet tells of his Satanic fall from a state of divine omniscience and absolute freedom into a subterranean prison, where he is condemned to silence. In the second, which ironically alludes to the biblical story of the Flood and the promise of divine redemption, the poet sees the natural innocence of childhood as being progressively corrupted by the rise of civilization, and he ends by conjuring up new floods that will sweep away the repressive work of society.

A second and related major theme, exemplified by such prose poems as "Villes I" ("Cities I"), "Villes II" ("Cities II"), and "Métropolitain" ("Metropolitan"), is that of the city. Although modeled in part on the Paris and London of Rimbaud's own time, the cities in *Illuminations* are phantasmagoric, shimmering cities of the future that present a vision of technological wonder and bleak sterility. Promised utopias, they repeatedly and rapidly degenerate into vast urban wastelands that devour their pitiful human prey. In the end, they are bitterly renounced by their creator and verbally banished back to the void from which they emerged.

A third major theme is that of metamorphosis—a theme that is a logical outgrowth of Rimbaud's own assertion that "I is an other." For Rimbaud, as his "Seer Letter" makes clear, the seemingly stable Cartesian I is merely an illusion that masks the presence of a multiplicity of repressed others. Humans have no central, defining essence. In *Illuminations*, the poet thus undergoes a continual series of metamorphoses. In "Parade," he appears as a procession of itinerant comedians; in "Antique," as the son of the pagan god Pan, at once animal, man, and woman; in "Bottom," as the character in William Shakespeare's *A Midsummer Night's Dream* (pr. c. 1595-1596) who seeks to appropriate all the other characters' roles; and finally, in "Being Beauteous," as the incarnation of beauty itself. There are no limits to humanity's being, Rimbaud suggests, if people will only realize the vast potential within them.

OTHER MAJOR WORKS

MISCELLANEOUS: *Œuvres complètes*, 1948 (*Complete Works, Selected Letters*, 1966); *Rimbaud Complete*, 2002-2003 (2 volumes; Wyatt Mason, editor).

BIBLIOGRAPHY

Ahearn, Edward J. *Rimbaud: Visions and Habitations*. Berkeley: University of California Press, 1983. Discusses the influence of Rimbaud's early life and surroundings on his brief poetic career, including the anticlerical and anticonventional guidance he received during his teen years, when he began writing poetry. Points out links between Rimbaud's poetic images and his actual physical environment.

Cohn, Robert Greer. *The Poetry of Rimbaud*. 1973. Reprint. Columbia: University of South Carolina Press, 1999. A critical analysis of the poetry that Rimbaud wrote during his short life.

Hackett, Cecil Arthur. *Rimbaud: A Critical Introduction*. New York: Cambridge University Press, 1981. A good introduction for those beginning to explore Rimbaud's poetry. Contains much poem-by-poem explication, as well as analyses of Rimbaud's overall poetic achievement and cultural influence.

Lawler, James R. *Rimbaud's Theatre of the Self*. Cambridge, Mass.: Harvard University Press, 1992. A unique book that translates Rimbaud's work into a theatrical progression, explaining why he stopped writing to explore the dark side of his personality.

Oxenhandler, Neal. *Rimbaud: The Cost of Genius*. Columbus: Ohio State University Press, 2009. An examination of the life of Rimbaud that argues that his talent had a destructive side to it.

Perloff, Marjorie. *The Poetics of Indeterminacy: Rimbaud to Cage*. Evanston, Ill.: Northwestern University Press, 2000. This work contains only one chapter on Rimbaud but is highly useful in placing him within his historical context. Discusses his influence on modernist poets such as Gertrude Stein, Ezra Pound, and William Carlos Williams, as a transitional force between Symbolism and modernism.

Robb, Graham. *Rimbaud: A Biography*. New York: W. W. Norton, 2000. Presents a "reconstruction of Rimbaud's life"; discusses the revolutionary impact his poetry had on twentieth century writers and artists, especially since Rimbaud's admirers primarily arose after his early death. Examines the influence of Rimbaud's early family life, in particular his stormy relationship with his mother, and presents thoroughly his checkered career after his abandonment of poetry at the age of twenty-one.

Steinmetz, Jean-Luc. *Arthur Rimbaud: Presence of an Enigma*. Translated by Jon Graham. New York: Welcome Rain, 2001. A comprehensive biography, this work focuses on Rimbaud's numerous self-contradictions and extremes of behavior, particularly in his stormy relationship with the older poet Paul Verlaine. The author analyzes Rimbaud's poetry primarily in its relation to the poet's life.

James John Baran

TRISTAN TZARA
Sami Rosenstock

Born: Moineşti, Romania; April 4, 1896
Died: Paris, France; December 24, 1963

PRINCIPAL POETRY
  La Première Aventure céleste de Monsieur Antipyrine, 1916
  Vingt-cinq Poèmes, 1918
  Cinéma calendrier du coeur abstrait, 1920
  De nos oiseaux, 1923
  Indicateur des chemins de coeur, 1928
  L'Arbre des voyageurs, 1930
  L'Homme approximatif, 1931 (*Approximate Man, and Other Writings*, 1973)
  Où boivent les loups, 1932
  L'Antitête, 1933
  Primele Poème, 1934 (English translation, 1976)
  Grains et issues, 1935
  La Deuxième Aventure céleste de Monsieur Antipyrine, 1938 (wr. 1917)
  Midis gagnés, 1939
  Une Route seul soleil, 1944
  Entre-temps, 1946
  Le Signe de vie, 1946
  Terre sur terre, 1946
  Morceaux choisis, 1947
  Phases, 1949
  Sans coup férir, 1949
  De mémoire d'homme, 1950
  Parler seul, 1950
  Le Poids du monde, 1951
  La Première main, 1952
  La Face intérieure, 1953
  À haute flamme, 1955
  La Bonne heure, 1955
  Miennes, 1955
  Le Temps naissant, 1955
  Le Fruit permis, 1956 (wr. 1946)
  Frère bois, 1957
  La Rose et le chien, 1958

De la coupe aux lèvres, 1961
Juste présent, 1961
Selected Poems, 1975

OTHER LITERARY FORMS

Although the largest part of the work of Tristan Tzara (TSAH-rah) consists of a vast body of poetry—filling more than thirty volumes—he did experiment with drama, publishing three plays during his lifetime: *Le Coeur à gaz* (pb. 1946; *The Gas Heart*, 1964), *Mouchoir de nuages* (pb. 1924; *Handkerchief of Clouds*, 1972), and *La Fuite* (pb. 1947; the flight). His important polemical writings appeared in two collections: *Sept Manifestes Dada* (1924; *Seven Dada Manifestos*, 1977) and *Le Surréalisme et l'après-guerre* (1947; Surrealism and the postwar period). Much of Tzara's critical and occasional writing, which is substantial in volume, remains unpublished, including book-length works on François Rabelais and François Villon, while the published portion includes *Lampisteries* (1963; English translation, 1977), *Picasso et la poésie* (1953; Picasso and poetry), *L'Art Océanien* (1951; the art of Oceania), and *L'Égypte face à face* (1954).

ACHIEVEMENTS

Tristan Tzara's importance as a literary figure of international reputation rests primarily on his relationship to the Dada movement. Of all the avant-garde movements that challenged the traditional foundations of artistic value and judgment at the beginning of the present century, Dada was, by consensus, the most radical and disturbing. In retrospect, the Dada aesthetic, which was first formed and expressed in Zurich about 1916, seems to have been a fairly direct response to World War I; the Dadaists themselves suggest as much in many of their works during this period.

The harsh, confrontational nature of Dada is notorious, and Tzara was one of the most provocative of all the Dadaists. In his 1930 essay, "Memoirs of Dadaism," Tzara describes one of his own contributions to the first Dada soiree in Paris, on January 23, 1920, in which he read a newspaper while a bell rang. This attitude of deliberate confrontation with the conventional, rational expectations of the audience—to which the Dadaists juxtaposed their illogical, satirical productions—is defended by Tzara in his most famous polemical work, "Manifeste Dada 1918" ("Dada Manifesto 1918"), in which he asserts the meaninglessness of Dada and its refusal to offer a road to truth.

To escape the machinery of human rationality, the Dadaists substituted a faith in spontaneity, incorporating the incongruous and accidental into their works. Even the name by which the Dadaists called themselves was chosen rather arbitrarily. According to most accounts (although this report is subject to intense difference of opinion among Dadaists), it was Tzara himself who chose the word *dada*, in February of 1916, by opening a French dictionary to a randomly selected entry.

Tzara's achievements are not limited solely to his leadership in the Dada movement.

Until recently, Tzara's later work—which is more optimistic in tone and more controlled in technique—has been overshadowed by his more violent and sensational work from the Dada period. It is now becoming apparent to many readers and critics that the Surrealist phase of Tzara's work, the little-known work of his post-Surrealist phase, and his early pre-Dada work in Romanian, are equally important in considering his contribution to modern literature. In the 1970's and 1980's, largely through the work of editors and translators such as Mary Ann Caws, Henrí Behar, and Sasa Pană, this work became more readily available.

Biography

Tristan Tzara, whose real name was Sami Rosenstock, was born on April 4, 1896, in Moineşti, a small town in the province of Băcău, in northeastern Romania. His parents were Jewish, his father a prosperous merchant. Tzara first attended school in Moineşti, where Romanian was spoken, but later, when he was sent to Bucharest for his secondary education, he attended schools where instruction was also given in French. In addition to languages, Tzara studied mathematics and music. Following his graduation in 1913, he attended the University of Bucharest for a year, taking courses in mathematics and philosophy.

It was during this adolescent period, between 1911 and 1915, that all Tzara's Romanian poems were written. His first published poems appeared in 1912 in *Simbolul*, a short-lived Symbolist review that he helped to edit. These first four poems were signed with the pseudonym S. Samyro. The subsequent poems in Romanian that Tzara published during this period were often signed simply "Tristan" or "Tzara," and it was not until near the end of this period, in 1915, that the first Romanian poem signed "Tristan Tzara" appeared.

In the fall of 1915, Tzara went to Zurich, in neutral Switzerland, where he became involved with a group of writers and artists—including Hugo Ball, Richard Huelsenbeck, Marcel Janco, and Hans Arp—who were in the process of forming an artistic movement soon to be called Dada. This period, between Tzara's arrival in Zurich in the fall of 1915 and February of 1916, was the germinating period of the Dada movement. The Dadaists' first public announcement of the birth of a new movement in the arts took place at the Cabaret Voltaire on the evening of February 5, 1916—the occasion of the first of many such Dada soirees. These entertainments included presentations such as "simultaneous poems," which confronted the audience with a chaotic barrage of words made incomprehensible by the din; recitations of "pure sound-poems," often made up of African-sounding nonsense syllables and recited by a chorus of masked dancers; satirical plays that accused and insulted the audience; and, always, the ceaseless manifestos promoting the Dada revolt against conformity. Tzara's work during this period was written almost entirely in French, and from this time on he used that language exclusively for his literary productions.

As the activities of the Zurich Dadaists gradually attracted notice in other countries, especially Germany and France, Tzara's own fame as an artist spread to an increasingly larger audience. The spread of Dada's fame from Zurich to other centers of avant-garde activity in Europe was aided by the journal *Dada*, edited by Tzara and featuring many of his most provocative works. Although this journal lasted only through five issues, it did draw the attention of Guillaume Apollinaire in Paris, and through him the devoted admiration of André Breton, who was later to be one of the leaders of the Surrealist movement. At Breton's urging, Tzara left Zurich shortly after the Armistice was declared, arriving in Paris in December of 1919.

For a short period between January of 1920, when the first public Dada performance in Paris was held, and May of 1921, when Breton broke his association with Tzara to assume the leadership of the developing Surrealist movement, Breton and Tzara organized an increasingly outrageous series of activities that frequently resulted in public spectacles. Following Breton's break with the Dada group, Tzara continued to stage public performances in Paris for a time, collaborating with those who remained loyal to the Dada revolt. By July of 1923, however, when the performance of his play *The Gas Heart* was disrupted by a Surrealist counter demonstration, even Tzara regretfully admitted that Dada was effectively dead, a victim of its own destructive impulses. Tzara gave up the Dada ideal reluctantly and continued to oppose the Surrealists until 1929, when he joined the Paris Surrealist group, accepting Breton's leadership. Tzara's resumption of activities with Breton's group was also accompanied by an increasing move toward political engagement.

The same year that he joined the Surrealists, Tzara visited the Soviet Union, and the following year, in 1930, the Surrealists indicated their dedication to the Communist International by changing the name of their own journal, *La Révolution surréaliste*, to *Le Surréalisme au service de la révolution*. For Tzara, this political commitment seemed to be a natural outgrowth of his initial revolt, for, as he wrote later in *Le Surréalisme et l'après-guerre*: "Dada was born . . . from the deep feeling that man . . . must affirm his supremacy over notions emptied of all human substance, over dead objects and ill-gotten gains."

In 1935, Tzara broke with the Surrealists to devote himself entirely to the work of the Communist Party, which he officially joined at this time. From 1935 to 1937, he was involved in assisting the Republican forces in the Spanish Civil War, salvaging art treasures and serving on the Committee for the Defense of Culture. This political engagement continued during World War II, with Tzara serving in the French Resistance, all the time continuing to publish his work, despite widespread censorship, under the pseudonym T. Tristan. In 1946 and 1947, he delivered the lectures that make up *Le Surréalisme et l'après-guerre*, in which he made his controversial assessment of Surrealism's failure to influence Europe effectively between the wars. In 1955, Tzara published *À haute flamme* (at full flame), a long poetic reminiscence in which he reviewed the stages of his lifelong revolt and reaffirmed his revolutionary aesthetic. Tzara continued to affirm the authenticity of his position until his death in Paris at the age of sixty-seven, a victim of lung cancer.

Analysis

Whatever else Tristan Tzara was—Dada instigator and polemicist, marginal Surrealist, Communist activist, or Romanian expatriate—his great skill as a poet is abundantly apparent. At his death, Tzara left behind a vast body of poems, extremely diverse in style, content, and tone. Important features of his work are his innovations in poetic technique and his development of a highly unified system of symbolic imagery. The first of these features includes the use of pure sound elements, descriptive ideophones, expressive typography, enjambment that creates complex syntactic ambiguities, and multiple viewpoints resulting in a confusing confluence of speaking voices. The second important feature includes such elements as Tzara's use of recurring verbal motifs and refrains, ironic juxtapositions, and recurring image clusters.

Tzara's earliest period extends from 1911 to 1915 and includes all the poetry he wrote in his native Romanian. Until recently, little attention has been given to Tzara's Romanian poetry. Several Romanian critics have noted the decisive but unacknowledged influence on Tzara of the Romanian poet Urmuz (1883-1923), virtually unknown in the West, who anticipated the strategies of Dada and Surrealism. Much of Tzara's early work, however, is relatively traditional in technique, although it must be remembered that this period represents his poetic apprenticeship and that the poems were written when he was between the ages of fifteen and nineteen. The poetry of this period often displays a curiously ambivalent tone, mixing a detached ironic perspective—which is sometimes gently sarcastic and at other times bitterly resentful—with an uncritically sentimental nostalgia for the past. In some of the poems, one of these two moods dominates, as in Tzara's bitterly ironic treatment of war's destructive effect on the innocence of youth in "The Storm and the Deserter's Song" and "Song of War," or the romantic lyricism of such highly sentimental idylls on nature as "Elegy for the Coming of Winter" and "Evening Comes."

Primele Poème

The most successful poems of this period—later collected as *Primele Poème*—are those which mix nostalgia with irony, encompassing both attitudes within a single poem. The best example of this type of poem is "Sunday," whose conventional images of leisurely activities that occupy the inhabitants of a town on the Sabbath are contrasted with the bitter reflections of the alienated poet-speaker who observes the scene. The scene seems idyllic enough at first, presenting images of domestic tranquillity. Then the reflecting consciousness of the alienated speaker intrudes, introducing images that contrast darkly with and shatter the apparently false impression he himself has just created. Into the scene of comfortable regularity, three new and disturbing elements appear: the inescapable presence of death in wartime, the helplessness of parents to protect their children from danger, and the futility of art stagnated by Decadence.

VINGT-CINQ POÈMES

This successful mixture of sentimental lyricism with ironic detachment is developed to an even greater degree in Tzara's first collection of poems in French, *Vingt-cinq Poèmes* (twenty-five poems), a collection that, although published after he had already arrived in Zurich, still resembles in technique and content the early Romanian poems. In "Petite Ville en Sibérie" ("Little Town in Siberia"), there are a number of new elements, the most important of which are Tzara's use of typography for expressive purposes, the complex syntactic ambiguity created by enjambment, the rich confluence of narrative voices, and the appearance of images employing illogical juxtapositions of objects and qualities:

> a blue light which flattens us together on the ceiling
> it's as always comrade
> like a label of infernal doors pasted on a medicine bottle
> it's the calm house tremble my friend

This disorienting confluence of voices is deliberate, and it evokes in the reader a futile desire to resolve the collage (based on the random conjunction of several separate discourses) into a meaningful and purposeful poetic statement.

DE NOS OISEAUX

In Tzara's second period—extending from 1916 until 1924—he produced the Dadaist works which brought him international fame. To the collage technique developed in *Vingt-cinq Poèmes*, the poems that make up *De nos oiseaux* (of our birds)—the major collection from this period—introduce several innovations, including pure sound elements such as African-sounding nonsense words, repeated phrases, descriptive ideophones, use of multiple typefaces, and catalogs of discrete, separable images piled one upon the other. Tzara's collage technique has become more radical in these poems, for instead of simply using the juxtaposition of speaking voices for creating ironic detachment, in the Dada poems the narrative itself breaks down entirely into a chaotic barrage of discontinuous fragments that often seem to lack any discursive sense. These features are readily apparent in "La Mort de Guillaume Apollinaire" ("The Death of Guillaume Apollinaire") and "Les Saltimbanques" ("The Circus Performers"), two of the best poems from *De nos oiseaux*.

"THE DEATH OF GUILLAUME APOLLINAIRE"

In his Dadaist elegy for Apollinaire, Tzara begins with a series of propositions that not only establish the resigned mood of the speaker but also express the feeling of disorder created in the reader by the poem itself. A simple admission of man's inability to comprehend his situation in the world is followed by a series of images that seem designed to convey the disparity the speaker senses between a world which is unresponsive to human needs (the unfortunate death of Apollinaire at such an early age is no doubt one aspect of this) and a world in which he could feel comfortable (and presumably learn to accept the death of his beloved friend):

>   if snow fell upward
>   if the sun rose in our houses in the middle of the night
>   just to keep us warm
>   and the trees hung upsidedown with their crowns . . .
>   if birds came down to us to find reflections of
>   themselves
>   in those peaceful lakes lying just above our heads
>   THEN WE MIGHT UNDERSTAND
>   that death could be a beautiful long voyage
>   and a permanent vacation from flesh from structures
>   systems and skeletons

The images of this poem constitute a particularly good illustration of Tzara's developing symbolic system. Although the images of snow falling upward, the sun rising at night, trees hanging upside down, and birds coming to earth at first appear unrelated to one another, they are actually related in two ways. First, Tzara is describing processes within the totality of nature which give evidence that "nature is organized in its totality." Humanity's sorrow over the inescapable cycles of life and death, of joy and suffering, is caused by a failure to understand that humans, too, are a part of this totality. Second, Tzara's images suggest that if one's perspective could only be reversed, one would see the reality of things properly. This method of presenting arguments in nondiscursive, imagistic terms was one of Tzara's primary poetic accomplishments, and the uses to which he put it in this elegy for Apollinaire were later expanded and developed in the epic scope of his masterpiece, *Approximate Man, and Other Writings*.

"THE CIRCUS PERFORMERS"

"The Circus Performers" illustrates Tzara's increasing use of pure sound elements in his work. The images of this poem attempt to capture the exciting rhythms of the circus performance that Tzara is describing. In the opening vignette of the poem, in what seems at first an illogical sequence of statements, Tzara merges the expanding and contracting rhythm of the verses with his characteristic use of imagery to convey thought in analogical, nondiscursive terms. Describing a ventriloquist's act, Tzara uses an image that links "brains," "balloons," and "words." In this image, "brains" seems to be a metonymic substitution for ideas or thoughts—that which is expressed by "words."

Here the brains themselves are inflating and deflating, as are the balloons. What is the unstated analogical relation between the two? These words are treated like the words and thoughts of comic-strip characters—where words are enclosed in the "balloons" that represent mental space in newspaper cartoons. To help the reader more easily identify the analogy, Tzara has included an explanatory aside, enclosed in parentheses. A second example of Tzara's use of sound in this poem is the presence of "ideophones"— words that imitate the sounds of the actions they describe. Pure sound images devoid of abstract meaning are scattered throughout the poem.

APPROXIMATE MAN, AND OTHER WRITINGS

By all standards of judgment, *Approximate Man, and Other Writings*, a long epic in nineteen sections, is Tzara's greatest poem. It was Tzara's most sustained effort, its composition and extensive revisions occupying the poet between 1925 and 1931, the year that the final version appeared. Another important characteristic of the work is its epic scope, for *Approximate Man, and Other Writings* was Tzara's attempt to discover the causes of modern humanity's spiritual malaise, drawing on all the technical resources he had developed up to the time of its composition. The most important feature of the poem, however, is its systematic presentation of Tzara's revolutionary ideology, which had begun to reflect, in a guarded form, the utopian vision of Surrealism.

Approximate Man, and Other Writings is about the intrusion of disorder into modern life, and it focuses on the effects of this disorder on the individual. Throughout the poem, Tzara makes it clear that what he is describing is a general disorder or sickness, not a personal crisis. This is one of the key ideas that is constantly repeated in the form of a refrain: "approximate man like me like you reader and like the others/ heap of noisy flesh and echoes of conscience/ complete in the only element of choice your name." The most important aspect of the poem's theme is Tzara's diagnosis of the causes of this debilitating universal sickness, since this indicates in a striking way his newly found attitude of commitment.

The first cause of humanity's sickness is the very condition of being "approximate." Uncertain, changeable, or lacking commitment to any cause that might improve the world in which he lives, Approximate Man wanders aimlessly. For Tzara, the lost key for curing the sickness is commitment, as Tzara himself declared his commitment to the work of the Communist Party in 1935, shortly after the completion of this poem.

Humanity's sickness arises not only from inauthentic relationships with others but also from an exploitative attitude toward nature—an attitude encouraged by the development of modern technology. In Tzara's view, this modern belief in humanity's preeminent importance in the universe is a mistaken one, as is evident in "The Death of Guillaume Apollinaire," and such vanity contributes to the spiritual sickness of humankind.

Tzara finds a third cause of humanity's spiritual sickness in humans' increasing reliance on the products of their own alienated consciousness, especially reason and language. In *Approximate Man, and Other Writings*, Tzara's efforts to describe this solipsistic entrapment of humans by their own systems gives rise to many striking images, as in the following passages: "vapor on the cold glass you block your own image from your/ sight/ tall and insignificant among the glazed frost jewels/ of the landscape" and "I think of the warmth spun by the word/ around its center the dream called ourselves." These images argue that human reason is like a mirror in which the reflection is clouded by the observer's physical presence, and that human language is like a silken cocoon that insulates people from the external world of reality. Both reason and language, originally created to assist humans, have become debased, and to attain a more accurate picture of the world, humans must learn to rely on instinct and imagination. These three ideas, which find their fullest expression in *Approximate Man, and Other Writings*, form the basis of Tzara's mature poetic vision and constitute the most sustained expression of his critique of the modern sensibility.

OTHER MAJOR WORKS

PLAYS: *Mouchoir de nuages*, pb. 1924 (*Handkerchief of Clouds*, 1972); *Le Coeur à gaz*, pb. 1946 (wr. 1921; *The Gas Heart*, 1964); *La Fuite*, pb. 1947.

NONFICTION: *Sept Manifestes Dada*, 1924 (wr. 1917-1918; *Seven Dada Manifestos*, 1977); *Le Surréalisme et l'après-guerre*, 1947; *L'Art Océanien*, 1951; *Picasso et la poésie*, 1953; *L'Égypte face à face*, 1954; *Lampisteries*, 1963 (English translation, 1977).

MISCELLANEOUS: *Œuvres complètes*, 1975-1991 (6 volumes).

BIBLIOGRAPHY

Browning, Gordon Frederick. *Tristan Tzara: The Genesis of the Dada Poem: Or, From Dada to Aa*. Stuttgart, Germany: Akademischer Verlag Heinz, 1979. A critical study of Tzara's Dada poems. Includes bibliographical references.

Caws, Mary Ann. Introduction to *Approximate Man, and Other Writings*, by Tristan Tzara. Translated by Mary Ann Caws. Detroit: Wayne State University Press, 1973. This book is an excellent selection of English translations of Tzara's poetry, and the introduction provides a helpful guide to each phase of his work.

_____, ed. *Surrealist Painters and Poets: An Anthology*. Cambridge, Mass.: MIT Press, 2001. Contains translations of several prose pieces by Tzara as well as works by many of his contemporaries, providing an overview of the context in which he operated. Includes many illustrations.

Forcer, Stephen. *Modernist Song: The Poetry of Tristan Tzara*. Leeds, England: Legenda, 2006. Traces Tzara's development and changing poetry from his early works to publications in the 1950's.

Marcus, Greil. *Lipstick Traces: A Secret History of the Twentieth Century*. 1989. 20th anniversary ed. Cambridge, Mass.: Belknap Press, 2009. A highly original and accessible study of nihilistic movements in art, music, and literature, from Dada to punk rock. Tzara is only one of many figures discussed here, but this book deserves mention because of its broad historical scope and excellent analysis of the relationship between popular culture and the avant-garde.

Motherwell, Robert, and Jack D. Flam, eds. *The Dada Painters and Poets: An Anthology*. 2d ed. Cambridge, Mass.: Harvard University Press, 1989. A collection of Dada documents including journals, reviews, and manifestos that hold valuable biographical and historical details of the life and work of Tzara.

Peterson, Elmer. *Tristan Tzara: Dada and Surrational Theorist*. New Brunswick, N.J.: Rutgers University Press, 1971. A study of Tzara's aesthetics. Includes bibliographical references.

Richter, Hans. *Dada: Art and Anti-Art*. New York: Thames & Hudson, 1997. Through selections from key manifestos and other documents of the time, Richter records Dada's history, from its beginnings in wartime Zurich to its collapse in the Paris of the 1920's.

Sandqvist, Tom. *Dada East: The Romanians of Cabaret Voltaire*. Cambridge, Mass.: MIT Press, 2006. Looks at Dadaism in Romania, where Tzara was born.

Steven E. Colburn

PAUL VERLAINE

Born: Metz, France; March 30, 1844
Died: Paris, France; January 8, 1896

PRINCIPAL POETRY
Poèmes saturniens, 1866
Fêtes galantes, 1869 (*Gallant Parties*, 1912)
La Bonne Chanson, 1870
Romances sans paroles, 1874 (*Romances Without Words*, 1921)
Sagesse, 1881
Jadis et naguère, 1884
Amour, 1888
Parallèlement, 1889, 1894 (English translation, 1939)
Bonheur, 1891
Chansons pour elle, 1891
Femmes, 1891 (English translation, 1977)
Liturgies intimes, 1892
Élégies, 1893
Odes en son honneur, 1893
Épigrammes, 1894
Dans les limbes, 1894
Chair, dernière poésies, 1896
Invectives, 1896 (English translation, 1939)
Hombres, 1903 (English translation, 1977)
Selected Poems, 1948
Femmes/Hombres, 1977 (includes English translation of *Femmes* and *Hombres*)

OTHER LITERARY FORMS

Most of the other published works of Paul Verlaine (vehr-LEHN) are autobiographical writings and critical articles on contemporary poets. During his lifetime, he published two plays that were performed—*Les Uns et les autres* (pr. 1884; the ones and the others) and *Madame Aubin* (pr. 1886)—and one short story, *Louise Leclercq* (1886). A collection of seven other short stories, *Histories comme ça* (1903; stories like that), was published posthumously.

The most significant of his critical writings were published under the title *Poètes maudits* (1884; *The Cursed Poets*, 2003), which includes articles on Tristan Corbière, Arthur Rimbaud, Stéphane Mallarmé, Villiers de L'Isle-Adam, and others. Verlaine's *Confessions* (*Confessions of a Poet*, 1950) was published in 1895. Many of his previ-

Paul Verlaine
(Library of Congress)

ously unedited writings were published posthumously in a 1903 edition of his works, which includes several autobiographical pieces as well as some original ink drawings. All his prose works were published in the 1972 Pléiade edition.

Achievements

Paul Verlaine is universally recognized as one of the great French poets of the nineteenth century. His name is associated with those of his contemporaries Charles Baudelaire, Rimbaud, and Mallarmé. His most famous and frequently anthologized poems, such as "Chanson d'automne" ("Song of Autumn"), "Mon rêve familier" ("My Familiar Dream"), "Clair de lune" ("Moonlight"), and "Il pleure dans mon coeur" ("It Is Crying in My Heart"), are readily recognized and often recited by persons with any knowledge of French poetry. Many of his poems, including those cited, have been set to music by serious composers.

Verlaine's admirers include both saints and sinners, for Verlaine is at once the author of one of the most beautiful collections of religious poetry ever published and the writer of some explicitly erotic poems. During his lifetime, Verlaine's poetic genius was recognized by only a handful of poets and friends. His penchant for antisocial and occasionally criminal behavior (he was jailed twice for potentially murderous attacks) undoubtedly contributed to his lack of commercial success or popular recognition during his lifetime. By the end of his life, he had gained a small measure of recognition and received some income from his royalties and lecture engagements.

Biography

Paul Marie Verlaine was born in Metz, France, on March 30, 1844, the only child of Captain Nicolas-Auguste Verlaine and Elisa Dehée Verlaine. The family moved often during Verlaine's first seven years, until Captain Verlaine retired from the army to settle in Paris. Verlaine attended the Lycée Bonaparte (now Condorcet) and received his *baccalauréat* in 1862.

Verlaine's adoring mother and equally adoring older cousin Elisa Moncomble, whose death in 1867 affected him profoundly, spoiled the sensitive child, encouraged his demanding capriciousness, and helped him become a selfish, immature, unstable young man.

After his *baccalauréat*, he worked in an insurance office and then found a clerical job in municipal government, which he kept until 1870. In 1863, he published his first poem, "Monsieur Prudhomme." He met Catulle Mendès, an editor of the literary magazine *Le Parnasse contemporain*, in which Verlaine published eight poems. In 1866, he published his first volume of poetry, *Poèmes saturniens*, and in 1869, a second volume, *Gallant Parties*.

Alcoholism began to take its toll on his personal life. Twice in drunken rages, he threatened to kill his mother . His family tried to marry him to a strong-willed cousin, a fate that he avoided by proposing to Mathilde Mauté, whom he married in 1870 and who inspired his third volume of poetry, *La Bonne Chanson*.

Having served as press officer to the Commune of Paris during the 1870 insurrection, Verlaine subsequently fled Paris and lost his government job. He helped to found a new journal, *La Renaissance*, in which he published many of the poems included in his 1874 volume, *Romances Without Words*.

Verlaine's drinking and his friendship with Rimbaud led to violent domestic scenes. Following several fights and reconciliations with Mathilde, Verlaine ran off to Brussels with Rimbaud in July, 1872. During the following year, the two poets lived together in Brussels and London and then returned to Brussels. On July 10, 1873, Verlaine, in a drunken rage, fired a revolver at Rimbaud, who had threatened to leave him. Verlaine was convicted of armed assault and sentenced to two years in prison.

In prison, Verlaine converted to a mystical form of Roman Catholicism and began to write the poems for the volume *Sagesse*, published in 1881. After his release in 1875 and until 1879, he held teaching positions in England and France. He formed a sincere and probably chaste relationship with one of his students, Lucien Létinois. They attempted a joint farming venture, which failed, and then returned to Paris, where

Verlaine tried to get back his old government job but was turned down because of his past record. This disappointment, coupled with the sudden death of Létinois in 1883, caused Verlaine to become profoundly discouraged.

After another ill-fated farming venture, Verlaine abandoned himself for a long period to drinking and sordid affairs. A drunken attack on his mother cost him a month in prison in 1885. During his last ten years, his economic distress was somewhat eased by his growing literary reputation. He continued writing and published several more significant volumes of verse.

From 1890 to his death in 1896, Verlaine moved in and out of several hospitals, suffering from a swollen, stiffened leg, the terminal effects of syphilis, diabetes, rheumatism, and heart disease. He lived alternately with two women who cared for him and exploited him. During his last years, he was invited to lecture in Holland, Belgium, and England.

Analysis

In two articles on Baudelaire published in *L'Art* in 1865, Paul Verlaine affirms that the overriding concern of a poet should be the quest for beauty. Without denying the role of inspiration and emotion in the process of poetic creation, Verlaine stresses the need to master them by poetic craftsmanship. Sincerity is not a poetic virtue. Personal emotion must be expressed through the combinations of rhyme, sound, and image that best create a poetic universe in which nothing is the result of chance.

The most obvious result of Verlaine's craftsmanship is the musicality of his verse. Sounds flow together to create a sonorous harmony that repetitions organize and structure as in a musical composition. In his 1882 poem "L'Art poétique," Verlaine gives a poetic recipe that begins with the famous line, "Music above everything else." He goes on to counsel using odd-syllabled lines, imprecise vocabulary and imagery (as if veiled), and nuance rather than color. The poet should avoid wit, eloquence, and forced rhyme. Poetic verse should be light and fugitive, airborne and slightly aromatic. The poem ends with the somber warning, "Anything else is literature."

The subject matter of Verlaine's carefully crafted poetry is frequently his personal experience, certainly dramatic and emotionally charged material. The prologue to *Poèmes saturniens* reveals his consciousness of his miserable destiny. Throughout the rest of his poetry, he narrates the various permutations of his self-fulfilling expectation of unhappiness. "Moonlight," which serves as a prologue to his second volume of verse, presents gallant eighteenth century lovers "who don't appear to believe in their happiness." This skepticism clouds the fugitive moments of happiness throughout Verlaine's poetic pilgrimage. *La Bonne Chanson* is Verlaine's homage to marital bliss. Poem 17, filled with images of love and faithfulness, begins and ends with the question, "Isn't it so?" Poem 13 ends with a similar worry: "A vain hope... oh no, isn't it so, isn't it so?" In *Sagesse*, which proposes Roman Catholic mysticism as the ultimate form of happiness, the fear of a return to his old ways haunts the poet's peaceful communion with God.

Because sex, love, God, and wine all fail to provide a safe haven from his saturnine destiny, Verlaine must seek another refuge. What he finds, perhaps not entirely consciously, is sleep. With surprising frequency the final images of Verlaine's poems are images of sleep; many of his musical pieces are thus lullabies whose delicate, soothing images—from which color, laughter, pompousness, loudness, and sharpness have been banished—lead the poet's battered psyche to the unthreatening harbor of sleep. Often, a maternal figure cradles the poet in his sleep or stands by watchfully. In many poems in which the sleep motif is not explicit, the imagery subsides at the end of the poem, leaving an emptiness or absence analogous to the oblivion of sleep.

POÈMES SATURNIENS

Verlaine's first volume of poetry, *Poèmes saturniens*, was published by Lemerre in November, 1866, at the author's expense. It drew very little critical or popular attention. The title refers to the astrological contention, explained in the prologue, that those like Verlaine who are born under the sign of Saturn are doomed to unhappiness, are bilious, have sick, uneasy imaginations, and are destined to suffer.

The volume is the work of a very young poet, some of the poems having been written as early as 1861. They are consequently of uneven quality, but among them is the poem "My Familiar Dream," which is perhaps the most frequently anthologized of all Verlaine's poems and which, according to Verlaine's friend and admirer H. Suquet, the poet preferred to all his others. It is a haunting evocation of an imaginary woman who loves the poet, who understands him, and who is capable of soothing his anguish.

The central section of the volume, titled "Paysages tristes" ("Sad Landscapes"), contains the poems most typical of Verlaine: vague, melancholy landscapes, inspired by his memories of the Artois region, whose fading colors, forms, and sounds reflect the poet's soul and whose ultimate disappearance translates as an innate desire for oblivion.

The first of these poems, "Soleils couchants" ("Setting Suns"), a musical poem of sixteen five-syllable lines, describes a rising sun so weakened that it casts a sunset-like melancholy over the fields, inspiring strange raddish ghosts in the poet's imagination. The short, odd-syllabled lines create a musical effect reinforced by alliteration and repetition—the phrase "setting suns," for example, is repeated four times in a poem about dawn.

"Promenade sentimentale" ("Sentimental Walk") presents a twilight scene through which the wounded poet passes. The vaguely lit water lilies that glow faintly through the fog in the evening light are swallowed up by the shroudlike darkness in the poem's final image.

" Nuit du Walpurgis classique " (" Classical Walpurgis Night") is full of allusions. Phantoms dance wildly throughout the night in a landscape designed by Johann Wolfgang von Goethe, Richard Wagner, Antoine Watteau, and André Le Nôtre. At dawn's approach, the Wagnerian music fades and the phantoms dissolve, leaving "absolutely" nothing except "a correct, ridiculous, charming Le Nôtre garden." Another noteworthy tone poem, "Song of Autumn," a melodic eighteen-line lyric composed of four- and three-syllable lines, combines *o*'s and nasal sounds to reproduce a melancholy autumn wind that carries off the mournful poet like a dead leaf.

Verlaine's first collection of verse reveals the influence of Baudelaire, Victor Hugo, Charles-Marie Leconte de Lisle, Théodore de Banville, and Théophile Gautier—and of Verlaine's young friends Louis de Ricard and Joseph Glatigny. It is a carefully crafted and original volume, demonstrating that at the age of twenty-four, Verlaine had already mastered the art of poetry and discovered most of the themes of his later works.

GALLANT PARTIES

The mid-nineteenth century's rediscovery of the paintings of Watteau is confirmed by several works dedicated to that artist and to his times, including one by the Edmond de Goncourt and Jules de Goncourt, *L'Art du dix-huitième siècle* (1859-1875; *French Eighteenth Century Painters*, 1948), which undoubtedly had a strong influence on Verlaine's choice of this subject and his interpretation of it. During the composition of the poems of *Gallant Parties*, Verlaine undoubtedly consulted some of the published reproductions of Watteau's works as well as his one painting in the Louvre collection, *Embarkation for Cythère*, a vast work devoted to eighteenth century gallantry, its rites, costumes, myths, poetry, and fashionable devotees. These aristocratic gallants and the characters from *The Italian Comedy*, also painted by Watteau, come alive in Verlaine's second published volume of poetry.

The often-anthologized "Moonlight" opens the volume and sets the mood. This musical evocation of the songs and dances of the masked characters and the relationship between their costumes and their souls insist on the underlying sadness of both. The gallant aristocrats are somewhat sad beneath their fantastic disguises because they do not really believe in the love and life of which they sing. Their dispersed song is absorbed by the moonlight.

These same characters sing, dance, walk, skate, and love through the rest of the volume, sometimes assuming stock character names from commedia del l'arte—Pierrot, Clitandre, Cassandre, Arlequin, Colombine, Scaramouche, and Pulcinella—and sometimes classical names—Tircis, Aminte, Chloris, Eglé, Atys, and Damis.

The landscapes of *Gallant Parties* are very different physically and psychologically from those of the *Poèmes saturniens*. They are sculpted, landscaped, arranged, and peopled. Paths are lined by rows of pruned trees and mossy benches. Fountains and statues are harmoniously placed around well-kept lawns. The relationship between the characters and the landscape is no longer a natural sympathetic mirroring. Nature has been artificially subdued to reflect the characters' forced gaiety and becomes a mocking image of the vanity of their pursuits. One of the obvious formal characteristics of the volume is the presence of dialogue and monologue, couched in the artificial, erotic language of gallantry. There are many allusions to "former ecstasies," "infinite distress," and "mortal languors."

The volume's overriding pessimism is orchestrated by the arrangement of the poems. The latent sadness of the apparently carefree gallants in "Moonlight" becomes the dominant feeling in the second half of the work. While humorous love play and inconsequential erotic exchanges dominate the first half, several disturbing images—such as the statue of a snickering faun who anticipates eventual unhappiness and the sad spectacle of a statue of Cupid overturned by the wind—foreshadow the volume's disastrous conclusion, the poem "Colloque sentimentale" ("Sentimental Colloquium"), in which a ghostly "form" tries to recall a past sentimental adventure. The cold, solitary park, witness to the scarcely heard dialogue, swallows up the desperate efforts to recall a past love as well as the negations of those efforts. One of the lovers tries unsuccessfully to awaken memories of their past love, which the other negates repeatedly: "Do you remember our former ecstasy?" "Why do you want me to remember it?" "Does your heart still beat at the sound of my name?" "No."

ROMANCES WITHOUT WORDS

The Franco-Prussian War of 1870 and the Commune separated Verlaine from his Parnassian friends and led him toward new friendships and a new form of poetry, toward a modernistic vision that replaced the artificiality of Parnassian inspiration with an attempt to capture the essence of contemporary life. During 1872 and 1873, Verlaine wrote the poems of *Romances Without Words*, which was published in 1874. All the poems precede the episode with Rimbaud that resulted in Verlaine's imprisonment. The period was emotionally difficult for Verlaine. Torn between love for Mathilde and dependence on Rimbaud, Verlaine was tormented by his vacillations. *Romances Without Words* fuses his new poetic ideal with his personal struggle.

The sad, lilting songs that make up the first part of the volume, titled "Ariettes oubliées" ("Forgotten Melodies"), include one of the most frequently quoted of Verlaine's poems, "It Is Crying in My Heart," in which the gentle sound of the rain falling on the town echoes the fall of tears within his heart. A more interesting poem, however, is the musical twelve-line poem "Le Piano que baise une main frêle" ("The Piano Kissed by a Fragile Hand"), in which the light, discreet melody rising from the piano corresponds to the faintness in the fading evening light of the visual impression of slight hands on a barely discernible piano. A series of vague, fleeting adjectives seep out of the perfumed boudoir to disappear through a slightly opened window into a small garden. The hushed sonorities of the poem coincide with the diminished intensity of the images. One remarkable phrase in the tenth line embodies both the musical effects and the characteristic tone of Verlaine's verse: "fin refrain incertain" ("delicate, uncertain refrain").

While the influence of music on Verlaine's poetry is certain, the importance of painting is no less significant. *Gallant Parties* is to a great extent a tribute to the painting of Watteau. The "Paysages belges" ("Belgian Landscapes") that Verlaine paints into *Romances Without Words*, are a tribute to the Impressionist school of painting, whose birth corresponds with the date of composition of the collection. Verlaine knew Édouard Manet and Ignace Henri Fantin-Latour and was certainly interested in their technique. The Impressionistic Belgian landscapes that Verlaine has painted are carefree and happy, carrying no reflection of the shadow of Mathilde that haunts the rest of the volume. The first poem in the section, "Walcourt" (a small, industrial town in Belgium), reflects the gaiety of the two vagabond poets (Verlaine and Rimbaud) in a series of brightly colored images that flash by, without help of a verb, in lively four-syllabled lines: tiles and bricks, ivy-covered homes, and beer drinkers in outdoor bars.

The gaiety of the Belgian countryside is interrupted by a bitter poem, "Birds in the Night" (original title in English), which Verlaine had first titled "La Mauvaise Chanson" ("The Bad Song") as an ironic counterpart to his previous book of poems, *La Bonne Chanson*, devoted to marital bliss. "Birds in the Night" accuses Mathilde of a lack of patience and kindness as well as of treachery. The suffering poet offers his forgiveness. The poem suggests a singular lack of understanding of the real causes of their marital discord.

The last section of *Romances Without Words* contains visions of Verlaine's London experience, but the image of Mathilde pierces through the local color with haunting persistence. All six of the poems have English titles. The most interesting is "Green," in which the poet presents to his mistress fruits, flowers, leaves, branches, and then his heart, which he commends to her care. The poem ends with the desire for a restful oblivion on the woman's bosom.

Sagesse

Only seven of the poems in *Sagesse* were actually composed while Verlaine was in prison. The rest were written between the time of his release in 1875 and the spring of 1880. The title refers to Verlaine's intention to live virtuously according to the principles of his new faith and should perhaps be translated not as "wisdom" but as "good behavior." The volume is divided into three parts, the first of which dwells on the difficulty of converting to a virtuous life, the almost daily battles with overwhelming temptation. The second part narrates the poet's mystic confrontation with God, primarily through a cycle of ten sonnets. The last part describes the poet's return to the world and contains many of the themes and images of his earlier nature poetry. These poems are not overtly religious; the prologue to this part, "Désormais le sage, puni" ("Henceforth, the Virtuous, Punished"), explains the virtuous poet's return to a contemplative love of nature.

Poems 6 and 7 of the first part, both sonnets, are the most poetic of Verlaine's evocations of the contrast between his former and his present preoccupations. Poem 6 presents his former joys as a line of clumsy geese limping off into the distance on a dusty road. Their departure leaves the poet with a welcome emptiness, a peaceful sense of abandonment as his formerly proud heart now burns with divine love. Poem 7 warns of the prevailing appeal of the "false happy days" that have tempted his soul all day. They have glowed in his memory as "long hailstones of flame" that have symbolically ravaged his blue sky. The last line of the poem exhorts the poet's soul to pray against the storm to forestall "the old folly" that threatens to return.

Three of the most moving poems of the third part were written in prison, one on the very day of Verlaine's sentencing: "Un Grand Sommeil noir" ("A Great Black Sleep"). This poem, as well as "Le Ciel est, par-dessus le toit" ("The Sky Is, Beyond the Roof") and "Gaspard Hauser chante" ("The Song of Kaspar Hauser"), sings of the poet's despair, plaintively expressing his self-pity, his regrets, and his total sense of shock in the early days of his imprisonment. The third part of *Sagesse* also contains two of Verlaine's most finely crafted sonnets. "L'Espoir luit comme un brin de paille dans l'étable" ("Hope Glistens Like a Blade of Straw in a Stable") is perhaps his most Rimbaudian and most obscure poem. An unidentified protector speaks to the poet reassuringly as he rests in a country inn. The voice is maternal and encourages the poet to sleep, promising to cradle him. The voice shoos away a woman whose presence threatens the poet's rest. The poem opens and closes with a fragile image of glistening hope, which, in the final line, opens up into a hoped-for reflowering of the roses of September.

The sonnet "Le Son du cor" ("The Sound of the Hunting Horn") is perhaps the best example of Verlaine's poetic art. It was written before his imprisonment, probably in the spring of 1873. This very musical poem blends the sound of the hunting horn, the howling of the wind, and the cry of a wolf into a crescendo that subsides to a mere autumn sigh as the falling snow blots out the last colors of the setting sun. The painful notes of the opening stanza are completely obliterated as day gives way to a cradling, monotonous evening.

OTHER MAJOR WORKS
SHORT FICTION: *Louise Leclercq*, 1886; *Histoires comme ça*, 1903.
PLAYS: *Les Uns et les autres*, pr. 1884; *Madame Aubin*, pr. 1886.
NONFICTION: *Poètes maudits*, 1884 (*The Cursed Poets*, 2003); *Mes hôpitaux*, 1891; *Quinze jours en Hollande*, 1892; *Mes prisons*, 1893; *Confessions*, 1895 (*Confessions of a Poet*, 1950); *Les Mémoires d'un veuf*, 1896; *Charles Baudelaire*, 1903; *Critiques et conférences*, 1903; *Souvenirs et promenades*, 1903; *Voyage en france par un français*, 1903.

BIBLIOGRAPHY
Blackmore, A. M., and E. H. Blackmore, eds. *Six French Poets of the Nineteenth Century: Lamartine, Hugo, Baudelaire, Verlaine, Rimbaud, Mallarmé*. New York: Oxford University Press, 2000. This anthology of poetry is preceded by an introduc-

tion, notes on text and translations, a select bibliography, and a chronology. Contains poems by and background information on Verlaine.

Ivry, Benjamin. *Arthur Rimbaud*. Bath, Somerset, England: Absolute Press, 1998. A biography of Rimbaud that details his two-year affair with Verlaine. Ivry delves deeply into the relationship, especially its sexual aspects, including possible dalliances with other men, misogynist outbursts, and graphically sexual poems.

Lehmann, John. *Three Literary Friendships: Byron and Shelley, Rimbaud and Verlaine, Robert Frost and Edward Thomas*. New York: Henry Holt, 1984. An examination of the way these friendships influenced each poet's work. Verlaine and Arthur Rimbaud each produced more poetry after their relationship.

Lepelletier, Edmond Adolphe de Bouhelier. *Paul Verlaine: His Life, His Work*. Translated by E. M. Lang. New York: AMS Press, 1970. The only English translation of the hefty 1909 biography.

Nicolson, Harold George. *Paul Verlaine*. 1921. Reprint. New York: AMS Press, 1997. This venerable biography remains useful.

Robb, Graham. *Rimbaud: A Biography*. New York: W. W. Norton, 2001. This biography of Arthur Rimbaud contains discussion of his affair with Verlaine, including the altercation at its end.

Sorrell, Martin. Introduction to *Selected Poems*, by Paul Verlaine. 1999. Reprint. New York: Oxford University Press, 2009. Sorrell's introduction is useful for beginning students in this bilingual edition of 170 newly translated poems by Verlaine.

Whidden, Seth Adam. *Leaving Parnassus: The Lyric Subject in Verlaine and Rimbaud*. Amsterdam: Rodopi, 2007. Notes the influence of Parnassian poetry on Verlaine and Arthur Rimbaud, even as they departed from it. One multichapter section is devoted to various aspects of Verlaine's poetry.

Paul J. Schwartz

FRANÇOIS VILLON

Born: Paris, France; 1431
Died: Unknown; 1463(?)
Also known as: François des Loges; François de Montcorbier

PRINCIPAL POETRY
Le Lais, wr. 1456, pb. 1489 (*The Legacy*, 1878; also known as *Le Petit Testament, The Little Testament*)
Le Grand Testament, wr. 1461, pb. 1489 (*The Great Testament*, 1878)
Ballades en jargon, 1489 (*Poems in Slang*, 1878)
Les Œuvres de Françoys Villon, 1533 (Clément Marot, editor)
The Poems of Master François Villon, 1878
Ballads Done into English from the French of François Villon, 1904
The Testaments of François Villon, 1924
The Complete Works of François Villon, 1928
The Poems of François Villon, 1954, 1977, 1982 (includes *The Legacy, The Great Testament*, and some shorter poems; Galway Kinnell, translator)

OTHER LITERARY FORMS

François Villon (vee-YOHN) indicates in *The Great Testament* that he also wrote a romance titled "Le Rommant du pet au diable" (romance of the devil's fart). This work, apparently about an elaborate student prank, is not extant, and Villon's mention of it is the only evidence that it ever did exist.

ACHIEVEMENTS

Of all the poets of the Middle Ages, perhaps only Dante and Geoffrey Chaucer are better known and more admired than François Villon. He has been widely praised since his own time by voices as diverse as those of Clément Marot in the sixteenth century and Nicolas Boileau-Despréaux in the seventeenth; by Robert Louis Stevenson (whose admiration for Villon's poetic genius was even stronger than his revulsion at the depravity of the poet's life) and Algernon Charles Swinburne; by Dante Gabriel Rossetti, Ezra Pound, and William Carlos Williams. Remarkably enough, Villon has found his way into popular culture as well. He has been the subject of motion pictures (*Beloved Rogue*, with John Barrymore, 1927), novels such as Francis Carco's *Le Roman de François Villon* (1926), and popular songs by George Brassens, Reggiani, and others.

The usual explanation for Villon's extraordinary popularity is exemplified by Pound's contention (in *ABC of Reading*, 1934) that Villon is the most "authentic" of poets and (in *The Spirit of Romance*, 1910) that he is the only poet without illusions. He is,

François Villon
(Library of Congress)

in this view, notable for accepting and admitting his own failures and depravity and speaking of them forthrightly, frequently with regret but always without shame. It is the presumed presence of the poet in his poetry, the fact that when he says "I" he is referring to himself rather than to a disembodied allegorical voice, that readers have found refreshing and appealing. Nor is the world around the poet an abstract or idealized place. His poetry is more firmly rooted in his own historical and geographical context (Paris at the end of the Middle Ages, a place and time of social and intellectual turmoil) than is that of any other medieval poet. His city, its students and thieves and judges, its priests and prostitutes, are both his dramatis personae and his subject.

The personal element in Villon's poetry—his honesty, sincerity, and authenticity—is related, according to the usual view, to his apparent lack of poetic artifice. Pound insisted that "Villon is destitute of imagination; he is almost destitute of art." He is considered to be without affectation, personal or literary. It is presumably the voice of a fallible, ordinary man and not the calculated utterance of a poet that the reader hears. Such is the reaction of many students, casual readers, poets, and critics alike. Such an assessment must represent, however, something of a misreading if it is intended literally. The Villon to whom readers are drawn is clearly a persona that he has crafted with great care and subtlety, and while that persona has much in common with the historical Villon, one is nevertheless the creature of the other. Villon is far from "destitute of art": While a very great poet and a very bad one might appear to be destitute of art, only the former is likely to be remembered. Perhaps one should say instead that Villon is destitute of obvious art: The impression of artlessness is his most artful illusion.

Although many generations have read and admired Villon, they have seen entirely different things in him—hero or coward, criminal or degenerate or tortured soul. This multiplicity of readings suggests that Villon is a great and complex poet, whose themes have universal appeal and whose command of his poetic resources is equal to the demands that his vision places on them.

Biography

François Villon was born François de Montcorbier (or perhaps des Loges) and later took as his own the name of his benefactor, Guillaume de Villon. He was a native of Paris, born there the year Joan of Arc died, and presumably reared there. He received his baccalaureate in 1449 and became a master of arts three years later.

Much of the fragmentary information that is available concerning Villon's life comes from legal documents dating back to 1455. In that year, he was involved in a brawl and killed a priest named Phillippe Chermoye or Sermoise, but he was later pardoned for justifiable homicide. The following Christmas season, he and others committed a burglary at the College of Navarre, after which he apparently fled Paris.

In 1461, Villon was in a dungeon at Meung. Incarcerated there for reasons unknown, he was (as he says in *The Great Testament*) cruelly mistreated by Bishop Thibault d'Aussigny, but along with other prisoners, he was released when the newly crowned King Louis XI passed through the town. Evidently unable to stay out of trouble, Villon was before long imprisoned once again, this time at the Châtelet in Paris. He was soon released again, but he had been incriminated in the College of Navarre burglary by a talkative accomplice, Guy Tabary, and had to agree to repay his share of the loot. Very soon, Villon was arrested yet again, following a brawl. This time, he was sentenced to be hanged; the sentence was commuted, however, and he was exiled instead. At that point, the trail ends, and further references to him (in François Rabelais's works, for example) are probably pure fictions. He died during or after 1463.

At some time, perhaps after he first fled from Paris, Villon spent a while at Blois, at the court of Charles d'Orléans, and a poem is preserved (titled "Je meurs de seuf auprès de la fontaine"/ "I Am Dying of Thirst near the Fountain") which he composed for a poetry contest held by Charles. His first long poem, *The Legacy*, was composed shortly after the 1456 Christmas burglary, while *The Great Testament* was written following his release from the Meung prison.

ANALYSIS

François Villon's poetry offers a depiction of his narrator so vivid and effective that readers have traditionally inferred that the narrator is the poet himself, assuming that Villon is dispensing with poetic mediation in order to express directly the thoughts and fears of a fifteenth century Parisian. That readers find themselves fascinated with Villon the man, even to the point of ignoring his poetry, is a testimony to the mastery of Villon the artist. The methods by which he creates and presents his narrator thus provide one of the most accessible keys to an analysis of his poetry. Foremost among his methods is the thematic inconsistency and apparent formlessness that one would expect to characterize not literary activity, but the thoughts of a complex human being.

Although Villon generally deals with sober and important themes (injustice and intolerance; disease, decrepitude, and death), the tone of his poetry is not always as heavy as these subjects would suggest. Villon can be lighthearted and playful one instant, sober and bitter the next. Throughout his work, he shows himself to be a master of irony. In many cases, that irony is directed at his enemies, whom he may characterize either as magnanimous friends or as needy and worthy citizens. (In a number of such cases, Villon's ironic intent was revealed to posterity only in the last century or the present one, when historical research permitted the identification of most of the people mentioned by the poet.) He also, however, directs his irony at himself; for example, he may present himself as love's martyr, the victim of an unhappy affair, when in fact it is clear that his "broken heart" is a thinly veiled reference to his criminal activity.

At times, Villon's irony and humor fall away, and he launches into a direct and abusive attack on his enemies. This invective, all the more striking because it brusquely interrupts a lighter tone and sometimes interrupts another thought, has convinced readers that this, at least, is the "real" Villon, yet such "outbursts" can also be regarded as carefully planned poetic effects designed to add realism to his persona. Similarly, Villon often suspends banter and invective alike to offer a simple, plaintive statement of regret or a plea for forgiveness—although he is likely to cancel such a statement in turn by a joke or another attack. His work is thus built on contrast and digression, on a systematic rejection of consistency. His poetry is carefully composed so as not to appear to have been carefully composed, and it is certainly as dynamic as any ever written.

THE LEGACY

Villon's first long poem, *The Legacy*, is a work of 320 octosyllabic lines arranged in eight-line stanzas. It was probably composed around the end of 1456, after the burglary at the College of Navarre, when Villon had fled from Paris or was preparing to do so. Characteristically, Villon uses events from his own life, and the premise for *The Legacy* is the necessity that he leave the city. The work is thus a *congé* (leave taking), a traditional genre describing one's reasons and preparations for a departure. Critics have sometimes interpreted *The Legacy* as an alibi intended to provide evidence that Villon was away from Paris when the Christmas robbery took place. It is more likely that his fictional absence was an "inside joke" for the benefit of his friends or accomplices who knew of his involvement in the burglary.

In any case, the robbery itself is not mentioned in the poem. Instead, the narrator tells us that he is leaving because a love affair has ended painfully. His discussion of the relationship and its end is replete with mock allegorical imagery drawn from the traditional vocabulary of courtly love. He thus speaks of the "prison of love," the "pain of love," and "sweet glances." He concludes that his only recourse is to flee, but his poetic intent quickly becomes clear when the reader notes that the word he uses, *fouïr*, means not only to "flee" but also to "copulate," and his double meaning is obvious when he insists, for example, that he must "plant in other fields." Specifically, he announces that his destination is Angers, but, as David Kuhn has pointed out, "going to Angers" was a slang reference to orgasm.

Following this introduction is a series of bequests, in which Villon, by antiphrasis, leaves to others fictitious possessions or exaggerated assets (his money, tents, and fame—the first two nonexistent, the third undesirable), makes obscene puns (his *branc*, which he bequeaths to Ythier Marchant, means either "sword" or "excrement"), and bestows otherwise ironic gifts (as when he leaves money to "three poor orphans"—who, research has revealed, were actually three rich merchants and usurers).

The third and final section of *The Legacy* offers a closure that is an elaborate parody of Scholastic language; typically, however, Villon's lines constitute not only an indictment of Scholasticism but also a system of sexual, specifically masturbatory, imagery. Thus, Villon closes the circle of his poem—although he does so in an unexpected way. He has told us that he is leaving a woman and that he is leaving Paris. He announces his destination (Angers), which indicates also his sexual intention, and that intention is enacted in the "Scholastic" section and achieved when, at the end, Villon's senses clear and, his "candle extinguished" and his "ink frozen," he is unable to continue writing. While some scholars have interpreted these details as realistic images of Villon's miserable existence, they are rather the burlesque conclusion of his sexual situation: He is spent. *The Legacy* thus relates travel, courtly and Scholastic thought, and poetic effort in a complex progression that ends in mock-pathetic autoerotic exhaustion.

THE GREAT TESTAMENT

The Great Testament, written five days after *The Legacy*, is longer (2,023 lines), generally less comical, and far more complex. It is considered to be a mature and serious recasting of *The Legacy*, and indeed many of the same persons and images recur in it. While this view can claim some justification, however, it would be unjust to the earlier poem to see in it nothing more than a prefiguration of Villon's mature work. *The Legacy* is a comic masterpiece in its own right; *The Great Testament* uses some of the same methods and materials to produce a masterpiece of an entirely different sort. Indeed, the two works have relatively little in common other than certain characters and the fact that each of them offers a series of ironic or burlesque bequests. Even the irony varies. That of *The Legacy* appears for the most part good-natured. In *The Great Testament*, the irony is most often bitterly vituperative, and at times, Villon suspends his ironic detachment altogether, as when, at the very beginning of the poem, he launches into a vicious attack on Bishop Thibault, who mistreated Villon in prison.

The subject of *The Great Testament* is no longer the loss of Villon's love, but the loss of his youth and the impending loss of his life. He is, he suggests, an aging and weak man who regrets his wasted youth and must put his life in order. However, there is another side of him, a side that has no desire to waste even a precious hour of life preparing for death: He has too much to do, perhaps too many friends to see and pranks to play, but especially he has too many scores to settle and too many enemies to malign. Thus the poet presents, developed in sharp relief, the two sides of his character: the heart and the flesh, the conscience and the appetites, the contrite sinner preoccupied with the hereafter and the mortal desperately clinging to life, preoccupied with the present. Much of the artistic tension of the work derives from the conflict of these opposing impulses, intercutting each other ever more quickly and more frantically as the poem progresses.

The form of *The Great Testament* could be described with a fair degree of accuracy as a structure of digression. The pattern is set when Villon interrupts his very first sentence to launch into the lengthy attack on Thibault, then soon after to offer elaborate praise of King Louis XI, before finally returning to the ostensible subject of the work. Although the ultimate destination of the poem (the narrator's death) is clear from the beginning, the path to it is circuitous, as the poet digresses repeatedly to offer details of his past, his associates, his fears, and his regrets.

The work incorporates a number of lyric pieces (ballades and rondeaux) which represent in most cases the illustration or crystallization of a thematic development. These lyric poems are thought by some scholars to have been composed earlier and chosen for use in *The Great Testament* (a contention that has not been proved and that is of no great consequence in any case, because whether they were written early or late, their inclusion indicates that they satisfactorily served Villon's purposes). The best known of these pieces is the "Ballade des dames du temps jadis" ("Ballad of Dead Ladies"), which, along with two accompanying poems, the "Ballade des seigneurs du temps jadis" ("Ballad of Men from the Past") and the "Ballade en vieil langage françoys" ("Ballad in Old French"), develops the *ubi sunt* motif in regard to illustrious persons from the past. While the "Ballad of Dead Ladies" is justly praised, its meaning has been distorted in English by the traditional translation of its famous refrain as "Where are the snows of yesteryear?" *Antan*, the last word of the refrain, means simply "last year," and the correct rendering of the line, while robbing it of a rather romantic poignancy, restores its effectiveness in another way: Villon is, after all, contrasting the passing of a fragile and rather commonplace phenomenon with the loss of remarkable, famous, and (by implication) equally fragile women from history.

It is in fact typical of Villon not to reach for the extravagant image or the elaborate paraphrase; often his most effective passages are, as here, impressive for their directness and simplicity. He also has a tendency to move from the distant to the immediate, from the abstract to the concrete. Thus, for example, while these early *ballades* effectively suggest the loss of life and fame, that theme is far more strikingly developed when he later refers simply to "skulls stacked up in cemeteries" or when he presents the lament of Belle Hëaulmiere, an aging prostitute who recalls the firm, attractive body she once had and contrasts it with the shriveled and repulsive form it has now, to her horror, become. Her contemplation is followed by a *ballade* in which she urges a group of prostitutes to seize the day.

These lyric poems are inserted irregularly, but with increasing frequency toward the end. The subject matter, moreover, follows a general evolution toward the realistic, direct, and sometimes coarse. From the three *ballades* treating illustrious people from the past (and from another early one, a masterful prayer to Notre Dame intended to be offered by Villon's simple and naïve mother), he goes on to present Hëaulmiere and, later, la Grosse Margot (Fat Margot, a prostitute whose consort Villon is, and the subject of a poem by Stevenson, who describes her as "grimy" and as "gross and ghastly"). Villon's themes—misery, aging, and death—are hardly subjects to be developed abstractly in pretty ballads, and indeed the appeal of his poetry for many is precisely that he is willing to suspend obvious poetic musing and present death in all its ugliness and pain—and himself as a man whose flesh is weak and whose spirit is only sporadically willing.

Even though *The Great Testament* is bitter, vituperative, and often uncompromisingly realistic, and even though its predominant tone is sober, it is by no means devoid of comedy, although the humor of *The Great Testament* is humor with a sharp edge. The "three poor orphans" reappear here, as do a number of other characters from *The Legacy*; in this case, however, Villon's banter only thinly covers a venomous attitude. He jokes about his legatees, but the jokes are mostly intimations of sexual and other disorders on the part of his adversaries. Nor does he spare himself: He indicates (as he did in his earlier poem) that he is a martyr to love, but the specific details he offers in support of that suggestion have led some scholars to theorize that his martyrdom took the form of advanced syphilis.

Throughout the poem, the reader hears Villon's two voices (sinner and penitent) clearly, but the work is also structured around a variety of other voices, and in some cases other narrators appear as well. The interplay of voices in *The Great Testament* is in fact very complex, and toward the end, as the tempo quickens and the realism intensifies, these complexities multiply. In the fiction of the poem, Villon presents himself as aging, becoming increasingly infirm, and approaching death. Indeed, at the end, he composes his own epitaph, and his fiction even includes looking back from beyond the grave to describe his death. In this section, some passages are not only in the past but also in the third person, as though another narrator were taking over. At one point, Villon comments in the first person on his third-person character: "Et je croy bien que pas n'en ment" ("And *I* do not think *he* is lying"; emphasis added). This is the culmination of a movement that has developed throughout the work, whereby Villon creates two entities, a persona and a character, who periodically merge and separate and who are finally established as entirely distinct from each other. The interplay of voices confirms the poet as partially independent of the character he creates; the latter follows the fictional course set for him (lamenting his age, preparing his will, and dying), while the poet uses him and the text to indulge in an examination of, and commentary on, life, death, sexuality, the judicial system, his friends, enemies, and accomplices—and above all, Villon himself.

The Great Testament is thus a remarkable portrait of its narrator, of Paris, of the life led by a medieval "student, poet, and housebreaker" (according to Stevenson's characterization), but it is also a remarkable poem, a masterpiece of verbal wit, of structural complexity, of poetic voice and virtuosity. *The Legacy* is in many ways a remarkable work of undeniable merit, but it is lighter not only in tone but also in literary weight. *The Great Testament* is the complex and mature masterpiece of a consummate poet.

POEMS IN SLANG

Whether *Poems in Slang* is also a masterpiece remains open to question: The poems included are virtually incomprehensible to modern readers. Many of the words and expressions, drawn from underworld slang, have been identified through documents that preserve them; the meaning of others can be deduced from their context. Still, enough mysteries remain to frustrate critical efforts. Scholar Pierre Guiraud has offered one of the more elaborate and controversial attempts to deal with these poems, proposing three distinct levels of meaning and consequently three translations for each. The first level deals with criminal activity, the second with cheating at cards, the third with sodomy. Whether Guiraud has successfully deciphered Villon's system—and a good number of scholars remain unconvinced—the fact remains that the *Poems in Slang* are still largely inaccessible. Modern scholars cannot adequately assess the poetic value of the volume because their attention is still on its meaning, in the most basic sense: the definition of words. For the present, these poems must remain an enigma, a closed system constructed in a language that is largely foreign even to the best specialists in Villon's Middle French.

His remaining miscellaneous poems are extremely varied in subject matter, style, date of composition, and literary value, and the very authorship of some of them is disputed. Certain of them are no more than playthings or poetic pastimes. Others, however, are very interesting, and two deserve brief comment here. "L'Épitaphe Villon" ("Villon's Epitaph") offers a horrible portrait of corpses on the gallows—swinging in the breeze, flesh rotting, eyes pecked out by birds—and asks for compassion and absolution. "Le Débat du cuer et du corps de Villon" ("The Dialogue of Villon's Heart and Body") provides a confrontation of basic human impulses, as the personified heart attempts to persuade the body to abandon its dissolute ways. Both poems are reminiscent in certain ways of *The Great Testament*, the former in the realistic images of death, the latter in the dramatization of the fundamental conflicts within Villon and within all of us, and both of them in the impressive poetic sensibility that informs them.

For Swinburne, Villon was "our sad bad glad mad brother." That is indeed what Villon has been for most readers. What is conspicuously absent from such assessments (except perhaps by implication) is precisely Villon's artistic status, his success in creating the persona that many readers mistake for the poet. When one looks directly at his poetry—stripping away the veneer of romantic imagery, bypassing Victorian revulsion at his manners and character, going beyond popular distortions and fanciful interpretations—it becomes clear that Villon is, quite simply, the finest French poet of the Middle Ages and an enduring artist for any age.

BIBLIOGRAPHY

Burl, Aubrey. *Danse Macabre: François Villon, Poetry, and Murder in Medieval France*. Stroud, Gloucestershire, England: Sutton, 2000. Biography studies Villon within the context of fifteenth century Paris, seeking out the truth behind the poet's crimes as well as the surpassing depth and beauty of his poetry.

Daniel, Robert R. *The Poetry of Villon and Baudelaire: Two Worlds, One Human Condition*. New York: Peter Lang, 1997. Daniel traces many themes that Villon shared with Charles Baudelaire, such as mortality and the *danse macabre*, or dance of death. The result is an illumination of the poetry of a modern and a medieval poet that highlights Villon's medieval and modern characteristics.

Fein, David A. *François Villon Revisited*. New York: Twayne, 1997. A basic biography of Villon that also examines his poetry.

Freeman, Michael. *François Villon in His Works: The Villain's Tale*. Atlanta: Rodopi, 2000. Arguing that no analysis of Villon is complete without taking into account the Paris in which he lived, this book describes that rough place and also tells how Villon consciously fashioned his own image.

Peckham, Robert D. *François Villon: A Bibliography*. New York: Garland, 1990. This comprehensive text is the starting place for anyone wishing to understand Villon's poetry, his influence, and his times. Peckham lists all the manuscripts containing Villon's poetry and translations of it, and he includes the critical texts relating to the poetry, even works inspired by Villon's poetry, up to 1985.

Simpson, Louis. Preface to *François Villon's "The Legacy" and "The Testament."* Ashland, Oreg.: Story Line, 2000. Simpson's preface provides a useful introduction to Villon's life and times, and the notes provide commentary on Villon's language and clarify the many obscure allusions that enrich Villon's poetry.

Taylor, Jane H. M. *The Poetry of François Villon: Text and Context*. New York: Cambridge University Press, 2001. Study highlights the flair and originality of Villon's poetry, showing how it appealed to his contemporary readers.

Norris J. Lacy

CHECKLIST FOR EXPLICATING A POEM

I. The Initial Readings

A. Before reading the poem, the reader should:
  1. Notice its form and length.
  2. Consider the title, determining, if possible, whether it might function as an allusion, symbol, or poetic image.
  3. Notice the date of composition or publication, and identify the general era of the poet.

B. The poem should be read intuitively and emotionally and be allowed to "happen" as much as possible.

C. In order to establish the rhythmic flow, the poem should be reread. A note should be made as to where the irregular spots (if any) are located.

II. Explicating the Poem

A. *Dramatic situation.* Studying the poem line by line helps the reader discover the dramatic situation. All elements of the dramatic situation are interrelated and should be viewed as reflecting and affecting one another. The dramatic situation serves a particular function in the poem, adding realism, surrealism, or absurdity; drawing attention to certain parts of the poem; and changing to reinforce other aspects of the poem. All points should be considered. The following questions are particularly helpful to ask in determining dramatic situation:
  1. What, if any, is the narrative action in the poem?
  2. How many personae appear in the poem? What part do they take in the action?
  3. What is the relationship between characters?
  4. What is the setting (time and location) of the poem?

B. *Point of view.* An understanding of the poem's point of view is a major step toward comprehending the poet's intended meaning. The reader should ask:
  1. Who is the speaker? Is he or she addressing someone else or the reader?
  2. Is the narrator able to understand or see everything happening to him or her, or does the reader know things that the narrator does not?
  3. Is the narrator reliable?
  4. Do point of view and dramatic situation seem consistent? If not, the inconsistencies may provide clues to the poem's meaning.

C. *Images and metaphors.* Images and metaphors are often the most intricately crafted vehicles of the poem for relaying the poet's message. Realizing that the images and metaphors work in harmony with the dramatic situation and point of view will help the reader to see the poem as a whole, rather than as disassociated elements.
   1. The reader should identify the concrete images (that is, those that are formed from objects that can be touched, smelled, seen, felt, or tasted). Is the image projected by the poet consistent with the physical object?
   2. If the image is abstract, or so different from natural imagery that it cannot be associated with a real object, then what are the properties of the image?
   3. To what extent is the reader asked to form his or her own images?
   4. Is any image repeated in the poem? If so, how has it been changed? Is there a controlling image?
   5. Are any images compared to each other? Do they reinforce one another?
   6. Is there any difference between the way the reader perceives the image and the way the narrator sees it?
   7. What seems to be the narrator's or persona's attitude toward the image?

D. *Words.* Every substantial word in a poem may have more than one intended meaning, as used by the author. Because of this, the reader should look up many of these words in the dictionary and:
   1. Note all definitions that have the slightest connection with the poem.
   2. Note any changes in syntactical patterns in the poem.
   3. In particular, note those words that could possibly function as symbols or allusions, and refer to any appropriate sources for further information.

E. *Meter, rhyme, structure, and tone.* In scanning the poem, all elements of prosody should be noted by the reader. These elements are often used by a poet to manipulate the reader's emotions, and therefore they should be examined closely to arrive at the poet's specific intention.
   1. Does the basic meter follow a traditional pattern such as those found in nursery rhymes or folk songs?
   2. Are there any variations in the base meter? Such changes or substitutions are important thematically and should be identified.
   3. Are the rhyme schemes traditional or innovative, and what might their form mean to the poem?
   4. What devices has the poet used to create sound patterns (such as assonance and alliteration)?
   5. Is the stanza form a traditional or innovative one?
   6. If the poem is composed of verse paragraphs rather than stanzas, how do they affect the progression of the poem?

7. After examining the above elements, is the resultant tone of the poem casual or formal, pleasant, harsh, emotional, authoritative?

F. *Historical context.* The reader should attempt to place the poem into historical context, checking on events at the time of composition. Archaic language, expressions, images, or symbols should also be looked up.

G. *Themes and motifs.* By seeing the poem as a composite of emotion, intellect, craftsmanship, and tradition, the reader should be able to determine the themes and motifs (smaller recurring ideas) presented in the work. He or she should ask the following questions to help pinpoint these main ideas:
1. Is the poet trying to advocate social, moral, or religious change?
2. Does the poet seem sure of his or her position?
3. Does the poem appeal primarily to the emotions, to the intellect, or to both?
4. Is the poem relying on any particular devices for effect (such as imagery, allusion, paradox, hyperbole, or irony)?

BIBLIOGRAPHY

GENERAL REFERENCE SOURCES

BIOGRAPHICAL SOURCES

Jackson, William T. H., ed. *European Writers*. 14 vols. New York: Scribner, 1983-1991.

Kunitz, Stanley, and Vineta Colby, eds. *European Authors, 1000-1900: A Biographical Dictionary of European Literature*. New York: Wilson, 1967.

Magill, Frank N., ed. *Critical Survey of Poetry: Foreign Language Series*. 5 vols. Englewood Cliffs, N.J.: Salem Press, 1984.

_____. *Critical Survey of Poetry: Supplement*. Englewood Cliffs, N.J.: Salem Press, 1987.

Serafin, Steven, ed. *Encyclopedia of World Literature in the Twentieth Century*. 3d ed. 4 vols. Detroit: St. James Press, 1999.

CRITICISM

Coleman, Arthur. *A Checklist of Interpretation, 1940-1973, of Classical and Continental Epics and Metrical Romances*. Vol. 2 in *Epic and Romance Criticism*. 2 vols. New York: Watermill, 1974.

Jason, Philip K., ed. *Masterplots II: Poetry Series, Revised Edition*. 8 vols. Pasadena, Calif.: Salem Press, 2002.

The Year's Work in Modern Language Studies. London: Oxford University Press, 1931.

DICTIONARIES, HISTORIES, AND HANDBOOKS

Auty, Robert, et al. *Traditions of Heroic and Epic Poetry*. 2 vols. Vol. 1, *The Traditions*; Vol. 2, *Characteristics and Techniques*. Publications of the Modern Humanities Research Association 9, 13. London: Modern Humanities Research Association, 1980, 1989.

Bede, Jean-Albert, and William B. Edgerton, eds. *Columbia Dictionary of Modern European Literature*. 2d ed. New York: Columbia University Press, 1980.

France, Peter, ed. *The Oxford Guide to Literature in English Translation*. New York: Oxford University Press, 2000.

Henderson, Lesley, ed. *Reference Guide to World Literature*. 2d ed. 2 vols. New York: St. James Press, 1995.

Oinas, Felix, ed. *Heroic Epic and Saga: An Introduction to the World's Great Folk Epics*. Bloomington: Indiana University Press, 1978.

INDEX OF PRIMARY WORKS

Hoffman, Herbert H. *Hoffman's Index to Poetry: European and Latin American Poetry in Anthologies.* Metuchen, N.J.: Scarecrow Press, 1985.

POETICS

Gasparov, M. L. *A History of European Versification.* Translated by G. S. Smith and Marina Tarlinskaja. New York: Oxford University Press, 1996.

Wimsatt, William K., ed. *Versification: Major Language Types: Sixteen Essays.* New York: Modern Language Association, 1972.

FRENCH POETRY

BIBLIOGRAPHY

Kempton, Richard. *French Literature: An Annotated Guide to Selected Bibliographies.* New York: Modern Language Association of America, 1981.

BIOGRAPHICAL SOURCES

Beum, Robert, ed. *Nineteenth-Century French Poets.* Dictionary of Literary Biography 217. Detroit: Gale Group, 2000.

Sinnreich-Levi, Deborah, and Ian S. Laurie, eds. *Literature of the French and Occitan Middle Ages: Eleventh to Fifteenth Centuries.* Dictionary of Literary Biography 208. Detroit: Gale Group, 1999.

CRITICISM

Coleman, Kathleen. *Guide to French Poetry Explication.* New York: G. K. Hall, 1993.

DICTIONARIES, HISTORIES, AND HANDBOOKS

Acquisto, Joseph. *French Symbolist Poetry and the Idea of Music.* Burlington, Vt.: Ashgate, 2006.

Aulestia, Gorka. *The Basque Poetic Tradition.* Translated by Linda White. Reno: University of Nevada Press, 2000.

Banks, Kathryn. *Cosmos and Image in the Renaissance: French Love Lyric and Natural-Philosophical Poetry.* London: Legenda, 2008.

Bishop, Michael. *Nineteenth-Century French Poetry.* Twayne's Critical History of Poetry Series. New York: Twayne, 1993.

Brereton, Geoffrey. *An Introduction to the French Poets, Villon to the Present Day.* 2d rev. ed. London: Methuen, 1973.

Caws, Mary Ann, ed. *The Yale Anthology of Twentieth-Century French Poetry.* New Haven, Conn.: Yale University Press, 2004.

Dolbow, Sandra W. *Dictionary of Modern French Literature: From the Age of Reason Through Realism.* New York: Greenwood Press, 1986.

France, Peter, ed. *The New Oxford Companion to Literature in French.* New York: Clarendon Press, 1995.

Gaunt, Simon, and Sarah Key, eds. *The Cambridge Companion to Medieval French Literature.* New York: Cambridge University Press, 2008.

_____. *The Troubadours: An Introduction.* New York: Cambridge University Press, 1999.

Levi, Anthony. *Guide to French Literature.* 2 vols. Chicago: St. James Press, 1992-1994.

Moss, Ann. *Poetry and Fable: Studies in Mythological Narrative in Sixteenth-Century France.* New York: Cambridge University Press, 2009.

Palmer, R. Barton, ed. and trans. *Medieval Epic and Romance: An Anthology of English and French Narrative.* Glen Allen, Va.: College Publishing, 2007.

Shaw, Mary Lewis. *The Cambridge Introduction to French Poetry.* New York: Cambridge University Press, 2003.

Switten, Margaret Louise. *Music and Poetry in the Middle Ages: A Guide to Research on French and Occitan Song, 1100-1400.* New York: Garland, 1995.

Thomas, Jean-Jacques, and Steven Winspur. *Poeticized Language: The Foundations of Contemporary French Poetry.* University Park: Pennsylvania State University Press, 1999.

Willett, Laura, trans. *Poetry and Language in Sixteenth-Century France: Du Bellay, Ronsard, Sébillet.* Toronto: Centre for Reformation and Renaissance Studies, Victoria University, 2004.

WOMEN WRITERS

Sartori, Eva Martin, and Dorothy Wynne Zimmerman. *French Women Writers: A Bio-bibliographical Source Book.* New York: Greenwood Press, 1991.

Shapiro, Norman R., ed. and trans. *French Women Poets of Nine Centuries: The Distaff and the Pen.* Baltimore: Johns Hopkins University Press, 2008.

Maura Ives
updated by Tracy Irons-Georges

GUIDE TO ONLINE RESOURCES

Web Sites

The following sites were visited by the editors of Salem Press in 2010. Because URLs frequently change, the accuracy of these addresses cannot be guaranteed; however, long-standing sites, such as those of colleges and universities, national organizations, and government agencies, generally maintain links when their sites are moved.

LitWeb
http://litweb.net
    LitWeb provides biographies of hundreds of world authors throughout history that can be accessed through an alphabetical listing. The pages about each writer contain a list of his or her works, suggestions for further reading, and illustrations. The site also offers information about past and present winners of major literary prizes.

The Modern Word: Authors of the Libyrinth
http://www.themodernword.com/authors.html
    The Modern Word site, although somewhat haphazard in its organization, provides a great deal of critical information about writers. The "Authors of the Libyrinth" page is very useful, linking author names to essays about them and other resources. The section of the page headed "The Scriptorium" presents "an index of pages featuring writers who have pushed the edges of their medium, combining literary talent with a sense of experimentation to produce some remarkable works of modern literature."

Poetry Foundation
http://www.poetryfoundation.org
    The Poetry Foundation, publisher of *Poetry* magazine, is an independent literary organization. Its Web site offers links to essays; news; events; online poetry resources, such as blogs, organizations, publications, and references and research; a glossary of literary terms; and a Learning Lab that includes poem guides and essays on poetics.

Poetry in Translation
http://poetryintranslation.com
    This independent resource provides modern translations of classic texts by famous poets and also provides original poetry and critical works. Visitors can choose from several languages, including English, Spanish, Chinese, Russian, Italian, and Greek. Original text is available as well. Also includes links to further literary resources.

Poetry International Web
http://international.poetryinternationalweb.org

Poetry International Web features information on poets from countries such as Indonesia, Zimbabwe, Iceland, India, Slovenia, Morocco, Albania, Afghanistan, Russia, and Brazil. The site offers news, essays, interviews and discussion, and hundreds of poems, both in their original languages and in English translation.

Poet's Corner
http://theotherpages.org/poems

The Poet's Corner, one of the oldest text resources on the Web, provides access to about seven thousand works of poetry by several hundred different poets from around the world. Indexes are arranged and searchable by title, name of poet, or subject. The site also offers its own resources, including "Faces of the Poets"—a gallery of portraits—and "Lives of the Poets"—a growing collection of biographies.

Western European Studies
http://wess.lib.byu.edu

The Western European Studies Section of the Association of College and Research Libraries maintains this collection of resources useful to students of Western European history and culture. It also is a good place to find information about non-English-language literature. The site includes separate pages about the literatures and languages of the Netherlands, France, Germany, Iberia, Italy, and Scandinavia, in which users can find links to electronic texts, association Web sites, journals, and other materials, the majority of which are written in the languages of the respective countries.

ELECTRONIC DATABASES

Electronic databases usually do not have their own URLs. Instead, public, college, and university libraries subscribe to these databases, provide links to them on their Web sites, and make them available to library card holders or other specified patrons. Readers can visit library Web sites or ask reference librarians to check on availability.

Canadian Literary Centre

Produced by EBSCO, the Canadian Literary Centre database contains full-text content from ECW Press, a Toronto-based publisher, including the titles in the publisher's Canadian fiction studies, Canadian biography, and Canadian writers and their works series; *ECW's Biographical Guide to Canadian Novelists*; and *George Woodcock's Introduction to Canadian Fiction*. Author biographies, essays and literary criticism, and book reviews are among the database's offerings.

Literary Reference Center

EBSCO's Literary Reference Center (LRC) is a comprehensive full-text database designed primarily to help high school and undergraduate students in English and the humanities with homework and research assignments about literature. The database contains massive amounts of information from reference works, books, literary journals, and other materials, including more than 31,000 plot summaries, synopses, and overviews of literary works; almost 100,000 essays and articles of literary criticism; about 140,000 author biographies; more than 605,000 book reviews; and more than 5,200 author interviews. It contains the entire contents of Salem Press's MagillOnLiterature Plus. Users can retrieve information by browsing a list of authors' names or titles of literary works; they can also use an advanced search engine to access information by numerous categories, including author name, gender, cultural identity, national identity, and the years in which he or she lived, or by literary title, character, locale, genre, and publication date. The Literary Reference Center also features a literary-historical time line, an encyclopedia of literature, and a glossary of literary terms.

MagillOnLiterature Plus

MagillOnLiterature Plus is a comprehensive, integrated literature database produced by Salem Press and available on the EBSCOhost platform. The database contains the full text of essays in Salem's many literature-related reference works, including *Masterplots*, *Cyclopedia of World Authors*, *Cyclopedia of Literary Characters*, *Cyclopedia of Literary Places*, *Critical Survey of Poetry*, *Critical Survey of Long Fiction*, *Critical Survey of Short Fiction*, *World Philosophers and Their Works*, *Magill's Literary Annual*, and *Magill's Book Reviews*. Among its contents are articles on more than 35,000 literary works and more than 8,500 poets, writers, dramatists, essayists, and philosophers; more than 1,000 images; and a glossary of more than 1,300 literary terms. The biographical essays include lists of authors' works and secondary bibliographies, and hundreds of overview essays examine and discuss literary genres, time periods, and national literatures.

Rebecca Kuzins; updated by Desiree Dreeuws

CATEGORY INDEX

AESTHETIC POETS
    Baudelaire, Charles, 69
AVANT-GARDE POETS
    Apollinaire, Guillaume, 47
    Aragon, Louis, 58
    Breton, André, 80
    Celan, Paul, 88
    Laforgue, Jules, 129
    Mallarmé, Stéphane, 149
    Reverdy, Pierre, 197
    Tzara, Tristan, 230

BALLADS
    Villon, François, 250

CHILDREN'S/YOUNG ADULT POETRY
    La Fontaine, Jean de, 118
CLASSICISM
    La Fontaine, Jean de, 118
CONCRETE POETRY
    Apollinaire, Guillaume, 47
CUBISM
    Apollinaire, Guillaume, 47
    Reverdy, Pierre, 197

DADAISM
    Aragon, Louis, 58
    Breton, André, 80
    Tzara, Tristan, 230
    Éluard, Paul, 97
DECADENT POETS
    Baudelaire, Charles, 69
    Laforgue, Jules, 129
    Rimbaud, Arthur, 218
    Verlaine, Paul, 240

DRAMATIC MONOLOGUES
    Laforgue, Jules, 129

ELEGIES
    Nerval, Gérard de, 170
    Rilke, Rainer Maria, 207
EPICS
    Hugo, Victor, 104
    Perse, Saint-John, 181
    Tzara, Tristan, 230
EXPERIMENTAL POETS
    Breton, André, 80
    Celan, Paul, 88
    Mallarmé, Stéphane, 149
    Reverdy, Pierre, 197
    Rimbaud, Arthur, 218
EXPRESSIONISM
    Celan, Paul, 88

FABLES
    La Fontaine, Jean de, 118
    Marie de France, 158

GAY AND LESBIAN CULTURE
    Rimbaud, Arthur, 218
    Verlaine, Paul, 240

IMPRESSIONISM
    Laforgue, Jules, 129
    Nerval, Gérard de, 170
    Verlaine, Paul, 240

JEWISH CULTURE
    Celan, Paul, 88
    Tzara, Tristan, 230
JUGENDSTIL
    Rilke, Rainer Maria, 207

LOVE POETRY
    Verlaine, Paul, 240
    Villon, François, 250
    Éluard, Paul, 97
LYRIC POETRY
    Apollinaire, Guillaume, 47
    Baudelaire, Charles, 69
    Celan, Paul, 88
    Hugo, Victor, 104
    Laforgue, Jules, 129
    Lamartine, Alphonse de, 140
    Nerval, Gérard de, 170
    Rilke, Rainer Maria, 207
    Villon, François, 250

MODERNISM
    Baudelaire, Charles, 69
    Rilke, Rainer Maria, 207

NARRATIVE POETRY
    Hugo, Victor, 104
    Laforgue, Jules, 129
    Lamartine, Alphonse de, 140
    Marie de France, 158
    Tzara, Tristan, 230
NATURE POETRY
    Verlaine, Paul, 240

ODES
    Hugo, Victor, 104
ORAL TRADITION
    Marie de France, 158

PARNASSIANISM
    Mallarmé, Stéphane, 149
    Verlaine, Paul, 240
PATTERN POETS
    Apollinaire, Guillaume, 47
    Mallarmé, Stéphane, 149

POLITICAL POETS
    Aragon, Louis, 58
    Prévert, Jacques, 189
POSTMODERNISM
    Tzara, Tristan, 230
PROSE POETRY
    Baudelaire, Charles, 69
    Mallarmé, Stéphane, 149
    Reverdy, Pierre, 197
    Éluard, Paul, 97

RELIGIOUS POETRY
    Verlaine, Paul, 240
ROMANTICISM
    Hugo, Victor, 104
    Lamartine, Alphonse de, 140
    Mallarmé, Stéphane, 149
    Nerval, Gérard de, 170

SATIRIC POETRY
    Hugo, Victor, 104
    Rimbaud, Arthur, 218
SOCIALIST REALISM
    Aragon, Louis, 58
SONNETS
    Nerval, Gérard de, 170
    Rilke, Rainer Maria, 207
    Verlaine, Paul, 240
SURREALIST POETS
    Apollinaire, Guillaume, 47
    Aragon, Louis, 58
    Breton, André, 80
    Celan, Paul, 88
    Reverdy, Pierre, 197
    Tzara, Tristan, 230
    Éluard, Paul, 97
SYMBOLIST POETS
    Apollinaire, Guillaume, 47
    Baudelaire, Charles, 69
    Laforgue, Jules, 129

Mallarmé, Stéphane, 149
Rimbaud, Arthur, 218
Verlaine, Paul, 240

VERSE DRAMATISTS
Hugo, Victor, 104
VISIONARY POETRY
Baudelaire, Charles, 69
Rilke Rainer Maria, 207
Rimbaud, Arthur, 218

WAR POEMS
Apollinaire, Guilaume, 47
Aragon, Louis, 58
Reverdy, Pierre, 197
WOMEN POETS
Marie de France, 158

SUBJECT INDEX

Adonis (La Fontaine), 121
Alcools (Apollinaire), 53
"All the Soul Indrawn . . ." (Mallarmé), 152
Amers. See *Seamarks*
Anabasis (Perse), 185
Ancel, Paul. *See* Celan, Paul
"Antéros" (Nerval), 178
Antschel, Paul. *See* Celan, Paul
Apollinaire, Guillaume, 47-57
    Alcools, 53
    Bestiary, 53
    Calligrammes, 54
    "The New Spirit and the Poets," 47
    poem about, 235
Apollinaris, WIlhelm. *See* Apollinaire, Guillaume
Approximate Man, and Other Writings (Tzara), 237
Aragon, Louis, 58-68
    "Elsa's Eyes," 65
    "Poem to Shout in the Ruins," 63
    "You Who Are the Rose," 66
Art for art's sake, 38, 72
"Art poétique, L'" (Verlaine), 243
"Artémis" (Nerval), 178
Automatic writing, 62

"Bad Blood" (Rimbaud), 224
Ballade (poetic form), 17
Ballades en jargon. See *Poems in Slang*
Baroque poetry, 28
Baudelaire, Charles, 69-79
    "Beacons," 73
    "A Carcass," 73
    Flowers of Evil, 72
    "Heautontimoroumenos," 76

Paris Spleen, 1869, 77
    "The Poor Child's Plaything," 78
    "The Swan," 75
    "To the Reader," 72
    "The Trip," 77
"Beacons" (Baudelaire), 73
Bertin, Antoine, 33
Bestiary (Apollinaire), 53
Birds (Perse), 186
Boileau-Despréaux, Nicolas, 28
Book of Hours, The (Rilke), 211
Book of Images, The (Rilke), 211
Breton, André, 80-87
    Communicating Vessels, 82
    Fata Morgana, 86
    Free Union, 86
    "In the Eyes of the Gods," 84
    "In the Lovely Half-light," 85
    Manifesto of Surrealism, 82
Buch der Bilder, Des. See *Book of Images, The*

Calligrammes (Apollinaire), 54
"Carcass, A" (Baudelaire), 73
"Carrefour" (Reverdy), 200
Celan, Paul, 88-96
    Mohn und Gedächtnis, 91
    Die Niemandsrose, 94
    Speech-Grille, 93
    Von Schwelle zu Schwelle, 93
Chansons de geste, 2
Chant des morts, Le (Reverdy), 204
Chants de Maldoror (Ducasse), 39
Charles d'Orléans, 18
Chimeras, The (Nerval), 176
Chrétien de Troyes, 11

Chute d'un ange, La (Lamartine), 146
Chénier, André-Marie, 34
"Circus Performers, The" (Tzara), 236
Comic and satiric poetry, 12
Communicating Vessels (Breton), 82
Complaintes, Les (Laforgue), 134
Contemplations, Les (Hugo), 113
Contes et nouvelles en vers. See *Tales and Short Stories in Verse*
Coup de dés jamais n'abolira le hasard, Un. See *Dice Thrown Never Will Annul Chance*
Courtly love, 9

Dadaism, 41
De nos oiseaux (Tzara), 235
"Death of Guillaume Apollinaire, The" (Tzara), 235
Decadent poets, 40
Defence and Illustration of the French Language, The (Du Bellay), 24
"Delfica" (Nerval), 178
"Deliria I" (Rimbaud), 225
"Deliria II" (Rimbaud), 225
Derniers Vers de Jules Laforgue, Les (Laforgue), 137
"Desdichado, El" (Nerval), 177
Dice Thrown Never Will Annul Chance (Mallarmé), 155
Didactic poetry, 33
Dieu (Hugo), 115
"Dimanches" (Laforgue), 136
Dinggedichte (Rilke), 213
Dramatic poetry, 27
"Drunken Boat, The" (Rimbaud), 222
Du Bellay, Joachim, 23, 24
Ducasse, Isidore-Lucien, 39
Duinese Elegies, 207
Duineser Elegien. See *Duino Elegies*
Duino Elegies (Rilke), 214

Early twentieth century poets, 40
Eleventh century, 2
"Eliduc" (Marie de France), 165
Éloges (Perse), 184
"Elsa's Eyes" (Aragon), 65
Éluard, Paul, 97-103
  "Enfermé, seul," 102
  "Première du monde," 101
  "A Woman in Love," 101
"Enfermé, seul" (Éluard), 102
"Enfin" (Reverdy), 204
"Equitan" (Marie de France), 164
"Et Maintenant" (Reverdy), 205
Existentialism, 43
"Expiation, L'" (Hugo), 112

Fables Written in Verse (La Fontaine), 30, 125
Fables choisies, mises en vers. See *Fables Written in Verse*
Fabliaux, 13
"Familiale" (Prévert), 195
"Farewell" (Rimbaud), 225
Fata Morgana (Breton), 86
Fêtes galantes. See *Gallant Parties*
Feudal society, 3, 6
Feuilles d'automne, Les (Hugo), 111
Fifteenth centuries, 14
Fin de Satan, La (Hugo), 114
Fleurs de bonne volonté, Des (Laforgue), 136
Fleurs du mal, Les. See *Flowers of Evil*
Flowers of Evil (Baudelaire), 72
Fourteenth century, 14
Free Union (Breton), 86
French Canadian poets, 43
French poetry
  origins to seventeenth century, 1-31
  eighteenth century to present, 32-46

Gallant Parties (Verlaine), 245
Grand Testament, Le. See *Great Testament, The*
Great Testament, The (Villon), 254
Grindel, Eugène. *See* Éluard, Paul
"Guerre" (Reverdy), 201
Guillaume de Lorris, 12

Harmonies poétiques et religieuses (Lamartine), 145
"Heautontimoroumenos" (Baudelaire), 76
"Her Pure Fingernails on High Offering Their Onyx" (Mallarmé), 153
Herodias (Mallarmé), 153
Homme approximatif, L'. See *Approximate Man, and other Writings*
"Horus" (Nerval), 177
Hugo, Victor, 104-117
    Les Contemplations, 113
    Dieu, 115
    "L'Expiation'," 112
    Les Feuilles d'automne, 111
    La Fin de Satan, 114
    The Legend of the Centuries, 114
    Odes et ballades, 110
    Les Orientales, 110
    Les Rayons et les ombres, 111

Igitur (Mallarmé), 155
Illuminations (Rimbaud), 226
Imitation de Notre-Dame la lune, L' (Laforgue), 135
"Impossible, The" (Rimbaud), 225
"In the Eyes of the Gods" (Breton), 84
"In the Lovely Half-light" (Breton), 85
"It Is Crying in My Heart" (Verlaine), 246

Jean de Meung, 12
Jocelyn (Lamartine), 146

Kostrowitzki, Guillelmus Apollinaris de. *See* Apollinaire, Guillaume

"Lac, Le." *See* "Lake, The"
La Fontaine, Jean de, 29, 118-128
    Adonis, 121
    Fables Written in Verse, 30, 125
    The Loves of Cupid and Psyche, 123
    Le Songe de Vaux, 122
    Tales and Short Stories in Verse, 123
Laforgue, Jules, 40, 129-139
    Les Complaintes, 134
    Les Derniers Vers de Jules Laforgue, 137
    "Dimanches," 136
    Des Fleurs de bonne volonté, 136
    L'Imitation de Notre-Dame la lune, 135
"Lake, The" (Lamartine), 143
Lamartine, Alphonse de, 140-148
    La Chute d'un ange, 146
    Harmonies poétiques et religieuses, 145
    Jocelyn, 146
    "The Lake," 143
    Nouvelles méditations poétiques, 145
    Poetical Meditations, 143
    "Les Revolutions," 145
    "Tristesse," 145
    "The Valley," 144
Langue d'oc (poetic form), 8
"Lanval" (Marie de France), 162
Legacy, The (Villon), 253
Legend of the Centuries, The (Hugo), 114
Légende des siècles. *See* *Legend of the Centuries, The*
Léger, Alexis Saint-Léger. *See* Perse, Saint-John
Léonard, Nicolas-Germain, 33
"Lightning" (Rimbaud), 225
"Little Town in Siberia" (Tzara), 235
Llyric poetry, 27
Loges, François des. *See* Villon, François

Loves of Cupid and Psyche, The (La Fontaine), 123
Luther, Martin, 22
Lyric poetry, 8

Madame de Staël, 35
"Main-Morte" (Reverdy), 203
Mal du siècle, 37
Malherbe, François, 28
Mallarmé, Stéphane, 149-157
    "All the Soul Indrawn . . .," 152
    Dice Thrown Never Will Annul Chance, 155
    "Her Pure Fingernails on High Offering Their Onyx," 153
    Herodias, 153
    Igitur, 155
    "My Old Books Closed at the Name of Paphos," 152
Manifesto of Surrealism (Breton), 82
Marguerite of Angoulême, 22-23
Marie de France, 158-169
    "Eliduc," 165
    "Equitan," 164
    "Lanval," 162
    "The Two Lovers," 163
Marot, Clément, 23
Méditations poétiques. See *Poetical Meditations*
"Mémoire" (Reverdy), 202
"Mes bouquins refermés sur le nom de Paphos." See "My Old Books Closed at the Name of Paphos"
Millevoye, Charles-Hubert, 34
Mir zur Feier (Rilke), 211
Modern poetry, 42
Mohn und Gedächtnis (Celan), 91
Montcorbier, François. See Villon, François
"Morning" (Rimbaud), 225
"My Familiar Dream" (Verlaine), 244

"My Old Books Closed at the Name of Paphos" (Mallarmé), 152
"Myrtho" (Nerval), 177

Nature poetry, 36
Nerval, Gérard de, 170-180
    "Antéros," 178
    "Artémis," 178
    The Chimeras, 176
    "Delfica," 178
    "El Desdichado," 177
    "Horus," 177
    "Myrtho," 177
    "Vers dorés," 179
New Poems (Rilke), 213
"New Spirit and the Poets, The" (Apollinaire), 47
Niemandsrose, Die (Celan), 94
"Night in Hell" (Rimbaud), 224
Nouvelles méditations poétiques (Lamartine), 145

Odes et ballades (Hugo), 110
Oiseaux. See *Birds*
Orientales, Les (Hugo), 110

"Panther, The" (Rilke), 214
Paris Spleen, 1869 (Baudelaire), 77
Parnassianism, 37
Parny, Évariste-Désiré de Forges de, 33
Perse, Saint-John, 181-188
    Anabasis, 185
    Birds, 186
    Éloges, 184
    Seamarks, 185
Petits Poèmes en prose. See *Paris Spleen, 1869*
Philosophes, 32
"Piano Kissed by a Fragile Hand, The" (Verlaine), 246

Pléiade poets, 23
Poe, Edgar Allan, French reception of, 72
"Poem to Shout in the Ruins" (Aragon), 63
Poems in Prose (Baudelaire). See *Paris Spleen, 1869*
Poems in Slang (Villon), 257
Poetical Meditations (Lamartine), 143
Poetics, 42
"Poor Child's Plaything, The" (Baudelaire), 78
Poèmes saturniens (Verlaine), 244
Pre-Romanticism, 34
"Première du monde" (Éluard), 101
Primele Poème (Tzara), 234
Prose poetry, 38
Précieux poets, 29
Prévert, Jacques, 189-196

Rambouillet, marquise de, 29
Rayons et les ombres, Les (Hugo), 111
Religious poetry, 33
Renaissance, 20
Reverdy, Pierre, 197-206
    "Carrefour," 200
    Le Chant des morts, 204
    "Enfin," 204
    "Et Maintenant," 205
    "Guerre," 201
    "Main-Morte," 203
    "Mémoire," 202
"Revolutions, Les" (Lamartine), 145
Rhétoriqueurs, 23
Rilke, Rainer Maria, 207-217
    The Book of Hours, 211
    The Book of Images, 211
    Dinggedichte, 213
    Duino Elegies, 214
    Mir zur Feier, 211
    New Poems, 213
    "The Panther," 214
    Sonnets to Orpheus, 214

Rimbaud, Arthur, 218-229
    "Bad Blood," 224
    "Deliria I," 225
    "Deliria II," 225
    "The Drunken Boat," 222
    "Farewell," 225
    Illuminations, 226
    "The Impossible," 225
    "Lightning," 225
    "Morning," 225
    "Night in Hell," 224
    A Season in Hell, 223
    "Seer Letter," 221
    "Vowels," 223
Roman de Renart, 13
Romance of the Rose, The (Guillaume de Lorris and Jean de Meung), 12
Romances, 11
Romances Without Words (Verlaine), 246
Romanticism, 35
Ronsard, Pierre de, 23
Rosenstock, Sami. *See* Tzara, Tristan

Sagesse (Verlaine), 247
Saison en enfer, Une. See Season in Hell, A
Scudéry, Madeleine de, 29
Seamarks (Perse), 185
Season in Hell, A (Rimbaud), 223
"Seer Letter" (Rimbaud), 221
"Ses purs ongles trés haut dédiant leur onyx." *See* "Her Pure Fingernails on High Offering Their Onyx"
Seventeenth century, 25
Sixteenth century, 19
Song of Roland, The (anonymous), 4
Songe de Vaux, Le (La Fontaine), 122
Sonnets to Orpheus (Rilke), 214
"Sound of the Hunting Horn, The" (Verlaine), 248
Speech-Grille (Celan), 93